A Kingdom of Priests

JEWISH CULTURE AND CONTEXTS

Published in association with the Center for Advanced Judaic Studies
of the University of Pennsylvania

David B. Ruderman, Series Editor

Advisory Board
Richard I. Cohen
Moshe Idel
Alan Mintz
Deborah Dash Moore
Ada Rapoport-Albert
Michael Swartz

A complete list of books in the series is available from the publisher.

A Kingdom of Priests

Ancestry and Merit
in Ancient Judaism

MARTHA HIMMELFARB

PENN

University of Pennsylvania Press

Philadelphia

10 9 8 7 6 5 4 3 2 1

Published by
University of Pennsylvania Press
Philadelphia, Pennsylvania 19104-4112

Library of Congress Cataloging-in-Publication Data

Himmelfarb, Martha, 1952–
    A kingdom of priests : ancestry and merit in ancient Judaism / Martha Himmelfarb.
        p. cm. — (Jewish culture and contexts)
    ISBN-13: 978-0-8122-3950-8
    ISBN-10: 0-8122-3950-4 (alk. paper)
    1. Priests, Jewish—History.   2. Holiness—Judaism.   3. Judaism—History—
Post-exilic period, 586 B.C.–210 A.D.   4. Dead Sea scrolls.   5. Apocryphal books—
Criticism, interpretation, etc.   I. Title.   II. Series.

BM651.H56 2006
296.4'95—dc22   2006046151

In memory of
Milton Himmelfarb (1918–2006)
My father, my teacher

Contents

Introduction

This book takes its title from God's promise to the children of Israel as they stand before Mt. Sinai: "If you will obey my voice and keep my covenant, you shall be my own possession among all people . . . you shall be to me a kingdom of priests and a holy nation" (Exod 19:5-6). While the phrase itself does not receive a great deal of attention in the literature of the Second Temple,[1] I hope to show that the idea it expresses and the tensions it hints at are of central importance to Jews during that period.

The promise that Israel will be "a kingdom of priests" reflects a milieu in which priests hold an honored position. The Israelites, like other peoples of the ancient Near East, entrusted priests with the delicate task of mediating between humanity and the divine through the sacrifices they offered in the temple. The rituals priests performed were understood to keep the cosmos functioning properly; if the priests failed at their duties, the consequences would be dire. Priests are by definition a minority; indeed the Torah limits priesthood to a single family or tribe. Clearly "a kingdom of priests" was not meant to advocate that all Israelites serve as priests in the temple, sacrificing and eating consecrated food. Rather, as the context suggests, the phrase serves to emphasize the holiness of all Israelites.

The idea of Israel as a holy people is of course a central biblical theme. But the notion that all Israelites are equally holy, as "a kingdom of priests" implies, is more problematic. After all, if all Israelites are equally holy, why bother with priests in the first place? The tension between the holiness of the whole people and the existence of priests receives dramatic expression in the story of the rebellion of Korah during the Israelites' wandering in the wilderness (Numbers 16–17). Korah is a Levite, a member of the tribe that had been singled out for a special role in the cult. His rebellion grows out of his unwillingness to accept the more exalted priestly status that one particular family of Levites, Aaron and his sons, has claimed. Korah rejects not the institution of priesthood but particular arrangements for it that exclude him and most of the rest of the tribe of Levi. Thus, as the narrative now stands, its main point is to counter an assault by other Levites on the prerogatives of the sons of Aaron. But one argument the rebels bring against Moses and Aaron hints at an earlier story in which the rebels demanded an end to any form of hierarchy among the people of Israel: "All the congregation are holy, every one of them, and the Lord is among them; why then do you exalt yourselves above the assembly of the Lord?" (Num 16:3).[2]

The Torah rejects both types of criticism in no uncertain terms: the earth swallows up all of the protestors together with their families. And it is not only the Torah, a document written in part by priests, that believes in priests and their prerogatives. The prophets denounce their listeners' belief that enthusiasm for the cult will make up for lack of kindness to one's fellows (e.g., Amos 5:21-26), but they do not reject the institution of the cult itself. Indeed, Isaiah of Jerusalem, who condemns the sacrifices of the wicked in the first chapter of his book (Isa 1:11-15), understands God to be present in the temple, as his vision of the Lord enthroned among the seraphim (Isaiah 6) indicates. Two of the great prophets who came after him in the kingdom of Judah, Jeremiah and Ezekiel, were themselves priests (Jer 1:1; Ezek 1:3). Yet despite the embrace of the institution of priesthood by all strands of biblical thought, the tension inherent in the idea of a "kingdom of priests" remained unresolved.

A different way to read "a kingdom of priests" that at first appears to offer a solution to the problem formulated by Korah's companions is to emphasize the role of Israel in relation to other nations: "You shall be my own possession *among all people* . . . a kingdom of priests and a holy nation." Thus a prophet active in Jerusalem after the return from Babylonia imagines Israel fulfilling its destiny as a nation that serves the other nations as priest:

Aliens shall stand and feed your flocks,
foreigners shall be your plowmen and vinedressers;
but you shall be called the priests of the Lord,
men shall speak of you as the ministers of our God;
you shall eat the wealth of the nations,
and in their riches you shall glory. (Isa 61:5-6)

Here the whole people is to enjoy the benefits that Israelite society conferred on priests. Recognizing the special status of the people of Israel, other nations will provide its needs in exchange for its role of mediating between God and humanity.[3] Yet the emphasis on Israel's special status in relation to other nations can also undercut the status of Israelite priests: the more Israel is differentiated from other nations, the less place there is for hierarchical distinctions within the holy people.[4]

Further, the idea of a holy nation is inherently unstable. Whether one chooses to emphasize the inner-directed or the outer-directed aspects of the phrase, the desire that God's special people be holy inevitably runs up against a less elevated reality, as the prophets tell us in considerable detail. The nature of that reality should come as no surprise since the criterion for membership in the people of Israel is ancestry, a criterion that does little to promote holiness. Yet the Torah imagines both the rewards and the punishments of the covenant in collective terms: the Israelites will together suffer exile for their sins, and they will together be restored to their land after they repent (Leviticus 26; Deuteronomy 28-30). The tension inherent in collective responsibility for the covenant was intolerable for the great prophet Isaiah, who has God warn Jerusalem, "I will turn my hand against you / And will smelt away your dross as with lye, / and remove all your alloy" (Isa 1:25); after this purification, "you shall be called the city of righteousness, / the faithful city" (Isa 1:26). Thus only a small portion of the people would enjoy restoration, as Isaiah indicates with the name he gives his son, *Šĕʾār yāšûb*, "a remnant shall return" (Isa 7:3).[5]

Implicit in Isaiah's vision of the purified remnant is a new criterion for membership in the people of Israel: piety rather than birth. Yet before the exile, it did not occur to anyone to apply that criterion to the present. As long as the land of Judah was ruled by a king from the house of David, the people of Israel was more or less co-extensive with those living in the land.[6] After the return from the Babylonian exile, however, with the land no longer under Israelite rule, the extent of the people became a subject of concern and controversy. In the face of widespread intermarriage with neighboring peoples, both Ezra and Nehemiah demand that the members of their community divorce their foreign wives and send away their offspring (Ezra 9-10; Nehemiah 13).[7] But despite their zeal for endogamy, the authors of Ezra and Nehemiah, living after the exile, could not help but be aware of the problems of defining Israel on the basis of ancestry alone. Their remarkable term for the community of the return, *zeraʿ haqqōdeš*, "the holy race" or, more literally, "the holy seed" (Ezra 9:2), offers a striking, if troubling, conflation of ancestry and merit.

The concern for merit is evident also in the Book of Ruth, which rejects Ezra and Nehemiah's definition of the boundaries of the community. It tells the story of a marriage that not only Ezra and Nehemiah but even the Book of Deuteronomy (23:4) would have condemned: the marriage of an Israelite man to a Moabite woman. The Book of Ruth, however, suggests that this marriage is not only acceptable but praiseworthy, because ancestry is not as important as merit. Its heroine's sacrifices for her beloved mother-in-law win her the admiration of all who encounter her and finally the benefits of marriage to a wealthy man. The connection to King David (Ruth 4:17) may be a later addition to the work,[8] but even without it the birth of Ruth's son removes any question about her place in the community. Still, though it was written in the Persian period, the Book of Ruth is set in the days of the judges and presents its case in pre-exilic terms: the willing non-Israelite spouse is assimilated into the people of Israel without fuss or ceremony. Only later in the Second Temple period does a notion of conversion emerge, and even then there is no unanimity about the rituals required for it.[9]

The possibility of conversion develops out of the Jews' encounter with the Greeks, which marks a new stage in thinking about the definition of the people of Israel.[10] The Greeks understood their culture to be available without regard to ancestry; even a barbarian could become "Greek in soul." This phrase comes from Clearchus of Soli's report of Aristotle's account of his encounter in Asia Minor with a learned Jew.[11] Although the passage does not say so explicitly, it is possible for a barbarian to become Greek in soul because Greek culture is acquired through education; thus it is potentially available not only to Greeks but to others as well. In the aftermath of the Maccabean Revolt some Jews come to understand their culture in similar terms, as the very term "Judaism" suggests, modeled as it is on "Hellenism."[12] Like Hellenism, Judaism could be learned, and thus gentiles could now become Jewish in soul.

The aftermath of the Maccabean Revolt also sees the emergence of sectarian definitions of the people of Israel that develop Isaiah's idea of the righteous remnant, leaving the rest of the people irrevocably behind. The Qumran sectarians understand themselves as children of light, fighting on the side of the angels in the eschatological battle, while the rest of the Jewish people belongs to the other side, the children of darkness. For these sectarians, Jewish ancestry is necessary, but far from sufficient, for membership in the holy community.

Both before and after the revolt it did not escape the notice of some Jews that the priesthood was subject to the same problem as was the people of Israel as a whole. The fact that priestly status was inherited meant that Jewish priests often fell short of serving as the models of holiness enshrined in the phrase "a kingdom of priests." Indeed, the difficulties posed by the hereditary priesthood are even more acute since priests should constitute an elite of holiness within the holy people, enjoying certain privileges even as they are held to higher standards than ordinary Jews. Thus it was more than a little troubling when priests failed to live up to the standards and did nothing to deserve the privileges. Recognition of this problem goes back as far as the Torah itself, which attempts to defuse it by telling two stories about how early occupants of the priestly office earned the right to it through their zeal for the Lord.

Although the stories come from different strands of the Torah and reflect different views of who is qualified to serve as priest, both recount their heroes' killing of idolatrous Israelites. The epic strand of Exodus reports that the Levites "ordained [themselves] for the service of the Lord" by rallying in response to Moses' cry and slaughtering worshipers of the golden calf among their fellow Israelites (Exod 32:25-29). The language of ordination, used by the P source only a few chapters earlier (Exodus 29) of Aaron and his sons, suggests that through this slaughter the Levites became priests. According to the priestly source,[13] as the Israelites mingled with the Midianite women at Baal Peor (Num 25:1-9), Phinehas, the grandson of Aaron, killed an Israelite man caught in flagrante delicto with a Midianite woman. This act wins its perpetrator and his descendants a "covenant of perpetual priesthood" (Num 25:13), and the story provides one priestly line with an origin in pious zeal like that the epic sources gave the Levites.

Still, even if these stories claim that the priestly line was originally chosen on the basis of merit, nowhere does the Bible suggest merit as an ongoing criterion for priesthood. Throughout the Bible there is widespread agreement that priesthood is hereditary and that it is connected to the tribe of Levi, although there is disagreement about the identity of the ancestor required for priestly status and about the types of personnel needed to staff the temple. Outside of the priestly sources, the Torah suggests a system in which all male descendants of Levi were priests.[14] This understanding is implicit in the J and E narratives of the Torah; it becomes explicit in the Book of Deuteronomy with its expressions "the Levitical priests" (Deut 17:9, 18; 24:8; 27:9) and "the priests, the sons of Levi" (Deut 21:5; 31:9).[15] On the other hand, P and H, the priestly sources, grant the priesthood only to descendants of Aaron, Levi's great-grandson. Through the Books of Exodus and Leviticus these sources are silent on the subject of the nonpriestly descendants of Levi, referring to priests as sons of Aaron and ignoring their more distant ancestor. Thus a first-time reader of the Torah would be somewhat surprised on reaching the Book of Numbers to discover the existence of the Levites as a group with a role to play in the Israelite cult (Numbers 3–18). Like the priestly sources in Exodus and Leviticus, the priestly material in Numbers understands priests as descendants of Aaron, but it departs from Exodus and Leviticus in treating the other descendants of Levi as a distinct group with cultic responsibilities of its own: the preparation of the tabernacle for breaking camp and its transportation (Numbers 4).

The historical developments reflected in the Book of Numbers' view of the Levites are unfortunately lost to us, but its picture of Levites as a distinct group standing in a subordinate relationship to priests became standard during the Second Temple period. Nehemiah's efforts at re-form on the Levites' behalf reflect Numbers' picture (Neh 13:10-13), as does, somewhat later, the Book of Chronicles' depiction of a well-defined priestly hierarchy with a high priest at the head, priests descended from Aaron officiating at the altar, and Levites serving as musicians, singers, and gatekeepers (1 Chronicles 23-26). The preference in post-exilic sources for the picture of the Book of Numbers is perhaps not surpris-ing. A reader who wished to reconcile the conflicting points of view he found in the Torah might understand the Levitical priests of Deuteron-omy as descended not only from Levi but also, as P and H require, from Aaron, while the existence of the Levites as a distinct group would satisfy the expectations raised by the prominence of the Levites in the other strands of the Torah. It is striking, however, that Numbers' picture of priests as a subgroup of Levites is at odds with the evidence for the ac-tual situation during the period of the return. According to the picture in Numbers, one would expect the number of nonpriestly Levites to be considerably larger than the number of priests, yet the census of those who returned to Judea with Zerubbabel lists more than twelve times as many priests as Levites (Ezra 2:36-42).[16]

The Torah says rather little explicitly about the apex of the priestly hi-erarchy, the high priest (Lev 21:10-15); most of what we learn about this figure emerges from the description of the activities of Aaron, the first occupant of the office. At his death, Moses strips Aaron of his special garments and dresses Aaron's son Eleazar in them to indicate that he has taken on his father's role (Num 20:23-28), but despite this story the Torah provides no guidelines for determining the high priestly succes-sion. Indeed, while in the post-exilic period the office seems to have passed from father to son, there is some evidence in the Deuteronomic history to suggest that the high priest of the monarchic period was a royal appointee.[17] Further, it is not until the Book of Chronicles that Zadok, one of the two high priests of David's court and the supposed an-cestor of all high priests until the hellenistic reform in the early second century B.C.E., is explicitly placed in a line of descent from Aaron, Eleazar, and Phinehas (1 Chron 6:34-38). The silence of earlier sources on this point and the Canaanite associations of the name Zadok have led some scholars to suggest that he began his career as a priest in the Canaanite shrine in Jerusalem before David's conquest of the city, though important voices have also argued in favor of Zadok's Aaronide descent.[18] Fortunately, what is important for my purposes in this book is not the actual development of the offices of priests, Levites, and high priests, now largely lost to us, but rather the way ancient Jews under-stood that history based on their reading of the Bible.

The prestige of the priesthood inevitably increased during the Second

Temple period. Under the monarchy, the temple was undoubtedly a central institution, yet as long as there was an Israelite king in power, it was under royal control. The priests who staffed it were royal retainers; the high priest exercised whatever power he held within the royal orbit. With the loss of kingship, the high priest became an important political figure in his own right, the recognized head of the people in the eyes of foreign rulers. Further, with the loss of the monarchy, the temple became by default Israel's preeminent institution. The status of priests in general, the anointed officials of the central institution, also rose. But as priests became more important, some of their countrymen began to wonder about their fitness for their office. While an observer of the priesthood could surely have noted some tension between ancestry and merit at any time in its history, the increased importance of priests made the tension more acute.

By the time of Ezra and Nehemiah, the temple was no longer the only institution at the center of the life of the people of Israel. Under Persian rule, the Torah became the law of the land in the province of Yehud. The authority of the Torah also served to support the existence of the priesthood and its hereditary character, which its laws ordained. But the Torah also constituted a new source of authority, and Nehemiah invokes it against priests who fail to operate according to its dictates.[19] The institutionalization of the Torah required a new class of religious officials: scribes, skilled interpreters of the Torah. Many of these scribes were themselves priests, but their allegiance to the Torah sometimes made them critics of priests who failed to exemplify the holiness the Torah demands. Scholars have often understood the relationship between priest and scribe, like the earlier one between priest and prophet, as one of antagonism. I have already suggested that such a reading is a misunderstanding of the prophets' attitude toward the cult and its ministers. It is equally a misunderstanding of the scribes' attitude. There was considerable tension in the relationship, as Nehemiah's behavior demonstrates, but Nehemiah's criticism of individual priests was in the service of an ideal of priestly behavior against which they offended. Indeed, as self-conscious guardians of the Torah, scribes could not but support the priesthood as an institution.

It is a reasonable assumption that most Jews in the ancient world lost little sleep over the fact that neither the people of Israel nor its priests regularly achieved the holiness the Torah demands of them. The subject of this book is the minority that found this reality intolerable. I argue that in Palestine in the three centuries preceding the destruction of the Second Temple members of this minority with quite different points of view used the idea of Israel as a kingdom of priests to criticize their contemporaries and to imagine the people of Israel as a holy nation in a wide variety of literature, including apocalypses, wisdom texts, and legal texts. These texts take a variety of positions, from insistence that Israelite ancestry marks an almost angelic status on one extreme to radical redefinition of the boundaries of Israel to include only the pious within them on the other, but all had to contend with the inevitable tension between ancestry and merit. Nor was concern for these questions limited to Jews in Palestine; the writings of Philo of Alexandria show the relevance of these questions in a more cosmopolitan milieu.

I begin in the first chapter by considering the attitude toward priests and priesthood in the *Book of the Watchers* from the last part of the third century B.C.E. and the Wisdom of ben Sira from the beginning of the second century. As I have noted, the Second Temple period saw the emergence of a new kind of religious functionary, the scribe. The scribe's qualifications for his task had to do with skill and learning rather than ancestry. The *Book of the Watchers* offers criticism of contemporary priests and depicts its hero, a scribe, in priestly terms, implying that merit can earn priest-like status. On the other hand, Joshua ben Sira appears to be a supporter of the priesthood of his time, though I suggest that he is by no means uncritical of his contemporaries. But he is clearly an admirer of the high priest of his youth, Simon, whom he depicts as Wisdom's twin, thus conferring some of the earned prestige of scribes on the hereditary occupant of the high priestly office. Finally I consider briefly *Aramaic Levi*, which appears to come from circles close to those of the author of the *Book of the Watchers*, yet embraces the status conferred by priestly ancestry without any evident anxiety about merit.

The second chapter treats the *Book of Jubilees*, which draws on the *Book of the Watchers* and other Enochic traditions. Through both narrative and legal means, *Jubilees* depicts the people of Israel as a true kingdom of priests and insists that it is indeed a holy nation. It emphasizes the priestly status of a series of ancestors of the people of Israel, and some of its laws claim that through their sexual behavior Israelites have a direct effect on the sanctuary, just as priests do. Israel's holiness is built into creation since God conceived of Israel as the human counterpart to the angels. This holiness is transmitted by heredity; thus no one born outside Israel can become part of the people. In other words, *Jubilees* claims that merit and ancestry are one and the same. *Jubilees* was regarded as an authoritative work at Qumran, yet I suggest that its emphasis on ancestry is a response to sectarian attempts to redefine the people of Israel on the basis of merit.

The third chapter considers the way two halakhic works found among the Dead Sea Scrolls, the *Temple Scroll* and the *Damascus Document*, use the purity laws of Leviticus to make all Jews more like priests. While the biblical laws apply to all Israelites, they have a far greater impact on priests, who must be in a state of purity in order to serve in the temple, and on their families, who must be in a state of purity to eat the consecrated food that belongs to priests. By making the biblical laws more elaborate and more restrictive, these legal works make all Jews share at least to some extent the limitations imposed on priests.

The fourth chapter turns to sectarian attitudes toward priesthood, exploring the tension between sectarian use of merit to define membership in the people of Israel and the hereditary status of priests. A comparison of the *Damascus Document* and the *Rule of the Community* shows that priests have become less important in the *Rule of the Community* because its more radically sectarian outlook makes hierarchy within the sect less palatable. So too the Book of Revelation, a Jewish sectarian work from a quite different milieu, takes the idea of a kingdom of priests with great seriousness. John's solution to the problem faced by the *Rule of the Community* is not to reduce the importance of priesthood but to make priests of all the pious, Jews and gentiles, men and women, alike.

The fifth chapter moves from Palestine to Alexandria to examine the tension between ancestry and merit in the picture of the Jewish people in the work of the philosopher Philo. For Philo, the Torah contains the true philosophy, and thus those who adhere to it are genuine philosophers. The hereditary priesthood decreed by the Torah and the cult in which it ministers are, unfortunately, anything but philosophical. Given his allegorical approach to the Torah and his preference for the soul over the body, Philo could have chosen to allegorize both priests and cult virtually out of existence. Yet, remarkably, despite his Platonism, Philo is deeply attached to the temple and its rituals, and while he often pursues allegorical interpretations of the cult, he refuses to let go of real-life priests and sacrifice. Thus he too must struggle to make sense of the significance of a priestly class for a kingdom of priests. His solution to the problem they pose is to suggest that the nation is the archetype for the priesthood rather than the priesthood for the nation.

In the final chapter I sketch the fate of the idea of Israel as a kingdom of priests after the destruction of the temple prevents priests from performing the tasks the Torah mandates for them. Rabbinic Judaism represents itself as a temporary substitute for the temple, and it prays for the restoration of the temple, its cult, and its personnel. Still, the absence of working priests serves to reduce anxiety about the tension between ancestry and merit. The status of the new elite class, the rabbis, is based at least in principle on merit rather than ancestry. And as Jews come to realize that loss of the temple is more than a temporary inconvenience, the rise of Christianity, culminating in its adoption as the official religion of the empire, changes the nature of Jewish minority status, and not for the better. No longer are Jews one among many ethnic groups in a pluralistic society, distinctive perhaps for their monotheism, but in many ways much like their neighbors. Rather, in the eyes of the authorities they have become the minority par excellence, and their minority status has theological significance. While rabbinic society recognizes the possibility of conversion, its dominant way of speaking about Jewish identity is as a function of birth, perhaps in response to the strong sense of distance from the surrounding society. Indeed, Jewish ancestry comes to be understood as carrying with it the presumption of salvation. Thus after discussing crimes to be punished by death, the Mishnah insists, "All Israel has a portion in the world to come" (*m. Sanh.* 10.1). So too the *'Amidah*, the central prayer recited three times a day, assures Jews that the God of Abraham, Isaac, and Jacob will remember the good deeds of the ancestors and bring a redeemer to their descendants. The connection to the ancestors, whose merit is beyond dispute, reduces the pressure on the conduct of ordinary Jews since the merit of the ancestors guarantees the salvation of the Jewish people, if not of individuals.

Experience taught ancient Jews how difficult it was to fulfill the Torah's demand that Israel be a holy people. It was certainly not made any easier by the fact that the usual mode of entrance into the people of Israel was birth. So too when priests fell short of the holiness required of them, their failure was perhaps not surprising since they attained their office on the basis of birth alone, but it was even more distressing than that of ordinary Jews given their status and responsibilities. Thus, while the phrase "a kingdom of priests" may have been little quoted in the Second Temple period and virtually ignored by the rabbis, the tensions it expresses are central to understanding ancient Judaism.

Chapter 1

Priest and Scribe

Ancestry and Professional Skill in the Book of the Watchers,
the Wisdom of Ben Sira, and Aramaic Levi

Of all the institutions of the period of the monarchy, the temple proved the longest lived. The First Temple was destroyed by the Babylonians in 586 B.C.E., but by 515 a new temple had replaced it, and the Judean priesthood was restored, more or less, to its old tasks.[1] Monarchy and prophecy, or at least prophecy in the style of the prophets who gave their names to biblical books, did not prove as resilient. No Davidic king ever again reigned in Jerusalem.[2] While prophecy flourished during the period of the exile (Ezekiel; 2 Isaiah), the beginning of the return (Zechariah 1-8; Haggai; 3 Isaiah), and even beyond (Zechariah 9-14; Malachi), it had more or less disappeared by the end of the Persian period. The prophets we glimpse later in Josephus's contemptuous descriptions are wonder-workers or leaders of penitential movements preparing for the imminent end.[3] The crucial factor in this change was probably not the demise of the monarchy—after all, as I have just noted, prophecy continued to flourish through the exile and into the period of the return—but the emergence under the Persians of a new institution, the Torah. This written constitution had been anticipated by the publication of Deuteronomy in the reign of Josiah toward the end of the monarchy, but with the demise of the monarchy, the text achieved a new type of authority. And because of the support of the Persian rulers, this authority was practical as well as theoretical.

The authority of a written text required a new type of religious functionary: the skilled interpreter of the text. Ezra is the first such "scribe [*sōpēr*] skilled in the Torah of Moses" (Ezra 7:6) known to us, but he was certainly not the last.[4] "Scribe" is a profession; to become a scribe skilled in the Torah of Moses required intelligence and education, and, as ben Sira indicates centuries later, education required wealth (Sir 38:24). Still, to be a scribe did not require particular ancestry. The profession was open to any Jewish man of requisite intelligence and sufficient means to undertake the education.

The potential for tension between priests, the hereditary guardians of tradition, and such learned custodians of the Torah was quickly realized. In his memoir, Nehemiah recounts a series of reforms he enacted that trod on the toes of the high priest Eliashib and his family (Nehemiah 13). Nehemiah is never called "scribe," and his profile is rather different from what one would expect of a scribe: he is a high official of the Persian court who uses his access to the king to become governor of Judah. Yet to justify his reforms Nehemiah invokes not his authority as Persian governor but the authority of the "book of Moses" (Neh 13:1). It is not clear whether Nehemiah has in mind here the Torah more or less as we know it or the Book of Deuteronomy alone, the only portion of the Torah that claims to be a book written by Moses (Deuteronomy 31), since the passage from the book of Moses on which Nehemiah relies appears in Deuteronomy (Deut 23:4-6). In either case, the written text allowed Nehemiah to trump the claim of the traditions passed on from priestly father to priestly son that Eliashib and his grandson surely would have flung back at him, a layman meddling in a sphere that from their point of view belonged to descendants of Aaron alone. Had Nehemiah not been the representative of the Persian crown as well as a careful reader of Deuteronomy, the dispute would surely have been resolved in Eliashib's favor, no matter what the text said. Yet the existence of the text allows Nehemiah to refer to a source of authority that might persuade his contemporaries even as the power of his office compelled them to accept his decision.

The occupation of scribe is not an innovation of the Second Temple period. The royal court of Judah employed officials called "scribe" (e.g., 2 Sam 8:17; 20:25; 2 Kings 12:11; 18:18, 37; 19:2) and "recorder" (*mazkîr*) (e.g., 2 Sam 8:16; 20:24; 1 Kings 4:3; 2 Kings 18:18, 37); in Judah as elsewhere the skills of reading and writing were essential for running the state. But the rather technical skills of these officials took on new significance in the era of Deuteronomy. The promulgation of Deuteronomy naturally elevated the status of reading and writing, the skills of the scribe. Furthermore, the scribe's role took on political dimensions, for society was now to be governed, at least ideally, on the basis of a text, which inevitably required interpretation. The practical wisdom of statecraft had been the sphere of the *ḥākām*, the wise advisor, who was apparently a standard figure in the courts of the ancient Near East. Joseph, for example, becomes second in command to Pharaoh by demonstrating that he is even wiser than the resident advisors, "all the magicians of Egypt and its wise men" (Gen 41:8). The demonstration consists of dream interpretation, a type of wisdom that biblical tradition understands as granted by God (Gen 40:8; 41:25, 39). But upon his appointment Joseph immediately takes action to soften the dire effects of the coming famine revealed by his interpretation of Pharaoh's dreams, giving evidence of a practical wisdom that the narrative of Genesis presents as his own, not as divinely inspired. Elsewhere we read of the wise men of Pharaoh (Isa 19:11), the wise men of Babylonia (Jer 50:35, 51:57), and the wise men of the Persian court (Esth 1:13). Haman, a vizier like Joseph rather than a king, has his own wise men (Esth 6:13). The tales of Daniel assume a class of royal advisors who serve to interpret dreams and other portents for their king, as Joseph did for Pharaoh, although they are not called wise men.[5] The Book of Proverbs suggests the presence of such wise men in the Judean royal court: "These also are sayings of the wise" (Prov 24:23), and "These also are proverbs of Solomon which the men of Hezekiah king of Judah copied" (Prov 25:1).

With the Babylonian conquest, Israelite wise men were out of work, at least on their home territory, for there was no longer a royal court in Jerusalem. The story of Joseph, it is true, provided a model for Jewish wise men serving foreign kings, a model developed in the Book of Daniel, but the fall of the monarchy was a severe blow to the profession of the wise man. Further, with the rise of the written text the understanding of wisdom inevitably underwent a certain redefinition. Daniel is not only, like Joseph, an interpreter of dreams (Daniel 2, 4); he also interprets the writing on the wall (Daniel 5) and is the recipient of an interpretation of a biblical text, the prophecy of Jeremiah that Israel's exile would endure for seventy years (Daniel 9). Dreams are a medium of divine revelation, just as is the writing on the wall or indeed the Torah. But it is surely not accidental that the Book of Daniel includes the interpretation of written texts as the story of Joseph does not. It is not surprising, then, that in the period of the Second Temple some of the functions once performed by wise men were taken over by scribes. Ezra the scribe serves as an official of the Persian crown. Nehemiah begins his career as the cup bearer of the Persian king, a position that suggests the role of court wise man, and while he is never called a scribe, as we have seen, he justified his reforms by reference to a book. Thus both Ezra and Nehemiah can be seen as examples of the scribe who not only studies the text but also serves rulers.

I have already noted that the Book of Deuteronomy laid the groundwork for Nehemiah's appeal to the written text in the last half-century before the Babylonian conquest. By placing a text at the center of Israel's communal life, Deuteronomy inevitably changed the nature of the priesthood both internally and externally. Priests had traditionally derived their authority from their role in the sacrificial cult, the purity laws associated with it, and certain mantic functions of the office. The centralization of the cult that Deuteronomy demanded brought with it radical changes for priests accustomed to serving the Lord outside

Jerusalem. But another aspect of the reform had implications even more revolutionary. No longer could priests count on an appeal to the traditional knowledge passed on by father to son through the generations to silence opposition to the way they conducted the affairs of the temple. The significance of this development may not have been immediately obvious. First of all, until the Babylonian conquest the temple remained under the control of the king. It is the power of the king that accounts both for idolatrous worship in the temple at the time of Manasseh and for the implementation of the Deuteronomic reform under Josiah. Only with the disappearance of the king in the Second Temple period do the full implications of the authority of the text become clear.

Still, though they may not have been able to foresee the ultimate results of their innovations, it hardly escaped the notice of Deuteronomy's authors that they had undercut the traditional basis of priestly authority. The evidence for their realization lies in their effort to redefine the role of priests. One aspect of the redefinition of the priesthood associates priests with the book of the Torah; the other makes them judicial officials. As part of its program to establish itself as the constitution of the people of Israel, Deuteronomy prescribes that the king himself write a copy of the Torah, that is, Deuteronomy, with all the limitations on his power that it specifies, *milipnē hakōhănîm halĕwiyîm* (Deut 17:18). The meaning of this phrase is not entirely clear;[6] what is clear is that Deuteronomy uses the phrase to associate the book of the Torah with the priests. The association of priests and text is also expressed in the teaching role Deuteronomy attributes to priests. Moses' blessing of the tribe of Levi juxtaposes teaching and sacrifice: "They shall teach [*yôrû*] Jacob thy ordinances, and Israel thy law; they shall put incense before thee, and whole burnt offerings upon thy altar" (Deut 33:10). It even transforms the role of priests in dealing with skin eruptions into teaching: "Take heed, in an attack of leprosy, to be very careful to do according to all that the Levitical priests shall teach [*yôrû*] you" (Deut 24:8).[7]

While Deuteronomy connects priests with the book of the Torah, it never calls them scribes. The office Deuteronomy adds to the priestly repertoire is the office of judge. As part of its constitution for the Israelite polity, Deuteronomy calls for a judicial system in which cases too difficult to be resolved at the local level can be referred to a central court of appeal (Deut 17:8-13). Priests participate in the upper level of the judicial system together with judges who are not priests, presumably lending some of the prestige of their traditional status to their new roles (Deut 17:9, 12). So too cases involving a malicious witness (Deut 19:16) are to be referred to "the priests and the judges" (Deut 19:17). Deuteronomy even makes a parenthetical reference to the judicial function of

priests in the course of delineating their quite different role in the ceremony for ridding a city of guilt for a murder victim found outside the
city (Deut 21:5).

Deuteronomy never directly associates priests with wisdom, but it does
treat wisdom as a qualification for judges. In the opening chapter of
Deuteronomy, Moses recalls how the people accepted his plan to relieve
him of some of the burden of their affairs by choosing officials to serve
as judges. These officials are described as "wise, understanding, and experienced men" (Deut 1:13) and "wise and experienced men" (Deut
1:15); in contrast, when Moses takes a similar step at the suggestion of
his father-in-law in the Book of Exodus, the men are described not as
wise but as "able men" (Exod 18:21, 25). Deuteronomy's condemnation
of bribery also associates wisdom with judges: "You shall not take a bribe,
for a bribe blinds the eyes of the wise and subverts the cause of the righteous" (Deut 16:19). A somewhat different set of associations for wisdom
emerges in Moses' exhortation to Israel to observe the "statutes and ordinances" (Deut 4:5) that he has taught them, "for that will be your wisdom and your understanding in the sight of the peoples, who, when
they hear all these statutes, will say, 'Surely this great nation is a wise and
understanding people' " (Deut 4:6). Although Deuteronomy here refers
to "statutes and ordinances" rather than the "book of the Torah," the association of wisdom with ordinances does suggest a connection between
wisdom and text. This is a connection that we take for granted, but it is
important to remember that the connection is possible only with the
emergence of a text at the center of Israel's life.

The association of priests with the Torah and wisdom does not mean a
merging of professions. Not all priests were trained as scribes, and not
all priests could offer wise advice. Furthermore, no matter how skilled
the scribe or how wise the sage, he could not serve as a priest unless he
was a descendant of Aaron. But it is worth dwelling on the fact that the
roles of priest and scribe are by no means diametrically opposed. Indeed, as the figure of Ezra himself shows, any theoretical contradiction
could be resolved through the combination of priestly heredity and
scribal training in a single person: even before identifying Ezra by his
profession, as scribe, the Book of Ezra introduces its hero with a lengthy
genealogy tracing his line back to Aaron (Ezra 7:1-5). In the hellenistic
period Joshua b. Eleazar b. Sira perhaps offers another example of this
combination. His book makes it clear that he was a scribe by profession,
while his name makes it plausible that he was a priest by ancestry.[8] Just as
in the period of the First Temple, then, when at least two of the most important prophets, Jeremiah and Ezekiel, were of priestly ancestry, there
was significant overlap in the Second Temple period between the
priestly elite and the scribal elite.

In this chapter I wish to examine two important works of the period before the Maccabean Revolt that depict their heroes as both priest and scribe: the *Book of the Watchers* (*1 Enoch* 1-36), which probably dates to the late third century B.C.E, and the Wisdom of ben Sira, composed around 180 B.C.E. The *Book of the Watchers* offers as its exemplar of true priesthood a virtuous scribe who performs priestly functions, while the Wisdom of ben Sira concludes with an ode to a high priest who has all the attributes of wisdom. Both works attribute prophetic status to scribes. But there are also some striking differences of outlook between the works; for example, ben Sira famously discourages speculation about matters beyond human understanding, while the *Book of the Watchers* depicts Enoch as the recipient of revelations about a variety of hidden matters. Recent scholarship has puzzled over the meaning of the similarities and differences, and some have detected in ben Sira's work a defense of the Jerusalem priesthood against the sort of criticism implicit in the *Book of the Watchers*. I shall explore the possible relation between the two works after discussing each individually. Finally I shall briefly consider *Aramaic Levi*, a text in which the ideal priest remains primarily a cultic functionary; if he has been granted some royal prerogatives, they are more limited than those of ben Sira's high priest, and it is quite clear that he is not understood as a scribe or wise man. I am inclined to date *Aramaic Levi* early, perhaps even earlier than the *Book of the Watchers*, but others place it as late as the Hasmonean period. Either way, its picture of the ideal priest is strikingly out of tune with the developments observed in the *Book of the Watchers* and ben Sira, and this difference requires consideration.

Enoch as Scribe and Priest

After the *Astronomical Book* (*1 Enoch* 72-82), the *Book of the Watchers* is the earliest extant apocalypse; the Aramaic fragments from Qumran can be dated on paleographical grounds to the early part of the second century B.C.E., making it likely that the work was composed in the third century. I use the term "composed" because the *Book of the Watchers* is not an authored work in the usual sense. It was composed in layers by authors who attached their work to the previous layers that inspired it.[9] Thus it is perhaps not surprising that the *Book of the Watchers* is a particularly difficult text to interpret. Despite this, it was extremely influential in the centuries immediately following its composition and even into the early Christian era. It is the first Jewish work to describe the ascent of a visionary to heaven; such ascents became an important form of expression for ancient Jews and Christians. It was also the fountainhead of a flourishing literature attributed to Enoch. While the status of first Enochic work belongs to the *Astronomical Book* rather than the *Book of the Watchers*, it is the narrative of the *Book of the Watchers* and its depiction of Enoch that serve as the point of departure for the *Epistle of Enoch* (*1 Enoch* 92-105), the *Book of Dreams* (*1 Enoch* 83-90), the *Similitudes of Enoch* (*1 Enoch* 37-71), and *2 Enoch*; its influence is felt as late as *Sefer Hekhalot*, the hekhalot text sometimes called *3 Enoch*.

The *Book of the Watchers* tells the story of the descent of a group of angels, the sons of God of Gen 6:1-4, who take human wives (*1 Enoch* 6-11). This violation of cosmic order has disastrous results. First, the giant offspring of the intermarriages between angels and women are soon ravaging the earth (*1 Enoch* 7). Further, the angels reveal forbidden knowledge to humanity, including the making of implements of war, jewelry, and cosmetics, which lead human beings to fornication and warfare (*1 Enoch* 8). This unhappy state of affairs is resolved only through divine intervention, with archangels punishing the angelic criminals and their sons as the flood cleanses the earth of human wrongdoing. Enoch enters this story as a messenger (*1 Enoch* 12-16). He is enlisted first by the Watchers who have remained in heaven to carry their words of condemnation to their fallen brothers (*1 Enoch* 12:1-13:3). Then the fallen Watchers ask Enoch to write a petition for mercy and deliver it to the Lord (*1 Enoch* 13:4-7). Enoch ascends to heaven, where the Lord rejects the petition and gives Enoch further words of condemnation for the fallen Watchers (*1 Enoch* 13:8-16:4). Following his ascent, Enoch travels to the ends of the earth in the company of angels (*1 Enoch* 17-36). The places he visits in the course of the tour allow him to learn about the wonders of creation and the future judgment.

Enoch makes a brief appearance in a genealogy in the Book of Genesis that manages to raise a host of questions in a mere four verses (Gen 5:21-24). His life span of 365 years, strikingly short in this genealogy, is fraught with calendrical significance. Furthermore, rather than simply living, begetting children, and dying like the other patriarchs, Enoch "walked with God and was not, for God took him" (Gen 5:24).[10] This passage hints at traditions about the figure similar to the ones that appear in the *Book of the Watchers*, traditions the authors of this passage or editors of the Torah preferred to play down, just as the account in Gen 6:1-4 suggests acquaintance with a more elaborate version of its problematic story.

The section of the *Book of the Watchers* of most interest for the treatment of Enoch as scribe and priest is chapters 12–16, which George Nickelsburg dates to the first half of the third century B.C.E.[11] It is here that Enoch makes his first appearance in the narrative of the *Book of the Watchers*; indeed this is probably the first place where Enoch is connected to the story of the descent of the Watchers. Enoch's professional identity is implicit in the earlier *Astronomical Book,* where Enoch writes down the revelations of Uriel (*1 Enoch* 74:2).[12] In chapters 12–16, it is immediately obvious that Enoch is a scribe: the Watchers who remain in heaven address him as "Enoch, righteous scribe" (*1 Enoch* 12:4), and later God calls him a scribe (*1 Enoch* 15:1).[13] Not only is Enoch called scribe; he also acts as scribe. He writes down the petition of the fallen Watchers (*1 Enoch* 13:6) and reads it (*1 Enoch* 13:7) before his ascent. The act of writing the petition involves more than taking dictation. The petition is a quasi-legal document, and it requires training to draw up such a document. Since the Watchers of heaven and the Lord address Enoch as scribe before they give Enoch the messages he is to take to the fallen Watchers, we should probably understand that Enoch wrote down these messages also. In other words, it is his ability to write and his knowledge of the proper forms that make Enoch a desirable messenger.

Enoch's scribal activity is of great importance to chapters 12–16, but it is also rather limited in its scope; it consists entirely of drawing up and reading petitions and messages. Thus at first glance Enoch appears to be at something of a disadvantage when compared to the ideal scribe of the Wisdom of ben Sira or even to the Enoch of the *Astronomical Book.* Ben Sira's scribe is no mere paralegal but a learned interpreter of the Torah and other ancient wisdom (Sir 39:1-11), while the *Astronomical Book,* as just noted, shows Enoch engaged in the learned task of copying down calendrical information to transmit to humanity. But, as Annette Reed has recently argued, one of the central concerns of chapters 12–16 is to depict Enoch as the positive counterpart to the fallen Watchers: while they wrongly reveal to humanity secrets best left in heaven, Enoch shows himself to be a worthy recipient of the heavenly knowledge he is granted, including his experience of the heavenly temple and his vision of God.[14] The continuation of the *Book of the Watchers* offers other forms of knowledge revealed to Enoch. Following his ascent to heaven, Enoch tours the ends of the earth in the company of the archangels, viewing the wonders of the cosmos (*1 Enoch* 17-36); the natural world's testimony to the greatness of its creator is an important theme of the classical wisdom tradition.[15] Thus the *Book of the Watchers* does complement Enoch's rather technical skills as a scribe with a higher wisdom, though it does not clearly link either the vision of the heavenly temple or the sights Enoch sees in the course of the journey to the ends of the earth to Enoch's role as scribe. Apparently it understands the skills of the scribe and the knowledge of heavenly secrets as two separate aspects of Enoch's wisdom.

The depiction of Enoch as priest in chapters 12–16 is not explicit, but it is nonetheless clear. But while Enoch's association with writing predates the *Book of the Watchers,* as far as I know there is no evidence that the picture of Enoch as priest draws on earlier traditions. In contrast to the account of Noah's career in Genesis, which reports that he offered sacrifices (Gen 8:20), the very spare biblical account of Enoch's life contains nothing that points to a priestly role. As we shall see, *Jubilees* places considerable emphasis on Enoch's priestly role, making him the founder of the incense offering (*Jub.* 4:25), but *Jubilees* is clearly indebted to the *Book of the Watchers*, among other Enochic works, for its picture of Enoch.[16]

Enoch's priestly status becomes evident in the course of his ascent to heaven, which the *Book of the Watchers* describes as a temple (*1 Enoch* 14-16).[17] In the ancient Near East, the temple was often understood as the earthly abode of the god, the counterpart to the god's actual dwelling place in heaven or on some far mountain. In ancient Israel during the monarchy God's presence was widely understood to be available in the temple. It is in the temple that Isaiah of Jerusalem sees the Lord enthroned among his angelic entourage (Isaiah 6), and the popular certainty that Jerusalem would never be conquered derived from the belief that the Lord was truly present in his house. There were always critics of this view, to be sure. Thus Jeremiah denied that the temple could protect a sinful people from harm (Jer 7:4), and when he prophesied its destruction (Jer 25:1-6), some of his listeners are said to have recalled a similar prophecy of Micah of Moreshet, a contemporary of Isaiah a century earlier (Jer 26:1-18; Mic 3:12). The Book of Deuteronomy also distances itself from the popular view. The temple is a holy place not because its location is inherently holy but because God has chosen it as the place to put his name (Deut 12:5 and elsewhere)—his "name," not his glory or his presence. Yet before the destruction of the temple, the dominant view is undoubtedly that God is truly available in his temple.[18]

The destruction, however, made necessary a new way of thinking about God's presence. To begin with, those who understood God to dwell in the temple needed a way to make sense of the destruction. The prophet Ezekiel's vision of idolatry in the temple (Ezekiel 8) is surely a figment of his imagination; Ezekiel had already been exiled to Babylonia, but Jeremiah, who lived in Jerusalem and welcomed any evidence of his people's sinfulness, never mentions this striking instance. Ezekiel's vision is meant to explain how the destruction was possible: the glory of God is unwilling to remain in the temple thus defiled and departs on a throne of cherubim (Ezekiel 10-11). Once the Lord is no longer present, the temple and the city can be destroyed. Ezekiel also sees the glory return to the eschatological temple in his vision at the end of the book (Ezek 43:1-3). In the meantime, the mobile throne on which the glory sits makes it clear that the Lord's presence is not restricted to any single location.

Roughly seventy years after the destruction of the First Temple, the Second Temple was dedicated. But the new temple never enjoyed the unquestioned status of its predecessor. The ark and the cherubim were gone, although their disappearance may have preceded the destruction by several generations.[19] The appearance of the new temple, at least at the beginning, was no match for that of the First Temple (Hag 2:3). Furthermore, those who brought sacrifice in the new structure were all too aware of what could happen to a temple if its people and priests were sinful. Disappointment and anxiety combined to call into question the holiness of the Second Temple. For the author of chapters 12–16 of the *Book of the Watchers*, the Lord's presence is better sought in heaven than on earth. He is the first to imagine his hero's ascent to heaven and the first to describe heaven as the true temple, of which the Jerusalem temple is merely a copy. Later apocalypses follow the *Book of the Watchers* by narrating ascents and picturing heaven as a temple. But while later apocalyptic authors claim that the Second Temple was defiled from the very start,[20] the *Book of the Watchers* is more moderate in its criticism. The preference for the heavenly temple over the earthly in *1 Enoch* 12-16 suggests that the affairs of the temple were not being conducted in a manner that lived up to the author's standards, but, as I shall try to show, he had no reservations about the temple as an institution, nor did he claim that the Second Temple was irreversibly defiled.

The *Book of the Watchers* never announces that its heaven is a temple, but it describes it in terms that make this clear.[21] The various biblical depictions of temple and sanctuary differ on many points, but all agree on an arrangement of three areas of increasing holiness.[22] The first is accessible to ordinary Israelites, the second to priests alone, while the third, the holy of holies, is entered only once a year, on the Day of Atonement, by the high priest (Leviticus 16). The series of heavenly structures that Enoch encounters in heaven—a wall (*1 Enoch* 14:9), an outer building (*1 Enoch* 14:10-14), and an inner building (*1 Enoch* 14:15-24)—reflects this structure. The cherubim on the ceiling of the outer room of the heavenly temple (*1 Enoch* 14:11) echo the cherubim on the walls of the earthly temple,[23] while the cherubim throne on which the Lord sits (*1 Enoch* 14:18) is the heavenly version of the cherubim in the holy of holies in the temple.[24] The priests of this heavenly temple are the crowd of angels who stand before the throne day and night (*1 Enoch* 14:21-23).[25]

If heaven is a temple, Enoch's safe passage through the court and the outer chamber to the entrance of the holy of holies, unhindered by any angelic objection, is a clear indication of priestly status. The words of the Lord to Enoch as he stands before him also point to an understanding of Enoch as priest: "Go and say to the watchers of heaven who have sent you to intercede on their behalf: 'It is you who should be petitioning on behalf of men, and not men on your behalf'" (*1 Enoch* 15:2). Intercession is a priestly task.[26] God's objection is to the unsuitability of Enoch's clients, not to his undertaking the task.

The understanding of the Watchers as priests in the heavenly temple is the contribution of chapters 12–16; it does not appear in the story of the descent of the Watchers in chapters 6–11. I suggested above that interest in the heavenly temple reflects lack of confidence in the earthly. But chapters 12–16 report that all is not well in the heavenly temple either. Some of the priests of the heavenly temple have abandoned their posts; they have descended to earth, undertaken marriages unsuitable to them, and revealed secrets that should not have been made known, to devastating effect. Why imagine troubles in the heavenly temple? Or, to be more precise, why imagine priests of the heavenly temple who break the rules of priesthood? Perhaps as a way of criticizing the behavior of priests in the earthly temple. But it is important to notice that the according to the *Book of the Watchers* many Watchers remain in heaven performing their duties. Thus the criticism of earthly priests that chapters 12–16 read in the story of the descent of the Watchers is not directed at all priests, and thus it appears that in the view of the author of these chapters, the earthly temple, despite its problems, remains a viable temple—just like the heavenly temple.

Priestly Marriage and the Watchers' Wives

Presumably the author of chapters 12–16 developed the picture of heaven as temple and treated the Watchers as priests because there was something about the story of their descent that reminded him of his concerns about the priests of his own day.[27] The sins of the Watchers, according to the ancient story on which chapters 12–16 drew, consist of marriage to women and revelation of heavenly secrets to humanity. We have seen that the contrast between the Watchers' revelation of heavenly secrets to humanity and God's revelation of secrets to Enoch is a central theme of chapters 12–16. But it is difficult to imagine any contemporary analogue for the revelation of secrets, and it seems to me more likely that the author of chapters12–16 is upset about the wives priests in his own day have chosen. Priestly marriages are of great importance for the future of the priesthood, and they are a subject of polemic in other texts of the Second Temple period.

But before we turn to some of those texts, it is worth remembering that there is a certain lack of symmetry between Watchers and priests in regard to marriage. While the Torah decrees that priests are more limited in their choice of wives than other Israelite men (Lev 21:7, 14; cf. Ezek 44:22), no ancient Jewish text suggests that priests should not marry. The Watchers' marriages to women, on the other hand, are wrong not because the Watchers should have married someone else, but because as immortal angels they should not have married at all:

> Why have you forsaken the high heaven, the eternal sanctuary;
>   and lain with women, and defiled yourselves with the daughters of men;
>   and taken for yourselves wives, and done as the sons of earth;
>   and begotten for yourselves sons, giants?
> You were holy ones and spirits, living forever.
> With the blood of women you have defiled yourselves,
>   and with the blood of flesh you have begotten;
> And with the blood of men you have lusted,
>   and you have done as they do—
>   flesh and blood, who die and perish. (*1 Enoch* 15:3-4)

This lack of symmetry makes it particularly difficult to decide what chapters 12–16 view as wrong in the marriages of the priests of Jerusalem sometime in the third century B.C.E. In his early work on the subject, Nickelsburg emphasized the parallels between Enoch's rebuke of the Watchers and Ezra's rebuke of the men of the community of the return in the middle of the fifth century B.C.E. who had taken foreign wives — or at least wives Ezra considered foreign. Like Enoch, Ezra, as we have seen, was both priest and scribe.[28] But Nickelsburg suggested another direction as well. He also connected the *Book of the Watchers'* language about the Watchers' defilement with women and the blood of women (*1 Enoch* 15:3-4) to texts that condemn the defilement of the temple by men who contracted impurity from sexual relations with women in a state of menstrual impurity.[29] In his commentary, however, Nickelsburg no longer makes reference to Ezra but concentrates instead on the defilement the Watchers incur through sexual relations with women (*1 Enoch* 15:3) and the even more severe defilement of sexual relations with women in a state of menstrual impurity (*1 Enoch* 15:4).[30] He does not comment on the change in his position, but I presume it reflects his desire to make the sins he deduces for the priests reflect as much as possible the language of the *Book of the Watchers*.

Yet I am not sure that Nickelsburg's current position solves the problem. According to Lev 15:18, the defilement caused by sexual relations is so short-lived that it is hardly an impediment to service in the temple: both man and woman must bathe, and at evening they become clean. True, a priest could fail to bathe, or he could fail to wait until evening to enter the temple. It is possible that such neglect of the requirements of Leviticus is what the *Psalms of Solomon* intends: "They trampled the altar of the Lord, *coming straight* from all *kinds of* uncleanness" (*Pss. Sol.* 8:12). But this possibility does not seem to have caused great anxiety in the literature of the period. Closer to the turn of the era, as we shall see, the *Temple Scroll* and 4QD extend the period of impurity and make more elaborate the process of purification required after sexual relations for all Jews.[31] As far as I know, however, the defilement caused by sexual relations is nowhere else the subject of polemic against priests.

The defilement incurred through sexual relations with a woman in a state of menstrual impurity is more severe than that incurred through ordinary sexual relations. It lasts for seven days, and it can be conveyed to others (Lev 15:24). Unlike many other ways of incurring impurity, such as ordinary sexual relations, it is also forbidden (Lev 18:19, 20:18). Nickelsburg points to instances of polemic against priests who pollute the temple through sexual relations with women in a state of menstrual impurity in the continuation of the passage from the *Psalms of Solomon* just quoted, "And with menstrual blood they defiled the sacrifices as *though they were* common flesh" (*Pss. Sol.* 8:12), and in the *Damascus Document* (CD 5.6-7). While the trampling of the *altar*, where only priests approach, in the first part of the verse from the *Psalms of Solomon* suggests that this work has priests in particular in mind,[32] the *Damascus Document* explicitly designates the pollution of the temple in this way a snare in which "Israel" is caught (CD 4.15-16). One did not need to be a priest to pollute the temple through menstrual impurity, for any Jew entering the temple for any purpose in a state of impurity would have caused pollution.

It is also worth paying careful attention to the language of the *Book of the Watchers*. The Watchers have "lain with women and defiled [themselves] with the daughters of men" (*1 Enoch* 15:3). Leviticus, on the other hand, emphasizes the seminal emission as the source of defilement:

And if a man has an emission of semen, he shall bathe his whole body in water, and be unclean until the evening. And every garment and every skin on which the semen comes shall be washed with water, and be unclean until the evening. If a man lies with a woman and has an emission of semen, both of them shall bathe themselves in water, and be unclean until the evening. (Lev 15:16-18)

Perhaps the language of the *Book of the Watchers* is intended to make the point that unlike men, the Watchers incur defilement not only through seminal emission but by the very fact of taking wives.

Furthermore, while the *Damascus Document* and the *Psalms of Solomon* leave no doubt that the men they are condemning are defiled by *menstrual* blood, the *Book of the Watchers* is much less clear:

With the blood of women you have defiled yourselves,
    and with the blood of flesh you have begotten;
And with the blood of men you have lusted[33]

and you have done as they do—
flesh and blood, who die and perish. (*1 Enoch* 15:4)

It is certainly possible that the "blood of women" means menstrual
blood, but what does "blood of flesh" mean? Perhaps the key to this passage is the phrase "flesh and blood," since all the appearances of "blood"
in the passage could be read as if part of that pair. Thus, rather than indicating menstrual defilement, "with the blood of women you have defiled yourselves" could mean that the very fact of marriage is defiling for
the Watchers.

But perhaps the most important reason to reject the view that the
Book of the Watchers condemns violations of the purity laws that could
lead to defilement of the temple is that the Watchers who are the objects
of the condemnations have in fact abandoned the heavenly temple. They
are doing just what priests (or anyone else) in a state of impurity should
do: staying away from the temple. Indeed, according to the Torah, there
is nothing wrong with becoming impure through sexual relations. One
must take care not to enter the temple or have contact with holy things
while in a state of impurity (Lev 12:4), and one must take proper steps
to bring an end to the state of impurity.[34] But for human beings, who
have been commanded to be fruitful and multiply, sexual relations are
not only permissible but desirable.

Thus it seems to me that whatever is at stake in the Watchers' marriages, it is not purity. To my mind, Nickelsburg's comparison of Enoch
to Ezra is a more promising direction.[35] Priests are prominent among
those condemned by Ezra and Nehemiah for marriage to foreign
women, or rather to women Ezra and Nehemiah considered foreign
(Ezra 9:1; 10:5, 18-22; Neh 13:28). According to Josephus, the same sort
of marriages continued to be a significant social problem a century
later. Josephus accounts for the building of the Samaritan temple on
Mt. Gerizim, which he places at the beginning of the conquests of Alexander, with a story about Manasseh, the brother of the high priest Jaddua
(*Jewish Antiquities* 11.303-12). Manasseh married Nikaso, the daughter of
Sanballat, the governor of Samaria. When Jaddua and the elders of
Jerusalem pressured Manasseh to divorce Nikaso, Sanballat built the
temple. Manasseh then left Jerusalem for Samaria, where he served as
high priest in the temple, accompanied by many other Israelites, including priests, who were married to Samaritan women.

This explanation for the building of the Samaritan temple certainly
does not inspire confidence, but the assumption that marriage with
Samaritan women was common in fourth-century Jerusalem is not implausible. Eibert J. C. Tigchelaar suggests that this incident, in which an
improper marriage led to abandoning the Jerusalem temple just as the

Watchers' marriages led to abandoning the heavenly temple, provides the context for understanding the criticism of priestly marriages in chapters 12–16.[36] While marriage to Samaritan women and other women of the land seems to have receded as an issue in the third and second centuries,[37] Nickelsburg's dating of chapters 12–16 to the first half of the third century puts them not too far from the background Tigchelaar proposes.[38] Yet Josephus's account reports widespread opposition to Manasseh's marriage; without such opposition, there would have been no need for the building of the Samaritan temple and Manasseh's departure from Jerusalem. Indeed, according to Josephus, both the high priest and the elders were opposed to Manasseh's behavior. It seems unlikely that the author of chapters 12–16 would have found behavior that was widely condemned so threatening.

Priests and Marriage in Second Temple Times

I would prefer to read the *Book of the Watchers* in light of *Aramaic Levi*,[39] a roughly contemporary text that appears to come from the same milieu.[40] Unfortunately, the text is fragmentary, but it is clear that *Aramaic Levi* is deeply concerned with questions of acceptable marriage partners.[41] It begins with Simeon and Levi's attack on the Shechemites (*Ar. Levi* 1-3), which it views as entirely praiseworthy. Indeed, it is this act of zeal that earns Levi the priesthood. The motive for Levi's attack on Shechem is the desire to prevent any possibility of intermarriage between Jacob's family and the people of Shechem (*Ar. Levi* supp. 22-supp. 26).[42] Once Levi has earned the priesthood, his grandfather Isaac teaches him the "law of the priesthood," a rather lengthy set of instructions that have to do primarily with procedures for sacrifice (*Ar. Levi* 13-61). The instructions begin, however, with an exhortation about choosing an appropriate wife:

> And now, my son, the true law I will show you, and I will not hide from you any word, so as to teach you the law of the priesthood. First, keep yourself pure of all fornication and uncleanness, and of all harlotry. And you, take for yourself a wife from my family so that you will not defile your seed with harlots. For you are holy seed, and holy is your seed, like the holy place. For you are a holy priest called for all the seed of Abraham. (*Ar. Levi* 15-17)

In insisting that Levi must marry a woman from "my family," Isaac must mean more than that Levi should not marry outsiders like the Shechemites, a prohibition that applies to all of Jacob's family.[43] The emphasis on Levi's priestly status—"For you are a holy priest called for all the seed of Abraham" (*Ar. Levi* 17)—suggests that as a priest Levi is subject to different rules from the rest of his family. Indeed Isaac's words contain an echo of the Torah's rule for the high priest: "A widow, or one divorced, or a woman who has been defiled, or a harlot, these he shall not marry; but he shall take to wife a virgin of his own people ['ammāyw]"[44] (Lev 21:14). Like Philo (*Special Laws* 1.110) and Josephus (*Antiquities* 3.277),[45] who claim that the high priest must marry a woman of priestly ancestry, *Aramaic Levi* appears to intend Isaac's "my family" in the sense of priests. Thus it interprets Lev 21:14's "people" in a restricted sense, not as Israelites generally but as other priests. The contrast between proper wives and harlots involves an expansion of the meaning of "harlot," *zōnâ*, to include any woman forbidden to Levi.[46] Surely Isaac could not mean that all women outside his family are harlots in the usual sense. Elsewhere in the literature of the Second Temple period, too, "harlotry" comes to mean any sexual practices to which the writer objects.

Levi in *Aramaic Levi* occupies an ambiguous place in the priestly hierarchy. As the only priest in his generation, he is at once the high priest (by default) and the ancestor of all priests. So it is not entirely clear whether Isaac's limits on marriage partners are intended to apply to the high priest alone or to all priests. Since the instructions as a whole are relevant to all priests, not merely the high priest, I am inclined to think that *Aramaic Levi* intends the restrictions to apply to all priests. Further, the exegesis of "harlot" implicit in *Aramaic Levi*'s understanding of Lev 21:14 might well have led in this direction. According to the Torah, ordinary priests are more limited in their choice of wives than ordinary Israelites, but less limited than the high priest: "They shall not marry a harlot or a woman who has been defiled; neither shall they marry a woman divorced from her husband; for the priest is holy to his God" (Lev 21:7). Thus, unlike the high priest, an ordinary priest is permitted to marry a widow, and there is no mention of a requirement that the bride be "of his own people." But once *Aramaic Levi* defined women from nonpriestly families as "harlots," that is, forbidden, to the high priest, the appearance of the term "harlot" among the women forbidden to ordinary priests might have suggested that all priests should restrict themselves to wives from priestly families.

The advice about marriage is the only part of the law of the priesthood that is polemical in tone.[47] The fact that it is polemical strongly suggests that the author recognized that his was a minority opinion—a fact confirmed by what we know from other sources. Ezekiel never mentions the high priest, but requires that all priests' wives be "of the seed [*zera'*][48] of the house of Israel" (Ezek 44:22). Perhaps this limitation could not be taken for granted at the end of the period of the First Temple. Ezra and Nehemiah show that it was by no means observed during the Persian period. Neither Ezekiel nor Ezra and Nehemiah insist that priests marry within the priesthood. In the first century neither Philo (*Special Laws* 1.111) nor Josephus (*Antiquities* 3.276) extends to ordinary priests the requirement that the high priest marry a woman of priestly family.

It is possible that *Aramaic Levi*'s restrictive opinion appears also in 4QMMT B 75–82.[49] The passage in question is unfortunately quite fragmentary, and its reconstruction and interpretation have been the subject of considerable discussion. It begins by referring to "harlotry" taking place among the people (B 75), quotes the laws against the mixing of kinds (B 76–78), designates Israel as holy and the sons of Aaron as most holy (B 76, 79), and then condemns the defilement of holy seed[50] with "harlots" (B 80–82). While the editors of the text read the passage as a prohibition of marriage between priests and women from nonpriestly families,[51] others have read it as a prohibition on marriage with gentile women.[52] A prohibition on intermarriage in 4QMMT seems to me unlikely. There was little need for polemic on this subject since the prohibition was widely accepted at least in theory and there is no reason to believe that intermarriage was a significant social reality in the second century B.C.E.[53] Christine Hayes has recently suggested that 4QMMT, like Ezra and *Jubilees*, rejects the possibility of conversion and is engaged in a polemic against marriage to women of gentile origin who have converted to Judaism.[54] The fact that Hayes assumes a clearer concept of conversion than is likely to have existed in the second century is not an insurmountable objection; indeed, I believe Hayes is correct in her reading of *Jubilees*, which I discuss in the next chapter. What is more, whether or not there was much "conversion" to Judaism, there was certainly considerable assimilation by gentiles of Semitic background such as the Idumeans during the period of Hasmonean expansion.[55] But Hayes's suggestion does not explain the passage's exclusive focus on men. *Jubilees*, in contrast, is very clear in rejecting the marriage of Jews of either gender to those it continues to regard as gentiles—of either gender (*Jub.* 30:11).

If, on the other hand, we understand 4QMMT's quotation of the prohibition on mixing kinds to be directed against mixing the holy Israelites and the most holy priests, the exclusively male frame of reference makes sense: priests are exclusively male. The harlots of the passage would then reflect the tradition of interpretation found in *Aramaic Levi*: a harlot is any woman prohibited to a priest, including a Jewish woman who is not from a priestly family.[56] If 4QMMT stands in the same tradition as *Aramaic Levi*, it helps resolve another difficulty as well. Hayes argues that it is impossible for the Israelites' holy seed to be defiled by contact with the priests' seed; the only seed that would be negatively affected in this situation is the priests' most holy seed, which would not be defiled but only "reduced in status."[57] Yet *Aramaic Levi* (*Ar. Levi* 17) refers to Levi and his descendants as "holy seed." Perhaps, then, the holy seed 4QMMT has in mind is that of priests, not of Israelites.

However we read 4QMMT, *Aramaic Levi* provides evidence for the view that priests should marry only women from priestly families in the circles in which the *Book of the Watchers* was written although it must be confessed that the exegetical moves of *Aramaic Levi* are not evident in the *Book of the Watchers*. Its polemical tone indicates that the position *Aramaic Levi* advocates is a minority position. This fact helps make sense of the behavior of the priests in Jerusalem: most of them did not think they were doing anything wrong, nor did most of their contemporaries.

To return to the *Book of the Watchers*, any conclusions about the marriage practices criticized in chapters 12–16 of the *Book of the Watchers* must be tentative. We know little about the setting in which these chapters were written, and their chosen mode of expression, the reworking of an ancient myth, makes interpretation particularly difficult. With these cautions in mind, I offer my conclusions in descending order of conviction: these chapters are surely intended to criticize some members of the contemporary Jerusalem priesthood; the criticism very likely has something to do with their marriage practices; and the most plausible possibility for the practice in question is marriage to women from lay families.

Enoch as Priest, Scribe, and Prophet

What is clear in chapters 12–16 is that the figure of Enoch stands in contrast to the delinquent Watchers and the contemporary priests they represent. Enoch's virtue is called to our attention as he enters the story: the Watchers address him as "Enoch, righteous scribe" (*1 Enoch* 12:4). Enoch willingly undertakes the mission to the fallen Watchers (*1 Enoch* 12:3-13:2), and just as willingly he agrees to intercede on behalf of the fallen Watchers, a task that, as we have seen, combines priestly and scribal elements (*1 Enoch* 13:4-7). Only after these acts of intercession, which have a priestly aspect, does Enoch ascend to heaven and enter the heavenly temple. If, as I have just suggested, the *Book of the Watchers* criticizes priests who marry women who are not from the right line, this is strong evidence that it does not consider priestly ancestry unimportant. Yet it presents Enoch is a model of priesthood because of his righteousness, not because of his ancestry. This righteousness, even the work of intercession, is related to his profession as scribe. Thus Enoch earns his right to priesthood.

It is almost tautological to say that the author of chapters 12–16, indeed the authors of all the layers of the *Book of the Watchers*, were scribes.

I will have more to say about what this means after discussing ben Sira's picture of the profession. It is possible that some of the authors were also priests, perhaps even likely since there appears to have been considerable overlap between priests and scribes in the Second Temple period. But I would argue strongly that interest in priests and temples on heaven and earth does not necessarily point to priestly identity, just as criticism of priests points neither toward nor away from priests. Pious Jews believed that the temple and the priesthood were central to the well-being of the whole Jewish people, perhaps even of the cosmos. Thus they could hardly avoid holding priests to a high standard and finding their inevitable failings deeply disturbing.

Before turning to ben Sira, I want to point out that for the *Book of the Watchers* Enoch is not only priest and scribe, but also prophet. In one sense this is obvious; delivering messages from the Lord serves to define the role of prophet in ancient Israel. But it is also important to note that the various layers of the book draw on prophetic models to depict Enoch. The language of chapters 1–5 implicitly compares Enoch to Moses and Balaam, the greatest prophets of Israel and the gentiles.[58] Elsewhere in the *Book of the Watchers* it is the Book of Ezekiel that is the dominant prophetic model. The influence of Ezekiel is apparent in both form and content. In chapters 12–16 the throne from which the Lord addresses Enoch has wheels although it is stationary, a clear indication that it is modeled on the mobile chariot throne of Ezekiel. The fire, lightning, and ice of the picture of the heavenly temple also echo Ezekiel's vision.[59] Some of the sights Enoch sees in the course of the tour to the ends of the earth (*1 Enoch* 17-36) are indebted to Ezekiel's picture of Jerusalem and the banks of the river flowing from it (Ezek 47:1-12) in his tour of the future temple and its surroundings (Ezekiel 40-48).[60] Enoch's ability to join the angel-priests in the heavenly temple and his tour to the ends of the earth in the company of the angels are a transformation of the prophet's claim to have participated in the deliberations of the divine council where the Lord sits enthroned among his angelic courtiers.[61] Ezekiel's tour of the future temple, the only account in prophetic literature of a journey through a temple, is the model not only for the tour to the ends of the earth, like it a horizontal tour, but also for Enoch's ascent to the heavenly temple, the first in ancient Jewish literature.[62]

The *Book of the Watchers* marks Enoch's experience as unique: "I, Enoch, alone saw the visions, the extremities of all things. And no one among humans has seen as I saw" (*1 Enoch* 19:3). Yet it also uses Enoch's story to encourage its audience not to despair of the ability of an exceptional human being to participate in the divine sphere. In the figure of Enoch, scribe of righteousness, priest in the heavenly temple, and prophet, priests would surely have heard a message: piety is a requirement for proper performance of the job. Perhaps scribes would have heard another message as well, although this one is only hinted at: a pious scribe has earned something of the privileges of a priest. No one would have understood the *Book of the Watchers* to suggest that Israelites not of priestly stock should officiate in the Jerusalem temple. But the pious might have been forgiven for feeling that Enoch's success implied that in the heavenly temple they might count themselves priests.

Scribe, Prophet, and Priest in the Wisdom of Ben Sira

Compared to other Jewish literature of the Second Temple period, certainly to the *Book of the Watchers*, the Wisdom of Joshua ben Sira is generous with information about its author. We know his name,[63] and we can date his activity with some precision to the beginning of the second century B.C.E. on the basis of his mention of the high priest Simon. At the end of the book a poem (Sir 51:13-30), an acrostic in the original, describes the speaker's pursuit of wisdom and invites students to his school.[64] The poem is sometimes read as autobiographical,[65] but there are grounds for skepticism about such a reading.[66] The language of the poem reflects the conventions of wisdom literature, and part of the poem was preserved in the Psalms Scroll from Qumran (11QPs^a = 11Q5, col. 21). Further, there is little evidence that institutionalized schools existed in Jerusalem in ben Sira's day.[67] Still, even if he did not run a school, ben Sira may well have taught the wisdom he wrote down for his book to a circle of students in a more informal setting. Some scholars have suggested on the basis of his sympathies that ben Sira was not only a scribe but also a priest.[68] In my view holding the priesthood in high regard is not enough to indicate priestly heredity. But whether or not he was a priest himself, ben Sira surely spent time with priests. As he points out, the opportunity to become wise requires the leisure that only wealth can buy (Sir 38:24), and among the Jews of ben Sira's day, priests were leading candidates for leisure. They made up a significant segment of the Jerusalem aristocracy at the turn of the third to the second century, and at least in theory their needs were provided for by the contributions of the people.

In his account of the various occupations that make the world run, ben Sira makes no secret of his view that the most exalted of all is that of the scribe:

He who devotes himself
to the study of the law of the Most High
will seek out the wisdom of all the ancients,

and will be concerned with prophecies;
he will preserve the discourse of notable men
and penetrate the subtleties of parables;
he will seek out the hidden meanings of proverbs
and be at home with the obscurities of parables.
He will serve among great men and appear before rulers;
he will travel through the lands of foreign nations,
for he tests the good and the evil among men. (Sir 39:1-4)[69]

The scribe ben Sira describes here is clearly both scribe and wise man,[70] a student of the Torah and of obscure texts on the one hand, an advisor to rulers on the other. Indeed, the book he wrote shows ben Sira to have been the kind of scribe he holds up as an ideal in chapter 39, devoting himself to the study of the law of the Most High, seeking out the wisdom of the ancients (Sir 39:1).

The great hymn to wisdom at the center of the book offers another glimpse of ben Sira's understanding of his profession. Earlier biblical wisdom literature sees wisdom as a way of life based on observing the workings of nature and humanity, available to all peoples. In this poem, modeled on Wisdom's praise of herself in Proverbs 8, ben Sira describes Wisdom, also personified as a woman, taking up residence in the Jerusalem temple, thus claiming her as the special heritage of Israel. Nor is wisdom any longer a way of life to be discovered by human contemplation; rather, after Wisdom finishes praising herself with comparisons to a variety of flourishing trees, ben Sira explains that Wisdom is the Torah: "All this is the book of the covenant of the Most High God, the law which Moses commanded us" (Sir 24:23).

After introducing a new set of similes comparing Wisdom/Torah to a river or sea (Sir 24:25-29), ben Sira turns to his own relationship to Wisdom/Torah, carrying forward the water imagery:

I went forth like a canal from a river
and like a water channel into a garden.
I said, "I will water my orchard and drench my garden plot";
and lo, my canal became a river,
and my river became a sea.
I will again make instruction shine forth like the dawn,
and I will make it shine afar;
I will again pour out teaching like prophecy,
and leave it to all future generations.
Observe that I have not labored for myself alone,
but for all who seek instruction. (Sir 24:30-33)

These are extraordinary claims ben Sira makes for himself and his chosen profession. He has already compared Wisdom/Torah to a river or sea. He himself begins as a channel, a narrow, man-made waterway, but he ends as a sea. His teaching is not merely teaching; it is "like prophecy."

The association of the scribe's teaching with prophecy is remarkable, but it is not as surprising as it would have been in an earlier period. During the First Temple period, prophecy was primarily auditory: the prophet heard God's word, which he then transmitted to the people. Zechariah at the beginning of the Second Temple period does indeed hear the word of the Lord (Zech 1:1-6, 2:10-17, 6:9-15, 7:1-8:23), but the dominant form of divine communication in his prophecy is the vision (Zech 1:7-17, 2:1-4, 2:5-9, 3:1-6:8). Most of these visions require interpretation, which is provided by an angel.[71] Visions in prophecy are not a new departure. Amos, the first of the classical prophets, sees visions (Amos 7:1-9, 8:1-3), as does Jeremiah at the end of the period of the First Temple (Jer 1:13-19, 24:1-10); God himself interprets the visions for both prophets. Despite the divine interpreters, the mode of interpretation in the symbolic visions of all three prophets recalls Joseph's interpretation of Pharaoh's dreams (Genesis 41).[72]

In contrast to Zechariah, however, symbolic visions make up only a very small portion of the prophecy of Amos and Jeremiah. Further, Zechariah's visions are considerably more complex than those of the earlier prophets or of Pharaoh in the Joseph story. Zechariah's clearest heir is the author/editor of the Book of Daniel, who never calls his hero a prophet but has him communicate predictions of the imminent end by means of the interpretation of visions and texts. The influence of visions to be deciphered can be felt even in Enoch's tour to the ends of the earth. There the sights Enoch sees are explained rather than deciphered, but the formal features of the explanations recall the language of vision interpretation in Zechariah and his predecessors.[73] The new prominence of symbolic visions in the prophecy of the Second Temple period reflects the growing importance of interpretation in communicating the divine will as Jews come to recognize the authority of the Torah.

In the Praise of the Fathers, his poetic account of Israel's history in the concluding section of his work, ben Sira treats prophecy as a thing of the past, a phenomenon of the period of the First Temple and earlier. The last prophet he mentions by name is Ezekiel (Sir 49:8-9). Immediately after Ezekiel, but before Zerubbabel, the leader of the community of the return (Sir 49:11-12), he praises "the twelve prophets" as a group (Sir 49:10). This placement is significant because two of the twelve, Zechariah and Haggai, explicitly locate themselves in the community of the return during the Persian period.[74] In other words, ben Sira could have placed the twelve or at least some of their number later in his account. Instead he prefers to leave the impression that prophets were no longer active in the period of the Second Temple. In his own day, he suggests, the mantle of divine inspiration has come to rest on the scribe.

Indeed, ben Sira's depiction of the prophets included in the Praise of the Fathers plays down their role in mediating God's will. The dominant characteristic of the prophet is instead great deeds, ranging from the standard prophetic task of anointing of kings (Sir 46:13, 48:8) to the less obviously prophetic role of leadership in battle (Sir 46:1-6).[75] The emphasis on deeds is somewhat less surprising when one considers the figures ben Sira treats as prophets: Joshua (Sir 46:1-8), Samuel (Sir 46: 13-20), Nathan (Sir 47:1), Elijah (Sir 48:1-12), and Elisha (Sir 48:12-14), as well as Isaiah (Sir 48:22-25), Jeremiah (Sir 49:6-7), Ezekiel (Sir 49:8-9), and the twelve (Sir 49:10). The second group of prophets, those from Isaiah on, whose primary achievement was verbal, are given somewhat less space than their more active predecessors. Furthermore, Isaiah and Jeremiah are described as doers of deeds in addition to speakers of prophetic words. Thus Jerusalem was saved from Sennacherib "by the hand of Isaiah" (Sir 48:20), while its destruction takes place "by the hand"[76] of Jeremiah (Sir 49:7). Of all the prophets ben Sira includes in the Praise of the Fathers, only Ezekiel and the twelve lack deeds of power. This lack of emphasis on prophetic words has the effect of playing down the link between prophet and scribe.

The figure in the Praise of the Fathers whose career provides the best model for the office of the scribe is Moses (Sir 45:1-5). Despite the brief treatment, there can be no doubt that Moses is the most exalted figure in ben Sira's history: he is the equal of the angels (Sir 45:2), God showed him part of his glory (Sir 45:3), and he spoke to him face-to-face (Sir 45:5). It is noteworthy that ben Sira never calls Moses a prophet, although he describes the power of Moses' words (Sir 45:3) and God's direct communication to him (Sir 45:5).[77] Still, it is other aspects of Moses' role that ben Sira emphasizes. The account of Moses' career culminates in the giving of the Torah and Moses' mission to teach it: "He made him hear his voice, and led him into the thick darkness, and gave him the commandment face to face, the law of life and knowledge, to teach Jacob the covenant, and Israel his judgments" (Sir 45:5).

From one point of view, the one-time-only nature of Moses' most important task, the mediation of God's revelation to Israel, ensures that Moses, unlike Aaron or David, has no successors.[78] His is not a role that can be institutionalized—nor need it be, since the Torah that he has brought to Israel survives him. But from another point of view, Moses does have successors, and ben Sira surely counted himself among them.[79] The successors are the scribes whose study of ancient texts ben Sira praises in chapter 39. Yet where ben Sira is straightforward in his account of Moses' glory and proximity to the divine, he relies on metaphors to claim glory for his own teaching activity at the end of the poem in praise of Wisdom (Sir 24:30-33). Presumably the metaphors betray an anxiety about the claims for himself that he did not feel for Moses. Yet despite the anxiety it is clear that ben Sira understands himself and his fellow learned teachers as following in the footsteps of Moses, just at the rabbis would later.

It is worth noting that ben Sira also assigns Aaron a teaching role in language similar to that he applies to Moses: "In his commandments he gave him authority in statutes and judgments, to teach Jacob the testimonies, and to enlighten Israel with his law" (Sir 45:17). Both passages echo Moses' blessing of Levi: his offspring "shall teach Jacob thy ordinances, and Israel thy law" (Deut 33:10). Making teaching a function of priests provides continuity for this important task.[80] But it also looks forward to ben Sira's presentation of Simon, the high priest of ben Sira's youth, as the embodiment of wisdom.

Priest and King in the Wisdom of Ben Sira

Though a second temple was built roughly seventy years after the destruction of the first one, the Davidic monarchy that fell with the First Temple was never restored. At the beginning of the Perisan period the prophet Zechariah describes his vision of two olive trees on either side of a lampstand (Zechariah 4). As the interpreting angel explains, the olive trees represent the "two sons of oil" (Zech 4:14)[81] who headed the community of the return, Zerubbabel the governor and Joshua the high priest. Zerubbabel's claim to anointing though he was not a king must be intended to call attention to his descent from the anointed kings of the line of David. Joshua's claim to anointing is clear; the office of high priest required it. Zechariah's pairing of high priest with governor suggests that in the new situation the high priest's power extends beyond the cult into the realm of politics.[82] While the evidence is spotty, it appears that this arrangement, rule by governor and high priest, continued throughout the Persian period. But the Persians must have decided that the appointment of Davidides was not good policy, probably because it raised hopes for restoration of a Davidic king. Sheshbazzar and Zerubbabel, the first two governors of Yehud, were descendants of David, but none of their successors was, though all who are known by name were Jews.[83] The office of high priest was a different matter. The very source of his authority, which gave him legitimacy in the eyes of his people, prevented him from claiming kingship. With the end of Persian rule, the status of the high priest rose even higher and his political power increased since the hellenistic kingdoms no longer placed a governor alongside him.[84]

Ben Sira's description of the glory of the high priest Simon at the conclusion of his work should be understood as a defense of this situation, in which, from one angle of vision, the high priest had come to replace the Davidic king of the period of the First Temple.[85] This angle of vision, it is true, required a certain amount of squinting to avoid the obvious and uncomfortable reality that the high priest was subservient to foreign kings. Still, while some Jews may have yearned for the restoration of a Davidic king,[86] ben Sira shows that the biblical tradition is not without resources for making the best of rule by high priest.

The prominence of priests in ben Sira's Praise of the Fathers has often been noted. Ben Sira devotes more lines (Sir 45:6-22) to Aaron than to any other figure from Israel's past; only Simon, who served as high priest while ben Sira was a young man, is described at greater length (Sir 50: 1-21). The most striking aspect of the passage about Aaron is the detailed description of his priestly garments, including a golden crown (Sir 45:12). The priestly document of the Torah provides the high priest with a turban with a gold plate inscribed "Holy to the Lord" (Exod 28:37-38), but the crown is ben Sira's own contribution. The phrase "golden crown" is drawn from Ps 21:4; there it describes the crown God has placed on the head of the king. Further, ben Sira notes that Aaron and his descendants are parties to a covenant that will endure "as the days of heaven" (Sir 45:1).[87] The source of the phrase is Psalm 89, a poem mourning the loss of the Davidic king: "I will establish his line for ever / and his throne as the days of heaven" (Ps 89:30[29]).[88] Thus the phrase is drawn from a royal context, but of a peculiar kind: the psalm laments the failure of the promise of an eternal dynasty. This context makes ben Sira's use of the phrase for Aaron's descendants all the more pointed.

After Aaron, ben Sira turns to Phinehas and his zealous violence against idolatry at Baal Peor (Num 25:12-13). Ben Sira's focus is the covenant Phinehas receives as a reward for his zeal rather than the nature of the deed he performs (Sir 45:23-24).[89] He notes the eternity of this covenant too and compares it to the covenant with David (Sir 45:24-25). The details of the comparison, which differ significantly in Greek and Hebrew, are not clear, but there can be no doubt about the point, the superiority of the priestly covenant to the Davidic covenant.[90] The comparison concludes with an apostrophe to the descendants of Phinehas, praying that God grant them wisdom (Sir 45:25-26).[91] The Hebrew speaks also of God "who crowns you with glory"; note that the verb "crown" has the same root as the golden crown ben Sira has already given Aaron (Sir 45:12). At the conclusion of the Hebrew version of the passage about Simon, which is also the conclusion of the Praise of the Fathers as a whole, the royal language applied earlier to Aaron's covenant appears again about the covenant with Phinehas: "May his love abide upon Simon and may he keep in him the covenant of Phinehas; may one never be cut off from him; and as for his offspring, (may it be) as the days of heaven" (Sir 50:24).[92]

Simon, too, is represented not only as the high priest but also as a royal figure. His works projects (Sir 50:1-4) recall those of Hezekiah (Sir 48:17-22).[93] His glorious appearance as he emerges from the temple evokes the glorious garments of his ancestor Aaron with their suggestion of a royal dimension to the high priest's role (Sir 45:7-13). The climax of the passage describes the people bowing before Simon to receive the blessing he mediates (Sir 50:20-21).

As ben Sira emphasizes the eternal covenants of priesthood made with Aaron and Phinehas, he downplays the covenant with David. The Hebrew does not even mention a covenant with David, and certainly not an eternal one; rather, God gave David "the law of kingship."[94] The Greek alludes to the covenant only in the concluding verse of its account of David's career: "The Lord took away his sins, and exalted his power for ever; he gave him the covenant of kings and a throne of glory in Israel" (Sir 47:11). It is noteworthy that it is the power rather than the covenant that is called eternal.[95] Not only does ben Sira try to play down the Davidic covenant; he also insists that the institution of kingship was flawed. In the course of its entire history it produced only three pious kings: "Except David and Hezekiah and Josiah they all sinned greatly, for they forsook the law of the Most High; the kings of Judah came to an end" (Sir 49:4).

But it is Solomon, the only other king mentioned by name in the praise of the fathers, who poses the most difficult problem for ben Sira. Solomon is surely the most eminent of biblical wise men. If wisdom is intimately associated with kingship, it calls into question ben Sira's claim that rule by high priest is preferable to rule by king. Thus ben Sira attempts to undercut Solomon's claim to wisdom, but only after confronting it head-on: "How wise you became in your youth! You overflowed like a river with understanding. . . . For your songs and proverbs and parables, and for your interpretations, the countries marveled at you" (Sir 47: 14, 17). The river simile recalls the description of Wisdom/Torah (Sir 24:25-27); the works Solomon wrote recall the subjects of the scribe's research (Sir 39:2-3).

But fortunately for ben Sira, Solomon was also a famous sinner:

You gathered gold like tin
and amassed silver like lead.

. . . You laid your loins beside women,
and through your body you were brought into subjection.
You put a stain upon your honor,
and defiled your posterity,
so that you brought wrath upon your children
and they were grieved at your folly,
so that the sovereignty was divided. (Sir 47:18-21)

Above I have slightly modified the translation of the RSV following the suggestion of Pancratius C. Beentjes.[96] The RSV takes the end of verse 18, the accumulation of silver and gold, as the last element of the praise of Solomon; it provides "but" to connect the praise to the criticism: "But you laid your loins beside women."[97] Against this view, Beentjes argues that ben Sira measures Solomon by the standards of Deuteronomy's law of the king: "And he shall not multiply wives for himself, lest his heart turn away; nor shall he greatly multiply for himself silver and gold" (Deut 17:17).[98] Thus the negative side of the picture begins in the middle of Sir 47:18, with the amassing of gold and silver. By appealing to the law of the king, ben Sira suggests that Solomon's betrayal of his wisdom was no accident. The stipulations of the law of the king reflect an understanding of kingship as inherently corrupting even as they attempt to check the potential for corruption. Ben Sira exploits this understanding: if even the wisest king in Israel's past fell victim to the temptations of his office, what hope was there for the institution? Further, the invocation of the law of the king suggests that ben Sira did not understand his rejection of kingship as a radical break with the traditions of Israel's past but rather as a working out of the implications of the Deuteronomic constitution and the centrality of wisdom for the life of the Jewish people. Thus Solomon is the crucial figure for ben Sira's argument.

At the conclusion of the passage about Solomon, ben Sira proclaims the continuation of David's line (Sir 47:22),[99] but the promise of "a root of [David's] stock" is apparently seen as fulfilled in the past, for ben Sira notes the continued existence of Judah under a Davidic king after the fall of the northern kingdom (Sir 48:16).[100] Ben Sira even manages to play down the royal status of the two pious kings who follow David, Hezekiah and Josiah. The career of Hezekiah (Sir 48:17-23) is intertwined with and largely subordinated to that of the prophet Isaiah (Sir 48:20-25), who, as we have seen, gets credit for the failure of the Assyrian siege. Josiah is praised highly, if briefly, for leading the people to repentance (Sir 49:1-3), but it is striking that some of the language of praise recalls the cult: "The memory of Josiah is like a blending of incense / prepared by the art of the perfumer" (Sir 49:1). This use of cultic language for Josiah is the mirror image of the praise of Aaron and Simon in royal language.

Unfortunately for ben Sira's effort to validate rule by high priest, the biblical resources for associating priests with wisdom are limited, although, as we have seen, Deuteronomy contains such elements, even if they are not fully developed. We have seen that ben Sira's account of the career of Aaron mentions the teaching role of priests in language that echoes Deut 33:10; otherwise, however, wisdom plays no role in ben Sira's characterization of Aaron.[101] Rather, it is with the figure of Simon that ben Sira takes his stand. The climax of the Praise of the Fathers is the description of Simon officiating in the temple (Sir 50:5-22). This description is clearly intended to recall the picture of Wisdom officiating in the temple (Sirach 24); the similes comparing the magnificence of Simon's appearance to a series of natural phenomena including trees and other vegetation (Sir 50:5-11) echo the tree similes Wisdom applies to herself there (Sir 24:13-17). Simon appears, if not as a scribe or teacher, then almost as Wisdom's double.

Yet even a reader persuaded by ben Sira's presentation of the claims of the high priest to rule over the people of Israel might be forgiven for remembering that the high priest must report to a foreign ruler. The Greek version of the conclusion of the Praise of the Fathers hints at the imperfections of the current situation, when it follows its description of Simon with a prayer: "May he entrust to us his mercy! / And let him deliver us in our days" (Sir 50:24). The Hebrew, which was quoted above, makes no mention at all of deliverance, thus avoiding any dissonant note in its retelling of Israel's history. Outside the Praise of the Fathers, ben Sira calls explicitly and in detail for the punishment of the nations (Sir 36:1-17), although the authenticity of this passage has been questioned.[102] Still, whether he committed his doubts to writing or not, ben Sira could hardly have been untroubled by the condition of foreign rule in his own time.

It is different for the circumstance of rule by high priest, however. Here, it seems to me, ben Sira is quite convinced, contrary to the dominant biblical view, that Israel has no need of a king. He has persuasively retold Israel's history so that there is no reason for nostalgia for kingship and he has shown wisdom embodied not in the king, whose power corrupts, but in the person of the high priest, heir to the eternal covenants of Aaron and Phinehas. Further, despite the inherent tension between his royal conception of the high priesthood and the ideal of the priest as scribe, ben Sira succeeds in integrating the two in the figure of Simon. By depicting the recent high priest in terms that recall Wisdom as she officiates in the temple in chapter 24, ben Sira implies that Simon bears not only the authority of the royal high priesthood but also the authority of the Torah.

Ben Sira, Enoch, and the Torah of Moses

If ben Sira's scribe is a student of the law of the Most High and the wisdom of the ancients, a conduit for the great sea of Wisdom, Enoch in the *Book of the Watchers* is a scribe in a rather technical and limited sense, an expert in drawing up legal documents. He could not be a student of the Torah since the *Book of the Watchers* is set in a time long before its revelation—nor has the world in Enoch's day been in existence long enough to provide much ancient wisdom. Yet though Enoch does not measure up to ben Sira's ideal of the scribe, the authors of the *Book of the Watchers* certainly do. They carefully studied the Torah: the narrative of *1 Enoch* 6-11 reworks extrabiblical traditions in light of the story of Gen 6:1-4, while the criticism of priests for improper marriage may reflect a particular exegesis of Leviticus 21. And they concerned themselves with the difficult writings of the ancients: *1 Enoch* 12-16 interprets the descent of the Watchers by means of a close reading of *1 Enoch* 6-11.

But many scholars would reject what I have just claimed about the importance of the Torah, especially its laws, for the *Book of the Watchers* and *1 Enoch* as a whole. These scholars understand the Enochic literature to expound a type of wisdom that stands if not in opposition to then at least apart from the Torah.[103] Thus Nickelsburg:

> To judge from what the authors of 1 Enoch have written, the Sinaitic covenant and Torah were not of central importance for them. . . . 1 Enoch employs a different paradigm or set of categories as the primary means of embodying the double notion that God has revealed the divine will to humanity and will reward and punish right and wrong conduct. Law and its interpretation are embodied in the notion of revealed "wisdom." . . . By using the epistemological term "wisdom" and emphasizing its receipt and transmission, the Enochic authors explicitly tie their soteriology to the possession of right knowledge. Actions are, of course, important, but they are possible only if one is rightly informed.[104]

If this formulation seems to contain echoes of faith versus works, a little later it emerges that Nickelsburg does have Paul in mind:

> 1 Enoch and the Wisdom of Solomon marginalize or ignore the Mosaic Torah, appealing more to revealed wisdom than to laws as the authority and criterion for human conduct. In all of these respects, one perceives a continuity from 1 Enoch and the Wisdom of Solomon back to the prophetic tradition and a disjunction with the Mosaic tradition. . . . The marginalizing of the Mosaic Torah in 1 Enoch, the Wisdom of Solomon, and the *Musar leMevin* [a text from the Dead Sea Scrolls] offers a precedent for the similar tendency expressed by Paul and attributed to Jesus of Nazareth in most strata of the gospel tradition.[105]

There is nothing inappropriate about using early Christian texts to illumine ancient Jewish texts. But in my view *1 Enoch* takes a stance very different from the one Nickelsburg attributes to it with Paul in mind. I will limit my quarrel with Nickelsburg to the *Book of the Watchers*, although I would be prepared to make the case about the centrality of the Torah for the entire corpus of *1 Enoch*. While there can be no denying that the understanding of the origins of evil in the *Book of the Watchers* stands in conflict with the Torah's understanding, I doubt very much that the authors of the *Book of the Watchers* understood their work to be in conflict with the Torah. The authors of some of the strands of *1 Enoch* 6-11 and 12-16 struggled to make sense of the relationship of divine wrongdoing to human culpability.[106] The author of the second tour to the ends of the earth (*1 Enoch* 20-36) felt compelled to include the Garden of Eden on the tour (*1 Enoch* 32:3-6) and, with it, the Torah's story of Adam and Eve; he works hard to cut down on conflict by ignoring the elements of the story that make it an etiology of evil in the world. In other words, the authors of the *Book of the Watchers* intended their work to clarify what the Torah really meant rather than to reject it or even ignore it. Nickelsburg is certainly right that the language of covenant, the figure of Moses, and the content of the Torah do not figure prominently in the *Book of the Watchers* or elsewhere in *1 Enoch*, but this absence is to a considerable extent a result of the fictive setting of the work, which places Moses many centuries in the future.

Nickelsburg's view that the *Book of the Watchers* stands apart from the Torah is related to his understanding of it and of the larger corpus of *1 Enoch* as sectarian. If the Enochic works are anti-establishment voices, it is easier to read the absence of a clear statement of loyalty to the central document of the establishment, the Torah of Moses, as an indication of less than wholehearted allegiance to that Torah. But as Annette Reed has pointed out, Nickelsburg arrives at his view of the *Book of the Watchers* as sectarian by reading it through the lens of the *Book of Dreams* and the *Epistle of Enoch* and assuming that it shares their rejection of the Jerusalem temple and sectarian or at least proto-sectarian attitude toward other Jews.[107] Yet, as we have seen, the *Book of the Watchers'* attitude toward the Jerusalem temple is not entirely negative, and there is little indication of sectarian identity anywhere in the work. The solar calendar of the *Astronomical Book* is at most hinted at in the *Book of the Watchers*, but even embrace of the calendar is not necessarily an indication of sectarian affiliation in the third century. It is not clear, after all, what the calendar of the temple was in the period before the Maccabean Revolt, and the absence of a polemic against the lunar or lunisolar calendar in the *Astronomical Book* is striking.[108] Finally, I would point out, the evidence of the Qumran community certainly suggests that it is possible to be both disaffected with the Jerusalem establishment and deeply loyal to the Torah.

The earliest readers of the *Book of the Watchers* certainly did not understand it as in any way aloof from Mosaic themes. The first non-Enochic work that reflects knowledge of the *Book of the Watchers* is the *Book of Jubilees*, a work that presents itself as the Torah-Testimony of Moses in contrast to the standard Torah, the Torah-Commandment in *Jubilees'* terminology. *Jubilees* depicts Enoch as an important link in its chain of priests and as the first author. *Jubilees* calls the text Enoch writes a "testimony" (*Jub.* 4:16-26), the same term it uses for itself, thus clearly a term of approbation. Altogether the Moses-centered *Jubilees* places a high value on the Enoch of the *Book of the Watchers*.

While *Jubilees* represents the response of a single reader, the Dead Sea Scrolls offer us the response of a community—a community well known for its commitment to a particularly strict reading of the laws of Moses. Yet the manuscript evidence shows that this community valued highly several Enochic works, including the *Book of the Watchers*. But they were certainly not the only texts it read—nor were they intended to be. To understand how evil came into the world, how knowledge is rightly and wrongly revealed, the authors of the *Book of the Watchers* might have said, read what we have written. To learn the details of the laws of impurity or Sabbath observance, look at texts that concern themselves with just these sorts of questions. In other words, the *Book of the Watchers'*—*1 Enoch's*—reticence about the laws of the Torah is a function of genre, not of distance or discomfort.

To reinforce this point, let me offer an example from another era. Nothing is more central to rabbinic Judaism and the tradition to which it gave rise than the Torah of Moses and its laws, yet members in good standing of this tradition wrote a variety of works—apocalyptic, ethical, liturgical—that say little about the Torah. Read in isolation, they might lead one to conclusions like Nickelsburg's for *1 Enoch*. In *Sefer Zerubbabel*, for example, the books of the prophets and traditions about David figure far more prominently than do the Torah and traditions about Moses. Yet it would not occur to anyone to suggest that the author of *Sefer Zerubbabel* did not see Moses and the covenant at Sinai as of central importance. It is true that for rabbinic culture the Torah is authoritative in a far more literal way than it was during the precanonical era in which the *Book of the Watchers* was written. Yet although the canon had not yet taken final shape and the contents of many works that would later be regarded as canonical still had a certain fluidity, the Torah was already widely accepted as the central document of Judaism in the third century BCE. If there ever was such a thing as an Enochic community, it surely read the Torah and many other works alongside Enochic texts.

The *Book of the Watchers* and Ben Sira in Conflict?

Several scholars have recently pointed out that despite their different genres, the *Book of the Watchers* and the Wisdom of ben Sira address similar issues.[109] Benjamin Wright has suggested not only that ben Sira is responding to the *Book of the Watchers* and the *Astronomical Book*,[110] but also that ben Sira understood these works as the teachings of a rival school of wisdom.[111] The central point of dispute between ben Sira and the early Enochic literature according to Wright is the Jerusalem priesthood, which ben Sira is defending against the critique of the *Book of the Watchers* and other like-minded works such as *Aramaic Levi*. Against those who cannot imagine that a writer in the wisdom tradition is genuinely enthusiastic about the cult, Wright insists quite rightly that ben Sira believes fully in its importance.[112] For Wright, ben Sira's advocacy of the priestly establishment is part of a conservative ideology that rejects many of the more radical ideas of the Enochic school. He identifies four themes in ben Sira's book that he reads as polemics against the Enochic school: insistence on the role of the moon for the calendar, rejection of speculation about hidden matters, criticism of the use of dreams and omens, and praise of the figure of Enoch. Wright is admirably straightforward about "the inevitably circumstantial character of the argument."[113] He also does an excellent job of sketching a social setting that makes sense of the polemic he detects in ben Sira's work, suggesting that Jerusalem was the scene of intellectual exchange among different groups in which priests would have been prominent and that people might even have moved from group to group.[114]

It seems to me that there is more agreement between ben Sira and the *Book of the Watchers* on these points than Wright allows. I would like to focus on two of the themes Wright considers—ben Sira's rejection of speculation about hidden matters and his criticism of reliance on dreams—but let me note in passing that it is also less than clear that ben Sira is engaged in polemic in relation to the other themes Wright points to. For the calendar, the polemic, if there is one, is quite muted. It consists of two brief passages noting the moon's role in determining festivals (Sir 43:6-8, 50:6).[115] While adherents of the calendar of the *Astronomical Book* would have rejected ben Sira's comments about the role of the moon, the tone of the passages hardly suggests that ben Sira is trying to make his case against those holding an opposing view.[116] For the figure of Enoch, Wright understands ben Sira's high opinion of Enoch (Sir 44:16, 49:14) as an effort to "domesticate" the figure his opponents had chosen as their standard-bearer.[117] But anyone not already persuaded that ben Sira is engaged in a polemic might be inclined to the more obvious reading: that ben Sira was an admirer of his ancient scribal predecessor.

It also seems to me difficult to read ben Sira's dismissal of dreams (Sir 34:1-8) as directed against Enochic writings. It is true that Enoch's ascent to heaven in the *Book of the Watchers* takes place in a dream, but the other revelations of the early Enochic literature—the conversation with Uriel in the *Astronomical Book* and the tour to the ends of the earth in the *Book of the Watchers*—do not. And only someone already persuaded that ben Sira has the *Book of the Watchers* in mind would find a reference to Enoch's ascent in his dismissal of fools to whom "dreams give wings" (Sir 34:1).[118] More important, the authors of the *Book of the Watchers* did not encourage their readers to seek revelations on their own by means of dreams, ascents, or any other visionary technique. The revelations granted Enoch are clearly meant to satisfy the revelatory needs of readers rather than to lead them to take up prophecy on their own.[119]

Ben Sira's attitude toward dreams fits well with his understanding of the phenomenon of prophecy. In his Praise of the Fathers, as we have seen, ben Sira firmly places prophecy in the past. The heir to the prophets, according to ben Sira, is the scribe, the interpreter of Torah—like ben Sira himself, who claims to pour out teaching "like prophecy" (Sir 24:33). Still it is surely significant that ben Sira's teaching is only "*like* prophecy"; full identification with the prophets would be going too far. Enoch in the *Book of the Watchers*, on the other hand, looks very much like a prophet as he speaks with God face-to-face and communicates God's words to others. But their depiction of an ancient figure in prophetic terms does not mean the authors of the *Book of the Watchers* were claiming to be prophets. If they had truly understood prophecy as a living phenomenon, they would not have needed to invoke the authority of Enoch but could have spoken in their own voices. Their approach to composing their work, as we have seen, suggests that they understood themselves as interpreters rather than recipients of revelation. From one angle, the authors of the *Book of the Watchers* are more conservative than ben Sira; they claim prophecy only for a hero of the past, while ben Sira claims prophecy, or at least something like prophecy, for himself and other contemporaries. This claim is perhaps related to another difference between ben Sira and the authors of the *Book of the Watchers*: ben Sira's willingness to write in his own name. Here, too, ben Sira is the radical, while the authors of the *Book of the Watchers* are the conservatives.

The passage in which ben Sira cautions against inquiring into matters too great for human beings is well-known:

Seek not what is too difficult for you,
nor investigate what is beyond your power.
Reflect on what has been assigned to you,

for you do not need what is hidden.
Do not meddle in what is beyond your tasks,
For matters too great for human understanding have been shown you.
For their hasty judgment has led many astray,
and wrong opinion has caused their thoughts to slip. (Sir 3:21-24)

Wright reads this passage as suggesting that ben Sira was offended by the cosmological content of the *Book of the Watchers* and the *Astronomical Book* as well as their interest in eschatology.[120] But this latter interest is not very prominent in either of the earliest Enochic works, nor is it clear that ben Sira is complaining about eschatological speculation. Indeed it is far from clear what he means by hidden matters; cosmology, a subject ignored by the books that became part of the Hebrew Bible, presumably purposefully, is a reasonable possibility but hardly a certainty. Further, the attitude toward knowledge in the *Book of the Watchers* is quite complicated. Indeed, the story of the descent of the Watchers in *1 Enoch* 6-11 views the angels' revelation of heavenly secrets to humanity as an unmitigated disaster. Annette Reed has argued persuasively that one of the primary concerns of *1 Enoch* 12-16 is to clarify the relationship between the forbidden knowledge the angels reveal to humanity and the knowledge properly revealed to Enoch.[121] In other words, ben Sira and the *Book of the Watchers* are hardly polar opposites on this important point. Reed imagines them rather as two voices in "a lively debate about the nature and scope of religious knowledge among scribes in the pre-Maccabean period."[122]

Wright does not consider ben Sira's allusions to the story of the fall of the Watchers in his discussion of the relationship between the two works. These allusions are probably the strongest evidence that ben Sira had actually read the *Book of the Watchers*.[123] Yet, Reed points out, ben Sira manages to use the material he found in the *Book of the Watchers* to serve his own purposes: he focuses on the giants, who serve as an example of sinners who are justly punished, and ignores the descent of the Watchers as the cause of evil in the world, an idea he must have found unpalatable.[124] Here, too, Reed's "debate" seems to me a better way than "polemic" to characterize the relationship between ben Sira and the *Book of the Watchers*.

This characterization seems to me applicable to the attitudes of ben Sira and the *Book of the Watchers* toward the Jerusalem priesthood as well. If the criticism of the *Book of the Watchers* is directed at priests who marry women from nonpriestly families, it clearly represents a minority opinion; the priests it criticizes would surely have argued that their critics misread the laws of Leviticus, and ben Sira might have agreed with them. But nothing in ben Sira's book responds to the specifics of the

Book of the Watchers' criticism. Though women and the dangers they pose are a subject of some interest to ben Sira, nowhere does he consider the problems women pose for priests in particular in order to defend them. Nor does he praise the pious observance of all the laws of wedlock by Aaron's heirs as the *Third Sibylline Oracle* in a different polemical context praises the Jews' piety in marriage in contrast to the nations' practice of pederasty (*Sib. Or.* 3:594-600). Perhaps it did not occur to ben Sira that his wisdom book was the appropriate place to address such an issue—or perhaps he was not offended by the rigorist ethic of the *Book of the Watchers*.

Much of ben Sira's attention to the priesthood is focused on the high priest. For ben Sira, the high priest is also Israel's head of state, and ben Sira goes beyond any other work I know in developing a theology of royal priesthood based on a careful if tendentious reading of biblical sources. Ben Sira is often pictured as a conservative advocate of priestly authority. Here is a clear instance where advocacy of priestly authority is anything but conservative. But it is noteworthy that Simon, the high priest whose appearance in the temple is depicted in such flattering terms in the final episode in the Praise of the Fathers, is the high priest of ben Sira's youth, no longer alive at the time ben Sira wrote. The fact that this idealized portrait is of the previous high priest may suggest a certain reticence toward the new high priest. Certainly a writer of mere propaganda would have made the current high priest the hero of his story or would at least have made explicit the transfer of glory from father to son. Further, by identifying Simon, the model high priest, with Wisdom, ben Sira suggests that the true high priest is defined not merely by ancestry but by merit as well. This definition need not be a rebuke to the occupant of the office, though it might be if the occupant were obviously not wise in ben Sira's sense. In any case, it holds the high priest to a standard that has nothing to do with ancestry.

Priest and Scribe in *Aramaic Levi*

The Wisdom of ben Sira and the *Book of the Watchers* show clearly that by the beginning of the second century B.C.E. some learned scribes had come to understand their profession in priestly terms and, conversely, to make wisdom a central aspect of the ideal priest's character. But the fragments of *Aramaic Levi* show that the association was by no means universal. Because of its extremely fragmentary nature, *Aramaic Levi* is not an easy text to interpret. It survives in fragments from Qumran and the Cairo Geniza as well as in Greek translation in several passages in MS e, the Mt. Athos manuscript, of the *Testament of Levi*. It was an important source for the *Testament of Levi*, but the *Testament of Levi* can be used to reconstruct *Aramaic Levi* only with great caution.[125]

Aramaic Levi tells the story of Levi's selection as priest as a reward for his pious zeal in destroying the city of Shechem to avenge the disgrace of his sister Dinah at the hands of its prince. The original account of the raid on Shechem in Genesis 34 is not terribly enthusiastic about the behavior of Levi and Simeon, the brother who shares the violent deed with him, or the brothers as a group. The brothers "deceitfully" (Gen 34:13) negotiate marriage arrangements with Shechem and Hamor that include the Shechemites' circumcision (Gen 34:8-17); Simeon and Levi then take advantage of Shechemites' weakness while they are recuperating from circumcision to murder them and to permit the other brothers to plunder the town (Gen 34:26-29). Jacob, who apparently took the negotiations at face value and was prepared to marry his daughter to her attacker, is furious at Simeon and Levi, not because he disapproves of the murder of the Shechemites but because he is afraid that they have jeopardized his position in the land (Gen 34:30). Indeed, Jacob's deathbed blessing condemns these two sons for their violent trickery (Gen 49:5-7). Yet the account of the incident in Genesis allows Simeon and Levi the last word when they reply to their angry father: "Should he treat our sister as a harlot?" (Gen 34:31).

If Genesis 34 is ambivalent about the brothers' deed, *Aramaic Levi* is not. It transforms the attack into an act of pious zeal on the model of the zealous violence that wins Phinehas the covenant of priesthood when the Israelites go astray after Baal Peor (Numbers 25; *Ar. Levi* 1-3). After the attack on Shechem, Levi sees a vision in which he is anointed as priest by seven angels (*Ar. Levi* supp. 20-supp. 27, 4-7). Following the vision, his father Jacob ordains him as a priest, he offers sacrifices, and they go to visit Levi's grandfather Isaac (*Ar. Levi* 8-12).

Now that Levi has been singled out to serve as priest, Isaac teaches him "the law of the priesthood" (*Ar. Levi* 13-61). These detailed instructions, primarily concerned with procedure for sacrifice, make up about a third of the surviving text of *Aramaic Levi*.[126] The law of the priesthood begins with the warning about proper marriage partners discussed above (*Ar. Levi* 16-18) but turns quickly to sacrifice: washing before and during sacrifice (*Ar. Levi* 19-21, 26, 53-55); the types of wood to be used for sacrifice (*Ar. Levi* 22-24); the order of sprinkling blood and laying the parts of the sacrificial animal on the altar, and the requirement to salt the parts (*Ar. Levi* 25-29); the sacrifice of flour, oil, wine, and incense that accompanies the animal sacrifice (*Ar. Levi* 30); the amount of wood necessary for different types of offerings (*Ar. Levi* 31-36); the weights of the salt, fine flour, oil, and frankincense that accompany different kinds of offerings (*Ar. Levi* 37-46); the relationships among the different weights (46–47); keeping the priest's garments free of blood (*Ar. Levi* 53); and covering and avoiding the consumption of blood of animals slaughtered for food (*Ar. Levi* 56).[127] Robert Kugler reads these instructions as a polemic against the contemporary priesthood. In his view, some of the details of the sacrificial practices Isaac enjoins purposefully contradict the laws of Leviticus. In particular Kugler points to the more elaborate washing, which he sees as intended to promote a higher level of purity. Thus, he claims, the instructions implicitly criticize the behavior of the priestly establishment descended from Aaron by describing an even more ancient figure as the ideal priest.[128]

While Kugler is certainly correct that Isaac's instructions differ at certain points from the laws of Leviticus, I have argued in detail elsewhere that the differences do not represent purposeful contradiction.[129] Rather, what the various topics of Isaac's teaching have in common is that all serve to supplement the rather sparse instructions the Torah provides for priests. To offer a single example, Leviticus decrees salting sacrifices (Lev 2:13) but neglects to tell us how much salt each sacrifice requires. Isaac's instructions fill in this gap (*Ar. Levi* 37-40). Indeed, Isaac's instructions look very much like the sort of instructions priests would pass on from father to son. The only item the rhetoric of the speech marks as polemical is the opening command to avoid harlotry by marrying a woman from Isaac's family (*Ar. Levi* 16-17). Here, as I suggested above, we find the same sort of criticism of priests' marriages to nonpriestly women that we find in the *Book of the Watchers*. Otherwise the presentation of the instructions is straightforward, without any implied contrast to the practices of others. If I am correct, *Aramaic Levi* holds a minority view on the issue of priests' marriages, an issue that was clearly the subject of controversy during a certain period of time. But I see no justification for calling the law of the priesthood sectarian. Finally, it is worth noting that nowhere does this central portion of *Aramaic Levi* hint at a scribal role for priests.

In a speech at the end of *Aramaic Levi* (*Ar. Levi* 82-105), Levi urges his sons to learn the scribal skills of reading and writing and praises wisdom as a treasure that will protect its possessor in foreign lands. Yet it is remarkable that the wisdom Levi praises is quite secular; the identification of wisdom with Torah is notably absent:

A man who learns wisdom, all [of his days will be long and his reputatio]n [will be great]. For every foreign land and country to which he goes [there he will have a brother....] in it. And he will not be like a traveler there.... His friend[s] are many, and those wishing him well are numerous. And people seat him on the seat of honor, so as to hear the words of his wisdom. Great abundance of glory is wisdom, and it is a good treaure to all who acquire it. Strong kings and a great people, and an army, and horsemen, and many chariots with them may come, and they may seize the possessions of the lands and countries and plunder everything that is in them, (but) the storehouses of wisdom they will not plunder. (*Ar. Levi* 91-95)

Wisdom as it is described in this passage sounds more like the wisdom of the Book of Proverbs than the Wisdom of ben Sira. In its reworking of this passage, the *Testament of Levi* supplies the association missing in *Aramaic Levi*. Its version of the speech has Levi urge his sons to teach their children to read so that they can study Torah: "And do you, too, teach your children letters that they may have understanding all their life, reading unceasingly the law of God. For everyone who knows the law of God will be honoured, and he will not be a stranger wherever he goes" (*T. Levi* 13:2-3).

It is also noteworthy that *Aramaic Levi* does not assume that wisdom, reading, and writing have a particular connection to the office of priest. The exemplar of wisdom Levi offers his sons is Joseph: "Observe, my children, my brother Joseph [who] taught reading and writing and the instruction of wisdom" (*Ar. Levi* 90). It is apparently Joseph's success in the Egyptian royal court to which Levi's praise of wisdom's powers of protection in a foreign locale alludes. The wisdom that got Joseph his start in Egypt is the wisdom of dream interpretation, a form of wisdom the Genesis story attributes to God, if only in passing (Gen 40:8, 41:16). But the wisdom Joseph displayed to keep his job is clearly a secular wisdom that has nothing to do with the Torah and even rather little to do with reading and writing, despite the claims of Levi's speech.

Aramaic Levi dates Levi's speech about wisdom to the one hundred eighteenth year of Levi's life, the year of Joseph's death (*Ar. Levi* 82). The speech follows Levi's account of the events of his life, an account that concludes, "And all the days of my life were one hundred [thirty]-seven years; and I saw my th[ird] generation before I died" (*Ar. Levi* 81). This placement is not the result of reconstruction; it is attested by the Cambridge Geniza manuscript. But the fact that the speech follows on a notice of the length of Levi's life that could well serve as the conclusion to the work suggests that the speech was added to *Aramaic Levi* after the work was complete.[130] Kugler is surely correct, however, that there is no reason to exclude the author of *Aramaic Levi* as the source of the addition.[131]

Kugler sees *Aramaic Levi*'s praise of Joseph, together with what he takes as criticism of the cultic practices of the Jerusalem priesthood in Isaac's instructions, as evidence for Samaritan authorship of *Aramaic Levi*.[132] If my reading of the law of the priesthood is correct, it provides no grounds for this claim, and the praise of Joseph just quoted is hardly sufficient grounds in itself. Yet the presentation of Joseph as the model wise man in a speech addressed to priests certainly requires explanation. Here *Aramaic Levi* turns back the clock. Its affinities with Enochic traditions suggest that *Aramaic Levi* was aware of the Enochic understanding of the relationship between priest and scribe. *Aramaic Levi* likely predates the Wisdom of ben Sira, but even if ben Sira was the first to make explicit the association of wisdom with the Torah, he drew on earlier developments in the understanding of wisdom, including Deuteronomy's view of God's commandments as wisdom. Nor is the association of priests with this type of wisdom ben Sira's innovation; it belongs to a tradition that goes back to Deuteronomy and the figure of Ezra. Yet *Aramaic Levi* appears untouched by these developments.

The author of *Aramaic Levi* is surely not engaged in a polemic against a blurring of boundaries between priest and wise man since he has Levi urge his sons to acquire the skills of the wise man. Yet the choice of Joseph as the model of the wise man reflects an attitude toward the priestly relation to wisdom quite different from the one found in the other works discussed here. For *Aramaic Levi*, the relationship between priests and wisdom is not a natural association, but one that requires priests to make the effort to follow the example of Joseph.[133]

Certainly it would not be surprising if a work devoted to the founder of the priestly line envisioned priestly rule as the most desirable of states, just as the Wisdom of ben Sira does. But there is no clear evidence for such a position in *Aramaic Levi*, though there are several suggestive passages. One is a fragment of an angelic speech to Levi during his anointment vision that contrasts the evils of "the kingdom of the sword" to the benefits of some other state. The kingdom of the sword "has fighting, the battle, the chase, exertion, conflict, and killing and hunger" (*Ar. Levi* 4-5), while the other state offers "peace, and all choice first fruits of the earth to eat" (*Ar. Levi* 4). The fragmentary condition of the text unfortunately leaves the identity of the positive state uncertain,[134] but the description appears to allude to the "covenant of peace" Phinehas earned for his zeal (Num 25:12) and the first fruits priests receive as their due (Num 18:13).[135] Still, there is no clear indication that this state involves priestly rule. Rather than praising rule by priests, the passage may instead be claiming that it is a greater privilege to hold the office of priest than the office of king.

Jonas Greenfield and Michael Stone read the passage in the section of *Aramaic Levi* that recounts the birth of Levi's son Kohath, who became the grandfather of Aaron and thus the ancestor of the priestly line, as favoring priestly political rule: "[And I call]ed his name [Kohath. And I saw] that he would ha[ve] an assembly of all [the people, that] he would hav[e] the high priesthood, [for all Is]rael" (*Ar. Levi* 66-67). They suggest that the phrase "he would have an assembly of all the people" is intended to recall a phrase from Jacob's blessing of Judah, "and to him shall be the obedience [*yiqhâ*][136] of the peoples" (Gen 49:10) and, by implicitly punning on the name Kohath (*Qĕhāt*), to transfer the role Jacob promises Judah's descendants to Levi's.[137] This is an appealing suggestion. Yet here too it is unclear whether this allusion is part of a larger effort to transfer political power from king to priest or whether it simply represents, as Kugler puts it, "the author's desire to elevate the sacerdotal office to preeminence in Jewish life."[138]

Finally, another passage, part of Levi's address to his descendants, makes mention of "your [pl.] kingdom" (*Ar. Levi* 100). The immediate context is too broken to be helpful, but the exhortation to wisdom that makes up most of the address is difficult to reconcile with support for political leadership for priests. The wisdom of *Aramaic Levi* is the wisdom of the highly placed retainer, not of the ruler himself. It earns favor in foreign lands, something of use only to an advisor, not to a sovereign.[139] Indeed, in the course of the wisdom speech Levi tells his sons that they will be "chiefs and judges" (*Ar. Levi* 99), perhaps echoing Deuteronomy's association of priests and judges.

Altogether, *Aramaic Levi*'s view of the priesthood is both patriotically priestly and remarkably conservative. It insists that it is better to be a priest than anything else: political power is inferior to priestly privilege; the skills of the scribe are a nice addition to one's resumé, but they are not an essential part of the priestly office. For *Aramaic Levi* priesthood is defined primarily by ritual activity, as prescribed by the priestly document of the Torah. It praises the founder of the priestly line for his zealous piety, claiming that he won the office on the basis of merit. But its warning that Levi's descendants will eventually go astray (*Ar. Levi* 102-6) is unaccompanied by any effort to describe priesthood in a way that would inject merit into the ongoing life of the institution.

It does not seem implausible that the sort of priestly pride *Aramaic Levi* demonstrates was more widespread than the surviving literature indicates. Several centuries after *Aramaic Levi*, the historian Josephus demonstrates a somewhat similar attitude. He begins his account of his life by expressing his pride in priestly ancestry: "My family is no ignoble one, tracing its descent far back to priestly ancestors. Different races base their claim to nobility on various grounds; with us a connexion with the priesthood is the hallmark of an illustrious line" (*Life* 1).[140] Josephus goes on to claim royal lineage as well; his mother was descended from the Hasmoneans (*Life* 2). The Hasmoneans were priests who eventually claimed kingship for themselves so that by Josephus's time some could claim royal and priestly descent through a single ancestor. It is surely noteworthy that Josephus chooses to begin his account with his priestly ancestry rather than his Hasmonean connection.

Josephus is not shy about claiming great learning for himself, yet he does not appear to connect his learning to his priestly ancestry.

While still a mere boy, about fourteen years old, I won universal applause for my love of letters; insomuch that the chief priests and the leading men of the city used constantly to come to me for precise information on some particular in our ordinances. (*Life* 9)

Later, in his account John of Gischala's plot, he reports that the hostile embassy was instructed to determine why the Galileans were devoted to Josephus.

> If they attributed it to my being a native of Jerusalem, they were to reply that so were all four of them; if to my expert knowledge of their laws, they should retort that neither were they ignorant of the customs of their fathers; if, again, they asserted that their affection was due to my priestly office, they should answer that two of them were likewise priests. (*Life* 198)

Again it is striking that Josephus does not suggest a connection between learning and priesthood.

Josephus's pride in his priestly ancestry goes together with concern for the integrity of the priestly line. In *Against Apion*, his case for the validity of the records of the Jews hinges in part on the unadulterated lineage of the priests: "Not only did our ancestors in the first instance set over this business [keeping the records] men of the highest character, devoted to the service of God, but they took precautions to ensure that the priests' lineage should be kept unadulterated and pure" (*Against Apion* 1.30). Josephus differs with *Aramaic Levi* on the particulars; he worries about the lineage of the brides of priests, but he does not insist that they come from priestly families (*Against Apion* 1.31-36).

Altogether Josephus's understanding of the glory of priesthood at the moment when it had ceased to be a functioning institution seems to me very much like *Aramaic Levi*'s: priestly ancestry is inherently desirable. Josephus lived to see priests deprived of the possibility of offering sacrifice, yet his pride in his ancestry remained. It is difficult to detect any anxiety about merit in his account.

In Jerusalem and its environs in the century before the Maccabean Revolt, there must have been considerable overlap between those who served as priests in the temple and those who received the education necessary to perform the tasks of the scribe. As ben Sira reminds us, that education required leisure. Leisure of course required financial resources, and many members of the small elite likely to have had those resources were from priestly families, precluded according to custom from farming, supported according to custom by the donations of the people. But despite the social proximity of priests and scribes, the two professions are in some ways quite opposed. The only necessary qualification for the priesthood is ancestry; the only necessary qualifications for the profession of scribe at least in principle are ability and education.

The fact that so many scribes were also priests must have made the tension between the nature of the two professions evident, not only to those who served in both capacities but to their friends, neighbors, and relatives. The authors of the *Book of the Watchers* and ben Sira were surely scribes, and whether or not they were priests, they were undoubtedly interested observers of the priesthood. As we have seen, despite some important differences, they share not only a range of concerns but even, to a considerable extent, specific opinions. For all of them the proximity of the two professions shed new light on the failings of priests. It was all too clear that ancestry alone was not enough; the ideal priest was one who shared the pious ethos of the learned scribe. The emphases are of course somewhat different. The *Book of the Watchers* depicts its hero explicitly as scribe, implicitly as priest. Ben Sira takes a rather different approach in his quest to demonstrate the desirability of rule by high priest. He praises the profession of scribe and makes the scribe a channel for wisdom, but he makes the high priest Simon Wisdom's twin.

Chapter 2

Jubilees' Kingdom of Priests

The *Book of Jubilees* draws on the *Book of the Watchers* and *Aramaic Levi*, and like the *Book of the Watchers* and the Wisdom of ben Sira, it is concerned with the tension between ancestry and merit. But unlike those earlier works, its anxieties focus not on the priesthood but on the people of Israel as a whole. Of all the works of the Second Temple period, *Jubilees* tries hardest to show that the people of Israel is indeed a kingdom of priests, a phrase it echoes twice (*Jub.* 16:18, 33:20). Its effort has both a narrative and a legal aspect. Its retelling of the stories of the patriarchs grants a priestly role not just to Levi but to all of the most important ancestors of the Jewish people, particularly its favorite, Jacob. Thus it manages to imply priestly ancestry for the entire Jewish people. In addition, it offers an understanding of the Torah's laws regarding sexual relations and the shedding and consumption of blood that gives ordinary Jews almost priestly status.

In some quarters, at least, *Jubilees* was highly regarded.[1] The *Damascus Document* refers to it by name (CD 16.3-4), claiming that the explication of the times of Israel's blindness are "specified" in it; in the previous line, it claimed that "everything" is "specified" in the "Torah of Moses" (CD 16.2).[2] A very fragmentary text perhaps describing eschatological destruction also appears to cite *Jubilees* and introduces the citation with terminology elsewhere used for quotations from scripture, "thus it is written" (4Q228 1 i 9), while the existence of a work or works labeled *Pseudo-Jubilees* (4Q225-27) indicates that *Jubilees* was of sufficient stature to warrant imitation. The number of manuscripts found at Qumran suggests that *Jubilees* had some kind of authoritative status there. There are more copies of *Jubilees*—fourteen or fifteen—than of any other work except the most popular biblical books: Psalms (thirty-six), Deuteronomy (twenty-nine), Isaiah (twenty-one), Exodus (seventeen), and Genesis (fifteen); to judge by the number of surviving manuscripts, then, *Jubilees* was hardly less popular than the biblical books whose stories it retells.[3]

Jubilees achieved this authoritative status despite what most modern readers cannot help but see as striking points of conflict with the Torah. To begin with, *Jubilees* takes its modern title from the chronological framework it imposes on its narrative of Israel's history from the creation of the world to the entrance into the land. The Holiness Code of the Torah decrees jubilees of forty-nine years of business as usual culminating in a fiftieth year in which slaves are set free and the land returns to its original owners (Leviticus 25). *Jubilees* transforms this schema by taking jubilees to be forty-nine-year periods, made up of seven "weeks" or seven-year periods, though its placement of the Exodus and the entrance of the Israelites into the land in the fiftieth jubilee echoes the Holiness Code's vision for the fiftieth year.[4] Still, the jubilee framework for the stories of Genesis and Exodus is foreign to the biblical account, and sometimes *Jubilees*' dating of events contradicts that of Genesis and Exodus.[5]

Counting by jubilees is related to *Jubilees*' advocacy of a 364-day calendar in which the moon plays no part (*Jub.* 6:23-32). This calendar imposes on the year the regularity that the jubilee system imposes on history. But "advocacy" is perhaps too mild a term; *Jubilees* attacks Israel for failure to follow the 364-day calendar and insists on the dire consequences of that failure (*Jub.* 6:32-38). Again, *Jubilees*' calendar cannot be said to stand in actual conflict with the Torah since the passages of the Torah devoted to the calendar never address the number of days in the year or the role of the sun and moon. But at the very least, *Jubilees* introduces into the stories of Israel's past a calendrical polemic entirely absent in the Torah.

Jubilees also retells the events described in Genesis and Exodus in a way that sheds quite a different light on them. Its version of events often improves on the Torah's, eliminating problematic behavior and emphasizing the virtues of its heroes and the failings of its villains, much as Chronicles improves on Samuel and Kings. And to ensure that readers are not left in any doubt about the conclusions to be drawn from the narrative, the angel of the presence periodically intervenes with little sermons. One particular concern of *Jubilees* is to demonstrate that many of the laws of the Torah were observed by the Israelites even before they were revealed at Mt. Sinai. This insistence on the eternal status of much of the Torah may be a response to a hellenistic critique of Judaism that admired monotheism but viewed the ritual laws, which they saw as superstitious and misanthropic, as a later addition.[6] The laws in question, according to *Jubilees*, could be found on the heavenly tablets. These heavenly tablets are central to *Jubilees*' thought.[7]

There can be no doubt that the Torah had achieved authoritative status among Jews by the second century B.C.E. when *Jubilees* was written. Thus *Jubilees* had to work very hard to present itself in a way that would make acceptance possible despite the tension between its account of Israel's early days and that of the Torah. *Jubilees* does not attempt to nudge the Torah out of its niche and replace it, but rather embraces the authority of the Torah even as it seeks to place itself alongside it. The heavenly tablets are a crucial element in this effort. *Jubilees* transforms the ancient conception of heavenly books containing the deeds of mankind and their fate into a veritable library of heavenly books. The Torah, in *Jubilees'* terminology the Torah-Commandment, and *Jubilees* itself, the Torah-Testimony, each contain some of the material in this heavenly library, and *Jubilees* also invents books of the patriarchs that contain a small share of the archive. This approach not only exalts *Jubilees* but also, perhaps less obviously, demotes the Torah, which must share its authoritative status with another text even as both are subordinated to the heavenly tablets.[8]

As I have just noted, scholars have often understood *Jubilees* as reacting against the hellenization of the period around the Maccabean Revolt, and most have placed it in the period after the revolt, some shortly after, others as late as the reign of John Hyrcanus.[9] The Maccabean Revolt also suggests a way to make sense of *Jubilees'* polemic about the calendar, though we know so little about the calendar in use in the Jerusalem temple during the Second Temple period in general and during the years before and after the Maccabean Revolt in particular that we must proceed with great caution. It makes a difference to our reading of *Jubilees* whether it is fighting on behalf of the once reigning calendar, which has been displaced, or has invented a calendar that conforms to ideals of order and the primacy of the number seven. There are some grounds for detecting a change in the calendar at the time of the hellenistic reform.[10] If a change took place at that time, *Jubilees'* polemic could reflect disappointment that the calendar it favors, set aside by the hellenizers, had not been restored after the revolt. The Qumran evidence is compatible with a post-revolt date, but does little to narrow the range of possibilities. The earliest manuscript evidence is the earlier hand in 4Q216, which dates to the last quarter of the second century.[11] The *Damascus Document*'s citation of *Jubilees* is certainly compatible with a second-century date but does little to limit the range, since the earliest manuscript evidence for the *Damascus Document* is dated to 75–50 B.C.E. Below I present new arguments in favor of a date in the second half or, even better, the last third of the second century.

Priests before Levi

According to the Torah the first Israelite priest was Aaron, Moses' brother; the office came into being when God ordained the sacrificial cult and other priestly responsibilities (Exodus 28-29). As just noted, one striking feature of *Jubilees'* rewriting of the narrative of the Torah is its claim that many of the laws revealed to Israel in the wilderness were practiced by the patriarchs. Indeed it claims that the sacrificial cult began with Adam; the first man was also the first priest. It also depicts Enoch and Noah as priests and then describes the transmission of the priestly office from Abraham through Isaac and Jacob to Levi, the ancestor of the priestly family descended from Aaron.

The Torah provides *Jubilees* with useful raw material for depicting Noah, Abraham, Isaac, and Jacob as priests. Noah offers a sacrifice upon emerging from the ark (Gen 8:20; *Jub.* 6:1-4), while Abraham performs a ritual that might be considered a sacrifice in the covenant between the pieces (Genesis 15; *Jub.* 14:11-20), and Jacob offers sacrifices at Beer Sheba on his way to Egypt to be reunited with Joseph (Gen 46:1; *Jub.* 44:1).[12] Further, Abraham (Gen 12:7, 13:18), Isaac (Gen 26:25), and Jacob (Gen 35:1-7) are all said to have built altars. But *Jubilees'* depiction of these patriarchs as priests goes far beyond what the Torah suggests. All except Isaac are given credit for founding a festival: Noah establishes the Feast of Weeks (*Jub.* 6:1-22); Abraham, the Feast of Tabernacles (*Jub.* 16:20-31); and Jacob, the Addition to the Feast of Tabernacles (*Jub.* 32:27-29).

For Adam and Enoch, the Torah offers less for *Jubilees* to work with. *Jubilees* certainly knew the *Book of the Watchers*, but there the picture of Enoch as priest is implicit rather than explicit. *Jubilees* depicts Enoch as priest in a more decisive way by making him the founder not of a festival but of a ritual it valued highly, the evening round of the twice-daily offering of incense (*Jub.* 4:25).[13] It makes Adam the originator of the morning incense offering (*Jub.* 3:27). Both Adam and Enoch are conveniently located in Eden, where spices are readily available.

The picture of the patriarchs as priests is not confined to *Jubilees*. *Aramaic Levi*, which *Jubilees* used as a source,[14] clearly understood Isaac as a priest; it gives him the honor of teaching Levi the "law of the priesthood" (*Ar. Levi* 13-61). In the course of these instructions, Isaac refers to what Abraham taught him, matters that Abraham himself learned from "the book of Noah concerning the blood" (*Ar. Levi* 57). Thus *Aramaic Levi* seems to have understood Abraham and Noah too as priests. The fact that it has Isaac rather than Jacob instruct Levi may mean that it did not view Jacob as a priest. The *Genesis Apocryphon* describes Noah's sacrifice (1QapGen 10.13-17), for which, of course, there is a strong foundation in Genesis, and it also depicts Abraham offering sacrifices at Bethel (1QapGen 21.1-2) where the Torah mentions only invoking the Lord at an altar (Gen 13:3-4). Unfortunately the poor preservation of the *Genesis Apocryphon* makes it impossible to know whether it treated other patriarchs as priests.

Even if the idea of a succession of priests in patriarchal times is not original to *Jubilees*, it takes considerable pain to delineate it. The succession is not, however, unbroken. According to *Jubilees'* chronology, Enoch could have learned priestly lore from Adam, and Noah could have learned from Enoch, though he would have had to visit him in the Garden of Eden. But there is a gap between Noah and Abraham. *Jubilees* hints at a solution to this problem: the gap was bridged by writing. In the course of instructing Isaac in the proper performance of the cult, Abraham cites authorities: "This is the way I found (it) written in the book of my ancestors, the words of Enoch and the words of Noah" (*Jub.* 21:10).[15] *Aramaic Levi*, as we have just seen, refers to a book of Noah on blood (*Ar. Levi* 57).[16]

Jubilees offers several reasons why Levi alone of all his father's sons was to succeed him as priest.[17] Jacob ordains Levi as part of his tithing of everything he has brought with him to Bethel; Levi is the tithe from among Jacob's sons because he is the tenth counting upward from Benjamin, then still in his mother's womb (*Jub.* 32:3). But *Jubilees* gives far more attention to Levi's role in the episode of the rape of Dinah (*Jubilees* 30), which *earns* him the priesthood and his descendants the right to be priests and Levites (*Jub.* 30:18). I shall have more to say about this incident below. Here let me note that while *Jubilees* reports that Levi himself "has been recorded on the heavenly tablets as a friend and a just man" (*Jub.* 30:20), it also insists that this exalted status is not reserved for Levi alone; *all* Israelites who keep the covenant are to be recorded as "friends" (*Jub.* 30:21). Thus any Jew who obeys God's commands follows in Levi's footsteps.

Finally, it is worth noting that.the one priest *Jubilees* never depicts in the act of sacrifice is Levi. Upon ordaining Levi, Jacob continues to offer sacrifice (*Jub.* 32:4-7).[18] While *Jubilees* reports that Levi served as priest, the notice lacks any detail: "Levi rather than his ten brothers served as priest in Bethel before his father Jacob" (*Jub.* 32:9). Jacob continues his priestly service after Levi's ordination as he establishes the Feast of Addition (*Jub.* 32:27-29). *Jubilees'* unwillingness to show Levi acting as priest is particularly striking in comparison to *Aramaic Levi*. There, upon his ordination, Levi learns the law of the priesthood from Isaac. *Jubilees'* version of the law of the priesthood is taught by Abraham to Isaac (*Jubilees* 21). Thus, while *Jubilees* glorifies Levi as the ancestor of the priestly line, it plays down his performance of priestly duties. I suspect this is because *Jubilees* is not entirely happy that with Levi priesthood came to be restricted to a single family within Israel. Before Levi, the people of Israel—a very small people, to be sure—was truly a kingdom of priests.

It is also noteworthy that *Jubilees* never mentions Aaron, the ancestor of the chosen family within the tribe of Levi, although its account of the exodus from Egypt covers ground in which he plays a significant role according to the Book of Exodus. This remarkable omission may reflect *Jubilees'* displeasure with some of the contemporary descendants of Aaron and particularly with the high priest, the heir to Aaron's singular position. If *Jubilees'* calendar is a protest against the contemporary temple establishment, this displeasure is hardly surprising. Still, like the silence about Levi's priestly activities after his ordination, Aaron's absence in *Jubilees* also contributes to picture of the people of Israel as a kingdom of priests by reducing the dissonance caused by the choice of a single family as priests.

Priests and Books

We have seen that *Jubilees* takes pains to depict its priests engaged in the most characteristic of priestly activities: sacrifice. Yet it also suggests an intimate association between priests and books. To begin with, the inventor of writing and first author, according to *Jubilees*, is Enoch (*Jub.* 4:17), who, as we have already seen, also serves as priest. Enoch writes a testimony about calendrical matters and the course of human history (*Jub.* 4:18-19). *Jubilees* also attributes books to Noah, Enoch's successor as priest. One of the books is a record of the division of the earth among his descendants (*Jub.* 8:11); another is a book of remedies revealed to him when his descendants were under attack by evil spirits (*Jub.* 10:13). Abraham copies and studies Hebrew books of unspecified content that he receives from his father; he is able to use them because the angelic narrator of *Jubilees* makes him understand Hebrew (*Jub.* 12:25-27). In the course of his instructions to Isaac about priestly matters, Abraham refers to "the book of my ancestors, . . . the words of Enoch and the words of Noah" (*Jub.* 21:10), suggesting that priestly lore could be transmitted by way of books. Abraham was also the author of a book according to *Jubilees*; Joseph resists the advances of Potiphar's wife, remembering what Jacob had read to him "from the words of Abraham" (*Jub.* 39:6). In a night vision an angel shows Jacob seven heavenly tablets on which the future of his descendants is recorded; Jacob awakens and writes down everything he has read (*Jub.* 32:21-26). Before his death, Jacob passes on "all his books and the books of his fathers" to Levi "so that he could preserve them and renew them for his sons until today" (*Jub.* 45:16).

Isaac's blessing of Levi glorifies first the cultic role of priests and then, paraphrasing Moses' blessing at the end of Deuteronomy, their role as teachers and judges:

May he make you and your descendants (alone) out of all
    humanity approach him

to serve in his temple like the angels of the presence and
    like the holy ones. . . .
They will be princes, judges, and leaders of all the descendants
    of Jacob's sons.
They will declare the word of the Lord justly
and will justly judge all his verdicts.
They will tell my ways to Jacob
and my paths to Israel. (*Jub.* 31:14-15)

For *Jubilees*, then, the roles of priest and scribe are intimately related. The discoverer of writing, the first author, is also a priest who establishes an important cultic act. The priests of future generations are also authors, and their assembled works ultimately become the property of Levi, the founder of the priestly line that continues to serve in the author's own day, sacrificing in the temple and teaching the Lord's word and judging according to it. Thus *Jubilees* follows the *Book of the Watchers*, which it obviously knew and drew on, rather than *Aramaic Levi*, which it also used, in its understanding of the relationship between priest and scribe. Yet there are important differences between the *Book of the Watchers* and *Jubilees*. In the *Book of the Watchers* the association of priest and scribe reflects concern for the idea of Israel as a kingdom of priests and anxiety about actual priests: if the learned man is a sort of priest and the priest is the ideal learned man, then the limits of ancestry are transcended, and priesthood is defined in some sense by merit. *Jubilees*, on the other hand, as we shall see, for all its desire to depict the entire people of Israel as priests, is deeply committed to a view of genealogy as the criterion for membership in the people; it implicitly rejects a definition of people or priests based on merit.

Priests and Kings

Despite the reference in Isaac's blessing to the descendants of Levi as "princes, judges, and leaders," and a curse on Levi's enemies including foreign nations (*Jub.* 31:17), *Jubilees* does not claim that priests should be the rulers of the people of Israel. In a scene reminiscent of Israel's blessing of Joseph's sons in Genesis 48, Jacob brings both Levi and Judah to Isaac to be blessed. Isaac takes Levi by his right hand (*Jub.* 31:12) and blesses him first. Though Isaac takes Judah by his left hand (*Jub.* 31:12), the blessing of Judah leaves no doubt that political power belongs in the hands of his descendants:

Be a prince—you and one of your sons—for Jacob's sons.
May your name and the name of your sons be one
that goes and travels around in the entire earth and the regions.

Then the nations will be frightened before you. . . .
May Jacob's help be in you;
May Israel's safety be found in you.
At the time when you sit on the honorable throne that is rightly yours,
there will be great peace for all the descendants of the beloved's sons. (*Jub.*
    31:18-20)

After this blessing, *Jubilees* gives the figure of Judah little more attention than the narrative of Genesis requires. The only addition to the
Genesis narrative is Judah's participation in the wars against the Amorite kings (*Jub.* 34:1-9) and Esau and his sons (*Jub.* 37:1-38:14), where he
plays a more prominent role than most of the brothers, although Jacob,
the hero of both wars, dominates the accounts. *Jubilees* omits Judah's
role in persuading his brothers to sell Joseph into slavery rather than to
kill him, perhaps to preserve his reputation (*Jub.* 34:10-12), but it does
not overlook Judah's embarrassing encounter with his daughter-in-law
Tamar (Genesis 38; *Jubilees* 41). As in Genesis, Judah responds honor-
ably when confronted with the evidence that he is the father of the ba-
bies Tamar is carrying, and as in Genesis (44:18-34) it is Judah who is the
hero of Joseph's effort to test his brothers (*Jub.* 43:11-13). But *Jubilees*
does nothing to develop the claim to leadership that Judah's behavior in
these stories might suggest.

Further, although Isaac promises Judah and his descendants an "honorable throne" (*Jub.* 31:20), he does not refer to them as kings but as
"prince[s]" (*Jub.* 31:18). The Ethiopic is a term for a high official, not
necessarily royal, and it is worth noting that Isaac's blessing promises
Levi's descendants the same office (*Jub.* 31:15, quoted above).[19] *Jubilees'*
avoidance of the term "king" for Judah's descendants is surely significant. *Jubilees* prefers a pair of leaders, one royal, the other priestly, to the
dominant biblical understanding of kingship exemplified in David and
his descendants during the period of the First Temple.

As we have seen, this type of dual leadership was a reality only briefly,
during the early days of the return. Through most of the Persian period,
the lay partner in the dual leadership of the community was not a descendant of David, probably because the Persians were unwilling to tol-
erate the expectations attached to a prominent descendant of David. In
the century and a half of rule by the Ptolemies and the Seleucids leading up to the Maccabean Revolt, the high priest stood alone as hereditary
leader of the Jewish people. This situation was the result of necessity, imposed by foreign rulers. Yet ben Sira represents rule by high priest as the
ideal regime since, he suggests, priests make better rulers than kings.
Soon after ben Sira wrote, of course, the political arrangements under
which the Jews lived changed dramatically. When their victory brought
an end to foreign rule, the Hasmoneans did not restore the traditional

high priestly family to office but quickly claimed the high priesthood for themselves. Later they called themselves kings as well, but even at the beginning, without a foreign overlord, they freely exercised political power.[20]

Given the exalted status *Jubilees* grants to the office of priest, one might have expected its ideal polity to be headed by a priest alone as for ben Sira. Below I argue for dating *Jubilees* to the reign of John Hyrcanus. If my dating is correct, *Jubilees* offered an account of Isaac's blessings of Levi and Judah that requires dual leadership, royal and priestly, at just the time the Hasmoneans were consolidating two kinds of power that had traditionally been distinct from each other. *Jubilees'* insistence that the throne belongs to Judah should then be read as criticism of the Hasmoneans. This is surely the motive for the expectation of two messiahs that is the dominant form of messianism in the Dead Sea Scrolls,[21] though there is no reason to view it as a peculiarly sectarian expectation.[22]

Jubilees and the Holiness Code

In addition to emphasizing the priestly ancestry of the entire people of Israel, *Jubilees* makes the remarkable claim that all Jews, not only priests, have the power to affect the proper functioning of the temple through their behavior *outside* the temple. If they fail to avoid eating blood, the sacrifices offered twice daily in the temple will not effect atonement for them (*Jub.* 6:14). So too if they permit marriage to foreigners, they defile the temple and render the sacrifices offered there unacceptable (*Jub.* 30:11-16). *Jubilees* arrives at its understanding of the implications for the temple of the behavior of laypeople through its innovative reading of the Holiness Code (Leviticus 17-26) and other H material in the Torah.[23] According to the Holiness school, the sins of idolatry, forbidden sexual relations, and bloodshed defile the land.

This view stands in contrast to that of the priestly source, which understands defilement as a purely ritual category, without any moral valence.[24] In the next chapter I discuss P's understanding of impurity in more detail. Here let me offer a brief sketch. According to P, human beings become impure through contact with human and animal corpses (Leviticus 11, Numbers 19), certain bodily fluids and skin conditions (Leviticus 12-15), and contact with implements used by people in certain relatively severe states of impurity as well as the people themselves (Lev 15:4-11, 20-27). It is not wrong to become impure; indeed it is natural and even desirable, since sexual relations (Lev 15:18) and childbirth (Lev 12:1-5), which P values highly, are causes of impurity. Nor are the consequences of impurity very onerous. People in a state of impurity must avoid entering the temple or touching the holy things associated with it so as to avoid defiling them (Lev 12:4). Unlike H, P does not understand the land as subject to defilement. Thus, while nonpriests are just as likely as priests to incur impurity in P's system, being in a state of impurity has a much greater impact on priests. Laypeople in a state of impurity can easily avoid entering the temple, and they are unlikely to have contact with holy things except in the course of bringing a sacrifice. Priests, on the other hand, enter the temple on a regular basis and rely on consecrated food for part of their diet, as do their families.

The Holiness school delineates a different type of impurity caused by three types of sins: Molech worship (Lev 20:1-5), forbidden sexual relations (Leviticus 18, 20), and bloodshed (Num 35:33-34). As the parenthetical references to biblical passages suggest, however, it does not give equal attention to the three types of sins. Forbidden sexual relations occupy more space and are treated with considerable rhetorical flourish in two chapters of the Holiness Code. Molech worship is given much less space, though it appears in one of the chapters concerned primarily with forbidden sexual relations. Murder does not figure in the Holiness Code itself, although the opening chapter of the Holiness Code (Leviticus 17) is devoted to laws concerning the shedding of animal blood in the course of sacrifice and slaughter. Rather, the defiling consequences of bloodshed in the sense of murder are noted in a brief H passage outside the Holiness Code that employs a somewhat different vocabulary of impurity.[25] The Holiness Code gives a central role to P's term for ritual impurity, ṭm', which means to make impure or to be impure depending on the conjugation. H's use of the term connects its category of impurity to P's even as it expands the range of the term.[26] The passage from Numbers about murder also uses ṭm' (Num 35:34), but it uses another verb as well, to defile, ḥnp, in the causative (Num 35:33).[27] The difference in the terminology of impurity and the appearance of this Holiness passage outside the Holiness Code suggest that the development of this Holiness material and its absorption into the Torah have a complex history.

While H's conception of a type of impurity caused by sinful actions is quite different from P's conception of impurity as a ritual state caused by contact with physical substances, it is important to note that the sins H describes as causing impurity have a ritual or cultic component. Molech worship is idolatry. While some instances of forbidden sexual relations such as adultery are clearly moral sins, other instances enumerated by the Holiness Code such as the prohibition of marriage with the widows of various relatives can be understood only in ritual terms. Murder is certainly a violation of moral law, but if it is considered a form of shedding blood, the terminology the Holiness school uses (Num 35:33), it also has a ritual aspect. What is more, H surely understood itself to be adding to P rather than replacing it. That is, it accepted P's view that contact with various physical substances caused ritual impurity. Thus, in P's system impurity is a ritual phenomenon; in H's system, impurity has both ritual and moral aspects.

The other crucial difference between P and H on impurity is that P believes that the people of Israel, the sanctuary, and holy things can become impure, while H claims that, depending on the sin, the people of Israel, the sanctuary, and the land of Israel are susceptible to impurity. H's understanding makes impurity more of a concern for nonpriestly Israelites. If the sanctuary is the only place subject to defilement, then priests must worry about impurity; other Jews can be rather relaxed. But if the entire land is subject to defilement, then impurity is a pressing concern for all Jews, not priests alone.

Though the author of *Jubilees* surely did not distinguish between the Holiness source and the rest of the Torah, he was clearly particularly drawn to H. The sins *Jubilees* singles out for special attention are two of the three sins H views as defiling the land. But *Jubilees'* treatment of these sins, though clearly indebted to H, is by no means identical. In contrast to the Holiness school, *Jubilees* understands the land defiled by bloodshed to be the whole earth rather than the holy land alone, for it connects H's warning about the defilement caused by bloodshed to the prohibition of bloodshed to Noah, the ancestor of all humanity. Yet while *Jubilees* devotes considerable attention to condemning forbidden sexual relations, it does not echo the Holiness Code's warning that forbidden sexual relations defile the land, much less the earth as a whole. It does, however, single out sexual relations with foreigners as defiling the sanctuary. On the face of it, the Holiness Code has nothing to say about sexual relations with foreigners, but as we shall see, *Jubilees* finds the prohibition and the warning about its consequences in the passages in the Holiness Code prohibiting Molech worship (Lev 18:21, 20:2-5).

Bloodshed and Defiling the Earth

The sin of bloodshed appears most prominently in *Jubilees* in the story of Noah.[28] Bloodshed, both murder and the slaughter of animals for food, is the main subject of God's instructions to Noah on his emergence from the ark (*Jub.* 6:5-14) and a central theme of Noah's account of the sins that caused the flood and his exhortation to his descendants to avoid God's wrath (*Jub.* 7:20-33). The association of laws about bloodshed with Noah reflects the narrative of the Torah in which God commands Noah and his sons upon their emergence from the ark to avoid eating the blood of animals and to avoid shedding human blood:

Every moving thing that lives shall be food for you; and as I gave you the green plants, I give you everything. Only you shall not eat flesh with its life, that is, its blood. For your lifeblood I will surely require a reckoning; of every beast I will require it and of man; of every man's brother I will require the life of man. Whoever sheds the blood of man, by man shall his blood be shed; for God made man in his own image. (Gen 9:3-6)

The biblical story of Noah, then, juxtaposes the two forms of avoidance of blood. *Jubilees* echoes this association of the prohibition of murder and the prohibition of eating animal blood (*Jub.* 6:7-8), but it goes beyond Genesis by linking these prohibitions of blood with the positive use of blood in sacrifice (*Jub.* 6:10-14). Here *Jubilees* is indebted to the Holiness Code, which connects the avoidance of eating blood with the atoning blood of sacrifices:

If any man of the house of Israel or of the strangers that sojourn among them eats any blood, I will set my face against that person who eats blood, and will cut him off from among his people. For the life of the flesh is in the blood; and I have given it for you upon the altar to make atonement for your souls; for it is the blood that makes atonement, by reason of the life. (Lev 17:10-11)[29]

Jubilees manages to integrate the concern for the blood of sacrifices into the story of Noah: because Noah and his sons swore to avoid eating blood in the third month, God has commanded Moses to sprinkle blood on the children of Israel in the same month so many years later on Mt. Sinai (*Jub.* 6:10-12). Further, *Jubilees* turns the negative formulation of the Holiness Code into a positive one:

Now you command the Israelites not to eat any blood so that their name and their descendants may continue to exist before the Lord our God for all time. This law has no temporal limits because it is forever. They are to keep it throughout history so that they may continue supplicating for themselves with blood in front of the altar each and every day. (*Jub.* 6:13-14)

The effect of this formulation is to emphasize the priestly powers of ordinary Jews. Even if they cannot offer sacrifices, they can avoid consuming blood, thus assuring that the blood of sacrifices is efficacious. Conversely, unless ordinary Jews avoid blood, priests cannot properly perform their duties.

Finally, by introducing the Holiness Code's connection between the avoidance of blood in food and the efficacy of sacrificial blood into the story of Noah, *Jubilees* links sacrificial blood to the avoidance of bloodshed in murder, which, as we have just seen, is the other side of the avoidance of blood in food according to God's command to Noah as he leaves the ark in Genesis. Thus *Jubilees* brings together all three aspects of blood behavior commanded in the Torah: avoiding the shedding of blood, avoiding the eating of blood, and offering blood to God in sacrifices.

The appearance of the laws regarding blood in the Noah story in Genesis and in *Jubilees* directs them not only to the people of Israel, but to all humanity. *Jubilees*, as we have just seen, immediately connects the avoidance of blood in food to sacrifice and thus appears to narrow the intended audience of God's words to the Jewish people. But Noah's exhortation to his descendants in the following chapter suggests that the laws of bloodshed are relevant for others as well. Here too we see that the author of *Jubilees* had not forgotten H's claim that bloodshed defiles the land despite its absence in God's address to Noah.

When Noah sees that the demons are leading his descendants astray (*Jub.* 7:27), he exhorts them to behave righteously and to follow the commandments he lays down for them (*Jub.* 7:20). He reminds them of the consequences of sin by reviewing the events leading up to the flood (*Jub.* 7:20-25). Alongside the fornication and uncleanness of the Watchers' relations with women, he points to the injustice caused by the Nephilim, the sons born from these relations. Injustice in Noah's account is more or less interchangeable with the shedding of blood:

When everyone sold himself to commit injustice and to shed innocent blood, the earth was filled with injustice .... Much blood was shed on the earth. . . . Then the Lord obliterated all from the surface of the earth because of their actions and because of the blood which they had shed in the earth. (*Jub.* 7:23-25)

The consequences with which Noah threatens his offspring if they shed or consume blood are dire indeed:

Everyone who sheds human blood and everyone who consumes the blood of any animate being will all be obliterated from the earth. . . . No blood of all the blood which there may be at any time when you sacrifice any animal, cattle, or (creature) that flies above the earth is to be seen on you. Do a good deed for yourselves by covering what is poured out on the surface of the earth. Do not be one who eats (meat) with the blood; exert yourselves so that blood is not consumed in your presence. Cover the blood because so was I ordered to testify to you and your children together with all humanity. Do not eat the life with the meat so that your blood, your life, may not be required from every person who sheds (blood) on the earth. For the earth will not be purified of the blood which has been shed on it; but by the blood of the one who shed it the earth will be purified in all its generations. (*Jub.* 7:28-33)

Here for the first time we see *Jubilees* explicitly invoke the view of the Holiness school that bloodshed defiles the land. The debt is particularly clear in the concluding clause of the passage just quoted, which echoes Numbers (35:33): "No expiation can be made for the land, for that blood that is shed in it, except by the blood of him who shed it." Yet *Jubilees* has transformed H's understanding in several significant ways. First of all, where for H the bloodshed that defiles the land is murder, *Jubilees* follows P in Genesis (9:3-6) in understanding the shedding of blood in animal slaughter to have consequences almost as profound as the consequences of murder, and it claims that not only murder but also the consumption of blood defiles the earth.

The second transformation *Jubilees* effects is the expansion of the space defiled by bloodshed. The prohibition of bloodshed in Genesis is addressed to Noah and his sons, and thus to all humanity (Gen 9:1), but the prohibition of murder in Numbers is addressed to the Israelites alone: "You shall not defile the land in which you live, in the midst of which I dwell; for I the Lord dwell in the midst of the people of Israel" (Num 35:34). Thus *Jubilees* goes beyond the Torah by making gentiles as well as Jews responsible for keeping the earth free from the defiling affects of bloodshed. To do this, *Jubilees* exploits the fact that H's term for the holy land is, simply, 'āreṣ, land or earth depending on context, as Betsy Halpern-Amaru notes in her study of *Jubilees*' view of the holy land.[30] Halpern-Amaru suggests that this transformation is a result of *Jubilees*' de-emphasis of the promise of the land in its retelling of the stories of the Patriarchs and the Exodus. For *Jubilees*, Israel's chosenness goes back to the creation of the world, and it claims that the land was allotted to Israel at the time of Noah. Thus the link between the land and the election of Israel is suppressed. With the origins of the relationship between God and Israel placed in the context of creation, *Jubilees*' eschatology looks forward to the restoration of the conditions of primeval times rather than to the restoration of the land. Halpern-Amaru sees this perspective as reflecting the conditions of the later Second Temple period, when the restoration to the land had been accomplished but without the hoped-for eschatological effects.[31]

Forbidden Sexual Relations

In the same address in which he warns against bloodshed, Noah also urges his descendants to avoid "fornication" and "uncleanness" (*Jub.* 7:20-21), which, he claims, led to the bloodshed that caused the flood. Abraham too warns his assembled descendants, not only Isaac and his sons but also Ishmael and his children and the sons of Keturah and their children, against "sexual impurity" and "uncleanness" (*Jub.* 20:3-6), threatening that sexual sin will lead them to destruction:

Now you keep yourselves from all sexual impurity and uncleanness and from all the contamination of sin so that you do not make our name into a curse, your entire lives into a (reason for) *hissing* and all your children into something that is destroyed by the sword. Then you will be accursed like Sodom, and all who remain of you like the people of Gomorrah. (*Jub.* 20:6)

According to Abraham, the dire consequences of forbidden sexual relations fall not only on those who engage in them but also on the people among whom they take place. So too the Holiness Code threatens those who engage in forbidden sexual relations with being cut off from among their people (Lev 18:29), and also warns that the whole people may suffer as a result (Lev 18:28). The suffering in question consists of expulsion from the land as a result of its defilement on which the Holiness Code places great emphasis (Lev 18:24-30). Abraham in his speech in *Jubilees*, however, makes no mention of defilement of the earth. Perhaps we can account for *Jubilees'* reluctance to treat forbidden sexual relations as it treated bloodshed by remembering that the Torah provides a way to undo the effects of bloodshed, shedding the blood of the party responsible for it (Gen 9:5-6; Num 35:33), but implies that there is no way to undo the defilement caused by forbidden sexual relations; even the punishments decreed in Leviticus 20 do not prevent the land's vomiting out the people among whom the defilers live (Lev 20:22). Like the Holiness Code, which explains the expulsion of the nations that preceded the Israelites in the land as a consequence of their sexual wrongdoing (Lev 18:24-28), *Jubilees* worries not just about Israel's sexual morality but about that of other peoples as well, as the inclusion of all of Abraham's descendants in the audience demonstrates. If the entire earth were to be susceptible to defilement, in light of *Jubilees'* low opinion of other peoples, it would be catastrophic to attribute the power to defile the earth to sexual wrongdoing.

Several stories in Genesis provide *Jubilees* with an opportunity to treat the laws of forbidden sexual relations for the people of Israel.[32] I shall concentrate on the two stories it uses to develop its view of Israel as a kingdom of priests: Reuben's relations with Bilhah (Gen 35:22; *Jub.* 33:1-20) and the rape of Dinah (Genesis 34; *Jubilees* 30).

It is perhaps an exaggeration to call Genesis' mention of the encounter of Reuben and Bilhah a story. But like so much of the narrative of Genesis, the brief mention of the violation of Jacob's concubine by his firstborn son manages to hint at a complex background and to raise a host of questions. While the narrative reports that "Israel heard"[33] about the incident, there is no clear indication of the consequences until the aged Jacob gives his sons their final blessing:

Reuben, you are my first-born,
my might, and the first fruits of my strength,
pre-eminent in pride and pre-eminent in power.
Unstable as water, you shall not have pre-eminence
because you went up to your father's bed;
then you defiled it—he[34] went up to my couch!
(Gen 49:3-4)

Yet clearly there were consequences even before Jacob's equivocal blessing. It has been suggested that Reuben's violation of Bilhah, which takes place while his father is mourning the death of Leah, is intended to assert his claim to lead the clan as the old leader begins to fail, just as Absalom publicly takes possession of his father's harem after David has fled Jerusalem (2 Sam 17:21-22).[35] If so, the effort was an utter failure. Following his sin, Reuben plays an important but negative role in the drama of the sale of Joseph; he serves as the foil to the hero of the story, his younger brother Judah. Reuben's plan for saving Joseph (Gen 37:21-22), perhaps an effort to get himself back in his wronged father's good graces, is thwarted when the brothers follow Judah's advice to sell Joseph to a caravan of merchants heading to Egypt (Gen 37:25-28). Later Reuben fails to persuade his father to permit the brothers to return to Egypt with Benjamin (Gen 42:37-38); it is Judah who succeeds (Gen 43:8-10). In the critical confrontation with Joseph (Gen 44:18-34), Reuben is nowhere to be found. Judah has emerged as the leader of the brothers; the firstborn, as usual, has been displaced.

But the author of *Jubilees* worried about a problem that did not occur to the authors of the narrative in Genesis. According to the Holiness Code, as *Jubilees* well knew, both Reuben and Bilhah deserved to die (Lev 20:11).[36] *Jubilees* supplies the unequivocal condemnation of Reuben's behavior lacking in Genesis and offers an explanation for Reuben's escape from the punishment due him according to biblical law: the law against sleeping with one's father's wife had not yet been "completely revealed" (*Jub.* 33:9-17). Presumably this is also the reason for Bilhah's escape although *Jubilees* does not say so. While *Jubilees* reiterates that, as the Holiness Code demands, both man and woman must die (*Jub.* 33:17), the angelic tirade against incest (*Jub.* 33:9-20) is otherwise directed exclusively at the man who commits the sin. The brief account in Genesis gives little indication of Bilhah's attitude toward the event in which she is so central a figure, but *Jubilees'* retelling emphasizes Bilhah's innocence: she is asleep when Reuben takes advantage of her, she is deeply distressed by the rape, and Jacob learns of the occurrence only when she warns him not to sleep with her because she has been defiled (*Jub.* 33:1-9). Thus it is not surprising that *Jubilees* prefers to play down the Holiness Code's call for equal punishment for both participants in the crime.

For *Jubilees*, the dire consequences of Reuben's sin are expressed in terms of impurity:[37]

For all who commit it on the earth before the Lord are impure, something detestable, a blemish, and something contaminated. No sin is greater than the sexual impurity which they commit on the earth because Israel is a holy people for the Lord its God. It is the nation which he possesses; it is a priestly nation; it is what he owns. No such impurity will be seen among the holy people. (*Jub.* 33:19-20)

The Ethiopic of *Jubilees* is a translation of a translation of the Hebrew original, but it seems safe to assume that the repeated use of the language of impurity[38] reflects the influence of the Holiness Code and particularly of the exhortation at the end of Leviticus 18's list of forbidden relations, which repeats the verb *ṭmʾ* six times (Lev 18:24-30). Yet for *Jubilees* the defilement caused by sexual immorality affects neither the holy land, as the Holiness Code claims, nor the earth as a whole, as *Jubilees* itself claims for bloodshed. Rather, as Abraham warned his descendants, the defilement falls on the parties to the relations and the people among whom they live. Such defilement, *Jubilees* insists, is particularly grave when the people in question is Israel, the priestly people.

In the society the narratives of the Bible depict, in which polygamy was the rule for men of high status, the sons of an older wife might well be as old as or older than a younger wife.[39] Thus, as those narratives indicate, the prohibition of sexual relations between sons and their father's wives was of more than theoretical interest. It is hard to imagine, however, that such relations were a major social problem for the society in which *Jubilees* was written, in which polygamy had been relegated to the past.[40] The intensity of the angelic tirade must reflect not the importance of this particular sin but rather *Jubilees'* attitude toward the violation of any of the incest laws of Leviticus 18 and 20, of which Reuben's sin with Bilhah is a readily available instance. Thus, while the angel's speech as a whole emphasizes the forbidden nature of Reuben's sin, sleeping with his father's wife, the concluding lines, quoted above, speak of sexual sin in general, thus extending the relevance of the association with impurity. Judah's relations with his daughter-in-law Tamar (*Jub.* 41:8-28), another violation of the incest laws (Lev 18:15; 20:12), is a much less attractive opportunity for the author of *Jubilees*. Not only does that story have a notably happy ending, but, as we have just seen, Judah eventually emerged as the leader of the brothers and ultimately was remembered as the ancestor of King David by way of one of the sons Tamar bore him.

Intermarriage and the Defilement of the Sanctuary

The influence of the Holiness Code on *Jubilees'* treatment of the rape of Dinah is even more striking. The account of this incident in *Jubilees* draws on traditions found in *Aramaic Levi*, but *Jubilees* reworks the incident with its own concerns in mind.[41] Like *Aramaic Levi, Jubilees* understands the murder of the Shechemites by Levi and Simeon as a highly praiseworthy defense of endogamy. Indeed, both works understand Levi to have won the priesthood by his leadership in this incident. According to Genesis (34:8-17), Jacob's sons "deceitfully" (34:13) negotiated terms for the marriage with the rapist and his father. *Jubilees* alludes to these negotiations, which are an embarrassment from its point of view, emphasizing the deceit: Jacob and his sons "spoke deceptively with them, acted in a crafty way toward them, and deceived them" (*Jub.* 30:3). But *Jubilees* never mentions them explicitly. For *Jubilees* it would be a terrible outrage to permit the marriage under any conditions, since *Jubilees* understands this marriage to fall under the prohibition of offering a child to Molech (Lev 18:21):

If there is a man in Israel who wishes to give his daughter or his sister to any foreigner, he is to die. He is to be stoned. . . . The woman is to be burned. . . . The man who has defiled his daughter within all of Israel is to be eradicted because he has given one of his descendants to Molech. (*Jub.* 30:7, 10)

The prohibition of such marriages, according to *Jubilees*, is to be found on the heavenly tablets (*Jub.* 30:9).

The Holiness Code's law that forbids giving a child to Molech follows the long list of forbidden sexual relationships in Leviticus 18. Its placement in this context and the peculiar language of the prohibition, literally, "You shall not give of your seed to cause to pass to Molech," led some rabbis and targumim to read the verse as a prohibition of sexual intercourse ("give of your seed") with pagan women.[42] While the passage from Leviticus is best suited to condemning the marriage of a Jewish man and a gentile woman or his sexual relationship with her, the speech of the angel of the presence following *Jubilees*' account of the rape of Dinah and its aftermath (*Jub.* 30:5-23) claims this verse to condemn the marriage of a Jewish woman to a gentile man.[43]

The Torah has rather little to say about intermarriage or sexual relations with gentiles, but it places somewhat more emphasis on the dangers posed by foreign women than by foreign men.[44] Of course, the concept of intermarriage does not apply very well to the narratives of Genesis; until the generation of Jacob's grandchildren, it would have been impossible for Israelites to marry other Israelites. But *Jubilees* works hard to provide the wives of even pre-Abrahamic patriarchs with what it views as desirable genealogical credentials, descent from Shem and then from Terah. It sees Canaanite women as particularly distasteful, and Abraham warns all of his descendants, not only Isaac and his sons, against marriage with them (*Jub.* 20:4).[45] Thus *Jubilees* is able to give meaning to the avoidance of marriage to foreigners even in the context of the patriarchal narratives.

The angelic narrator's speech after the incident at Shechem expresses *Jubilees*' understanding of the implications of the observance of the law it has just invented forbidding sexual relations with foreigners: unlike the sin of Reuben with Bilhah, violation of this law has an impact on the people as a whole and defiles the sanctuary.

If one does this [marries a foreigner] or shuts his eyes to those who do impure things and who defile the Lord's sanctuary and to those who profane his holy name, then the entire nation will be condemned together because of all this impurity and contamination. There will be no favoritism nor partiality; there will be no receiving from him of fruit, sacrifices, offerings, fat, or the aroma of a pleasing fragrance so that he should accept it. (So) is any man or woman in Israel to be who defiles his sanctuary. (*Jub.* 30:15-16)

Jubilees' warning that marriage to a foreigner defiles the temple reflects its interpretation of the Holiness Code's threat about Molech worship: "And I will set My face against that man and will cut him off from among his people, because he gave of his offspring to Molech and so defiled My sanctuary and profaned My holy name" (Lev 20:3). The language of the angel of the presence's condemnation of intermarriage echoes the language of the passage from the Holiness Code: "those . . . who defile the Lord's sanctuary," "those who profane his holy name" (*Jub.* 30:15).

In the passages under discussion, both the Holiness Code and *Jubilees* confer a sort of priestly responsibility on ordinary Jews, who must avoid idolatry or intermarriage in order to keep the temple from becoming impure.[46] But *Jubilees* makes ordinary Jews even more priest-like. Only if they observe God's commandment regarding sexual relations with foreigners will sacrifices, the priestly work par excellence, be acceptable. We have already seen *Jubilees'* appeal to the idea of Israel as a kingdom of priests in the exhortation to sexual purity after the account of Reuben's rape of Bilhah (*Jub.* 33:20). The speech of the angel of the presence in the aftermath of the rape of Dinah takes this idea further by giving the idea practical implications: failure to observe the ban on intermarriage results in defilement of the temple.

It is particularly striking that *Jubilees* confers these priestly responsibilities on all Jews in its reflection on the implications of the episode that earned Levi the priesthood. Clearly *Jubilees* wants to emphasize that the emergence of the Levitical priesthood does not mark the end of a sort of priesthood for all Israel. In *Aramaic Levi*, Isaac instructs his grandson Levi in the "law of the priesthood." The instructions conclude with a blessing:

You will be more beloved than all your brothers. And blessing will be pronounced by your seed upon the earth and your seed will be entered in a book of a memorial of life for all eternity. And your name and the name of your seed will not be blotted out for eternity. And now, (my) child Levi, your seed will be blessed upon the earth for all generations of eternity. (*Ar. Levi* 58-61)

Jubilees transfers the themes of this blessing to the comments of the angel of the presence on the incident of Shechem. The language echoes the passage from *Aramaic Levi*, but *Jubilees* has made some significant changes:

> Levi's descendants were chosen for the priesthood and as levites to serve before the Lord as we (do) for all time. Levi and his sons will be blessed forever because he was eager to carry out justice, punishment, and revenge on all who rise against Israel. . . . He has been recorded on the heavenly tablets as a friend and a just man. . . . Tell the Israelites not to sin or transgress the statutes or violate the covenant which was established for them so that they should perform it and be recorded as friends. (*Jub.* 30:18-21)

There can be no doubt that *Jubilees* shares the view of *Aramaic Levi* that Levi's zealous deed at Shechem won the priesthood not only for him but also for his descendants. But where *Aramaic Levi* insists that the names of Levi's offspring are to be entered in a heavenly book, *Jubilees* restricts the entry to Levi himself while promising all Israelites that their names too can be entered if they observe the laws of the covenant. What *Aramaic Levi* reserves for priests, *Jubilees* promises to all Israel.

Jubilees and Intermarriage

Jubilees places great emphasis on the avoidance of intermarriage not only in its interpretation of the rape of Dinah but also, as noted above, in its efforts to provide genealogies for the wives of the patriarchs that make them descendants of Shem and Terah. Some scholars have suggested that *Jubilees* was responding to a practice common among the hellenizing Jews in the period leading up to the Maccabean Revolt.[47] Yet there is very little evidence to support this claim.[48] "They joined with the gentiles" (1 Macc 1:15) may point to intermarriage, but it is hardly unambiguous; it could also refer to other types of interaction with non-Jews.[49] The silence of texts such as the Wisdom of ben Sira and 2 Maccabees, from which one would expect clear and unambiguous condemnation of such behavior if it existed, is particularly striking.[50]

The lack of concern about intermarriage in texts from either side of the revolt makes the task of explaining why intermarriage loomed so large for the author of *Jubilees* more difficult. Here I would like to shift the discussion forward in time to the second half of the second century, when Hasmonean rule was already established, and to look beyond the evidence for intermarriage as such and consider the evidence for the absorption of gentiles into the Jewish people during this period. I believe that this shift permits us to explain both the intense concern about intermarriage of the author of *Jubilees* and the lack of concern of most other observers, who would not have seen the problem *Jubilees* saw for reasons I will suggest below.[51]

The population of Palestine on the eve of the Maccabean Revolt was mixed. In addition to Jews, it included not only Greeks but also long-established groups such as the Idumeans, the descendants of the ancient Edomites. The inhabitants of the hellenistic cities were primarily non-Jews, some of Greek descent, others drawn from the local gentile population. There was also a considerable population of non-Jewish peasants in the villages outside Judea proper.[52] The events of the 160s changed the balance of power between Jews and gentiles in Judea in a significant way. During the revolt the Maccabees fought against the inhabitants of some of the hellenistic cities (1 Maccabees 5), and although they never made a systematic effort to eradicate paganism in the biblical land of Israel, they are occasionally reported to have destroyed a pagan cult site.[53] Nor, having achieved sovereignty in Judea, were the Maccabee brothers content to rest; they began a program of annexation of neighboring areas. Uriel Rappaport has suggested that as a result of the Maccabees' success some of their gentile neighbors might have decided to throw their lot in with the Jews.[54] One need not accept his claims about Jewish "religious propaganda" to be persuaded by other aspects of the scenario he proposes, such as his suggestion that Idumeans still attached to their traditional way of life might have felt that they had more in common with their ancient neighbors, the Jews, than with the Greeks. The Edomites, the ancestors of the Idumeans, appear to have practiced circumcision,[55] and it seems likely that many of their descendants continued to do so in the Maccabean era. For such gentiles moving toward the religious practices of the newly dominant Jewish population might have seemed a sensible and even congenial path.

On the other hand, Josephus reports two instances of the Hasmoneans' imposition of Judaism on a gentile population by force. The first is the conquest and conversion of the Idumeans by John Hyrcanus, which Josephus places shortly after 130. The second is the conquest and conversion of the Itureans by Aristobolus in 104–103 (*Antiquities* 13.318). I shall focus on the Idumeans because of their particular relevance for *Jubilees*.

After subduing all the Idumeans, [Hyrcanus] permitted them to remain in their country so long as they had themselves circumcised and were willing to observe the laws of the Jews. And so, out of attachment to the land of their fathers, they submitted to circumcision and to making their manner of life conform in all other respects to that of the Jews. And from that time on they have continued to be Jews. (*Antiquities* 13.257-58)

Josephus's account receives some support from a certain Ptolemy, a writer of unknown date, who also claims that the Jews conquered the Idumeans and forced them to be circumcised.[56]

The concept of conversion implicit in *Jubilees'* account developed gradually during the Second Temple period. During the monarchy, outsiders who married Israelites and came to live among them were absorbed into the people. The idea of "Judaism" as a set of beliefs and practices theoretically available to those who were not born into it emerged out of the encounter with Greek culture.[57] If Greek culture was available even to barbarians, why could not Judaism be available to gentiles? Though there was not yet a well-developed ritual marking conversion, men commonly underwent circumcision as part of their embrace of Judaism.[58]

But if circumcision was standard practice for the ancient Edomites, why did Hyrcanus need to require the Idumeans to undergo circumcision? In contrast to Josephus and Ptolemy, Strabo reports that the Idumeans "joined" the Jews and took on their customs (*Geography* 16.2.34); his terse account mentions neither conquest nor circumcision. Rappaport suggests that Idumeans who had held on to the traditional practice of circumcision were well on the way to becoming Jews even without Hyrcanus's conquest. Perhaps Hyrcanus's threat of exile was directed at the more hellenized Idumeans resident in the cities of Adora and Marisa, who no longer maintained the ancestral practice. The evidence for an increased Idumean presence in Egypt in the early part of the first century B.C.E. suggests that some of them preferred exile to conversion.[59]

Jubilees and Conversion

Whether of their own free will or under threat of exile, whether through conscious conversion or less conscious assimilation, it is clear that a significant number of gentiles joined the Jewish people during the Hasmonean period. This must have caused the author of *Jubilees* considerable distress for, although he never says so explicitly, he makes it quite clear that he does not recognize the possibility of conversion. For *Jubilees*, it was simply impossible for a gentile to become a Jew. Thus *Jubilees* sees intermarriage where others do not. From the point of view of most onlookers, including the partners to them, marriages between the new Jews of the Hasmonean period and the "native" Jewish population were marriages between two Jews. For *Jubilees*, however, they were marriages between a Jew and a foreigner.

As already noted, *Jubilees* takes great care to provide the patriarchs with wives descended first from Shem and then from Terah; Halpern-Amaru points out that the implication of *Jubilees'* attention to maternal ancestors is that "the only legitimate mode of entry into the community . . .

[is] birth."[60] Rejection of the possibility of conversion can also be seen in *Jubilees'* reworking of the story of the rape of Dinah.[61] In the biblical account, circumcision plays a crucial role. The brothers tell Shechem and Hamor that they will agree to Dinah's marriage to Shechem only if the men of Shechem circumcise themselves (Gen 34:13). The narrative informs us that the brothers spoke "with guile because [Shechem] had defiled their sister Dinah"; their real intentions emerge when Simeon and Levi take advantage of the communal convalescence that follows the acceptance of their terms to slaughter the population of the city. The narrative of Genesis does not know a concept of conversion, and nothing in the story suggests that the circumcised Shechemites would have been regarded as Israelites. Yet Jacob's silence during the negotiations and his angry reaction to the violent deeds of his sons indicate that, all other things being equal, circumcision would have served to make the Shechemites appropriate marriage partners.

Jubilees is troubled by Jacob's apparent willingness to accept Shechem as a son-in-law. It insists that father and sons were of one mind in rejecting the possibility: "They spoke deceptively with them, acted in a crafty way toward them, and deceived them" (*Jub.* 30:3). Yet someone who did not know the story in Genesis would not know of what the deceptive behavior consisted since *Jubilees* makes no mention of the negotiations or of the group circumcision to which the negotiations led. The elimination of any hint of circumcision from its version of the story suggests that *Jubilees* wanted to avoid a reading of the Genesis narrative that understood the circumcision of the Shechemites in Second Temple terms, as conversion. Indeed, the emphasis on deceit, which is rather surprising given *Jubilees'* usual tendency to gloss over any questionable behavior by its heroes, is perhaps intended to imply that the brothers' claim (in Genesis, never mentioned in *Jubilees*) that circumcision would have made the Shechemites acceptable marriage partners was itself an act of deception.

It is worth remembering that many of the gentiles who were becoming Jews in the Hasmonean period were Idumeans, and from the point of view of *Jubilees*, the Idumeans were not just any gentiles.[62] The connection between the Idumeans and the biblical Edomites had certainly not been lost in *Jubilees'* time; 1 Maccabees refers to the Idumeans as the sons of Esau (5:3). For *Jubilees*, Esau represents all that is evil in gentiles. Jacob as the first patriarch to engender only Israelite offspring is perhaps the most important hero of *Jubilees*. Just as *Jubilees* represented Jacob as altogether pious and virtuous, no easy task in light of the narrative in Genesis, it shows Esau as wicked despite the not unsympathetic treatment of Genesis.[63] The contrast between the brothers is evident from their youth: Jacob learns to write, while Esau learns to make war

(*Jub.* 19:14). In Genesis Esau marries Hittite women who are a source of distress to Rebecca (Gen 27:46). In *Jubilees* Esau's wives are Canaanites, forbidden by Abraham to his descendants (*Jub.* 20:4) and, according to their mother-in-law, a source of "sexual impurity and lewdness" (*Jub.* 25:1).[64] Genesis's account of Esau's gracious behavior toward Jacob on his return from his sojourn with Laban (Gen 33:4-16) is condensed into the bland report, "They were reconciled with one another" (*Jub.* 19:13). Esau abandons his parents for Mt. Seir, taking their flocks with him, while Jacob sends his parents anything they need, thus earning their blessings (*Jub.* 29:19-20). Ultimately Jacob must kill Esau in self-defense (*Jub.* 38:2) in the course of the war Esau started (*Jubilees* 37-38); his death is a richly deserved punishment for violating the oath he swore to his mother (*Jub.* 35:18-24). This picture of the ancestor of the Idumeans is better read as a result of the internal logic of *Jubilees*' delineation of the holy people than as a response to contemporary conditions, but with such a picture of Esau, a large influx of Idumeans into the Jewish people would surely have gotten the attention of the author of *Jubilees*.[65]

A connection between *Jubilees* and the conversion of the Idumeans is not a new idea. A century ago R. H. Charles suggested that *Jubilees*' war between Jacob and his sons and Esau and his sons (chaps. 37–38), an episode without parallel in the biblical narrative, reflects Judah Maccabee's conquest of Idumea, but he took the reference to the continued subjugation of the sons of Edom (*Jub.* 38:14) as an allusion to Hyrcanus's conquest of the Idumeans.[66] More recently, Rapapport has argued that the war of Jacob and Esau reflects not Judah's campaign, but that of Hyrcanus. He even finds evidence in *Jubilees*' story for the division he sees between the Idumean city dwellers and their rural relatives. It is Esau's sons who take the initiative against Jacob according to *Jubilees* (37:1-13); in Rappaport's view, Esau's sons represent the inhabitants of the cities of Adora and Marisa, deeply hostile to the Hasmonean state. They must persuade their initially reluctant father, who represents the rural Idumeans, more kindly disposed toward the Jews, to violate the oath he swore to his mother to live in peace with his brother.[67]

Though I have become persuaded that *Jubilees* was written against the background of the Hasmonean expansion of the Judean state, it seems most unlikely that *Jubilees* would have been willing to use the figure of Jacob, its favorite patriarch, to represent John Hyrcanus, a high priest who followed the calendar against which much of *Jubilees*' ire is directed. Indeed one might argue that *Jubilees* intends the story of the defeat of Esau and his sons at the hands of Jacob and his sons as a critique of Hyrcanus's actions. Rather than subduing the sons of Esau and misguidedly attempting to turn them into Jews, Jacob and his sons subdued them and kept them in an inferior position—"until today" (*Jub.* 38:14). But there is good reason to be cautious about any attempt to take the war between Esau and Jacob and their sons as a direct reflection of historical events since the wars fill a need of the narrative itself.[68]

Furthermore, any attempt to connect *Jubilees* to Hyrcanus's conquest of the Idumeans runs up against the problem of dating. Until quite recently Hyrcanus's conquest was usually dated on the basis of its placement in Josephus's account to shortly after 130.[69] The earliest manuscript of *Jubilees* is dated on paleographic grounds to 125–100 B.C.E. Thus it would have been possible to understand *Jubilees'* anxiety about intermarriage as a response to a mass conversion of the Idumeans after Hyracanus's conquest. But recent numismatic evidence taken together with the evidence of the tomb inscriptions, which was already known, suggests that the date deduced from Josephus is wrong and that the conquest of Idumea took place in 112/11, perhaps too late to have influenced a work that was certainly in existence by 100.[70]

On the other hand, as we have seen, it seems likely that the conversion of the Idumeans was not so much an event as an ongoing process that dates back to the beginning of Hasmonean rule. The conversion of the Idumeans under Hyrcanus is only the most dramatic instance of a process that had been going on quietly for decades. Thus even if *Jubilees* was written before the conquest of Idumea, it might still be responding to the Judaization of the Idumeans. Its rejection of conversion and consequent anxiety about intermarriage make sense in a period in which gentiles are being absorbed into the Jewish population in significant numbers. These considerations point to a date for *Jubilees* somewhat later than the one James VanderKam suggests, probably in the last third of the second century, a date that fits well the paleographic evidence.

It is perhaps worth noting here that several texts from Qumran demonstrate a rather hesitant attitude toward converts. Some scholars have suggested that they reflect priestly discomfort with conversion.[71] But there is a significant difference between the hesitance of most of these texts and *Jubilees'* opposition. The *Temple Scroll,* for example, appears to decree, though the text is quite broken, that *gērîm* are not to pass beyond the outer court of the temple until the fourth generation (*TS* 39.5, 40.5-6), an attitude that is cautious, but ultimately accepting. So too the *Damascus Document*'s provision for *gērîm* as one of the categories into which the membership of the sect is divided (CD 14.3-6) keeps *gērîm* separate from native Jews while accepting them as members of the sect. The text that stands closest to *Jubilees* is 4QFlorilegium, which insists that no *gēr* will enter the eschatological temple (4Q174 1 i 3-4). Here, it seems, the very possibility of conversion is denied.[72]

One passage that has not been considered in this context as far as I know comes from an eschatological timetable in 4Q390, part of the fragmentary *Apocryphon of Jeremiah*. Among the evils that will take place in the period shortly before the dawn of the eschaton, it appears, is intermarriage: *ûbĕbnê* [*nēkar*] *yĕhalĕl*[*û*] *et zar*[*'a*]*m*, "and with fo[reign]ers [t]he[y] will profane their offspr[ing]" (4Q390 2 i 10).[73] "Foreigners" is literally, "sons of a foreign place." "Sons" is preserved, but "foreign place" is a restoration; nothing is preserved of the word. The use of the term "Angels of Mastemot" (4Q390 1 11, 2 i 7) suggests sectarian provenance or at least connections for the work. If the restoration is correct, the condemnation of intermarriage in this passage is perhaps best read as I have suggested reading the condemnation in *Jubilees*, that is, as directed against marriages between native Jews and former gentiles who now view themselves and are viewed by most others as Jews. As we saw in the last chapter, Hayes reads 4QMMT as another example of opposition to marriage between native Jews and converts;[74] as I indicated there, I believe that 4QMMT should be read as opposing marriage between priests and women from lay families.

Jews and Gentiles in *Jubilees*

Jubilees' rejection of conversion needs to be understood against the background of its picture of the differences between Jews and gentiles. The reason *Jubilees* believes it is impossible for a gentile to become a Jew, as Cana Werman points out, is that Israel and the nations are essentially different.[75] For *Jubilees* the nations of the world live in subjugation to the demons. Only Israel is free of their rule: "For there are many nations and many peoples and all belong to [the Lord]. He made spirits rule over all in order to lead them astray from following him. But over Israel he made no angel or spirit rule because he alone is their ruler" (*Jub.* 15:31-32).

The only exceptions to *Jubilees*' division of humanity into two opposing camps are the descendants of Ishmael and the sons of Keturah, that is, Abraham's descendants through sons other than Isaac. In his farewell address to all his offspring, Abraham exhorts them to act kindly to each other, to circumcise their sons, to avoid sexual impurity, and to worship God rather than idols (*Jub.* 20:10). But it is not clear how to reconcile the more positive picture of the status of the descendants of Abraham in this passage with their apparent consignment to the fate of all the other nations, subjugation to the evil spirits, in the speech of the angel of the presence quoted above. Indeed, that speech, which comes after Abraham receives the command of circumcision, takes care to exclude the other descendants of Abraham from the covenant: "For the Lord did not draw near to himself either Ishmael, his sons, his brothers or Esau.

He did not choose them (simply) because they were among Abraham's children, for he knew them. But he chose Israel to be his people" (*Jub.* 15:30). Thus, although *Jubilees* shows a certain consideration for the descendants of Abraham through Ishmael and the sons of Keturah, it does not appear to be willing to adjust its binary view of humanity to allow for a third status.

Werman suggests that *Jubilees* understands Ishmael as a *gēr*, not as a convert, but rather in the sense the Torah uses the term: as a gentile living among the people of Israel.[76] Such gentiles are obligated to observe some of the laws of the Torah, and they enjoy certain protections legislated there.[77] Still, as Werman points out, the status of the *gēr* is by definition marginal. This is perhaps most clearly seen in Deuteronomy's juxtaposition of the *gēr* with the widow and the orphan (e.g., Deut 24: 17, 19). But if Ishmael is treated gently by *Jubilees*, Esau and his descendants, as we have seen, are not.

One source for the radical divide between Jews and gentiles in *Jubilees* is the Book of Ezra's idea of the people of Israel as "holy seed" (Ezra 9:2), as Halpern-Amaru and Hayes have pointed out.[78] Hayes notes that *Jubilees'* rejection of intermarriage is based not on the fear that the foreign spouse will be a bad influence on the Jewish partner but rather on genealogical unsuitablity.[79] She also notes the priestly dimension of holy seed ideology: it transfers to all Israel the holiness that some strands of the Bible reserve for priests.[80] Halpern-Amaru suggests that *Jubilees'* genealogical definition of membership in the people of Israel reflects its view of the people of Israel as a kingdom of priests; priestly status is after all defined by ancestry alone.[81] Finally, because it views differences between Jews and gentiles as inborn, the holy seed ideology does not recognize the possibility of conversion.[82]

But while it may embrace Ezra's conception of Israel as holy seed, *Jubilees* goes beyond Ezra in differentiating Israel from the nations.[83] For according to *Jubilees* the people of Israel is the earthly counterpart of the angels. As God and the angels prepare to keep the first Sabbath, he tells the angels,

> I will now separate a people for myself from among my nations. They, too, will keep the sabbath. I will sanctify the people for myself and will bless them as I sanctified the sabbath day. . . . I have chosen the descendants of Jacob among all of those whom I have seen. (*Jub.* 2:19-20)

For *Jubilees*, then, the people of Israel was part of God's plan from the very beginning. Its existence does not depend on particular contingent historical developments, nor does its relationship to God. Both Israel and its covenant with God were written into creation. Later, when *Jubilees* recounts how God ordained the covenant of circumcision with Abra-

ham, we learn that the angels were created circumcised, further strength-
ening the link between Israel and the angels (*Jub.* 15:25-27): "For this is
what the nature of all the angels of holiness was like from the day of their
creation. In front of the angels of the presence and the angels of holiness
he sanctified Israel to be with him and his holy angels" (*Jub.* 15:27).

Like so many other works from the Second Temple period, *Jubilees* assumes that heaven is a temple. Thus when Isaac blesses his grandson
Levi, he compares the role of priests to that of the angels: "May he make
you and your descendants (alone) out of all humanity approach him /
to serve in his temple like the angels of the presence and like the holy
ones" (*Jub.* 31:14). In this blessing the tension between *Jubilees'* enthusiasm for the idea of Israel as a kingdom of priests and its acceptance of,
indeed its admiration for, the Levitical priesthood surfaces again. It is
Levi and his descendants "out of all humanity" whom Isaac blesses as
serving like angels and yet *Jubilees* asserts elsewhere, quite emphatically,
that all Israel are like the angels, and thus, one must conclude, like
priests.

Jubilees and Sectarianism

The dominant reading of *Jubilees* in recent scholarship sees it as a response to hellenizing Jews. According to 1 Maccabees, some Jews com-
plained that things had gone better before Israel separated itself from
the nations (1 Macc 1:11). *Jubilees* insists that there never was such a
time: God chose Israel and set it apart from other peoples during the
very process of creation. Against the critique of Judaism current in the
hellenistic world, *Jubilees* claims that the ritual laws are not a later development but date back to deepest antiquity. Before the people of Israel
came into existence, the angels practiced circumcision, the Sabbath,
and the festivals in heaven. On the basis of these considerations and
other indications, this reading places the composition of the book in
the period shortly after the Maccabean Revolt.[84]

I argued above that *Jubilees'* view of an irreducible difference between
Jews and gentiles responds to a different concern—the influx of gentiles
to Judaism in the second half of the second century—when Jewish ascendancy encouraged the Idumeans and perhaps other gentiles living
under Hasmonean rule or at the edges of their kingdom to identify as
Jews. This somewhat later date is by no means incompatible with the
claim that *Jubilees* is responding to the hellenistic critique of Judaism;[85]
Jews living under Hasmonean rule, after all, were hardly untouched
by the larger culture in which they lived, and the debate about the proper
understanding of Judaism was not resolved by the triumph of the
Maccabees.

Here I would like to suggest that *Jubilees'* view of the gulf between Jews
and gentiles hints at another aspect of the context in which it was written. The period after the Maccabean Revolt saw the "flourishing" of
sects, as Albert Baumgarten has put it.[86] Not all of the groups Josephus
calls sects fit the modern sociological definition of a sect, which includes
the belief that the sect alone is in possession of the truth and that the
rest of the world is irredeemably lost.[87] But there can be no doubt that
the definition applies to the literature of Qumran *yaḥad,* whose emergence is usually connected to the events of the revolt and its aftermath,
and associated texts such as the *Damascus Document.*[88] The *Damascus Document* makes it clear that the true Israel consists of the members of its
community alone: "The first ones who entered the covenant became
guilty through it. . . . But out of those who held fast to God's ordinances,
who remained of them, God established his covenant with Israel forever" (CD 3.10-13).[89] The *Rule of the Community* is even more radical than
the *Damascus Document*; it abandons Israel altogether as a defining category and divides humanity into children of light and darkness. True, all
children of light are also Jews, but most Jews are children of darkness.[90]

Because of the shared solar calendar and its evident status at Qumran,
Jubilees has often been read as a proto-sectarian text.[91] I would like to
suggest that *Jubilees* should be read instead as an antisectarian work. I do
not mean by this that it opposes particular aspects of the Qumran sect's
program or practice; indeed the links between the calendar of *Jubilees*
and the calendars found at Qumran are indisputable. Yet in striking
contrast to the sectarians *Jubilees* insists that all Jews were singled out by
God from the beginning of the world, and they continue to be his holy
people for all time. My claim is that *Jubilees'* understanding of the people
of Israel as a group defined by heredity should be understood as developing in opposition to the sectarian definition that excludes most Jews
from the people of Israel.

The insistence on including all Israel among the elect is particularly
evident in the two passages in which *Jubilees* describes the course of history to the eschaton.[92] In *Jubilees* 1, the Lord predicts to Moses the exile
of the people and the return to the land in language that echoes
Deuteronomy. The account of the events leading up to the exile suggests that not all Israelites were equally implicated in the sins that
caused it: "I will send witnesses to them so that I may testify to them, but
they will not listen and will kill the witnesses. They will persecute those
too who study the law diligently" (*Jub.* 1:12). It is perhaps not surprising
that even those who study the law diligently are not spared the fate of
the people (the witnesses are no longer alive to suffer or to be spared);
it is typical of Deuteronomic thought that the whole people suffers together. But it is more surprising that *Jubilees* does not reserve the reward

of return for the deserving. Rather, *all* will turn back to God, return to the land, and undergo transformation into "a righteous plant" (*Jub.* 1:15-16) so that God will build his temple and live among them (*Jub.* 1:17). While the Deuteronomic picture is of restoration for the whole people, there is ample precedent for restricting restoration to the pious. Centuries before *Jubilees* was written, indeed as far back as Isaiah of Jerusalem (Isa 1:25-27, 10:21-22), some of the prophets had given up on an inclusive definition of Israel; it seemed more reasonable to suggest that a pious remnant would carry on the destiny of Israel.

The eschatological scenario of the Apocalypse of Weeks from the *Epistle of Enoch* (*1 Enoch* 92-105), roughly contemporary with *Jubilees*, offers a particularly striking contrast to *Jubilees* 1:

> After this, in the seventh week, there will arise a perverse generation,
>   and many will be its deeds,
>   and all its deeds will be perverse.
> And at its conclusion, the chosen will be chosen,
>   as witnesses of righteousness from the eternal plant of righteousness
>   to whom will be given sevenfold wisdom and knowledge.
>   (*1 Enoch* 93:9-10)

As in *Jubilees*, a whole generation is held responsible for bad behavior. But in *Jubilees* the entire people becomes a righteous plant, while in the Apocalypse of Weeks, the righteous plant consists only of the chosen.[93]

The second relevant passage is the *Jubilees* apocalypse (*Jub.* 23:11-32), which predicts the events leading up to the eschaton.[94] The passage follows *Jubilees'* account of the death of Abraham (*Jub.* 23:1-7), and it responds in part to Abraham's life span, which is quite short compared to those of the antediluvian patriarchs (*Jub.* 23:8-15). One central theme of the passage is that the diminution of the human life span, the result of sinfulness, will be corrected at the eschaton. Leading up to the eschatological turning point is a period of devastation and warfare (*Jub.* 23:18-20). The antagonists in the eschatological war are clearly Jews, for they are accused of having forgotten "covenant, festival, month, sabbath, jubilee" (*Jub.* 23:19). But the antagonists divide not into good and evil, but in the first instance into young and old: "One group will struggle with another—the young with the old, the old with the young; the poor with the rich, the lowly with the great; and the needy with the ruler—regarding the law and the covenant" (*Jub.* 23:19). It is not clear whether the other categories, poor/rich, lowly/great, needy/ruler, are distinct from young/old, or whether they echo that distinction in somewhat different terms.

The young make war against the old because of the sinfulness of the older generation (*Jub.* 23:16-17), yet the young are not clearly described as good. Indeed the war is not depicted as a war of good against evil but as a chaotic reflection of a society lacking true morality. Those who survive the war continue their evil ways, even defiling the holy of holies (*Jub.* 23:21). God then turns the sinful people over to the nations for punishment (*Jub.* 23:22-23). In this time of trouble, all Israel suffers (*Jub.* 23:23).[95]

Finally the moment of redemption arrives:

> At that time they will cry out and call and pray to be rescued from the power of the sinful nations, but there will be no one who rescues (them). . . . In those days the children will begin to study the laws, to seek out the commands, and to return to the right way . . . until their lifetimes approach 1000 years. (*Jub.* 23:24-27)

The use of generational language to describe the plan of salvation serves to underscore the unity of the people. Disaster is the result of the actions of an entire generation, as is salvation.

Nowhere in this account or in *Jubilees* 1 is Israel divided into a doomed majority and a righteous remnant. Rather, *Jubilees* chooses language that includes the entire people of Israel in the restoration it envisions. This can hardly be accidental. I would like to suggest that this position represents a reaction to the emergence of the strongly sectarian outlook we find in some of the Dead Sea Scrolls. The author of *Jubilees* was deeply distressed by the many transgressions of his contemporaries. The most pressing was the calendar in use in the temple, which institutionalized violation of the sacred order for the vast majority of Jews. But he was also distressed by the tone of those he might otherwise have considered allies. They shared his rejection of the calendar of the temple establishment and his disappointment with the lack of piety of their contemporaries, but they were willing to follow their criticism to what they must have viewed as its logical conclusion: they simply wrote the sinners out of Israel.

For the author of *Jubilees*, this mode of securing the piety of Israel at the expense of most of its people was unacceptable. *Jubilees'* view that all Jews are part of a people singled out before creation does not mean that it hesitates to criticize them. On the contrary, the book is full of denunciations of Israel's failings. Yet *Jubilees* insists that Jews cannot so easily be deprived of membership in the angelic people—something like the way the rabbis would later claim that all Israel had a portion in the world to come.

We have seen that some of *Jubilees'* predecessors were troubled by the lack of connection between the status of priest and the virtues they valued, such as wisdom and piety. In response they conflated categories.

Their heroes were wise priests or priestly scribes. *Jubilees'* problem is somewhat different. It accepts the association of scribal virtues with priests and attributes these qualities to its priestly heroes. But *Jubilees* is worried not about the Israelite priesthood, a group it skillfully maneuvers into the background, but about the whole people of Israel. One important aspect of *Jubilees'* claim that the whole people of Israel is a kingdom of priests is that membership in the people is defined strictly by ancestry, just as the Torah defines membership in the priesthood. But just as definition by ancestry stands in tension with the requirement of holiness for the priesthood, so too there is considerable tension between *Jubilees'* use of ancestry as the criterion of membership in the priestly people and the exalted status it confers on this people.

Jubilees itself is hardly unaware of this tension. It is far from content with the state of the Jewish people of its own day. Through the tirades of the angel of the presence, it condemns Israel for eating blood (*Jub.* 6:13-14, 38), failing to follow the true calendar (*Jub.* 6:32-38), neglecting circumcision or performing it improperly (*Jub.* 15:33-34), and engaging in forbidden sexual relations (*Jub.* 30:5-23, 33:13-20). Perhaps it is not surprising that *Jubilees* does not indicate how to reconcile the theory of Israel's exalted status with the reality of Israel's sinfulness. It is possible that *Jubilees'* emphasis on avoiding blood and forbidden sexual relations is at least in part an effort to make it relatively easy to be a pious Jews by singling out laws it was safe to assume most Jews obeyed—in contrast to its calendar. Yet despite the tension, *Jubilees'* account precludes a sectarian understanding of the Jewish people. While it excludes converts, it emphatically includes all born Jews.

Chapter 3

Priesthood and Purity Laws
The Temple Scroll *and the* Damascus Document

In this chapter I focus on two legal works found at Qumran, the *Temple Scroll*[1] and 4QD,[2] the material from the *Damascus Document* discovered in Cave 4, that develop the purity laws of the Torah to make them more intricate and more demanding. Unlike the *Book of Jubilees*, neither text ever calls the people of Israel a kingdom of priests, but I shall argue here that both of these texts constitute evidence for an understanding of the people of Israel as a priestly people or at least for the hope that all Jews could be made more like priests. The central aspect of their effort to make the hope a reality is their elaboration of the Torah's laws of purity. Although they take different approaches, both works lengthen the periods of impurity decreed by the Torah, make rituals of purification more elaborate, and otherwise impose more severe restrictions on those in a state of impurity. Yigael Yadin, the first editor of the *Temple Scroll*, claimed that it extended the laws of purity for priests to all Jews.[3] Despite my sympathy for the thrust of his argument, I cannot entirely agree with him, for while he was certainly right to point to the elaboration of purity laws in the *Temple Scroll*, his characterization of its program is not quite accurate. To begin with, as the Torah formulates them, the laws of purity apply to all Israelites, though for reasons I shall explain in a moment they have a greater impact on priests and their families than on other Israelites. Further, as we shall see, the *Temple Scroll* by no means ignores the differences between priests and other Jews, nor does 4QD. Rather, both make the purity laws more relevant to nonpriests. Their intensified purity laws affect all families with greater stringency than the laws of the Torah, but far more than those of the Torah, their laws have a major impact on lay as well as priestly families. The result is, inevitably, to make all Jews a little more like priests.

For most modern readers, the laws of purity as the Torah formulates them appear formidably complicated and strict. Yet the *Temple Scroll* and 4QD are by no means the only evidence that some ancient Jews believed that taken at face value the Torah was insufficiently worried

about impurity. I have chosen to discuss the *Temple Scroll* and 4QD because both are relatively well preserved and because both treat the laws
of genital discharge of Leviticus 12 and 15, of particular interest for our
purposes for reasons explained below. There are several other halakhic
texts from Qumran that treat these laws, such as 4QTohorot A (4Q274)[4]
and 4QOrdinances[c] (4Q514);[5] they are unfortunately so fragmentary
that it is difficult to draw any conclusions from them, though it is clear
that they share the tendency to intensify the laws of the Torah. Another
text from Qumran very much concerned with questions of purity is
4QMMT, the "halakhic letter" that contrasts the opinions of the author
and his community with those of another group.[6] Like virtually all the
texts found at Qumran, it is incomplete, but it is considerably better preserved than the texts just listed. It too exhibits a tendency toward intensification. It does not, however, include a treatment of the laws of genital
discharge in the extant text, although it does include a rule for skin
eruptions (B 64-72).[7] Finally, it should be noted that texts preserved at
Qumran are not the only place where the Torah's laws of purity are intensified. The Pharisees did not leave us any texts of their own, but the
picture that emerges from the gospels of the New Testament and the
references in rabbinic literature suggest that they too went beyond a
straightforward reading of the Torah's purity laws.[8]

For the Priestly Document of the Torah, impurity is an objective physical state caused by contact with the corpses of animals, childbirth, skin
eruptions, eruptions in houses and fabrics, genital discharge, and contact with human corpses (Leviticus 11-15; Numbers 19). P provides rules
to determine when someone is impure, whether the impurity can be
transmitted to others and if so, how, and, finally, how to perform the rituals necessary to restore the affected person to a state of purity. These
laws are "priestly" in the sense that they are found in the P source and
that many of the conditions they define require priestly participation for
the process of purification. Priests must judge the status of those afflicted with skin eruptions, priests must offer the sacrifices brought by
those concluding the process of purification from childbirth, skin eruptions, or abnormal genital discharge, and priests must produce the
ashes of the red heifer to be mixed with the water required for purification from corpse impurity. But the purity laws apply to laypeople as
much as to priests. Still, they undoubtedly had more of an impact on
priests and their families than on laypeople for an impure person is forbidden to enter the sanctuary or to have contact with consecrated
things, most important, consecrated food. For a priest, then, being in a
state of purity was a professional necessity during the weeks in which his
watch served in the temple: an impure priest could not offer sacrifices
nor eat of the sacrificial meat. But for a priest's family as well as for the

priest himself, being in a state of purity was economically desirable at all times, for it permitted the eating of the consecrated food due the priest from the contributions of laypeople. Laypeople, on the other hand, entered the temple and ate consecrated food only on special occasions; being impure usually did not matter for them. Thus the purity laws apply to all Israel, laypeople as well as priests, but they are more important in the everyday lives of priests and their families than of laypeople.

I have chosen to concentrate on the laws of the impurity of genital discharge because they regulate the most common types of impurity and they are preserved in both the *Temple Scroll* and 4QD. In the course of a lifetime everyone experienced the impurity of at least one type of normal genital discharge. While almost everyone would also have experienced corpse impurity, the surviving material in 4QD does not treat this subject. Further, as just noted, while priests play a role at some point in the process of purification from corpse impurity, childbirth, abnormal genital discharge, and skin eruptions, purification after normal genital discharge does not require the participation of a priest. It is thus a relatively private matter. Observance of regulations governing normal discharge, then, is hardly subject to priestly control or social pressure. The development of the elaborate regulations considered in this chapter means that the authors of the *Temple Scroll* and 4QD imagined that other Jews would be willing to observe more stringent regulations for their own sake.

Purity According to P and H

P understands impurity as a natural and unavoidable state, often the result of desirable conditions or actions such as menstruation and sexual relations, which make childbearing possible, and childbirth itself.[9] Nor are the consequences of most types of impurity dire: as just noted, the impure person is barred from the sanctuary and from contact with holy things (Lev 12:4).[10] The consequences of skin eruptions are somewhat more severe: the afflicted person must be quarantined away from home during his period of impurity (Lev 13:46). The rituals of purification and the duration of the process of purification appear to be related to the severity of the impurity. Thus, for example, the impurities caused by childbirth, skin eruptions, and abnormal genital discharge require sacrifice in addition to the bathing and laundering required for the impurity of normal genital discharge (Lev 12:6-7; 14:1-32; 15:14-15, 29-30).

For all their complexities and difficulties, the purity laws constitute a coherent system, reflecting P's distinctive understanding of the nature of God and the cult. Like others in the ancient Near East, the authors of P understood the temple as the home of the god; the sacrificial cult P delineates has its origins in the practice of propitiating and currying favor with the gods by feeding them. But by the time of P,[11] Menahem Haran points out, no one in the ancient Near East any longer understood the gods and their cult in "crudely anthropomorphic terms."[12] The monotheism of the biblical writers had drastically reduced anthropomorphism by removing God from the interactions characteristic of myth. Still, P's rejection of anthropomorphism is striking even in comparison to other strands of biblical literature. P takes considerable care to transform the practice of sacrifice to reflect its understanding of God as beyond bribing by human beings. Elsewhere in the Bible the sweet aroma, *rêaḥ nîḥōaḥ*, of the sacrifices soothes God's anger toward human beings. But, as Knohl points out, P uses the phrase in relation to burnt offerings and whole offerings, avoiding it entirely for guilt offerings and using it only once for sin offerings (Lev 4:31). Further, P orders that incense be added to the freestanding meal offering (Lev 2:2, 9; 6:8, 14), but avoids incense for the meal offering that accompanies the sin offering (Lev 5:11-12; Num 5:15). These variations in practice, Knohl argues, are intended to avoid the suggestion that the sinner could cool God's anger by offering him a sacrifice with a smell he enjoyed, a view of God that P finds unacceptably anthropopathic.[13]

P's purity rules are distinctive in relation to both other ancient near eastern cultures and other strands of the Bible. For P the demonic realm that plays so large a part in other cultures of the ancient Near Eastern is simply nonexistent.[14] P does not see skin eruptions or abnormal genital flows as afflictions caused by demons, requiring a cure. The priest's role in dealing with these states does not involve healing. In the case of skin eruptions the priest is required to diagnose the condition, or perhaps more accurately, to identify it officially, and for both types of impurity a priest participates in the process of purification. But this process does not cause the condition to disappear, but rather follows on its disappearance.[15] Yet despite P's rejection of the realm of the demonic, it incorporates into its regulations certain rituals that reflect the assumption that impurity is a demonic force. These rituals must have been so firmly entrenched in practice that P had no choice but to integrate them into its system. The ritual of the Day of Atonement, in which one goat is slaughtered and another is sent into the wilderness to the demon Azazel, is perhaps the most spectacular example; the beginning of the ceremony of purification from skin eruptions in which one bird is set free and another killed offers an example relevant to the purity laws.[16]

One striking indication of P's distance from the world of demonic forces is the nominalist view of impurity that emerges in its instructions for the house that develops the equivalent of skin eruptions. When the homeowner suspects that the house is thus afflicted, he calls a priest for a diagnosis. But before the priest enters the house, he orders that everything in the house be removed so that the contents of the house will not be affected if the priest does find the house impure (Lev 14:35-36). In other words, the house is incapable of conveying impurity to its contents until the priest actually declares it impure.[17]

Another distinctive aspect of P's view of impurity is that P sees it as an objective, ritual state, not a moral one. Impurity is wrong only if one neglects purification (Lev 5:1-13). This understanding was clearly not the popular view in ancient Israel. Elsewhere in the Bible, for example, skin eruptions are associated with sin. God punishes Miriam's slander of Moses with skin eruptions (Num 12:10), and he similarly afflicts King Uzziah just in time to prevent him from offering incense, a usurpation of the role of the priests (2 Chr 26:16-21). Some biblical writers apply the term *niddâ*, which P uses for the state of menstrual impurity, to idolatry and other types of sin (e.g., Ezek 36:17; 2 Chr 29:5). The Book of Lamentations claims a causal relationship between sin and impurity: "Jerusalem sinned grievously, / therefore she became a *niddâ*" (Lam 1:8).[18] Lamentations also uses the terminology of impurity to describe Jerusalem's humiliation at the hands of her enemies (Lam 1:17: *niddâ*; Lam 4:15: the person with skin eruptions warning others away [Lev 13:45]). While some of these examples are drawn from texts that postdate P, their association of impurity with sin and humiliation surely reflects a view with a long history. P's understanding of impurity in purely objective terms is a rejection of this more widespread view.[19]

If the purity laws of the Torah constitute a system, it seems reasonable to assume that they have implications for each other.[20] It is striking, for example, that the text of the Torah fails to spell out the consequences of impurity except in the case of the woman after childbirth: she is not to have contact with consecrated things or to enter the sanctuary (Lev 12:4). Most readers, ancient and modern, assume that these restrictions apply to other types of impurity as well: the high priest Jehoiada is reported to have placed guards at the gates of the temple to keep out anyone impure for any reason (2 Chr 23:19). So too Leviticus 15 decrees laundering and bathing for the man with abnormal genital discharge at the end of the period of purification (Lev 15:13) and bathing for a man who has had a seminal emission and for a woman who has had contact with semen in sexual relations (Lev 15:16, 18). Yet it mentions neither bathing nor laundering for the menstruant and the woman with abnormal discharge. Its failure to specify surely reflects its confidence that the analogy with the man with a flow and the man with a seminal emission would be obvious.[21] The narrative of 2 Samuel appears to imply that the bath that brings Bathsheba to David's attention was for purification after menstruation (2 Sam 11:4), suggesting that the practice of bathing after menstruation was an accepted one in biblical times.

But the assumption that P's laws form a system does not explain all aspects of their literary expression. If the silence of Leviticus 15 on bathing and laundering for women with genital discharge is due to its already having laid out the rules in relation to men in the first portion of the chapter, why does its discussion of the woman with abnormal flow repeat the requirement of sacrifice (Lev 15:29-30) in language virtually identical to that it uses for the man with a flow (Lev 15:14-15)? Once the text has become authoritative, the peculiarities of its mode of expression invite exegesis, as we shall see. Clearly, as these difficulties of the text indicate, the priestly document reflects a long and complex process of compilation and editing. The complexity is also evident in the appearance of the laws of corpse impurity in the Book of Numbers at some distance from the larger body of purity laws found in Leviticus.

P's idea of impurity is transformed in the second corpus of priestly law, the Holiness Code (Leviticus 17-26 and elsewhere in the Torah).[22] To begin with, H uses P's terminology of impurity to claim that certain *sins* are defiling: idolatry (Lev 20:1-8), forbidden sexual relations (Leviticus 18 and 20), and bloodshed (Num 35:33-34). P insists that the bearer of impurity be excluded from the sanctuary to avoid defiling it. As we saw in the previous chapter, H worries that idolatry will defile the sanctuary (Lev 20:3) but that forbidden sexual relations and bloodshed will defile the land. P provides rituals of purification for all the impurities it delineates. H provides a remedy for the defilement caused by bloodshed: shedding the blood of the murderers (Num 35:33). But H does not suggest any means to undo the defilement of the land by forbidden sexual relations. The punishment Leviticus 18 threatens for prohibited sexual relations is directed not only at the sinners—"For whoever shall do any of these abominations, the persons that do them shall be cut off from among their people" (Lev 18:29)—but at the community as a whole—"lest the land vomit you out, when you defile it, as it vomited out the nation that was before you" (Lev 18:28). Unlike Leviticus 18, Leviticus 20 includes punishments with each of the forbidden sexual relations it lists, but it appears that even the proper punishments will not prevent the land from becoming defiled, with the same dire effects for the whole people: "You shall therefore keep all my statutes and all my ordinances, and do them; that the land where I am bringing you to dwell may not vomit you out" (Lev 20:22).

H does not claim that all sins bring impurity in their wake, but only the three particularly severe sins it singles out. Sexual sin, the variety to which H devotes the most attention, spans the categories of morality and ritual.[23] While adultery and some of the forms of incest forbidden

by H are moral offenses, sexual relations with a woman and her daughter or granddaughter (Lev 18:17), for example, are not so much moral
offenses, offenses against other human beings, as offenses against a concept of right order. Further, given the prominent place of genital discharge in the purity system of P, it is perhaps not surprising that H
understands immoral actions involving the genitals to have consequences for purity even when they do not violate the purity laws. The
conflation of ritual and morality is well illustrated in Lev 20:21, which
terms relations between a man and his brother's wife *niddâ*, menstrual
impurity (RSV: "impurity"). In this passage *niddâ* is used as a parallel to
the terms *tebel* (Lev 20:12; RSV: "incest") for sexual relations with a
daughter-in-law, *tô'ebâ* (Lev 20:13; RSV: "abomination") for sexual relations between men, *zimmâ* (Lev 20:14; RSV: "wickedness") for sexual relations with a woman and her mother, and *ḥesed* (Lev 20:17; RSV:
"shameful thing") for sexual relations with a sister. In the course of
branding a moral transgression ritually impure, this passage also implies
that the ritual impurity of the menstruant is morally problematic. Furthermore, through this use of the term, H, unlike P, singles out menstrual impurity from among other types of impurity. I have already
noted the use of *niddâ* for idolatry and immorality generally elsewhere
in the Bible. But the use by the Holiness Code in the laws of sexual
morality is more pointed, reflecting the close relationship of P and H,
and it is particularly striking to the reader because the Holiness Code appears in Leviticus almost immediately following P's purity laws.[24]

Indeed, H's understanding of menstrual impurity as the impurity par
excellence highlights the distinctiveness of P's position in which gender
plays a remarkably small role. P does not single out menstruation as
qualitatively different from the other types of impurity; indeed, as a normal discharge, it is one of the less severe types of impurity. It is true that
the impurity of menstruation lasts longer than the impurity of seminal
emission, but menstruation itself lasts longer than seminal emission. It is
also true that the menstruant conveys impurity in a way that a man who
has had a seminal emission does not, but given the difference in the duration of the two types of impurity, this difference may not be a result of
gender. Gender does play a role in determining the length of impurity
after childbirth, twice as long for a woman who has given birth to a
daughter as for one who has given birth to a son (Lev 12: 2-4), but it does
not make the consequences of abnormal genital flow more severe for
women than for men. Further, the process of purification from menstruation is like that of purification from seminal emission, simple in comparison to the process of purification from abnormal genital flow in men
or women or from skin eruptions, both of which involve sacrifice. Not
only does P reject the association of menstrual impurity and immorality

found in other biblical sources, it also treats menstrual impurity as one among several varieties of impurity, and not one of the most severe varieties at that, rather than as the most noteworthy impurity.

The legacy of P, then, is a radical separation between the realms of purity and morality. It is wrong to try to enter the sanctuary or have contact with holy things in a state of impurity, and it is wrong not to undergo purification. But being impure is not a sign of any moral lack. For H, on the other hand, some sins that span the categories of morality and ritual have ritual consequences: they render the sinner impure (Lev 18:24, 30) and the land as well (Lev 18:25-28), thus threatening the safety of the community as a whole especially since in some cases there is no means to repair the damage. Conversely, H's use of the term *niddâ* for forbidden sexual relations suggests that impurity is morally suspect.

The two texts considered in this chapter agree that P did not take impurity seriously enough, but they develop their laws of impurity very much in the spirit of P. Their laws, different though they are, share P's view of impurity as an objective, ritual state without moral implications. In this they are close to the Mishnah, though the rabbis of the Mishnah are perhaps less inclined to exceed the demands of P than are the *Temple Scroll* and 4QD. The absence of any association of impurity with sin in the *Temple Scroll* and 4QD will be evident in the discussion that follows. It bears emphasizing since several scholars have argued recently that such an association is characteristic of the Qumran sect; I shall return to this point at the end of my discussion of 4QD.

The *Temple Scroll*

The *Temple Scroll* is a legal document that goes the Torah one better by speaking in God's own voice, unmediated by Moses. The most complete of the three manuscripts (11Q19) is sixty-six columns long, making it the longest work found at Qumran.[25] The *Temple Scroll* gets its modern name from its focus on the temple and its workings, but it covers a range of related topics including purity laws and the festivals and their sacrifices, as well as subjects less closely related to the temple, such as laws of kingship.[26] Some portions of the work appear to reflect preexisting sources,[27] but Lawrence Schiffman seems to me correct that the "author/redactor" selected only sources compatible with his own views.[28] Often the *Temple Scroll* reworks passages from the Torah, leaving much of the Torah's language intact while introducing small but significant changes. Sometimes the changes reflect the *Temple Scroll*'s effort to integrate material that appears in different places in the Torah. Because of their subject matter, some portions of the *Temple Scroll* are more independent of the text of the Torah, but they, too, are written in a style intended to echo the Torah.[29] There is no consensus about the date of the *Temple Scroll*, but 4Q524, a very fragmentary manuscript of the *Temple Scroll*, provides paleographic grounds for a dating no later than 150–125 B.C.E.[30]

Much of the scholarship on sectarian halakhah assumes that the *Temple Scroll* is a sectarian document, but this assumption is not unproblematic.[31] The *Temple Scroll*'s purity laws, as we shall see, are significantly more stringent than those of the Torah, but its rhetoric is neither sectarian nor polemical: there is no suggestion that it addresses a community of the faithful set apart from a faithless majority. The date of 4Q524, which places it before the earliest sectarian documents, offers support for the view that the *Temple Scroll* is not a sectarian composition but a work the sect inherited.[32] Still, the community at Qumran clearly continued to find it of interest, as the copies made around the turn of the era show.[33]

In keeping with its model, the Torah, the *Temple Scroll* treats the laws of genital discharge as part of a larger category of laws of impurity, including, as in the Torah, the laws of skin eruptions and contact with corpses. These purity laws appear in columns 45–51 among other laws intended to maintain the purity of the city of the sanctuary and the other cities of the holy land.[34] They are phrased as prohibitions of entry into the city of the sanctuary (*TS* 46.16-18) and ordinary cities (*TS* 48.14-17) for those in particular states of impurity and as mandates for them to remain outside those cities in places specially set aside for them. The idea for such places is indebted to several passages in the Torah. The purity laws of Leviticus decree banishment for those with skin eruptions (Lev 13:46), though not for any other bearers of impurity. A passage in the Book of Numbers orders the exile from the camp of Israel in the wilderness not only of those with skin eruptions, but also of two further groups of the impure, those with abnormal genital flow and those with corpse impurity (Num 5:2). Finally, Deuteronomy's law of the war camp requires men who have had a nocturnal emission to remain outside the camp (Deut 23:11).

Of the three places the *Temple Scroll* decrees to the east of the city of the sanctuary (*TS* 46.16-18), two are intended for those with skin eruptions and those with abnormal genital flow, the first two categories of those excluded from the wilderness camp of Numbers. In place of bearers of corpse impurity, the third category in the passage from Numbers, the *Temple Scroll* places Deuteronomy's men who have experienced a nocturnal emission. The places are presumably intended for people who contract their impurities while already inside the city of the sanctuary; if the impurity had been contracted elsewhere, the bearer of impurity would not have entered the city of the sanctuary in the first place.

The *Temple Scroll* sets aside places for the first two categories of Num 5:2, those with skin eruptions and those with abnormal genital flow, outside ordinary cities too, but the third group to be confined outside ordinary cities consists not of men with nocturnal emissions but of women after childbirth and menstruants (*TS* 48.14-17). It is noteworthy that there is no place for such women outside the city of the sanctuary though women are permitted limited access to the city (*TS* 39.7).

In contrast to the *Temple Scroll,* the laws of the Torah assume that menstruants live at home with their families. Leviticus 15 describes in some detail how contact with the menstruant herself, her bedding, and other implements causes impurity to those around her (Lev 15:19-24). The case of the woman after childbirth is not as clear, but the comparison of the first stage of her impurity to the impurity of the menstruant (Lev 12:2) perhaps confirms what one would in any case assume on other grounds: that a new mother was expected to remain at home. Nor does the passage from Numbers about the wilderness camp include these women among those exiled from the camp. Deuteronomy's camp is irrelevant to the discussion because the fact that it is a war camp means that there are no women in it. For those with abnormal genital discharge, on the other hand, the Torah contains two different rules. As we have seen, the *Temple Scroll* follows Num 5:2, which exiles them from the camp of Israel, but Leviticus 15 clearly assumes that they remain at home because, as for menstruants, it devotes considerable space to the impurity others may incur by contact with them or things they have touched (Lev 15:4-12 for a male; Lev 15:26-27 for a female).[35] Thus the *Temple Scroll* not only prefers the more stringent of the possibilities the Torah offers for those with abnormal genital discharge, but also expands the purview of the stringency to include menstruants and women after childbirth.

The *Temple Scroll*'s intensification of laws governing impurity is not restricted to exiling the impure from cities. It also lengthens the duration of some types of impurity and requires more elaborate rituals of purification. The Torah treats the impurity of seminal emission as easy to remedy and of short duration: a man who has experienced a seminal emission need only bathe and wait for the sun to set (Lev 15:16). According to Deuteronomy, a man who has experienced a nocturnal emission is excluded from the war camp because of its special holiness: God himself is present in it (Deut 23:15). Yet even for the war camp the period of impurity and the procedure for purification of Leviticus 15 are deemed adequate (Deut 23:12). The *Temple Scroll* not only excludes the man who has had a nocturnal emission from the city of the sanctuary, but also requires that he undergo a three-day process of purification involving bathing and washing his clothes on the first and third days.

Only after the sun has set on the third day does it consider the man pure (*TS* 45.7-10). A man who has had a seminal emission as a result of sexual relations is also excluded from the city of the sanctuary for three days (*TS* 45.11-12).[36] No ritual of purification is specified, but since the Torah requires the same process of purification after nocturnal emission and sexual relations (Lev 15:16-18), it seems likely that the *Temple Scroll* assumes that the process of purification required of the man who has had a nocturnal emission also applies to the man who has had sexual relations. There is no place set aside outside the city of the sanctuary for men impure as a result of sexual relations because the *Temple Scroll* cannot imagine sexual relations taking place in the city of the sanctuary. It is worth noting here that the *Damascus Document* contains an explicit prohibition of sexual intercourse in the city of the sanctuary (CD 12.1-2; 4Q271 5 i 17-18). Although 4QD devotes considerable attention to laws of genital discharge, nowhere else in what survives does it refer to the "city of the sanctuary," and the *Damascus Document*'s use of language that echoes the *Temple Scroll*'s characteristic phrasing has not been adequately explained. Further, the prohibition on sexual relations stands apart from its context in both CD and 4QD.[37]

Yadin suggests that the *Temple Scroll*'s intensified rules for purification after seminal emission derive from God's instructions for the Israelites as they camp before Mt. Sinai: "Go to the people and warn them to stay pure today and tomorrow. Let them wash their clothes. Let them be ready for the third day . . . . Be ready for the third day; do not go near a woman" (Exod 19:10-11, 15). Because it sees the city of the sanctuary as analogous to the camp of Israel before Sinai, the *Temple Scroll* derives the process of purification necessary to enter the city from the process of purification imposed before the revelation at Sinai. As the passage just quoted shows, Exodus 19 includes both of the innovations of the *Temple Scroll*: the three-day period of impurity and washing clothes.[38] But the influence of Exodus 19 accounts for the *Temple Scroll*'s treatment of only one type of impurity, and we have seen that the *Temple Scroll* intensifies the effects of and elaborates the rituals for other types of impurity as well.

Exodus 19 also figures in Sara Japhet's argument that the *Temple Scroll*'s laws reflect a strong sense of opposition between the sexual and the sacred, like that found in Exodus 19 and 1 Samuel 21, the story of David and the priests of Nob. This opposition goes well beyond P's rather mild view of the impact of normal genital discharge. In Japhet's reading, the *Temple Scroll*'s failure to provide places for the corpse impure reflects a more lenient stance toward corpse impurity than toward "source" impurity.[39] But while it is true that the *Temple Scroll* does not include the corpse impure on the list of those to remain outside cities as Num 5:2

might lead us to expect, the *Temple Scroll* does say explicitly that the corpse impure are banned from the city of the sanctuary until they are again pure (*TS* 45.17), and in other respects the *Temple Scroll*'s treatment of corpse impurity is in keeping with its intensification of the impurity of genital discharge. While it does not increase the seven-day period of impurity the Torah decrees for corpse impurity, it expands the ritual of purification. It decrees bathing and washing clothes on the first day, for which the Torah prescribes no ritual, and adds bathing and washing clothes to the biblical procedure of sprinkling on the third day (*TS* 49.16-50.4; Num 19:18-19). Indeed, the *Temple Scroll* engages in considerable elaboration of the Torah's terse command to sprinkle the tent in which someone has died and the vessels that were in it on the third and seventh days (Num 19:18-19) with a more rigorous cleansing of the house (no longer a tent) and a list of the various types of vessels and other belongings requiring purification; the process is to take place "on the day on which they bring the dead man out from it," perhaps the first day (*TS* 49.11-21).[40] Thus, despite its failure to set aside a place for bearers of corpse impurity, the *Temple Scroll* can hardly be said to take corpse impurity lightly.

In a series of publications over the last two decades, Jacob Milgrom has argued that the *Temple Scroll*'s elaboration of biblical laws of purity reflects a consistent program found throughout the legal texts from Qumran, a program based on an understanding of impurity as layered.[41] Removal of the first layer of impurity permits contact with the realm of the ordinary, but it is only with removal of the second layer that contact with the realm of the sacred can resume. Thus, for example, the *Temple Scroll* requires bathing on the first and third days for those with seminal emissions before they can enter the city of the sanctuary (*TS* 45.7-12).[42] For contact with the ordinary, the first day's ablution, prescribed by Leviticus as well, is enough. It is for this reason that there is no place of confinement outside ordinary cities for men who have had a seminal emission. There is simply no need to confine them because at the end of the first day they can become sufficiently pure for life in an ordinary city. For contact with the sacred, however, the second layer must be removed—thus the ablution of the third day is required before entering the city of the sanctuary.

Milgrom's understanding helps to make sense of the groups designated for places of confinement outside ordinary cities: those with skin eruptions; those with abnormal genital flow; and women after childbirth and menstruants. In Milgrom's view, bearers of impurity for whom the process of purification removes a layer of impurity on the first day need not be excluded from an ordinary city. Thus, as just noted, there is no need to confine men who had had a seminal emission, whose ablution on the first day is of biblical origin, or the corpse impure, for whom the *Temple Scroll* decrees bathing on the first day.

On the assumption that the *Temple Scroll* designates places outside the city of the sanctuary only for those whose impurity comes upon them suddenly and through circumstances beyond their own control, there is clear logic to the choice of skin eruptions, abnormal genital flow, and nocturnal emission as relevant causes of impurity. Even without regard to the *Damascus Document*'s explicit prohibition, it is clear that the *Temple Scroll* cannot imagine sexual intercourse taking place in the city of the sanctuary; thus it is not necessary to designate a place outside it for men who have had a seminal emission as a result of sexual intercourse or for their wives. Nocturnal emissions, on the other hand, are beyond the individual's control and could occur even within the city of the sanctuary. Similarly, one might discover abnormal genital flow or skin eruptions while already in the city of the sanctuary. Milgrom's theory does not explain the absence of a place of confinement outside the city of the sanctuary for menstruants. While it would not be difficult to avoid giving birth in the city of the sanctuary, surely menstrual impurity might overtake a woman while she was there. Perhaps the *Temple Scroll* regards such an occurrence as unlikely because menstruation is a regular event rather than an entirely unexpected one like the outbreak of skin eruptions or abnormal genital flow. Further, it probably does not imagine women spending a great deal of time in the city of the sanctuary, thus limiting the likelihood that such a problem would arise.

Corpse impurity poses another problem for Milgrom's understanding. As we have seen, the *Temple Scroll* prohibits those with corpse impurity from entering the city of the sanctuary, but it is impossible to guard against a sudden death that would introduce corpse impurity there. Thus, on Milgrom's theory there should be a place outside the city of the sanctuary set aside for those who contract corpse impurity in the city; the *Temple Scroll*'s first-day ablution, while sufficient to permit entrance to an ordinary city, does not remove the second layer of impurity necessary for entrance to the city of the sanctuary. Milgrom's discomfort with the absence of such a place can be felt in his suggestion that one once did appear in the lacuna at the top of column 47.[43] But though the absence of a place for the corpse impure is puzzling, the insistence of the *Temple Scroll* that there be a separate place for each type of impurity (*TS* 46.17) makes it unlikely that the corpse impure were to share a place with one of the other groups of the impure.

By now I hope it is clear that though Yadin's claim that the *Temple Scroll* extends the priestly laws of purity to all Israel has an element of truth to it, it is not quite accurate.[44] Like the priestly code of the Torah, the *Temple Scroll* does not understand the laws of purity to apply particularly to priests; indeed they apply equally to priests and laypeople. In the order the *Temple Scroll* envisions, the special impact of purity laws on priests would remain, but the *Temple Scroll* brings ordinary Jews closer to priests by making the purity laws more elaborate and thus heightening their impact on lay people as well as priests. For example, P's treatment of menstrual impurity means that priestly families will experience far more inconvenience than lay families. Only in priestly families, which regularly eat consecrated food, would the menstruant be forbidden to prepare food for the family. By requiring menstruants to stay outside their cities, away from their families, the *Temple Scroll* ensures that lay families too will feel the impact of menstrual impurity.[45] The *Temple Scroll*'s extension of the impact of the laws of purity is not accomplished by conflating the categories of priest and layperson. Indeed, the *Temple Scroll* emphasizes the boundaries between priests and laity in passages such as the instructions for preventing the mixing of the sin and guilt offerings of the people with those of the priests (*TS* 35.10-15).[46] Rather, the *Temple Scroll* extends the realm affected by impurity and heightens the intensity of impurity, thus increasing its impact on nonpriests.

4QD

Unlike the *Temple Scroll*, the *Damascus Document* is indisputably a sectarian document in the sociological sense. The concerns of its laws make clear, however, that it is not a document of the Qumran *yaḥad* but of an associated group that lived in families among the general population. The work contains a historical introduction describing the origins of the community, often referred to as the "Admonition," followed by a lengthy corpus of law. The Geniza version of the *Damascus Document* includes only a small portion of this legal material; the only passage relevant to the laws of Leviticus 12-15 is the prohibition on sexual relations in the city of the sanctuary mentioned above. The version of the *Damascus Document* found at Qumran, 4QD, devotes considerable attention to the laws of skin eruptions and genital impurity, although what survives is unfortunately quite fragmentary. The extant material does not, however, treat the laws of corpse impurity (Numbers 19). The earliest manuscript of 4QD, 4Q266, dates to the first century B.C.E.,[47] while the *Damascus Document*'s reference to *Jubilees* (CD 16.3-4, 4Q270 6 ii 17, 4Q271 4 ii 5) does not permit a date much earlier than that for the composition of the work as a whole.[48] As for the *Temple Scroll*, the author drew on sources so that some portions of the work are somewhat earlier than the work as a whole.

Each section of the purity laws in 4QD refers to itself as a rule, *mišpaṭ*, in construct with the appropriate category. Thus, for example, the unit on skin eruptions concludes, "This is [the rule (*mišpaṭ*) of skin] eruptions"[49] (4Q272 1 ii 2),[50] while the section on male genital discharge begins, "[And the r]ule [*mišpaṭ*] concerning one who has a discharge . . ." (4Q266 6 i 14, 272 1 ii 3).[51] In this usage, *mišpaṭ* appears to be an interpretation of the term *tôrâ* as it is used in Leviticus 11-15, where it appears in the construct, introducing and more frequently concluding discussion of the different types of impurity, for example, "This is the law [*tôrâ*] for her who bears a child" (Lev 12:7), or "This is the law [*tôrâ*] for him who has a discharge" (Lev 15:32).[52] The substitution of *mišpaṭ* for *tôrâ* may reflect the eclipse of the meaning "law" or "teaching" that *tôrâ* carries in Leviticus 11-15 as the term came to designate the Book of the Torah; it may also be a way of signaling that these laws are not intended as competition for the laws of the Torah but rather as interpretation.

The term *mišpaṭ* appears several times in the *Damascus Document*, but only in one other instance does it have the same meaning it has in the passages discussed here: "Concerning the law [*mišpaṭ*] of donations" (CD 16.13, 4Q271 4 ii 12-13).[53] This title belongs to a larger group of headings with *'al*, "concerning" (CD 10.10/4Q270 6 iv 20, 10.14, 16.10, and perhaps 4Q266 6 iii 3-4/4Q270 3 ii 12 [54]); the others lack *'al*. An instance of this type of heading is also found in 4QOrdinances[a] (4Q159 1 ii 6).[55] Elsewhere the *Damascus Document* uses the term *serek*, "rule," as a heading in a fashion similar to *mišpaṭ* in the purity laws, either with the demonstrative or without: "And this is the rule [*serek*] for the judges of the congregation" (CD 10.4; also 12.19, 22-23; 13.7; 14.3, 12). The term *serek* appears to be associated particularly with sectarian communal regulations. Most instances of all three types of heading are preceded by a *vacat*. The *'al* and *serek* headings appear exclusively at the beginning of sections. The use of *mišpaṭ* in at least one instance as a conclusion echoes the practice of the Torah in Leviticus 11-15, where "This is the law [*tôrâ*]" is used only once as a heading but six times as a conclusion.[56]

Before turning to 4QD's laws of genital discharge, I would like to look briefly at its laws for skin eruptions, which appear in 4QD immediately before the laws of genital discharge.[57] The point of most relevance for the discussion of the laws of genital discharge is that the laws of skin eruptions have a clearly exegetical aspect; I shall argue that the same is true of the laws of genital discharge. The laws of skin eruptions contain the only instance of an explicit interpretation of a passage from the Torah in 4QD's purity laws (Lev 13:33 in a form otherwise unknown; 4Q266 6 i 8-9/4Q272 1 i 17),[58] and they also devote considerable attention to clarifying the difficult language of Leviticus 13.[59] Thus they define the obscure *sapaḥat* (Lev 13:2; 14:56) (RSV: "eruption"; NJPS: "rash"), as a scab caused by a blow (4Q269 7 1-2/4Q272 1 i 1-2), clearly distinguishing it from other types of skin eruption, and they adopt the term *mam'eret* ("malignant"), used in Leviticus only of eruptions of fabric (Lev 13:51-52) and houses (Lev 14:44), to clarify the status of skin eruptions in human beings (4Q266 6 i 5/4Q272 1 i 13).

While 4QD's laws of skin eruptions follow the order of discussion of Leviticus 13,[60] its laws of genital discharge clearly and purposefully rearrange the laws of Leviticus 12 and 15. Leviticus 15 opens with the laws of abnormal male genital flow (Lev 15:1-15), moves on to normal male genital discharge, that is, seminal emission (Lev 15:16-18), then to normal female genital flow, that is, menstruation (Lev 15:19-24), and concludes with abnormal female genital flow (Lev 15:25-30). The laws of 4QD follow the lead of Leviticus 15 by treating the varieties of male genital discharge together before female genital discharge. But unlike Leviticus they place the discussion of the woman after childbirth (Leviticus 12) together with that of the menstruant and the woman with abnormal genital flow in the rule of the *zābâ* (4Q272 1 ii 7).[61] While Leviticus does not use the crucial root *zwb*, "flow," in its discussion of the woman after childbirth, it compares the first stage of the impurity of the woman after childbirth to menstrual impurity (Lev 12:2, 5).

The key to this reconfiguration of the laws of Leviticus as well as to the radical rereading of the laws of male genital discharge to which I shall turn in a moment is the interpretation of the root *zwb*. In the portion of Leviticus 15 devoted to the impurity of male genital discharge, the priestly source uses the root for abnormal discharge only: *zwb* means "flow" and thus is not properly applied to seminal emission, which involves ejaculation.[62] For normal male genital discharge, that is, seminal emission, P uses the term *šikbat-zera'* (Lev 15:16-18, 32). It does not make any difference whether the seminal emission takes place in the course of sexual relations or without sexual relations; the purity consequences are the same. For women, both normal and abnormal genital discharge are flow. Thus the discussion of menstruation begins: "When a woman has a flow [*tiḥĕyeh zābâ*], her flow being blood from her body, she shall be in her impurity seven days" (Lev 15:19).[63] For the priestly authors of the body of Leviticus 15, then, the root *zwb* has nothing to do with abnormality; it has only to do with the mode of discharge.

But the Hebrew of the Torah lacks a term equivalent to English "discharge" that includes both flow and seminal emission. The absence of such a term caused confusion as far back as biblical times. This confusion is evident in the contribution of the editors of Leviticus 15, who employ the root *zwb* as an umbrella category for all the types of genital discharge with which Leviticus 15 is concerned, including seminal emission, in their concluding summary of the chapter: "This is the law for one who has a flow [*hazzāb*]: for him who has a seminal emission [*šikbat-zera'*] and becomes impure from it, and for her who is sick with her impurity, and for a man or woman who has a flow [*hazzāb 'et-zôbô*], and for a man who lies with an impure woman."[64] In other words, they use the root *zwb* to mean not only its proper referents, the various types of genital flow, but also seminal emission.

The rule for male genital discharge in 4QD is only four and one-half lines long,[65] and it is not well preserved, but it is clear that it uses the term *zāb* in the extended sense of the conclusion of Leviticus 15 rather than in the more limited sense of the laws of Leviticus 15:

[And the r]ule concerning one who has a discharge [*hazzāb 'et zôbô*]: Any man / with a [dis]charge from [his] flesh, [o]r one [who] brings upon himse[lf] lustful thoughts or one[66] who/ [ ] his contact is like that of [/ he shall launder his clo[th]es and [bathe in water[67]]/ him, who touches him shall ba[the]. (4Q266 6 i 14-16/ 4Q272 1 ii 3-7) [68]

Baumgarten's translation of *hazzāb 'et zôbô* (4Q266 6 i 14/4Q272 1 ii 3) as "one who has a discharge" is in the spirit of the editors of Leviticus 15, and it responds to the inclusion of the one whose discharge is caused by lustful thoughts in the category. Such discharge is surely an instance of seminal emission without sexual relations (Lev 15:16).[69] Like the editors of Leviticus 15, then, the purity laws of 4QD make no distinction between flow and seminal emission. Thus I suggest that the third type of *zāb*, whose existence is indicated by the second *'ô 'ăšer*, "or who," but whose description is unfortunately lost to us, is the man who has had a seminal emission in the course of sexual relations (Lev 15:18). As far as I can see, Leviticus 15 provides no other candidates for the role, and the evident inclusion of the man who has had a seminal emission outside of sexual relations in the category *zāb* makes plausible the inclusion also of the man who has had one in the course of sexual relations. The missing line after *'ô 'ăšer* might have read something like *yiškab 'iššâ šikbat zera'*, "has a seminal emission in the course of sexual relations with a woman."[70] This restoration is drawn from the language of Lev 15:18; it is certainly possible that the language of the description was less closely related to Leviticus 15, as for the second type of *zāb*.

The process of purification Leviticus decrees for the man with abnormal discharge is very different from the process for the man with a seminal emission. The man who has had a seminal emission has only to bathe and wait for sundown to become pure (Lev 15:16, 18). The man with abnormal discharge, on the other hand, washes his clothes and bathes on the seventh day after the cessation of the flow; on the eighth day, he offers a sacrifice (Lev 15:13-15). Anyone who has physical contact with the man with abnormal discharge, or with his spittle, or anything he lies, sits, or rides upon also becomes impure (Lev 15:5-10); he must wash his clothes and bathe, and he remains impure until evening (Lev 15:11-12). The touch of a man who has had a seminal emission does not convey impurity; only the semen itself does so. The impurity it causes is removed by bathing for human beings and laundering for garments and skins, and then waiting until evening (Lev 15:16-18).

Unfortunately the text of 4QD is too fragmentary to permit certainty about the nature of its procedures for purification for the man with genital discharge. Still, the brevity of the text makes it extremely unlikely that it offered different procedures for men with abnormal discharge and men with seminal emission. The references to laundering as well as bathing (4Q272 1 ii 6) and the emphasis on the problem of contact with the *zāb* (4Q272 1 ii 5, 7) appear to reflect Leviticus's rules for the man with abnormal discharge.[71] The fragmentary conclusion of the preceding line suggests that the subject of the laundering and bathing is the one who has had contact with the *zāb* rather than the *zāb* himself. It is not clear from what is preserved whether the rule ordains laundering and bathing for the man with the discharge himself or indicates the length of his period of impurity. One aspect of Leviticus's purification procedure that is almost certainly missing is the sacrifice the man with abnormal discharge must bring on the eighth day. I shall return to this problem in my discussion of the treatment of the sacrifice of the woman after childbirth, but it is worth noting here that the purity laws of 4QD appear to assume participation in the temple cult.[72]

Despite their fragmentary state, it is virtually certain that the purity laws of 4QD understand the man who had had a seminal emission without sexual relations to convey impurity to others. If I am correct that the third type of *zāb* is the man with a seminal emission in the course of sexual relations, he too was understood to convey impurity by his touch. This is an extraordinary intensification of the impurity of seminal emission, but it is not without parallel; 4QTohorot A (4Q274) claims that the impurity of seminal emission can be communicated by contact: "And when [a man has] has an emiss[ion] of semen his touch is defiling" (1 i 8).[73] Indeed, the recognition that the purity laws of the Torah constitute a system might encourage such intensification. Seminal emission is exceptional among the types of discharge discussed in Leviticus 15: the period of impurity it causes is far shorter than those caused by other types of discharge, and only the discharge itself, but not the one with the discharge, conveys impurity to others.

As just noted, the state of the text does not permit certainty about whether it reiterated Leviticus's requirements of laundering and bathing for the man with abnormal discharge or indicated the duration of the impurity. It is perhaps more likely that it did not. Yet since it is clear that the purity laws of 4QD offer only a selective treatment of the laws of Leviticus, this surely means not that they rejected those requirements but that they assumed them. But how could the authors of these laws have ignored the plain sense of Lev 15:16-18 and applied the longer period of impurity and more complex rituals of purification for a man with abnormal discharge to a man with seminal emission? Perhaps they noted that while the Torah refers to the man with abnormal discharge becoming pure (Lev 15:13), it states that the man with seminal emission bathes and remains impure until evening (Lev 15:16, 18). This mode of expression clearly implies the return of a state of purity, but the absence of explicit mention may have made it easier to argue that the Torah intended the longer period it decrees for the man with abnormal discharge to apply also to the man with a seminal emission. Arguing for laundering in addition to Leviticus's requirement of bathing would have been relatively easy since the text of Leviticus 15 elsewhere fails to mention a ritual it surely assumed: bathing for the purification of the menstruant.[74]

If, as I have suggested, the laws of 4QD treat a man with a seminal emission as belonging to the category of the *zāb* and thus as bound by the laws of purification for a man with abnormal discharge, the consequences for married life are profound. Even nonpriests would need to plan carefully so as to be in a state of purity for the occasions on which they wished to bring sacrifices. But for priests and their families, ordinary married life would have been virtually impossible if they wished to be able to eat consecrated food, including not only portions of various sacrifices but also tithes. Thus the impact of 4QD's laws would have been felt beyond the two-week period of service of a particular priestly watch. Nor is this intensification of the regulations for seminal emission the only place where the laws of 4QD go beyond the laws of Leviticus in a way that would seem likely to wreak havoc on everyday life. As we shall see, they also require that infants be nursed by a wet nurse as long as the mother is in a state of postpartum impurity (4Q266 6 ii 10-11). This requirement is presumably the result of the quite reasonable inference that according to the principles of the Torah's purity laws the new mother would convey impurity to her baby. Yet the priestly source apparently did not find the idea of a baby in a state of impurity troubling.

Despite their radical intensification of the laws of Leviticus, the laws of 4QD are presented in a matter-of-fact manner without any rhetorical flourish, as if there were nothing surprising about them at all. They appear to be directed at all Israel, not at a pious remnant; they give no hint of the communal organization reflected in other portions of the *Damascus Document*.[75] Yet surely most Jews would have found their demands intolerable. They would have been quite suitable, however, for one group of Jews: the married Essenes who, according to Josephus, did not have sexual relations during pregnancy because they saw the purpose of marriage as procreation, not pleasure (*Jewish War* 2.160–61). Among such Jews, sexual activity would at least ideally be quite limited. It is worth noting that 4QD's list of transgressors appears to include a man who has had sexual relations with his pregnant wife (4Q270 2 ii 15-16).[76] The rule in 4QD's version of the penal code for the man "who comes near to fornicate with his wife contrary to the law" (4Q270 7 i 12-13) may also be relevant.[77] Further, if sexual relations were to be limited to efforts at procreation, the purity laws of 4QD might have been somewhat easier to observe. Perhaps a man did not undertake the full process of purification after each act of sexual intercourse but waited until his wife had become pregnant to undergo the process. Such an approach would do little to mitigate the impact of these laws on priests, however.

It is worth dwelling for a moment on the attitude toward women implicit in the purity laws of 4QD.[78] Denigration of the female was widespread among the ascetically minded in antiquity. The famous saying 114 at the end of the *Gospel of Thomas* is typical: "For every woman who will make herself male will enter the Kingdom of Heaven."[79] The body tends to be understood as female, the soul as male. Even Platonists such as Philo, who viewed the body as good, understood it as inferior to the soul.[80] Yet while the restrictive attitude toward sexual relations in the purity laws of 4QD is a striking Jewish antecedent to a more radical Christian asceticism, it is noteworthy that it is not linked to a negative attitude toward women. Indeed these laws achieve the limiting of sexual relations by intensifying Leviticus 15's laws of *male* impurity.

Following the rule of the *zāb*, 4QD moves on to "the rule of the *zābâ*" (4Q272 1 ii 7).[81] We have seen that 4QD reads Leviticus's three types of male genital discharge—abnormal genital flow, seminal emission outside of sexual relations, and seminal emission in the course of sexual relations—as instances of the discharge of the *zāb*. Leviticus also delineates three types of genital discharge for women, the discharge of childbirth, menstruation, and abnormal genital flow. While the fragmentary nature of the text makes it impossible to be certain, it appears that 4QD treats all three types of female genital discharge under the rule of the *zābâ*. Leviticus's comparison to menstrual impurity of the first stage of the impurity of the woman after childbirth (Lev 12:2) and of the impurity of the woman with abnormal flow and of her bedding (Lev 15:25, 26) provides a warrant for doing so. The menstruant, who, as we have seen, is introduced in Lev 15:19 with the term *zābâ* (4QD 272 1 ii 7-18/4QD 266

6 ii 1-2),[82] comes first, followed by the woman with abnormal discharge (4QD 266 6 ii 2-4) and the woman after childbirth (4Q266 6 ii 4). In the single surviving manuscript that preserves the relevant portion of the passage (4Q266 6 ii 4-5), the discussion of the woman with abnormal flow concludes in the middle of a line, and the discussion of the woman after childbirth begins on the next line. But despite this possible indication that a new unit is beginning, the discussion is not introduced with a phrase involving *mišpaṭ*, "rule," suggesting that 4QD understands the woman who has given birth too as a type of *zābâ*. Yet while 4QD's treatment of the three types of male genital discharge was remarkable for offering a single set of rules for all three, for the three types of female discharge, in contrast, 4QD delineates a separate set of rules for each. Thus the treatment of female genital discharge is considerably longer than that of male discharge.

The discussion of the menstruant begins by following the order of topics in Lev 15:19-24. It notes the seven-day duration of menstrual impurity (Lev 15:19; 4Q272 1 ii 8-9) and goes on to consider contact with the menstruant (4Q272 1 ii 9-10). At this point, with almost half a column remaining, the text of 4Q272 1 ii becomes extremely fragmentary. The model of Leviticus 15 suggests that it considered both how the menstruant conveys impurity to objects on which she sat or lay and how those objects then convey impurity to people who have contact with them. The discussion of the menstruant in Leviticus, as noted above, is remarkable for neglecting to explain how the menstruant rids herself of her impurity. It does, however, explain how those who have had contact with her bedding or seat get rid of their impurity. At the right margin of the bottom of the column, which is mostly lost, are visible the words *mê niddâ*, "waters of purification," and *haḥayyî[m]*, in this context, "fresh" (4Q272 1 ii 15-16). According to Leviticus, the man with an abnormal discharge is to wash himself in *mayim hayyîm*, "fresh water," at the end of the process of purification (Lev 15:13). P uses the term "waters of purification" for the special water sprinkled on those with corpse impurity in Numbers 19. The fact that the waters are called *mê niddâ* may contribute to their association with menstrual impurity. Indeed Joseph Baumgarten suggests that the Qumran community used sprinkling following bathing to remove genital impurity and other types of impurity as well as corpse impurity.[83] The loss of so much of this passage means that it is impossible to discern the contours of the process of purification, but it is certainly clear that water of some kind plays a role. It is possible that 4QD solved the problem of Leviticus 15's striking omission of the process of purification for the menstruant herself, but it is impossible for us to be sure.

Still following the order of the discussion in Leviticus 15,[84] 4QD now turns to the man who has sexual relations with the menstruant (Lev

15:24). I have emphasized the way the laws of 4QD understand the
Torah's laws of genital discharge as a system. But they also reflect the influence of another relevant part of the Torah, the laws of forbidden sexual relations in the Holiness Code. Nowhere in the course of Leviticus
15 does P prohibit sexual relations with a menstruant;[85] rather, it mentions such relations in order to lay out their implications for the purity
of the man who engages in them. The Holiness Code, however, twice
prohibits them (Lev 18:19, 20:18). Well aware of these prohibitions, the
laws of 4QD change the rather neutral description of the result of sexual
relations with a menstruant in Leviticus 15, *ûtĕhî niddātāh 'ālāyw*, "her
impurity is upon him" (Lev 15:24), to [*ă*]*wōn niddâ 'ālā[y]w*, "the sin of
menstrual impurity [is] upon him" (4Q266 6 ii 2). It is not the impurity
of the menstruant that 4QD associates with sin; the sin is the fact of sexual relations with her. [86]

The formulation of these forbidden relations in the purity laws of
4QD is also indebted to the Holiness Code. The verb Leviticus 15 uses
for sexual relations with a menstruant is emphatic and straightforward,
šākōb yiškab, "lies," or as the King James Version translates in an effort
to capture the emphasis, "lie with her at all." One of the prohibitions of
sexual relations with a menstruant in the Holiness Code uses the same
verb without the infinitive absolute (Lev 20:18), but the other uses the
euphemism *tiqrab*, "shall approach" (Lev 18:19). The laws of 4QD
adopt the euphemism, apparently without an infinitive absolute, although lacunae in the text make it impossible to be certain (4Q266 6
ii 1). The behavior was perhaps sufficiently shocking to require a
euphemism.

Following its discussion of the menstruant, 4QD turns to the woman
with abnormal flow. It defines abnormal flow as blood seen "again" not
during the seven-day span of menstrual impurity (4Q266 6 ii 2-3). Here
4QD describes the consequences of impurity for the first time, at least in
the material preserved: "She shall not eat any hallowed thing,[87] nor
co[me] into the sanctuary until sunset on the eighth day" (4Q266 6 ii
3-4). An understanding of the purity laws of the Torah as a system is visible here also. The only place the laws of Leviticus spell out the restrictions on someone in a state of impurity is in relation to the first case it
discusses, the woman after childbirth: "She shall not touch any hallowed
thing, nor come into the sanctuary, until her days of purifying are completed" (Lev 12:4). The laws of 4QD assume, as most readers do, that
the Torah makes explicit in relation to the first type of impurity it discusses prohibitions that apply to the bearers of other types of impurity
as well. Thus they apply them to the woman with abnormal discharge as
well, but with some significant changes in the wording. The language of

4QD is more pointed than that of Lev 12:4, indicating more precisely the nature of the contact to be avoided by changing Leviticus's "touch" to "eat"; eating was the primary way in which a nonpriest, whether a layperson or a member of a priestly family, might have contact with holy things.[88] According to the Torah, consecrated or holy food (*qōdeš*) consists of tithes or of portions of sacrifices consumed by priests and the person who brought the sacrifice. The Torah contains no general prohibition on eating this food in a state of impurity, but rather a number of specific rules, some directed at priests alone, some at laypeople.[89] The laws of 4QD apparently repeated at least a portion of Leviticus 12's prohibitions for the woman after childbirth; only the prohibition on eating survives, and the manuscript does not appear to have room for a time limit (4Q266 6 ii 9).

The passage in Leviticus 12 refers to the period of the purification of the woman after childbirth without mentioning the actual length of time: "until her days of purifying are completed" (Lev 12:4). This is a convenient expression in its context because the actual length of the period differs depending on the sex of the baby (Lev 12:4-5). But while the language of Lev 12:4 could be applied to any type of impurity, the laws of 4QD prefer to specify the length of time for the woman with abnormal flow: "until sunset on the eighth day." Perhaps they were wary of confusing the time required for purifying the woman with abnormal flow with the time required for the woman after childbirth. But they may also have intended to resolve another question raised by the text of Leviticus: When does the woman suffering from abnormal genital flow become pure? On the one hand, the Torah tells us that after counting seven days from the cessation of the flow, the former sufferer returns to a state of purity (Lev 15:28; Lev 15:13 for men). On the other hand, she (or he) is required to bring a sacrifice on the eighth day (Lev 15:29; Lev 15:14 for men). Despite the Torah's explicit reference to becoming pure on the seventh day, the fact that the procedure is not complete until the eighth day permits the laws of 4QD to decide that purity is restored only on the eighth day.

The stringent approach of the laws of 4QD does not stop there, for they insist also that the state of purity returns not early on the eighth day but at sunset. This rule too reflects a reading of the Torah's purity laws as a system. While Leviticus 15 does not indicate at what point on the last day of impurity the process of purification is complete for the other categories of genital impurity, it says explicitly that the impurity of seminal emission lasts until evening (Lev 15:16-18). It also notes repeatedly that the impurity caused by contact with bearers of impurity (Lev 15:7, 19) or with those of their belongings that convey impurity (Lev 15:5-11,

21-23, 27) lasts until evening.[90] The conclusion of the purity laws of 4QD that the Torah intended the same timing to apply to the purification of the woman with abnormal flow is not at all unreasonable.

Some scholars have read the insistence that purification is complete only at sundown as representing the Sadducean side of a debate with the Pharisees;[91] adherents of this point of view see the Sadducees and the communities of the Dead Sea Scrolls as proponents of the same stream of halakhah, which is priestly in character. They identify the Pharisees' position on the basis of the remarkable report in *m. Parah* 3:7 that the "elders of Israel" used to render impure the priest who was to burn the red heifer. Thus he would have to perform the task after he had bathed but before the sun had set, making him, in the terminology of the rabbis, a *ṭĕbûl yôm*. I have argued elsewhere in some detail that passages in the Dead Sea Scrolls that have been read as preserving a polemic against the idea of the *ṭĕbûl yôm* are better understood as reflecting the type of systematizing exegesis just described for the relevant passage in 4QD.[92] Here let me note only that neither the content nor the rhetoric of the passage from 4QD on the woman with abnormal flow and the relevant passages in the *Temple Scroll* offers any indication that these works understood the requirement of waiting for sunset to be the subject of polemic.

The treatment of the woman after childbirth in 4QD is remarkable for how much of the relevant passage in Leviticus it includes, or to put it more precisely, how much it appears to have included. The passage begins by delineating the different lengths of the two periods of impurity depending on the sex of the child (Lev 12:1-5). It then repeats a version of the prohibition on contact with holy things of Lev 12:4, again substituting eating holy things for touching them (4Q266 6 ii 9). The lacunae are of considerable size, but Baumgarten's restoration quite persuasively includes all of the information of Lev 12:1-5, although with some rearrangement.

The text continues with laws not to be found in Leviticus 12. First, it terms the violation of the prohibitions a "capital offense," [*mi*] *špaṭ māvet* (4Q266 6 ii 10). This threat of severe punishment for violation of the laws of purity provides an emphatic supplement to the matter-of-fact tone of Leviticus 12 and 15.[93] Next 4QD forbids the new mother to nurse her child. Rather, she is to give the child to a nurse who can nurse the child "in purity" (4Q266 6 ii 11).[94] While the practical implications of this ruling are astonishing, the logic of 4QD's position is quite powerful. As already noted, P explicitly compares the initial impurity of the woman after childbirth, which lasts one or two weeks depending on the sex of the child, to menstrual impurity (Lev 12:3, 5). Enough of the text of 4QD is preserved to see that it makes the same comparison

(4Q266 6 ii 6, 8). According to P, a person who touches a woman in a state of menstrual impurity becomes impure until evening (Lev 15:19); presumably this person must launder and bathe since laundering and bathing are required for a person who touches the menstruant's bedding or any object on which she has sat (Lev 15:21-22). Since the initial impurity of the woman after childbirth is like menstrual impurity, 4QD perhaps concluded that during that initial period the infant she nurses would incur impurity by touching her, its clothes would require laundering, and it would require bathing daily in order to become pure again at sundown. The extra work that such bathing and laundering would have caused in a society without running water, much less washing machines, is so considerable that the wet nurse might have seemed a more practical solution.

It is hard not to agree with 4QD that the ground rules of P's system mean that a woman in the first stage of impurity after childbirth conveys impurity to those who touch her. Surely it would not have escaped P's notice that the newborn baby could not avoid such contact. Yet Leviticus 12 betrays no anxiety about this contact, presumably because the consequences of impurity are hardly relevant to a newborn.[95] A newborn baby is unlikely to have the opportunity to enter the sanctuary or to touch holy things and is certainly incapable of eating sacrificial meat and other kinds of consecrated food. For P the undesirability of impurity is primarily practical: it prevents contact with the holy for those who need to be in contact with it—priests ministering in the sanctuary—and for those who are entitled to eat consecrated food—priests, their families, and laypeople who have brought certain sacrifices. The insistence in 4QD on a nurse to replace the mother so as not to convey impurity to the newborn baby suggests a somewhat different point of view in which purity is valued for its own sake.

This is an appropriate point at which to raise the question of the relationship between impurity and sin in 4QD. For P, the two categories are quite separate, but several scholars have suggested that at Qumran, they were not.[96] The heightened concern for purity for its own sake in 4QD might seem likely to lead in the direction of such a melding, but as far as I can see, 4QD offers no evidence for such a view. Indeed, as I have written elsewhere, I think the view is mistaken;[97] here, however, I restrict myself to comments on the purity laws of 4QD. These laws give no indication of the understanding, foreign to P but important elsewhere in the Bible, that skin eruptions are punishment for sin. The lewd thoughts that according to 4QD cause the condition of one kind of *zāb* reflect not an association of the *zāb* with sexual impropriety, but rather the effort to bring seminal emission outside of sexual relations under the heading of the rule of the *zāb*. The man who has sexual relations with a woman in a state of menstrual impurity bears the sin of her impurity according to 4QD, but this is because Leviticus forbids sexual relations with a woman in a state of menstrual impurity, not because 4QD associates menstrual impurity with sinfulness. In addition to its purity laws, 4QD also contains laws regarding marriage to a woman of bad reputation, but these are presented as an elaboration of the law of the bride accused of lacking signs of virginity in Deut 22:13-24; they do not invoke the language of impurity for promiscuity (4Q271 3 10-15).[98] Only in the Admonition of the *Damascus Document,* which is homiletical rather than legal, does the term *niddâ,* drawn from the technical vocabulary of impurity in P, appear to condemn sinful behavior (CD 2.1, 3.17); this usage echoes H's use of *niddâ* for sexual relations between a man and his brother's wife.[99] Altogether, despite the value the requirement of a nurse for the newborn baby places on purity for its own sake, I think it is accurate to say that 4QD maintains P's view of impurity as a ritual state without moral implications.

I return to 4QD's rule of the *zābâ.* The rule treats the sacrifice of the woman after childbirth (Lev 12:6-8; 4Q266 6 ii 12-13), but it appears to have skipped the standard sacrifice (Lev 12:6-7) in order to clarify the somewhat unusual provision for a less expensive bird sacrifice if the woman cannot afford a lamb (Lev 12:8). The passage from the Torah uses the phrase *timṣā' yādāh,* literally, "her hand finds," to mean, "affords." This uncommon phrase[100] is replaced in 4QD by the expression *hiśîgâ yādāh,* literally, "her hand reaches" (4Q266 6 ii 12); the Torah uses the imperfect of this expression for all other sacrifices that permit the substitution of less expensive alternatives to the preferred sacrifice.[101] The remaining words in the fragment also appear to be intended to clarify the nature of the procedure in Leviticus: *vě]hēmîrâ 'et ha[,* "[and she] shall substitute [it for the ...]" (4Q266 6 ii 13). The term "substitute" does not appear in the Torah's laws for this sacrifice or the others in which a less expensive alternative is indicated, but it does use the term in the prohibition on exchanging one animal for another that has been set aside for sacrifice (Lev 27:10, 33). If an allusion to that passage is intended, it is presumably meant to contrast permitted substitution with forbidden.

The sacrifice of the woman after childbirth (4Q266 6 ii 12-13) is the only purification sacrifice of Leviticus 12-15 treated in 4QD. Enough of the text is preserved to show that in the portions of the text devoted to skin eruptions[102] and the woman with abnormal flow, the absence of the sacrifices is not merely the result of partial preservation.[103] The text of 4QD breaks off in the midst of the sacrifice of the woman after childbrith, and there is a little more than half a column lost before the beginning of a new topic, the laws of agriculture. Thus it is possible that mention of some other sacrifices followed. The feature of the sacrifice of the woman after childbirth that attracted attention was the possibility of substituting a less expensive offering. This is a feature it shares with the sacrifice after skin eruptions (Lev 14:21-31), but not with the sacrifice after abnormal discharge (Lev 15:14-15, 29-30), and I am not sure how to explain the absence of discussion of the former.

To sum up: unlike the *Temple Scroll*, which integrates types of impurity treated in different portions of the Torah, 4QD offers a close reading of Leviticus 12-15; its development of the laws of impurity is to a considerable extent an attempt to resolve difficulties it found in the text of the Torah. It understands the purity laws of these chapters to constitute a system, but it believes that the Torah fails to present the system as clearly as it might. Thus 4QD reorganizes the purity laws of Leviticus and makes explicit connections that the Torah fails to make while clarifying difficult language. The best explanation for the contours of these laws, as far as their partial preservation allows us to discern it, is that they focus on difficulties in the text of Leviticus. It is in this light that we should understand the absence of significant portions of Leviticus's laws of skin eruptions, the lack of purification procedures for men with genital discharge, and the treatment of only one type of purification sacrifice. The subjects not treated were those where the text of the Torah was sufficiently clear—or sufficiently in line with the thinking of the authors of the laws.

The mode of intensifying the impurity laws in 4QD also differs significantly from that of the *Temple Scroll*. Rather than lengthening the period of impurity and making the ritual of purification more elaborate for each type of impurity, 4QD's approach extends the more stringent requirements of certain types of impurity to other types. Thus 4QD applies the more severe restrictions placed on a man with abnormal genital discharge to a man who has had a seminal emission. It also comes to the remarkable but logical conclusion that a nursing mother in the first stage of postpartum impurity conveys impurity to her child.

Like the *Temple Scroll*, 4QD intensifies P's laws of impurity to make certain that they will have a significant impact on the lives of nonpriests as well as priests. But again like the *Temple Scroll* 4QD does not collapse the distinction between priests and nonpriests. Indeed, 4QD attempts to strengthen the boundaries of the priesthood by inventing further limitations on who can serve as priest. P disqualifies priests with certain physical imperfections from offering sacrifices, although they are permitted to eat of them (Lev 21:16-23), and 4QD adds to P's limitations with a prohibition on priests with weak voices reading from the Torah (4Q266

5 ii 1-4), a prohibition on service by a high priest who has been captured by gentiles (4Q266 5 ii 4-7),[104] and a prohibition on service by priests who have lived in foreign lands (4Q266 5 ii 8-14).

4QD, the *Temple Scroll*, and Priestly Halakhah

Despite their shared desire to remedy what they see as P's too lenient approach to impurity, the *Temple Scroll* and 4QD go about the task quite differently. Though the *Temple Scroll* presents itself not as exegesis but as an alternative torah, it reads the text of the Torah carefully. The most distinctive development of its purity laws is the exclusion of the impure from the city of the sanctuary and the other cities of the holy land; while the system of places for the impure outside the cities is not biblical, it clearly derives from a close reading of several relevant passages in the Torah. The approach of 4QD to the purity laws of the Torah is perhaps more conservative, but its reading of Leviticus 12-15 manages to discover a far more stringent approach to impurity in the Torah than the P source itself intended.

The differences between the intensified purity laws of the *Temple Scroll* and 4QD have significant implications for the now popular theory that the legal texts from Qumran reflect a priestly halakhah to which the Sadducees too adhered and which stood in opposition to proto-rabbinic halakhah.[105] Not only do the *Temple Scroll* and 4QD take different approaches and emphasize different aspects of the purity laws, but at some points they contradict each other, making it difficult to see them as parts of the same legal system. Let me offer a single example. The *Temple Scroll* extends the very brief period of impurity decreed by P for nocturnal emission (Lev 15:16), until the sun sets, to three days; it also adds laundering clothes to the simple bathing decreed in Leviticus as the ritual of purification (*TS* 45.7-10). For seminal emission in the course of sexual relations, the *Temple Scroll* also decrees a three-day period of purification (*TS* 45.11-12); here it does not mention bathing and laundering, presumably assuming them by analogy with the practice after nocturnal emission. I argued above that 4QD (4Q266 6 i 14-16/4Q272 1 ii 3-7) subsumes both of these types of seminal emission under the heading of the *zāb*. Thus, although the text is poorly preserved here, it seems clear that the period of impurity is, remarkably, the eight days Leviticus decrees for the man with abnormal discharge. Because the text is so poorly preserved, I confess to being on firmer ground with seminal emission outside of intercourse than with seminal emission in the context of intercourse. But even if I am correct only about seminal emission outside of sexual intercourse, for this type of impurity at least

4QD and the *Temple Scroll* define periods of impurity of different lengths.

The idea of a well-defined priestly halakhah becomes even more problematic if we consider the purity laws of the *Book of Jubilees*, which proponents of the theory of such a legal tradition include among the priestly legal texts. Despite their differences, the *Temple Scroll* and 4QD are both engaged in intensifying and elaborating the purity laws of the Torah. There is no evidence that *Jubilees* has any interest in doing so. As we have seen, *Jubilees* is deeply influenced by the Holiness Code and develops laws about bloodshed and sexual relations on the basis of its reading of H. But only once does *Jubilees* treat a purity law from P, and when it does, *Jubilees* seems quite content with it. This is the law for purification for the woman after childbirth with its different periods of time depending on the sex of the newborn child. In keeping with its tendency to retroject into the primeval history and the period of the patriarchs laws that the Torah presents as revealed to Israel in the wilderness, it places the establishment of the laws of impurity for a woman after childbirth with Adam and Eve, at the very beginning of human history. It then uses the creation to explain why, as Leviticus 12 decrees, the two periods of impurity for the new mother after the birth of a girl are double the length of the periods of impurity following the birth of a boy. It does so by relating the first, more severe period of impurity to its chronology of the creation of Adam and the separation of Eve from his body. The second period of impurity, longer but less severe, is taken as reflecting the chronology of the entrance of first Adam and then Eve into the Garden of Eden.[106] But while *Jubilees* attempts to explain the impurity laws of the woman after childbirth, it makes no effort to intensify them. While the *Temple Scroll* required the exclusion of the woman after childbirth from its cities and 4QD prohibited her to nurse her baby, the restrictions *Jubilees* suggests do not go beyond those of Leviticus 12. Thus, in the one place that we can test it, *Jubilees*' attitude toward P's purity laws stands in striking contrast to the attitude of the *Temple Scroll* and 4QD, which insist on a more rigorous approach to impurity.

The substantial differences of approach among these three works seem to me to raise significant questions for the theory of a system of priestly halakhah. Surely there must have been agreement on the practices required for running the temple, public halakhah, or if not agreement, then enforcement of a single set of practices by those in control. Of course the practices so enforced could change gradually over time or more drastically in response to changes of those in charge. But for more private matters, there might well have been diverse practices even among the pious who wished to go beyond what the Torah required.

The library at Qumran preserves for us a variety of different traditions that share to some degree a basic orientation: the desire to develop the laws of P to give due weight to the seriousness of impurity. These texts all serve to strengthen the impact of the laws of purity on all Jews, thus making them a little bit more like priests, but they do so in different ways.

Chapter 4

Priesthood and Sectarianism

The Rule of the Community, *the* Damascus Document,
and the Book of Revelation

Before the Babylonian exile our sources show little interest in defining membership in the people of Israel. It must have seemed obvious that with a few exceptions those who lived within the boundaries of the kingdoms of Israel and Judah were Israelites. After the exile matters were quite different. To begin with, geography was no longer as relevant as it had been. Most of the Judean exiles chose to remain in Babylonia even after the Persians offered them the opportunity to return to their homeland, and there was by now a significant Jewish presence in Egypt, which grew and flourished in the later centuries of the Second Temple period. Even in the homeland itself, boundaries had become blurred. In the middle of the fifth century, Ezra and Nehemiah felt the need to take action against marriages between Jewish men and women from among the neighboring peoples (Ezra 9-10; Neh 10:31; 13:23-29); Nehemiah complains that many of their offspring could not even speak the language of Judah (Neh 13:24). At the same time, after two centuries of intermarriage and residence in the land, descendants of the colonists the Assyrians had placed in the defeated northern kingdom were demanding equal standing in the cult of the God of Israel. Ezra and Nehemiah regarded the offspring of those long-ago intermarriages in the same light that they regarded the offspring of the contemporary ones: they had no place in the people of Israel.

It is clear, however, that many Jews of the Persian period, and not only those who were themselves connected to families of questionable descent, felt quite differently. The author of the Book of Chronicles, for example, appears to have been sympathetic to the descendants of the Assyrian settlers who wanted to worship the Lord since he takes pains to show that at least some northerners participated in Hezekiah's Passover after the fall of the northern kingdom (2 Chronicles 30).[1] The Book of Ruth presents a more direct challenge to the attitude of Ezra and Nehemiah, who would have demanded that Boaz send its Moabite heroine packing. Ruth's explicit embrace of her mother-in-law's people (Ruth 1:16) announces that even under foreign rule, with the natural boundaries of sovereignty gone, birth is not the only path to membership in the Jewish people.

The idea that outsiders can join the Jewish people develops more fully in the course of the hellenistic period. Alone of all the subject peoples of the hellenistic empires the Jews were monotheists, and thus they alone avoided participation in the religious rituals of the rest of the hellenistic world. Yet from one point of view the Jews were perhaps more similar to the Greeks than any of the other subject peoples. Unlike the Israelites' previous overlords, the Greeks understood their culture, *Hellenismos*, to be accessible to outsiders, who could become Hellenes through education. As the Book of Ruth recognized, Jewish culture too could be acquired by outsiders. At least since the time of Ezra, Jewish culture had at its center the Torah, and a culture based on a book is a culture that can be learned, though the process of education need not be formal, as the Book of Ruth shows. The author of 2 Maccabees for one recognized the parallel between Jewish culture and Greek as his invention of the term *Ioudaismos*, Judaism, on the model of *Hellenismos*, shows.[2] The period after the Maccabean Revolt, as we have already seen, saw a significant number of gentiles joining the Jewish people. In most cases, no doubt, the absorption was accomplished without a conscious effort at education. Nonetheless, this influx of gentiles to the Jewish people in combination with the developing understanding of Judaism as a culture that could be learned opened up new possibilities for defining the people of Israel.

These factors I have just noted had a particular impact on the thinking of sectarian movements, for the demands of membership in a sect require more committed members than birth alone can assure.[3] To translate into the terms I have used of ancient Jewish attitudes toward priesthood, membership in a sect requires merit rather than ancestry. In this chapter I consider definitions of membership in the people of Israel in which birth plays a considerably diminished role and the implications of these definitions for the idea of Israel as a kingdom of priests. The definitions emerge in the most important Jewish sectarian movements of antiquity, the communities reflected in the Dead Sea Scrolls and the early followers of Jesus. The use of the category "sect" for ancient Judaism is not unproblematic,[4] but the groups I discuss here fit the sociological definitions of sects very well; their beliefs and practices separate them from the mainstream, and the boundaries are clearly defined.

The Scrolls and Priesthood

My discussion of the Dead Sea Scrolls centers on the *Damascus Document* and the *Rule of the Community*.[5] Both are rules intended for a pious few, and both were found among the scrolls from Qumran, although a version of the *Damascus Document* was already known from the Cairo Geniza. But as scholars have noted for more than half a century now, the rules regulate different communities: the *Rule of the Community* regulates the affairs of the *yaḥad*, a group of apparently celibate men living in isolation from the rest of society, while the *Damascus Document* legislates for families living among gentiles and Jews who are not members of the sect. The historical relationship between the communities reflected in these two texts is crucial for our understanding of the history of the sectarian movement or movements they represent. But the complexity of the texts makes it difficult to arrive at clear answers to historical questions;[6] both rules are composite works, and both have undergone redaction at Qumran.[7] I am inclined to follow those who see the more radical *yaḥad* as an offshoot of the more moderate sectarian community of the *Damascus Document*, and I believe that the results of my discussion are compatible with such a picture.[8] But the singular "sect" that appears frequently in the discussion below is a convenience made possible by the undoubted connections between the two works, and it is not intended to express a judgment about the details of their relationship. Fortunately, the historical question is not of central importance for my discussion.[9]

The sectarian communities of the Dead Sea Scrolls have often been characterized as priestly, and with good reason. Many scholars believe that the sect's origins lie in a dispute about the high priesthood,[10] and criticism of the way the temple was run is a central theme in several of the sectarian scrolls.[11] Despite their reservations about the actual temple, however, members of the sect were deeply devoted to the institution: they seem to have considered the sect a sort of temple,[12] and they wrote works reflecting on the eschatological temple[13] and the heavenly temple and its liturgy.[14] Priestly concerns are evident also in the sect's legal works, which give considerable space to matters of purity, temple procedure, and qualification for priestly service.[15] Further, the sect appears to have looked forward to a priestly messiah, either alone or in the company of a presumably Davidic messiah of Israel.[16] Finally, priests play a significant role in the organization of the sect, both in rules for life in the present and the future.[17]

Still, despite these strong indications of priestly connections, I shall argue that the sect's relationship to priesthood and purity is more complicated than this summary would suggest. I begin by comparing the role of priests in the *Damascus Document* and the *Rule of the Community*. We shall see that while the *Damascus Document* understands priests to play a significant role of leadership in the sect, the *Rule of the Community* gives them only a very limited role. I also compare the understanding of purity in these two documents. In the last chapter I argued that the purity laws of the *Damascus Document*, which strengthen and elaborate the laws of the Torah, serve to make all Jews more like priests, as do the laws of the *Temple Scroll*. The *Rule of the Community* too shows considerable interest in purity, but unlike the *Damascus Document* or the *Temple Scroll*, it contains no purity laws. Rather it applies the technical terminology of purity to spiritual states.

Children of Light, Children of Darkness

The biblical tradition imagines all humanity divided between Israel and the nations. This is a division of the utmost importance, but it is not a division between the saved and the damned. Israel has a special relationship with God that the nations do not, but that relationship is by no means a guarantee of salvation, as the prophets never cease to remind their listeners. Nor are gentiles necessarily excluded from a positive fate; some of the prophets imagine the nations flowing to Jerusalem as they come to recognize the Lord (Isa 2:2-4; Zech 8:20-23).

Like the biblical tradition, the *Rule of the Community* divides the world in two, but it is an absolute division between the saved and the damned. Only members of the sect are children of light, while all others, Jews and gentiles alike, are children of darkness. This view is only implicit in the *Rule of the Community*, in which no gentiles appear, but it is explicit in the *War Scroll* (1QM 1.1-2), a text of the *yahad* in which gentiles play a central role.[18] The division of humanity into children of light and children of darkness has nothing to do with Israel's history; rather, the *Rule of the Community* tells us, it goes back to the beginning of the cosmos:

From the God of knowledge comes everything that is and will be. Before they existed he fixed all their plans, and when they come into existence they complete their work according to their instructions in accordance with his glorious plan, and without changing anything. In his hand are the laws for all things, and he sustains them in all their concerns.

He created man to rule the world, and he assigned two spirits to him that he might walk by them until the appointed time of his visitation; they are the spirits of truth and of injustice. From a spring of light come the generations of truth, and from a well of darkness the generations of injustice. Control over all the sons of righteousness lies in the hand of the prince of lights, and they walk in the ways of light; complete control over the sons of injustice lies in the hand of the angel of darkness and they walk in the ways of darkness. It is through the angel of darkness that all the sons of righteousness go astray, and all their sins, their iniquities, their guilt, and their deeds of transgression are under his control in the mysteries of God until his time. All their afflictions and their times of distress are brought about by his rule of hatred, and all the spirits of his lot make the sons of light stumble. But the God of Israel and his angel of truth help all the sons of light. (1QS 3.15-25)[19]

The view that man was created to rule the world is certainly the view of Genesis 1, but the *Rule of the Community* does nothing to signal its connection to that passage. Indeed it is remarkable how little the *Rule of the Community* refers to Israel's history and its covenant with God in formulating its view of the universe. Apart from the faint echo of Genesis just noted and the reference to the God of Israel, there is nothing in this passage to connect it to the biblical tradition.

The *Damascus Document*'s categories for insiders and outsiders, on the other hand, are much more traditional. It is true that it refers to other Jews as those whom "God did not choose . . . primordially" (CD 2.7),[20] it ordains ranking new members according to their "inheritance in the lot of light" (CD 13.12), and it may even refer to the community it addresses as the children of light (4QD266 1 1).[21] But more often it condemns Jews who are not members of the sect in language that alludes to prophetic condemnation of the people of Israel:

But during all those years, Belial will run unbridled amidst Israel, as God spoke through the hand of the prophet Isaiah, son of Amoz, saying, "Fear and a pit and a snare are upon you, O inhabitant(s) of the land" [Isa 24:17]. This refers to the three nets of Belial. . . . The first is unchastity, the second arrogance, and the third defilement of the sanctuary. (CD 4.12-18)

They also polluted their holy spirits, and with a tongue of blasphemies they opened (their) mouth against the statutes of God's covenant, saying, "They are not right," and abomination they are speaking against them. They are all lighters of fire and burners of brands [Isa 50:11], webs of a spider (are) their webs and eggs of vipers (are) their eggs [Isa 59:5]. (CD 5.11-14)

Further, unlike the *Rule of the Community*, the *Damascus Document* has no shorthand term to refer to those outside the sect. It never uses the phrase "children of darkness." The closest equivalent to such an epithet is "children of the pit," from whom the *Damascus Document* orders its audience to separate (CD 6.14-15);[22] these undesirables are apparently other Jews. This epithet appears also in the *Rule of the Community* (1QS 9.22), where the context gives little help in deciding whether Jews or gentiles are meant.

Priests, Levites, Israelites

If the biblical tradition imagines the world divided between Israel and the nations, it also imagines Israel divided into priests, Levites, and Israelites. And just as the division into Israel and the nations fits poorly the sectarian division of humanity into children of light and children of darkness, so too the divisions within Israel pose problems for the sectarian view of the saved. The tension between sectarian preoccupations and biblical heritage is strikingly expressed in the *Damascus Document*'s famous *pešer* (CD 3.21-4.4) on Ezek 44:15, "the Levitical priests, the sons of Zadok, who shall attend on me to offer me the fat and the blood." The passage from Ezekiel refers to a single group, descendants of Zadok, who are also, by definition, Levitical priests, but the *Damascus Document*'s citation of the passage supplies conjunctions for Ezekiel's appositives so as to create three separate groups: "the priests, and the Levites, and the Sons of Zadok" (CD 3.21-4.1). One might thus imagine that the *Damascus Document* reads Ezekiel as ordaining a more elaborate hierarchy, with sons of Zadok at its apex, atop priests and Levites. But in the *Damascus Document*'s interpretation the hierarchy evaporates. The priests are the original penitents of Israel, presumably the founders of the sect; the Levites are those who joined them; and the sons of Zadok are the elect of Israel of the last days. The message is clear: the members of the sect are the true priests; Ezekiel's categories reflect not hierarchical divisions but chronology.

Despite the conceptual conflict between biblical hierarchy and sectarian worldview reflected in this passage, both the *Damascus Document* and the *Rule of the Community* make use of the biblical division of the people of Israel into priests, Levites, and Israelites. Although the use of these categories is largely ornamental, it is nonetheless significant that both rules employ the inherited categories despite their unsuitability for the sect.

As we have seen, the incorporation of the Levites into the Torah's vision of the people of Israel was not as smooth as it might have been. Still, the Book of Chronicles treats them as an essential element of the body of the people of Israel, noting their presence at several important moments when the people are assembled (1 Chr 23:2; 2 Chr 30:25, 34:30). Both the *Damascus Document* and the *Rule of the Community* show the influence of this picture in their arrangements for assemblies of the sect. Thus the *Damascus Document* decrees: "They [the members of the sect] shall all be mustered by their names; the priests first, the Levites second, the sons of Israel third, the proselyte(s) [*gēr*] fourth. Thus shall they sit and thus shall they inquire" (CD 14.3-6; the list of the four categories appears twice in the passage). I shall return to the fourth category, proselytes, below.

A similar picture appears in the *Rule of the Community*:

The priests shall enter into the order first, one after the other, according to their spiritual status. And the Levites shall enter after them. And thirdly all the people shall enter into the order, one after the other, by thousands, hundreds, fifties, and tens, so that every man of Israel may know his own position in the community of God. (1QS 2.19-22)

The Levites also play an important role in the covenant ceremony that precedes the assembly in the *Rule of the Community*. In this ceremony the Levites recite the negatives to the priests' positives, Israel's sins versus God's mighty deeds (1QS 1.21), curses on the lot of Belial versus blessings on the lot of God (1QS 2.1-9), and then join with the priests to recite curses on those who enter the covenant without abandoning their evil ways (1QS 2.11-17). According to Chronicles the primary role of the Levites is liturgical; the needs of the ceremony might well have been understood to require Levites.

Yet the Levites disappear from the *Rule of the Community*'s picture rather quickly. The seating plan for "the session [*môšāb*] of the many" divides the sect into priests, *elders*, and people (1QS 6.8-9). The status of elder is presumably achieved by merit, not heredity. Indeed, there is a certain tension in the description quoted above of the assembly after the covenant ceremony between the ordering of the sect by groupings based on hereditary status and the ordering within the groupings by "spiritual status." This mode of ordering requires constant striving since status is not fixed:

They shall register them in order, one before another, according to their insight and their deeds, that they may all obey one another, the one of lower rank obeying the one of higher rank. They shall review their spirits and their deeds every year that they may promote each man according to his insight and the perfection of his way, or demote him according to his perversity. (1QS 5.23-24)

It is worth noting that there is nothing in this passage to suggest that such ordering took place within the hereditary categories of priests, Levites, and Israelites.

The assemblies just described are the only places in either rule where the sect is grouped into priests, Levites, and Israelites, unless we include a reference in the *Rule of the Community* to the community as "all those who willingly offer themselves to holiness in Aaron and to the house of truth in Israel, and . . . those who join them in community" (1QS 5.6). "Those who join them in community" appears to contain a pun on Levites: the root of the verb join, *nilwîm*, is the root of the name Levi. More often, when they wish to indicate the totality of the sect, the rules refer to Israel and Aaron without mentioning Levites. Thus the *Damascus Document* in its account of the emergence of the sect: "He turned his attention to them and caused to grow out of Israel and Aaron a root of the planting" (CD 1.7); "And he raised from Aaron men of discernment

and from Israel wise men" (CD 6.2-3). The *Rule of the Community* refers
to the eschatological community as "a holy house for Israel and a most
holy assembly for Aaron . . . a most holy dwelling for Aaron . . . a house
of perfection and truth in Israel" (1QS 8.5-9). But while Aaron and Israel indicate the totality of the Jewish people, these passages indicate no
difference in their function. This lack of differentiation may not be particularly significant in the highly rhetorical contexts in which these
phrases appear, but, as we shall see, when the *Rule of the Community* attributes authority to priests and the rest of the community, it also fails to
distinguish between them.

The appearance of the division of the sect into Aaron and Israel
alongside the division into priests, Levites, and Israelites may reflect the
development of the rules over a period of time, although the link between the tripartite division and assemblies seems to suggest an explanation based on context rather than chronology. But the reason that
different types of division can coexist is that neither type of division is
central to the group's self-understanding. The crucial division for both
rules is between those in the sect and those outside it. Within the sect,
individuals are carefully ranked, but the rankings depend on merit, not
lineage.

Given their rather limited use of the category Levite, it is perhaps not
surprising that the rules offer Levites little to do. Their role in the
covenant ceremony of the *Rule of the Community* is their most significant
assignment. While four of the ten judges of the congregation in the *Damascus Document* are to come from "the tribe of Levi and Aaron" (CD 10.4-
5), the phrase probably designates priests, who are descended from both
Levi and Aaron, while Levites are descended from Levi alone. If both
Levites and priests were required, it would certainly have been possible to
say so more clearly. The *Rule of the Community*'s council of the community
(*'aṣat hayaḥad*) requires three priests and twelve "men," presumably nonpriests (1QS 8.1); Levites are not mentioned at all in this context. The
only certain role for a Levite in the *Damascus Document* is as substitute
priest: wherever ten members of the group are found, a priest learned in
the "Book of Hagi" is to serve as the group's authority; when no such
priest can be found, a Levite may be substituted (CD 13.2-4).

Some scholars have suggested that the sect, living on the margins of
Jewish society, at odds with the Jerusalem establishment, felt a special
kinship with the Levites because of the Levites' marginality within the
biblical schema.[23] But, as we have just seen, the rules provide little support for this claim. Indeed, such an understanding of the status of the
Levites requires a better historical imagination than a pious ancient Jew
was likely to have had. The Levites' precariously liminal situation, after
all, was decreed by the Torah. Further, although some scholars have

claimed to find examples of the elevation of the status of the Levites relative to the biblical text in the Dead Sea Scrolls, to my mind the only persuasive instances are those from the *Temple Scroll*.[24] But it is unlikely that they reflect sympathy for the biblical underdog. Rather, as Jacob Milgrom now argues, the innovations in the Levites' favor appear to reflect harmonizing exegesis of the Torah, not the pro-Levite *Tendenz* he originally saw in them.[25] It is also worth remembering that, as I noted in the previous chapter, the relationship of the *Temple Scroll* to the sect is not clear; some important voices have argued that it is at most proto-sectarian and perhaps even non-sectarian.

Jews and Gentiles

It is perhaps not surprising that the *Rule of the Community* has nothing to say about relations with gentiles since the members of its audience probably had few occasions to deal with them. Even if they had had such dealings, "gentile" is simply not a relevant category for them, because, as we have seen, gentiles are part of the larger category of children of darkness. Like the *Rule of the Community*, the *Damascus Document* focuses its antagonism on Jews outside the sect, as in the invective of the passage quoted above. When it considers gentiles, however, its treatment is not entirely negative. It prohibits selling them animals that they might sacrifice, grain and wine, or slaves (CD 12.8-11), but it also warns against killing them and stealing from them so as to prevent blasphemy (CD 12.6-8).[26]

These laws provide some context for understanding the fourth grouping, proselytes, into which the *Damascus Document* decrees that the members of the sect arrange themselves at their sessions, alongside priests, Levites, and Israelites. The only biblical precedent I know for such a fourfold division of the people of Israel is the account of Hezekiah's Passover in Chronicles, which mentions not only "the whole assembly of Judah, and the priests and the Levites, and the whole assembly that came out of Israel," but also "the sojourners [*gērîm*] who came out of the land of Israel and the sojourners [*gērîm*] who dwelt in Judah" (2 Chron 30:25). As we have seen, in the Bible the *gēr* is usually a non-Israelite who has come to live among the Israelites. As a concept of conversion emerges during the Second Temple period, the term *gēr* comes to be used of converts, proselytes. The picture in the *Damascus Document* of a group of *gērîm* parallel to priests, Levites, and children of Israel certainly points to an understanding of *gēr* as proselyte. The only other reference to the category in the *Damascus Document*, "to support the poor, destitute, and proselyte" (CD 6.21), is not decisive but also points in this direction.[27]

We have already seen that *Jubilees* rejects the possibility of conversion and thus the new understanding of the category of the *gēr*; similarly 4QFlorilegium prohibits the *gēr* along with a series of foreigners from entering its eschatological temple (4Q174 I 3-4). The presence of the *gēr* among the members of the sect shows that for the *Damascus Document*, in contrast, gentiles were not so essentially different from Jews that it was impossible to cross the boundary. Or, to put it differently, for the *Damascus Document*, just as most Jews walked in the stubbornness of their hearts and strayed from the path, so some gentiles overcame their heritage and found the path. On the other hand, the fact that proselytes are treated as a separate category is also significant; the *Damascus Document* apparently does not recognize proselytes as Jews just like any others. Indeed, taken together with the juxtaposition of the proselyte with the poor in that passage, the existence of the proselyte as a separate category in the assembly suggests that for the *Damascus Document*'s community, proselytes are a marginal group, like the poor and the biblical sojourner. It also shows that for the *Damascus Document*, unlike the *Rule of the Community*, the distinction between Jews and gentiles has not been completely displaced by the division between children of light and children of darkness.

Priests

I suggested above that the division that dominated the sectarians' consciousness was the division between the sect and the rest of the world, a division beside which all others pale. In the *Damascus Document*, the tension between this outlook and the ancient prestige of priests is largely ignored. As we have seen, the *Damascus Document* understands priests as figures of authority: four out of ten judges are to be priests, and whenever ten members of the group assemble there must be a learned priest present to serve as an authority. A priest learned in the Book of Hagi and the laws of the Torah is to preside over the assembly in which the people are seated as priests, Levites, Israelites, and proselytes (CD 14.6-8). But here too, as in the group of ten, heredity is not enough; the priest must also be learned. The laws of the *Damascus Document* disqualifying priests from serving in the temple if they have lived among the gentiles, either as captives or of their own free will (4Q266 5 ii and parallels), reflect a similar outlook. Although they are concerned with the temple rather than the life of the sect, their view of the high standards of purity to which priests must adhere indicates great respect for the office.[28]

Like the *Damascus Document*, the *Rule of the Community* requires that a priest preside whenever ten members of the group assemble (1QS 6.3-4).

There is no requirement that the priest be learned, but the members are to be arranged before him by rank; such a ranking implicitly undercuts hereditary claims such as that of the priest. Further, when ten members are assembled, one of them must always be engaged in studying the law (1QS 6.6). In contrast to the *Damascus Document*, the priest is not singled out; indeed the ten are to take turns studying.

Further, although the *Rule of the Community* often mentions priests in its definition of the sources of authority in the community, they always appear alongside the rest of the community. The rules of organization of the *Rule of the Community* contain several relevant passages. Twice the priests are referred to as sons of Aaron, twice as sons of Zadok:

They shall be answerable to the sons of Zadok, the priests who safeguard the covenant, and to the authority of the multitude of the men of the community who hold fast to the covenant. (1QS 5.2-3)

He shall undertake by a binding oath to return to the law of Moses . . . in accordance with all that has been revealed from it to the sons of Zadok, the priests who keep the covenant and seek his will, and to the multitude of the men of their covenant who together willingly offer themselves for his truth and to walk according to his will. (1QS 5.8-10)

They shall examine his spirit in common, distinguishing between one man and another, with respect to his insight and his deeds in regard to the law, under the authority of the sons of Aaron, who have willingly offered themselves in the community to establish his covenant and to pay attention to all his statutes which he has commanded men to perform, and under the authority of the multitude of Israel who have willingly offered themselves to return in the community to his covenant. (1QS 5.20-22)

If, on the advice of the priests and the multitude of men of their covenant, the decision is taken for him to draw near to the fellowship of the community, both his wealth and his property shall be handed to the overseer of the property of the many. (1QS 6.18-20)

The publication of the Cave 4 fragments of the *Rule of the Community* has raised some unexpected questions about the status of the sons of Zadok in these passages for they lack the references to the Zadokites of the first two passages quoted above. In the parallel passages in 4QS^b (4Q256) and 4QS^d (4Q258), authority belongs exclusively to the multitude (parallels to 1QS 5.2-3 in 4QS^b IX 3 and 4QS^d I 2) or to the council of the community (parallels to 1QS 5.9 in 4QS^b IX 8 and 4QS^d I 7). On paleographic grounds, the Cave 4 manuscripts of the *Rule of the Community* appear younger than the Cave 1 manuscript, but in the fullest discussion of the development of the *Rule* to date, Sarianna Metso has argued that the form of the rule in the Cave 4 fragments is older than the Cave 1 form.[29] Thus the references to the Zadokites were added at some point in the development of the rule. The Cave 4 fragments have not shed any new light on the two passages referring to the sons of

Aaron; no parallel to the passage from column 6 is preserved, and the parallel to 1QS 5.19-21 in 4QS^d II 1 includes them.

Almost from the moment of the discovery of the Dead Sea Scrolls, Zadokite priests have played a central role in discussions of the emergence of the sect and its development.[30] The dominant theories, despite differences of detail, understand the Teacher of Righteousness as a Zadokite priest alienated from the Jerusalem priestly establishment by the Hasmonean usurpation of the high priesthood, perhaps even as himself the legitimate claimant to the office of high priest.[31] Few adherents of these theories worried about the tension between the Zadokite ascendancy they perceived and the undermining of hereditary distinctions by the division of humanity into children of light and children of darkness. One who did was Daniel Schwartz, who attempted to resolve the tension by attributing the differences to historical development: the original members of the sect valued priestly ancestry, but as the sect failed to gain a wide following, its adherents became more and more alienated from other Jews and so came to understand the world as divided into two camps defined not by ancestry but by deeds.[32] If Metso is correct, however, Schwartz's reconstruction becomes untenable. The sect moved not from priestly embrace of lineage toward sectarian attention to quality of spirit, but rather from radically downplaying ancestry as a source of prestige toward a limited acceptance. Albert Baumgarten suggests that this direction of development may reflect the problems the community encountered in an early, egalitarian stage. One important aspect of the community's worldview is the belief that revelation is ongoing. In that early phase, in which all members could be seen as potential recipients of revelation, revelations would surely have multiplied, and with them, fissures within the community. As the difficulties of maintaining a community in the face of conflicting revelations became obvious, one faction of the original group, like other sects such as the Pauline communities and the Shakers, would have felt the need to bring the chaos under control. Placing considerable authority in the hands of members distinguished by the prestige of Zadokite ancestry would help to do so.[33]

What I would like to stress here, however, is that even in the Cave 1 version of the *Rule of the Community*, authority rests in the community as a whole, priests and Israel, not in the priests alone or even in the priests more than the rest of the community. The fact that the priests are singled out for mention is an acknowledgment of their status, but it is ultimately an acknowledgment without content. It is worth noting that in one passage in which 1QS assigns authority to the sons of Zadok and the many (1QS 5.9), the Cave 4 fragments grant authority to the council of the men of the *yaḥad*, *'ăṣat 'anšê hayaḥad* (4QS^b IX 8 and 4QS^d I 7). If the "council" here is a subgroup of the community, this is the only instance in which either version of the passages in which the Cave 1 text mentions the sons of Zadok grants authority to a portion of the community rather than to the community as a whole. That portion of the community, as we have already seen (1QS 8.1), consists of twelve laymen and three priests; here too, then, priestly ancestry is singled out for attention, but it is not a prerequisite for authority.[34]

The strongest attribution of authority to priests in the *Rule of the Community* refers not to Zadokites but to sons of Aaron: "Only the sons of Aaron shall rule in matters of justice [*mišpaṭ*] and wealth, and on their word the decision shall be taken with regard to every rule of the men of the community" (1QS 9.7, with parallel in 4QS[d] VII 7).[35] It is difficult to evaluate this claim since no procedural details follow, but it is perhaps relevant that the *Damascus Document* gives priests particular privileges in matters involving property. If a wronged party has no heirs, the priests are to receive the restitution due him, as Num 5:5-8 decrees, and the priests are to receive any ownerless lost property, "for the one who found it does not know its judgment [*mišpaṭ*]" (CD 9.13-15). The use of *mišpat* in *the Damascus Document* in relation to matters of property might suggest that the "matters of justice," or, perhaps better, judgment in the *Rule of the Community* (1QS 9.7) has to do with matters of property only. Yet even if this limitation applies, that passage in the *Rule of the Community* represents a very different point of view and perhaps a different source from the passages in columns 5 and 6 that attribute authority to the community as a whole. The *Rule of the Community* also grants priests the right to be first to bless food and wine at a communal meal (1QS 6.4-6), but these are ritual roles comparable to the recitation of priests and Levites in the covenant ceremony and not indications of authority.

While the *Rule of the Community*'s rhetoric is revealing of the values it embraces, it is certainly true that its grant of authority to the community reveals almost nothing about how decisions were actually made. It is worth noting that both the *Rule of the Community* and the *Damascus Document* mention several officials who lead the community.[36] The most prominent in both rules, or at least the one mentioned most frequently, is the *mĕbaqqēr*, the "examiner";[37] the relationship of this official to the *pāqîd*, the "officer," mentioned once in the *Rule of the Community*, is not clear. The *pāqîd* may well be a priest since the *Damascus Document* twice uses the verb from the same root for the priest who serves at the head of community (CD 14.6-7, 4Q267 9 v 11; 4Q266 11 8). In addition, the rules mention judges and the *maśkîl*, usually translated sage or master. But despite scholarly speculation, there is no clear indication in either rule that any of the other officials were priests, a silence that is surely significant at least in indicating a lack of emphasis.

Both the *Damascus Document* and the *Rule of the Community*, then, continue to use traditional biblical language to describe the sect. Sometimes they describe the sect as composed of priests, Levites, and Israelites, while at other times they omit the Levites and speak of the sect as Israel and Aaron. In both rules the influence of the biblical tradition seems to have preserved some of the traditional prestige of priests. Yet the roles set aside for priests in both rules are largely ornamental: a hierarchy based on ancestry is of limited relevance to a community in which members are ranked by their deeds. Still, it is important to emphasize that the diminished prestige of actual priests is by no means a rejection of the ideal of priesthood. The *Damascus Document*, for example, insists on the exclusion of men with physical blemishes from the community (CD 15.15-17), echoing the prohibitions on blemished priests.[38] There is, after all, more than one way to achieve a kingdom of priests. On the one hand, all members of the community become more priest-like, while on the other, priests become less different from others. The *Damascus Document*'s identification of the community with the sons of Zadok in its *pešer* on Ezek 44:15 is a fine example of how the process cuts both ways.

The Transformation of Biblical Language at Qumran

Important differences between the *Damascus Document* and the *Rule of the Community* are evident also in their development of the purity laws of the Torah. The legal section of the *Damascus Document*, as we have seen, contains a significant body of material devoted to the purity laws of Leviticus 12-15. In contrast to the *Damascus Document*, the *Rule of the Community* has nothing to say about the sources of impurity so important to the Torah. This silence is due, at least in part, to the character of the regulations found in the *Rule of the Community*. Unlike the *Damascus Document*, the *Rule of the Community* does not elaborate laws of the Torah. Rather, it delineates the special rules that govern the life of the community while, apparently, assuming the laws of the Torah. Since the *Rule of the Community* has nothing to say on a whole range of topics discussed by the Torah—laws of social life, laws of sacrifice, the festival calendar, to offer some examples—it would be a mistake to read any special significance into its lack of attention to purity laws. The members of the sect were surely expected to observe the laws of the Torah. Still, although it does not concern itself with purity laws, the *Rule of the Community* does use the language of purity, primarily in highly rhetorical passages that represent those outside the community as sinful and impure in contrast to those who join the community and are cleansed of their sin and impurity. The description of this cleansing draws on P's terminology of impurity and ritual purification, but deploys it in a very different way. Terms that in P refer to specific physical states and ritual equipment are applied in the *Rule of the Community* to spiritual states and processes. This lavish use of the technical terminology of purity stands in contrast to the virtual absence of biblical language typical of long stretches of the *Rule* such as the passage describing the struggle between good and evil in the cosmos quoted above. Yet the *Rule* uses the terminology of purity in a way that undermines the biblical meaning in the service of its quite different vision.[39]

The first extended passage to use the language of purity is the condemnation of one who refuses "to enter into the covenant," apparently after having shown interest in joining the community:

No one who refuses to enter [into the covenant of Go]d so that he may walk in the stubbornness of his heart [shall enter into the comm]unity of truth. . . . He shall not be made clean by atonement, or purified by waters for purification, or made holy by seas and rivers, or purified by any water for washing. Unclean, unclean shall he be as long as he rejects the precepts of God by refusing to discipline himself in the community of his counsel. For it is through a spirit of true counsel with regard to the ways of man that all his iniquities shall be wiped out so that he may look on the light of life. It is through a holy spirit uniting him to his truth that he shall be purified from all his iniquities. It is through a spirit of uprightness and humility that his sin shall be wiped out. And it is through the submission of his soul to all the statutes of God that his flesh shall be purified, by being sprinkled with waters for purification and made holy by waters for cleansing. (1QS 2.25, 3.4-9)

This passage draws liberally on P's language of purity: the root *ṭhr*, purify or become pure (1QS 3.4, 5, 7, 8); the technical term *mê niddâ*, waters of purification, the waters made from the ashes of the red heifer to be sprinkled on those suffering from corpse impurity (1QS 3.4, 9); and finally, "Unclean, unclean shall he be" (1QS 3.5), an allusion to Lev 13:45, which requires one suffering from skin eruptions to call out, "Unclean! Unclean!" to warn others to stay away from him. But the passage goes beyond P's language. It constructs terms that have no biblical parallels such as *mê raḥaṣ*, water for washing (1QS 3.5), and *mê dûkî*, waters for cleansing (1QS 3.9). It also uses biblical vocabulary in ways not found in the Torah: the root *qdš* (1QS 3.4, 9) is never used in the Torah with regard to purification by ablutions or sprinkling.[40] Only at the very end of the passage does the purification of the body come into view. Until then, the purification described is purification of the soul, a topic that P would have found quite incomprehensible. The *Rule of the Community* uses the language of purity in an almost poetic fashion to condemn those who have rejected the community in the strongest language it can.

A similar use of the language of purity appears in the *Rule*'s description of the eschatological purification of humanity:

> Then God will purify by his truth all the deeds of man and will refine for himself the frame of man, removing all spirit of injustice from within his flesh, and purifying him by the spirit of holiness from every wicked action. And he will sprinkle upon him the spirit of truth like waters for purification (to remove) all the abominations of falsehood (in which) he has defiled himself through the spirit of impurity. (1QS 4.20-22)

This passage blends the terminology of purity with a more abstract language: purification takes place by means of God's truth and the spirit of holiness. The verb "he will sprinkle," from the root *nzh*, used in the Torah to indicate sprinkling sacrificial blood (e.g., Lev 4:6, 17) as well as the waters of purification (Num 19:4, 18, 19), takes as its object not any liquid but "the spirit of truth," which, though it is compared to "waters of purification," is not a physical entity.

As we have seen, H also associates impurity with sin, but in a manner quite different from the *Rule of the Community*. H's view of sin as causing impurity appears clearly at the conclusion of the first set of laws of forbidden sexual relations:

> But you must keep My laws and My rules, and you must not do any of those abhorrent things . . . for all those abhorrent things were done by the people who were in the land before you, and the land became defiled. So let not the land spew you out for defiling it, as it spewed out the nation that came before you. (Lev 18:26-28)

Despite the rhetorical flourishes, the sins the passage refers to are those it has just detailed at some length: forbidden sexual relations (Lev 18:6-20) and idolatry (Lev 18:21). These are specific sins, quite different from the *Rule of the Community*'s spirit of injustice, abominations of falsehood, and spirit of impurity (1QS 4.20-22).

Further, while the Holiness Code uses P's language of impurity to exhort the people of Israel to stop certain sins from taking place, it never invokes language of purification. It decrees punishments for the sins that defile the land and the sinner (Leviticus 20; Num 35:30-31), but it is noteworthy that it does not use purity terminology to explain how the impurity of the land is removed (Lev 26:43; Num 35:33).[41] The *Rule of the Community*, on the other hand, prescribes modes of purification for the impurity caused by sin. Of course the means of purification are just as abstract as the sins from which they purify: "a spirit of true counsel" (1QS 3.6); "a holy spirit uniting him to his truth" (1QS 3.7); "a spirit of uprightness and humility" (1QS 3.8); "submission of his soul to all the statutes of God" (1QS 3.8); God's "truth" (1QS 4.20); "the spirit of holiness" (1QS 4.21); and "the spirit of truth" (1QS 4.21). The *Rule of the Community*, then, draws on both sides of P's language of purity, the language of defilement and the language of cleansing, but uses the language in a way considerably further removed from its concrete applications in P than does H, which draws only on the language of defilement.

A similarly metaphoric use of the language of P's technical terminology of purity is found in 4Q512, an extremely fragmentary text that contains blessings to be recited upon completion of purification.[42] But unlike the *Rule of the Community*, 4Q512 is concerned with actual states of ritual impurity together with the spiritual impurity that accompanies them. The difficulty of identifying the types of impurity to which individual blessings are connected is due not only to the text's poor state of preservation.[43] Rather, despite the poor preservation, it is clear that 4Q512 purposely blurs the distinctions among the various categories of impurity found in the Torah. The phrase *nega' niddâ* (4Q512 V 17, XII 16) provides a good example of 4Q512's slippery use of the terminology of impurity. The phrase combines a term that refers to skin eruptions (*nega'*) with the term for menstrual impurity (*niddâ*). Further, the second instance of the phrase appears in the context of holy ashes (4Q512 XII 3) and sprinkling (4Q512 XII 6), as well as water for washing (4Q512 XII 5); according to the biblical purity laws, the only type of impurity treated by sprinkling with water mixed with ashes is corpse impurity (Numbers 19). The fragmentary text of 4Q Tohorot B[b] (4Q277) 1 ii 7–10 appears to ordain both sprinkling and immersion for purification from corpse impurity and other types of impurity as well.[44] If this was standard practice at Qumran, there is then a halakhic dimension to the conflation of categories of impurity.[45] Still, it is clear that the thrust of the blessings in 4Q512 is not halakhic definition but the evocation of human imperfection. Phrases such as *'erwat běśārênû*, the shamefulness of our flesh (4Q512 III 17), and *'erwat niddâ*, the shamefulness of (menstrual) impurity (4Q512 VII 9), appear to point to impurity associated with the genitals: *bāśār* is used as a euphemism for the genitals in Leviticus 15 (2, 19), *'erwâ* in the sense of nakedness is used repeatedly in the list of forbidden sexual relations in Levitcus 18, and *niddâ* in its most limited sense refers to menstrual impurity. But Baumgarten points out that *'erwâ* and *bāśār* are used elsewhere at Qumran to indicate the inferiority of the corporeal aspect of human nature to the spiritual.[46] It is worth noting that despite the prominence of the term *niddâ* in 4Q512 the speaker in all of the liturgies is male.[47] For 4Q512, then, the significance of the various types of impurity carefully delineated by P is the same: all point to human frailty and failing.

Impurity and Sin and the Status of Law at Qumran

Jonathan Klawans has argued that passages like the ones from the *Rule of the Community* and 4Q512 considered here reflect the belief that sin in general causes impurity, a view that goes far beyond H's claim that idolatry, sexual sin, and murder defile the land. But, as Klawans himself notes, the *Rule of the Community* marks as impure not so much specific sins as "sinfulness in general."[48] This lack of specificity might suggest that the association of sin and impurity is not a halakhic claim, and the only halakhic implications Klawans can point to are the punishment of exclusion from the pure food and drink of the community prescribed for certain sins in the *Rule of the Community* (1QS 7.2-3, 15-16, 18-20; 8.16-18, 20-24).[49] Klawans does not spell out his argument, but it appears that he reads the *Rule of the Community* as treating the food of the community as equivalent to consecrated food.[50]

But I think there is reason to doubt that the *Rule of the Community* understood exclusion from the community's food in terms of the purity laws of the Torah. In the *Rule* the pure food is closely associated with membership in the community (1QS 8.16-19, 21-24).[51] Exclusion from the purity means exclusion from the community. But surely if the *Rule* was concerned with enforcing the purity rules of the Torah relevant to consecrated food, members of the community in good standing would also have been excluded from time to time on the basis of physical impurity, which would have been impossible to avoid entirely even in a community of celibate men. The *Rule of the Community* does not legislate at all for this eventuality.

Further, as Moshe Weinfeld has shown, the penal code of the *Rule of the Community* has close parallels in the rules of other Greco-Roman cult organizations and guilds.[52] These rules contain a number of instances of exclusion from the organization as punishment; sometimes the exclusion is temporary, sometimes permanent.[53] Exclusion from the pure food and drink of the community is probably best understood not as a measure related to purity concerns but as a way of enforcing exclusion from the community. The punishment is thus independent of concepts of purity, although no doubt the *Rule*'s view of outsiders as impure made it a particularly resonant punishment.

Klawans is certainly correct that the *Rule of the Community* and other sectarian texts such as 4Q512 reflect an understanding of purity and impurity that goes beyond anything to be found in the Torah. But the only practical implications I can see in the intimate relationship the sectarians found between sin and impurity is their fondness for baptism and bathing, ceremonies that operate on two levels to address both sin and impurity. The blessings of 4Q512 make frequent reference to water for sprinkling and bathing. Even in their very fragmentary state it is possible to see that some of the blessings give thanks not only for purification from impurity but also for forgiveness of sin:

[to] ask mercy for all the hidden guilty acts . . . you who are righteous in all your deeds . . . from the affliction of impurity [*nega' niddâ*]. (4Q512 V 15-17)

Blessed are you [God of Israel, who have saved me from al]l my sins and purified me from the indecency of impurity[54] [*'erwat niddâ*]. (4Q512 VII 8-9)

Still, it is important to note that in both passages, while impurity and sin stand side by side, they remain separate. The fragmentary phrase "[to serv]e you in the purity of righteousness" (4Q512 XIII[?] 4-5) is the closest 4Q512 comes to applying the language of impurity to sin or rather, the language of purity to righteousness, as in the *Rule of the Community*.[55] The passages quoted suggest rather that sin and impurity are understood as two aspects of human finitude, corresponding to soul and body. Bathing removes impurity, as Leviticus dictates; repentance, which is enacted by undertaking to bathe, atones for sin.

This view is quite similar to the understanding of the significance of baptism for new members of the community in the *Rule of the Community*. Joseph Baumgarten argues that the language of spiritual baptism in the passages cited above points to some sort of actual baptismal rite as part of the ritual for joining the Qumran community.[56] The clearest indication of such a practice in the *Rule of the Community* is a passage that appears in the instructions for new members of the community: "He shall not enter the waters in order to touch the purity of the men of holiness, for men are not purified unless they turn from their evil" (1QS 5.13-14). The passage is difficult. It fits poorly in its context,[57] and while the 4QS fragments contain some elements of this passage, they do not mention water at all (4QS[b] IX 8-9, 4QS[d] I 7-8). Still, the point seems clear. Since "purification" has come to mean more than removal of ritual impurity, baptism does not "purify" people who have not repented; thus those who have not repented should not be permitted the rite of baptism, which entitles them to partake of the community's food, which represents full membership in the community. This double meaning of bathing applies both to initiatory baptism and bathing as an ongoing practice. Further, it hardly needs to be pointed out that the use of bathing to mark repentance is by no means restricted to Qumran. John the Baptist and his followers and the other groups of baptizers alluded to in ancient sources made the same connection.[58]

I argued in the previous chapter that the intensification of the purity laws in the *Damascus Document* and the *Temple Scroll* served to make ordinary Jews more like priests by making those rules more relevant to their lives. The *Rule of the Community*, on the other hand, has nothing to say about the physical states that P designates as impure, although it surely assumes the observance of these laws, at least in as much as they are relevant to an all-male, celibate community. Rather, the *Rule*'s transformation of P's purity terminology might be said to work in the opposite direction from the *Damascus Document* and the *Temple Scroll*'s intensification of purity laws. It bridges the gap between priests and others by implying that the true significance of purity laws lies not in the physical realm, but in the spiritual, in metaphors for sin and repentance. In this realm there is no difference between priests and others.

An earlier generation of Christian scholars claimed that hellenistic Jews found the demands of the law deeply problematic; the solution to the problem was of course Christianity. More recently Daniel Schwartz has suggested that the sectarians at Qumran also found the law problematic, for not unrelated reasons. Schwartz acknowledges that some sectarian works such as the *Damascus Document* wholeheartedly embrace halakhah as the way to achieve holiness, but he argues that for other sectarian texts such as the *Rule of the Community* and the *Hodayot*, the laws of the Torah presented a problem not dissimilar to the problem Paul identified and solved after his own fashion.[59] Schwartz identifies several factors that contributed to the ambivalent attitude toward the Torah of these sectarian texts. One was the sect's belief that revelation was ongoing and thus that the revelation of the Torah was not final.[60] Another was the sect's alienation from the Jerusalem temple, which led it to seek substitutes for the rituals of the temple in its own life, such as prayer to replace sacrifice.[61] The most relevant for the passages from the *Rule of the Community* discussed above is the sectarians' distress about their sense of falling short in the observance of God's laws. Their pessimism about human nature led them to conclude that human beings are incapable of doing right without divine aid. But what is the value of the commandments if success in fulfilling them is entirely in God's hands? [62]

Schwartz explicitly compares the sectarians' attitude toward the Torah to Paul's, but he parts company from Christian scholarship by hinting that Christianity was not the only solution to the problem facing Paul and the sectarians: rabbinic Judaism, too, constitutes a solution.[63] For the rabbis, the laws of the Torah do not point to a truth beyond themselves; they are the end in themselves. Further, the rabbis were more optimistic than the sect about the possibility of fulfilling the law, for God the creator had surely taken account of the frailty of his creatures in his Torah.[64]

Schwartz's argument is both provocative and problematic. Let me begin by noting that one could represent Pauline Christianity quite differently from the way Schwartz does. It has been more than forty years since Krister Stendahl argued that the traditional view that Paul rejected the law out of despair at the impossibility of keeping it told us more about Luther than about Paul.[65] More recently, an influential body of scholarship has suggested that Paul's objections to the law pertained only to its observance by gentiles, not by Jews.[66] So too Schwartz's characterization of rabbinic Judaism is open to objection. No doubt there are strands of rabbinic thought that hold the view that the laws of the Torah are an end in themselves, but it is by no means clear that this view is dominant, and its presence is certainly more prominent in some layers of rabbinic literature than others.[67] Still, Schwartz is surely correct that some sectarian texts reflect the belief that observance of the laws of the Torah is not in itself sufficient for piety or salvation. Indeed such an attitude appears to lie behind the use of the language of ritual purity for spiritual states discussed above.

But does the tension between commitment to the laws of the Torah and a sense that those laws are somehow inadequate necessarily make a system unstable? In my view, Schwartz underestimates the ability of religious systems to maintain positions that from a certain angle of vision may be incompatible. In the particular case of the Qumran sectarians and in many other cases as well, the authoritative texts of the community reflect different and even divergent points of view. Not only the sectarians, but other pious Jews throughout the ages, could be moved by the evocative personal language of sin and redemption of many of the psalms without any desire to abandon the laws of the Torah. (So too, as I suggested in chapter 1, the failure of the *Book of the Watchers* to mention Moses and his covenant reflects not rejection or lack of interest in the Torah but rather the specific concerns of the work.)

Despite the powerful catalyst of intense eschatological expectation, the evidence from Qumran shows that the sectarians were able to maintain their ambivalent attitude toward the Torah and its laws through several generations. It was not the inherent instability of their system of thought that brought an end to the sectarian community, as far as we can tell, but rather the devastation caused by the revolt against Rome and the new situation caused by the destruction of the temple.

Priests in the Book of Revelation

Finally, I would like to turn to a Jewish sectarian work that, rather than de-emphasizing the role of priests in the new order, understands all of the righteous as priests. The work in question is the Book of Revelation, and the sect is, of course, the followers of Jesus.[68] John announces the new understanding of priesthood and its importance for him at the beginning of the book in his address to Jesus Christ as "him who loves us and has freed us from our sins by his blood and has made us a kingdom, priests to his God and Father" (Rev 1:5-6); the priesthood of the saved is a recurring theme of the book.[69]

The claim that the Book of Revelation should be read as a Jewish work perhaps requires some defense. Here I am particularly indebted to John Marshall, who has argued persuasively that it is anachronistic to apply the label "Christian" to Revelation.[70] The category Christian hardly existed in John's day, and "Israel" and "Jews" are clearly positive categories in Revelation. Some recent scholarship has rightly insisted that the letters of Paul constitute evidence for Judaism in the first century. But if Paul counts as evidence for Judaism, all the more should the Book of Revelation.

Unlike Paul, who discouraged his converts from observing the laws of the Torah, John criticizes followers of Jesus who are insufficiently loyal to those laws. The Book of Revelation begins with "letters" to the seven churches in Asia Minor accusing them of various failings. David Frankfurter has recently argued that the specifics of the accusations suggest that they are directed at followers of Paul.[71] The letters to the churches of Pegamum and Thyatira condemn members of those communities for committing harlotry[72] and eating food sacrificed to idols (Rev 2:14, 20). As Frankfurter admits, it is difficult to determine the specific sins characterized as "committing harlotry," a term that evokes the biblical association of idolatry and sexual sin. But the charge of eating food sacrificed to idols is more pointed. It is hard not to think of Paul's advice to the Corinthians:

If one of the unbelievers invites you to dinner and you are disposed to go, eat whatever is set before you without raising any question on the ground of conscience. (But if some one says to you, "This has been offered in sacrifice," then out of consideration for the man who informed you, and for conscience' sake—I mean his conscience, and not yours—do not eat it.) (1 Cor 10:27-29)

Either the churches at Pergamum and Thyatira were unwilling to make the concession to John's conscience that Paul encourages, or it was not enough for John. In any case, Paul's own words make it clear that his position aroused opposition.

Frankfurter also proposes to understand the groups in Smyrna (Rev 2:9) and Philadelphia (Rev 3:9) that John denounces as "synagogues of Satan" in light of Paul's teachings. The standard view has been that those who "say they are Jews but are not" are ethnic Jews who reject Christ, a reading that, as Marshall points out, reverses a straightforward reading of John's words.[73] Frankfurter suggests rather that those who "say they are Jews but are not" are gentile followers of Jesus. While they remain uncircumcised, they view themselves, following Paul, as circumcised in the heart, Jews inwardly if not outwardly (Rom 2:27-28). From John's point of view, however, they are gentiles who claim for themselves the honorable title "Jew" without having any right to it.[74] The attack on those who "say they are Jews but are not" could well be John's entry into the debate about whether circumcision was required of gentile followers of Jesus, a subject of controversy in the Galatian community Paul addresses (Gal 5:2-12).[75]

Frankfurter also suggests that John's concern for purity is an indication of his commitment to Jewish practices.[76] The insistence that the new Jerusalem be kept free of all sources of impurity (Rev 21:27) is noteworthy. While on the one hand John claims that the city needs no temple because God and the Lamb are to be available without mediation, the explicit retention of purity rules suggests that in another sense the temple has not been eliminated but expanded to include the whole of the city. So too in the *Temple Scroll* purity laws apply to the whole "city of the sanctuary."

Altogether, it is clear that John continued to embrace many aspects of Jewish practice. There is no positive evidence that he rejected any aspect. Indeed, John addresses his readers as "those who keep the commandments of God and the faith of Jesus" (Rev 14:12). He calls the people against whom the dragon makes war, "those who keep the commandments and bear testimony to Jesus" (Rev 12:17). Most commentators assume that John means only that his audience observes some portion of the commandments of the Torah, such as the ethical commandments. But, as Marshall points out, this assumption is based not on any internal evidence but on a preexisting view of which commandments a Christian should be expected to keep.[77]

Finally, Marshall argues that if we start from the assumption that John values Jewish practice, the lack of explicit reference to certain Jewish practices in Revelation reads quite differently. One example he points to is John's silence on the Sabbath, an observance that many commentators have suggested John rejected. Yet no reader can fail to note that the Book of Revelation is full of the number seven. In light of John's attitude toward other aspects of Jewish practice, it may well be that the lack of explicit reference to Sabbath observance means not that John rejected it but that he took it for granted.[78]

Jews and Gentiles, Holy Ones and Damned

Yet to call Revelation a Jewish work is not to question that the place of gentiles in the scheme of salvation was a central concern for John as it was for Paul and others in the Jesus movement. When the Qumran community replaced the biblical division between Israel and the nations with the division between children of light and children of darkness, the new division left gentiles as a group outside. The sectarians alone were children of light, while most Jews together with all gentiles were children of darkness. John also superimposes on the biblical division between Israel and the nations a division between the saved and the damned, in his terms, the "holy ones"[79] and everyone else, or, as he sometimes puts it, those whose names are written in the book of life of the Lamb and those whose names are not (Rev 13:8; 21:27). Further, just as the *Rule of the Community* claims that the division between children of light and children of darkness goes back to the beginning of time, John places the writing of names in the book "before the foundation of the world" (Rev 13:8).

John shares the Qumran sectarians' view of their fellow Jews: only a minority is counted among the holy ones, the 144,000 Israelites sealed by the angel (Rev 7:3).[80] Here I part company from Marshall. Marshall points out that the change in status of those gentiles whom the Lamb ransoms and makes holy ones is a central theme of the Book of Revelation, but there is no indication that any Jews undergo a corresponding change in status from inclusion among the holy ones to condemnation.[81] In the standard reading, of course, the 144,000 are not Jews at all but Christians, and the synagogues of Satan are Jews condemned for their opposition to Christians. But if we accept Marshall's view that when John says Jews, he means Jews, the picture is quite different; there is no reference to condemned Israelites in Revelation. Marshall argues that for John the salvation of Jews is never at issue: there is no indication in his book that John saw himself in opposition to Jews who were not followers of Jesus; his anger is directed at followers of Jesus who are insufficiently punctilious about Jewish practices and insufficiently zealous in their rejection of the evil empire under whose rule they found themselves.

Yet is it possible that John believed that the names of all Jews were written "in the book of life of the Lamb" (Rev 13:8)? If so, it would certainly require that most of the Jewish names written in the book belonged to Jews who did not share John's allegiance to the Lamb. To me this seems unlikely. It is worth noting that while the seal used on the foreheads of the 144,000 is first referred to as the "seal of the living God" (Rev 7:2), we later find that the foreheads are inscribed with the name of the Lamb and his father (Rev 14:1). It is also worth remembering that in the passage from Ezekiel that provides the model for the sealing of the 144,000, the angel is to mark the foreheads "of the men who sigh and groan over the abominations that are committed in [Jerusalem]" (Ezek 9:4). Clearly these men constitute only a minority of the inhabitants of Jerusalem.

Marshall's view that John included all Israel among the holy ones seems to me an overcompensation for the standard reading of Revelation in which almost all Israel belongs among the damned. John's sectarian view of humanity makes such an inclusive view of the saved highly unlikely. Marshall is surely correct that the opponents John addresses in the letters at the beginning of the book are followers of Jesus insufficiently committed to Jewish practice. The fact that John has nothing to say about Jews who are not followers of the Lamb may reflect not acceptance but a lack of interest in them. Jews who do not recognize Jesus as Christ are simply not relevant to John; they did not show up at the gatherings he attended, nor did they pay much attention to him.[82] Marshall is surely correct that for John the name "Israel" is always a positive one. But the same is true at Qumran. The sectarian approach, whether at Qumran or Patmos, is not to reject the name Israel but to limit membership in it.

But there is a crucial difference between John and the Qumran sectarians. Gentiles do not seem to have been very much on the minds of the Qumran sectarians, who had little contact with them. But the fate of gentiles, as I have already noted, was an important concern of the early Jesus movement, and gentiles appear to have made up a significant number of the followers of Jesus in Asia Minor. Perhaps for this reason John follows the sectarian logic of merit over ancestry farther than did the Qumran sectarians: a central task of the Lamb is to redeem gentiles with his blood (Rev 5:9-10). The gentiles ransomed by the Lamb stand in contrast to the rest of the gentiles, who are condemned for their allegiance to the beast (e.g., Rev 13:7-8, 17:15). Perhaps it is unnecessary to note, given John's sectarian outlook, that only a minority of gentiles are thus promoted to salvation.

Unfortunately for us, John never lays out explicitly what he expected of gentile followers of Jesus. But on the basis of what John criticizes and what he praises, it seems to me that John must have believed that for a gentile part of becoming a follower of Jesus was becoming a Jew. While there was not yet an agreed-upon ritual for conversion to Judaism, it seems likely that John would have expected a gentile embracing Judaism (or Jesus) to undergo circumcision and to observe the laws of the Torah such as the dietary laws and purity laws.

A Kingdom and Priests

Above I suggested that the *Rule of the Community* resolved the tension between the meritocratic criteria for membership in the sect and the ancestral right to Israelite priesthood in favor of merit: whatever prestige priests retain in the *Rule*, their role is almost entirely ornamental. The Book of Revelation faced the same problem, but resolved it quite differently. Unlike the *Rule of the Community*, which does not entirely divest itself of priests, as its logic would require, John carried his solution through to its logical conclusion. For Revelation, merit completely trumps ancestry, so that all of the righteous, Jews and gentiles alike, are understood as priests. The two solutions are not, however, truly opposites as they may at first glance appear to be. A community in which everyone is a priest is really not very different from a community in which there are no priests.

As I noted above, John introduces the idea that the saved are priests at the very beginning of the book (Rev 1:6). The inclusion of gentiles in John's priesthood is announced in the first vision of the Lamb in the heavenly temple (Revelation 5). There the living creatures and the elders praise the Lamb for ransoming gentiles with his blood and making them "a kingdom and priests to our God" (Rev 5:10), a phrase that echoes Rev 1:6 (with the addition of the conjunction "and") and, more distantly, Exod 19:6. The praise is realized in the vision John sees after the sealing of the 144,000 Israelites, "a great multitude which no man could number, from every nation, from all tribes and peoples and tongues," dressed in white robes, acclaiming God and the Lamb (Rev 7:9-10); they stand "before the throne of God/and serve him day and night within his temple" (Rev 7:15). The 144,000 righteous Israelites sealed by the angel (Rev 7:2-8) also act as priests, for later John sees them standing with the Lamb on Mt. Zion, singing a song that only they could learn (Rev 14:1-5), a liturgical function. The 144,000, we learned earlier, consist of 12,000 from each tribe of Israel (Rev 7:5-8). Thus a twelfth of them can claim Levitical descent and only a smaller portion, Aaronide descent. So John's Israelite priests too transcend the traditional definition of priesthood.

Furthermore, John's priests must include women since some of the holy ones in the communities John knew were surely women. Yet the 144,000 are explicitly described as male for they "have not defiled themselves with women" (Rev 14:4), while the gender composition of the great multitude is never specified. As their number indicates, the 144,000 are intended as symbolic of the true Israel.[83] The presence among them of members of the long-vanished tribes of the northern kingdom makes this conclusion unavoidable. The identification of the 144,000 as male works to obscure the fact that John's picture implies women as priests in the heavenly temple. Apparently the idea of women as priests was more shocking than the idea of Jews without Levitical descent or even gentiles in that role.

While the passages just considered distinguish between Jewish priests and gentile priests, John twice represents martyrs as priests without differentiating between Jews and gentiles. Before the pouring out of the seven plagues, John sees "those who had conquered the beast" standing with harps before God's throne and singing (Rev 15:2-4); their identification as priests is not explicit, but it is nonetheless clear. Later, the martyrs who reign with Christ for a thousand years at the end are called "priests of God and of Christ" (Rev 20:4-6). It is as if having established that holy ones of both Jewish and gentile origin can be priests in the heavenly temple, John can finally treat the two groups as a single body. It is also worth noting that, as elsewhere in apocalyptic literature, priesthood and angelic status are closely related.[84] John depicts the holy ones joining in the praise offered by the personnel of the heavenly temple, the clearly angelic holy creatures, the cherubim of Ezekiel's vision, and the twenty-four elders, who also appear to be heavenly beings. John himself is assured by his angelic interlocutor that he is his "fellow servant" (Rev 22:9).

John's picture of a gentile priesthood finds an antecedent in the prophecy in the last chapter of the Book of Isaiah. As the beginning of the book looks forward to a day when all nations will recognize the Lord and come to Jerusalem for his teaching (Isa 2:2-3), thus making Israel's way the way of all nations, so the last chapter of the book prophesies that at the end of days God will take priests and Levites from among the nations (Isa 66:21), allowing all nations a place on the highest rung of the Israelite hierarchy.[85] John frequently draws on the last chapters of Isaiah, and surely he would not have failed to notice this striking passage. But John's picture of gentile priests differs from 3 Isaiah's picture in a very important way. The prophet imagines God choosing a portion of the gentiles to serve as priests just as he had once chosen a portion of the Israelites. For John all of the redeemed gentiles are priests—just as all of the redeemed Jews are.

The attitude toward the temple in the Book of Revelation fits well with the attitude toward priests. It is clear that Revelation, like many Jewish apocalyptic texts, understands heaven as a temple.[86] As we saw for the *Book of the Watchers*, interest in the heavenly temple can be an indication of discontent with the state of affairs in the earthly temple, but it is surely also an indication of respect for the ideal of the temple.[87] Although the new Jerusalem that descends from heaven at the end of the Book of Revelation (Rev 21:2) contains no temple, John's description of the city makes it clear that the ideal of the temple has not been rejected. John tells us that the eschatological city no longer needs a temple, for "Its temple is the Lord God the Almighty and the Lamb" (Rev 21:22). But despite the availability of the presence of God and the Lamb, John's angelic interlocutor measures the new Jerusalem (Rev 21:15-21), just as Ezekiel's angelic guide measured the dimensions of the eschatological temple in the concluding vision of that book (Ezekiel 40-42). In other words, from one point of view the entire city of Jerusalem has become a temple. Further, as I noted above, John insists that purity laws apply to this city without a temple just as they once applied in the temple (Rev 21:27). Here, as in his treatment of priesthood, in which all the holy ones are priests, John transforms the temple by expanding its limits rather than by eliminating it.

The tension between ancestry and merit for the definition of the people of Israel was deeply troubling for the sectarian Jews considered in this chapter. The *Damascus Document* saw the sect as the true Israel, the Israel defined by merit, but it remained loyal to the thought and language of texts with a more inclusive view of an Israel defined by birth. The *Rule of the Community* and the Book of Revelation, on the other hand, found the tension intolerable and decided in favor of merit. The logic of the *Rule of the Community*'s division of humanity into children of light and children of darkness dictates that a hierarchy based on ancestry has no place among the children of light, whose status is determined by merit alone. The rejection of such a hierarchy of course has negative implications for the Jewish priesthood. Yet like the more moderate *Damascus Document*, the *Rule of the Community* fails to follow through on its program. Priests retain a place, if only an ornamental one, and their importance appears to increase from the earlier version of the *Rule* (4QS) to the later version (1QS). Further, while in the *Rule of the Community* the division between children of light and children of darkness has superceded the division between Israel and the nations, a significant aspect of the old division is preserved because the *Rule* cannot imagine gentiles as children of light. The Book of Revelation is more consistent in its application of the principle of merit over ancestry. John's holy ones are drawn not only from Israel but also from the nations. And since all of them are worthy, John does not de-emphasize the importance of priesthood as the *Rule of the Community* does but makes them all priests, a priesthood defined by merit.

Chapter 5

Priesthood and Allegory
Philo and Alexandrian Judaism

With the exception of John of Patmos, the authors of the texts I have considered so far lived in the land of Israel and wrote in Hebrew or Aramaic. The temple stood in easy reach, and its cult was familiar. In this chapter I turn to Philo of Alexandria, the great philosophical exegete of the Torah. Alexandria was one of the cultural centers of the Greco-Roman world, and like its other residents, Philo spoke and wrote Greek.

Alexandria at the turn of the era was home to a well-established Jewish population of considerable size, and Philo came from one of its leading families. Philo's brother Alexander was the one of the wealthiest men of the age;[1] Alexander's son Tiberius Julius Alexander became a high Roman official and is reported to have abandoned Judaism.[2] Philo's writings leave no doubt that he received an excellent Greek education. His interpretation of the Torah reflects his conviction that the Torah teaches the same truths as Plato, though he would have put it the other way, that Plato teaches the same truths as Moses.

Philo probably did not know Hebrew and Aramaic, and thus he could not have read most of the works considered in previous chapters.[3] Like the authors of those works, however, Philo worried about the meaning of priesthood and the tension between ancestry and merit in constituting the Jews as a holy people. It is possible that Philo came from a priestly family,[4] and although Jerusalem was far away, he visited the temple at least once (*On Providence* 2.64). Yet I think the key to understanding why Philo was interested in these issues lies not in his ancestry, if indeed it was priestly, but in the Torah itself. For these questions are relevant not only to Jews living in proximity to the temple for whom the special role of priests was an everyday reality, but to any Jew who reflected on the problems inherent in the Torah's picture of the holiness of the people of Israel and its provision for a priestly caste. Acceptance of the authority of the Torah, then, is the element common to Philo's writings and the texts considered in previous chapters.

Philo himself insisted that there was no tension between the Torah and philosophy; indeed, their messages were the same. Yet Jews with an education like Philo's would have known the judgment of many philosophically inclined men of Greek culture that while Jewish monotheism was admirable, indeed philosophical, the ritual laws of the Jews deserved no such praise.[5] Philo's older contemporary Strabo, for example, praises Moses and his followers for their piety and righteousness; later, however, Moses' successors introduced superstitious practices such as the dietary laws and circumcision.[6] It is thus not surprising that some members of the Alexandrian Jewish community were inclined to treat the ritual laws as symbolic. The point was to grasp the truths the laws impart, not to observe them. We learn of such Jews from Philo, who complains about their behavior in the course of one of his allegorical commentaries:

It is quite true that the Seventh Day is meant to teach the power of the Unoriginate and the non-action of created beings. But let us not for this reason abrogate the laws laid down for its observance, and light fires or till the ground or carry loads or institute proceedings in court. . . . It is true also that the Feast is a symbol of gladness of soul and of thankfulness to God, but we should not for this reason turn our backs on the general gatherings of the year's seasons. It is true that receiving circumcision does indeed portray the excision of pleasure and all passions, and the putting away of the impious conceit, under which the mind supposed that it was capable of begetting on its own power: but let us not on this account repeal the law laid down for circumcising. Why, we shall be ignoring the sanctity of the Temple and a thousand other things, if we are going to pay heed to nothing except what is shewn us by the inner meaning of things. Nay, we should look on all these outward observances as resembling the body, and their inner meanings as resembling the soul. It follows that, exactly as we have to take thought for the body, because it is the abode of the soul, so we must pay heed to the letter of the laws. If we keep and observe these, we shall gain a clearer conception of those things of which these are the symbols; and besides that we shall not incur the censure of the many and the charges they are sure to bring against us. (*On the Migration of Abraham* 91–93)[7]

Philo singles out the sanctity of the temple for mention among the "thousands" of things those who care only for the symbolic meaning of the laws might ignore, suggesting that the temple and its cult belonged among the laws that his enlightened friends preferred to understand rather than observe. Against them, Philo insists that the laws of the Torah must be observed as well as understood. But as a thoroughgoing Platonist, he cannot help admitting through his analogy of body and soul that the inner meaning of the laws ranks above the outward observance. For in Philo's view there could be no doubt that the immortal soul is of greater importance than the mortal body. Thus Philo might have been expected to treat the temple and its cult as something to make the best of, to ignore as much as possible, and to allegorize when ignoring was out of the question. Yet, although his position may not be entirely consistent with other aspects of his philosophical outlook,[8] we shall see that Philo's embrace of the temple and its cult is anything but grudging.

In the passage quoted above Philo writes that observance of the laws not only provides a clearer understanding of their inner meaning, but also allows one to avoid "the censure of the many." In other words, one reason for Philo's embrace of the bodies of the laws as well as their souls is his loyalty to the Jewish community and his desire to adhere to its norms. Philo wrote at a time of significant tension between the Jews of Alexandria and their neighbors. The beginning of Roman rule in 30 B.C.E. made the status of the Jews in Alexandria a subject of debate and cause for antagonism. Many Alexandrians opposed Jewish efforts to persuade the Romans to treat them as citizens of Alexandria and thus to allow them to enjoy the privileges the Romans reserved for citizens of Greek cities.[9] In 38 C.E. a mob desecrated synagogues, sacked Jewish homes and businesses, and attacked and killed Jews. Philo not only provided us with his view of this outburst (*Against Flaccus*) but also played an important role in the Jewish response to it, serving as leader of the delegation to Rome that sought to make the community's case to the unsympathetic emperor Gaius against the competing claims of a delegation representing the leadership of the Alexandrian anti-Semites (*On the Embassy to Gaius*). Philo's delegation was still in Rome awaiting a decision from Gaius when the emperor was assassinated in 41. With the death of Gaius, some Alexandrian Jews attempted to take revenge on their enemies, and the turmoil that followed led to the arrival in Rome of another Jewish delegation, this one apparently less moderate in its views. When Claudius finally issued a decree intended to resolve the problems caused by Roman policy, he reaffirmed the Jews' right to observe their ancestral laws, but he definitively denied them Alexandrian citizenship.[10]

Philo must have been deeply disappointed over the failure to recognize the rights his delegation had claimed though no account of his reaction has come down to us. Yet while some of the Alexandrian Jewish elite would have found the Roman rejection of their self-image as true Greeks unsettling, Philo surely remained secure in his belief that the Torah was the most philosophical of books and that a pious Jew was thus the truest Greek.

To some Jews in Alexandria the presence of the temple and its cult at the center of Judaism, though not at the center of their own religious life in Egypt, might have seemed to provide common ground with their neighbors, who also frequented temples and offered sacrifices to the gods. With his Greek education, however, Philo was well aware that philosophers tended to view this mode of worshiping the gods with skepticism.[11] There are certain points of contact between the philosophical critique and Jewish texts from the Bible and later works that insist on the impossibility of human beings providing for the needs of a transcendent God and on the primacy of morality. But unlike the Jewish sources, the philosophical critique points toward abolition of the cult. Philo clearly shares aspects of the views of the philosophers. Yet as a Jew Philo is committed to the sanctity of the Jerusalem temple and its cult, and his reading of the Torah works to justify their existence.

Philo's most elaborately allegorical treatises are devoted not to the legal portions of the Torah in which the cult is a central concern but to passages from the narrative of Genesis in which, according to the biblical story line, the cult had not yet been institutionalized nor a special priestly caste designated. Most of the passages from elsewhere in the Torah that Philo draws into his discussion in these treatises are also narrative; few are legal. The limited amount of narrative in the Torah about priests and cult may explain one of the peculiarities of Philo's treatment of the subject in the allegorical works: he has far more to say about the high priest and the Levites, to whom, at least in these works, he attributes priestly status,[12] than about ordinary priests. But unlike ordinary priests, both Aaron, the first high priest, and the Levites play a significant role in the narrative of the Torah.[13] Nowhere does Philo lay out systematically the allegorical interpretation of the cult on which his discussion of particular passages depends. The account that follows here is pieced together from several passages.[14]

Philo tells us explicitly that his allegorical interpretation of the cult has two interrelated aspects, one macrocosmic, the other microcosmic:

For there are . . . two temples of God: one of them this universe, in which there is also as High Priest His First-born, the divine Word, and the other the rational soul, whose Priest is the real Man; the outward and visible image of whom is he who offers the prayers and sacrifices handed down from our fathers. (*On Dreams* 1.215)

In the macrocosmic reading, the temple is the universe, and the high priest is the logos ("Word" in the translation quoted above) that orders the universe.[15] The elaborate robe Exodus ordains for the high priest points to the variegated elements of the cosmos,[16] just as do the rich materials used in the building of the tabernacle.[17] In the microcosmic reading, the temple is the soul, and the high priest, the "real Man" of the passage quoted above, is the logos that orders the soul, the counterpart to the logos that orders the cosmos. This logos appears, for example, in Philo's allegorical interpretation of the cities of refuge. There Philo takes the high priest whose death permits one who has committed manslaughter to return to his home as a symbol of the logos of the soul, whose absence permits unintentional sin to return to the soul (*On Flight and Finding* 116–18).[18]

The two allegorical possibilities are closely linked, and Philo moves easily from one logos to the other. Thus, for example, he follows an interpretation of the extremities of garments of the high priest as cosmic logos, in which the signet on the high priest's head (Exod 28:32) signifies the intellectual principle by which God created the universe, while the flower patterns and bells at the bottom of the garment (Exod 28:29-30) signify qualities that the senses can perceive, with an interpretation of the sound of the bells (Exod 28:31) that takes the high priest to be the soul (*On the Migration of Abraham* 102–4).

But what of the cult itself in Philo's allegorical interpretation? The strand of interpretation that takes the temple as cosmos does not have much to say about sacrifice. The passage about the two temples quoted above (*On Dreams* 1.215) goes on to suggest that the high priest's garments with their cosmic symbolism allow the universe to participate with humanity in the temple ritual. The cosmic correlate of earthly sacrifice, however, is not specified, and it appears that Philo was simply not interested in working out that aspect of the cosmic allegory. Thus his interpretation of the pillar Jacob set up at Bethel as a symbol of dedicating notes that the entire cosmos is an offering dedicated to God (*On Dreams* 1.242-43), a symbolism that would be most suitable for the cosmic allegory, but to the best of my knowledge Philo never makes the connection.

The meaning of sacrifice is much clearer in the allegory of the soul. One striking example is Philo's interpretation of the Torah's rules for the cereal offering:

When any one brings a cereal offering as an offering to the Lord, his offering shall be of fine flour; he shall pour oil upon it, and put frankincense on it, and bring it to Aaron's sons the priests. And he shall take from it a handful of the fine flour and oil, with all of its frankincense; and the priest shall burn this as its memorial portion upon the altar. . . . (Lev 2:1-2)

The interpretation runs as follows:

What then is the offering of an unembodied soul? What but the fine flour, the symbol of a will, purified by the councils of instruction, fit to produce nourishment that gives no sickness and life that knows no guilt. From such a sacrifice is the priest bidden to take his handful, take it with his whole hand, that is with all the grips of the mind, to offer the best of sacrifices, even the whole soul, brimful of truths of all sincerity and purity—a soul, too, rich with fatness, gladdened by light divine and perfumed with the breaths exhaled from justice and the other virtues, thus fitted to enjoy for ever a life of all fragrance and sweetness. For this is signified by the oil and the frankincense with which the priest fills his hand as well as with the wheaten flour. (*On Dreams* 2.73-74)[19]

This understanding of the sacrifice of the soul-priest as the soul itself is by no means isolated but appears in a number of other passages. Sometimes the sacrifice is virtues or aspects of the soul, and sometimes the whole soul.[20]

Philo's understanding of the true cult as spiritual is hardly surprising in light of his philosophical views. What is noteworthy is the high value Philo places on the actual practice of sacrifice.[21] This value emerges most clearly in *On the Special Laws*, where Philo offers a systematic discussion of the laws related to the cult in the course of his discussion of all the laws of the Torah. Philo's allegory of the temple as cosmos prepares us for the cosmic significance he finds in the Jerusalem cult (*Spec. Laws* 1.97), an understanding he shares with the priestly source of the Torah, as Valentin Nikiprowetzky points out.[22] Yet, as Nikiprowetzky also notes, the fact of Philo's commitment to the cult is of a piece with his treatment of other laws of the Torah. For while Philo's allegorical interpretations of narrative portions of the Torah sometimes suggest the elimination of the literal meaning and certainly its subordination to the allegorical meaning, his allegorical treatment of the legal portions of the Torah never does so.[23] Indeed, as I noted above, Philo is famously critical of those who draw what would appear to be the logical conclusion of the platonizing view of the Torah to which he subscribes and, having understood the spirit of the laws, jettison the body.

In *On the Special Laws* Philo organizes the laws of the Torah according to what he sees as their relationship to the Ten Commandments. Under the heading of the second commandment, the prohibition of idolatry, he includes the laws of the temple itself (1.60-78), the priests (1.79-161), and sacrifices (1.162-256). On the whole, Philo's approach in *On the Special Laws* is not allegorical but didactic and moralizing. But he does employ allegory at a number of points in *On the Special Laws*, including several topics related to the cult such as the high priest's robe (1.84-97), the burnt offering (1.198-211), and the ritual of the red cow (1.269-72), to offer some of the most striking and elaborate examples. In each of these passages and in many others, Philo signals the allegorical interpretation through the use of the term "symbol" or its derivatives.[24] Yet these allegorical interpretations are quite straightforward as compared to the complex allegories in the treatises interpreting Genesis.

Philo's discussion of the burnt offering (Lev 1:3-17), the first of the sacrifices he treats, is a good example of the less elaborate allegorical technique of *On the Special Laws*. After describing the appropriate victims for the offering and the procedure for the sacrifice, Philo explains that the animal to be sacrificed must be male because the male corresponds to the rational mind rather than irrational sense perception, which is female. Thus the burnt offering is the purest of sacrifices (*Spec. Laws* 1.200-201). He goes on to offer similarly allegorical interpretations of the sacrificer's laying hands on the sacrificial beast, the pouring of blood around the altar, the washing of belly and feet, and the division of the victim into pieces (1.202-9). His treatment of the command to wash belly and feet, which he designates as "highly symbolical," is typical. The belly represents lust, which of course requires cleansing, and washing the feet signals that the steps of one who loves God should tread not the earth but heaven (1.206-7).

But one peculiarity of Philo's treatment of the burnt offering must be noted: there is no allegorical interpretation of the man who brings the sacrifice or the priests who officiate. Philo's unwillingness to turn the human participants into souls as he often does in his treatment of the cult in the allegorical works serves to remind us of the continuing importance of the actual practice of sacrifice for Philo. So too while in *On the Migration of Abraham* the symbolism of his robe helps establish that the high priest represents the logos, in the course of the detailed allegorical treatment of the robe in *On the Special Laws* (1.84-97), the high priest remains a human being.

Even in *On the Special Laws* Philo is not always so restrained. In his interpretation of the ritual of the red cow, for example, the one who has been sprinkled with the waters of purification to prepare to offer a sacrifice is in fact offering himself to God (1.270-72). I suspect that the decision to treat the ritual of the red cow differently from the burnt offering was not a conscious one. In *On the Special Laws* Philo must have felt himself pulled in different directions. On the one hand, he wanted to lay out the meaning of the laws of the Torah, including the ritual laws, as clearly as possible and to insist on the value of performing them as well as of understanding them. We have already seen Philo's anxiety lest a really compelling allegorical interpretation of a ritual undermine its performance. Yet as for the laws of forbidden foods, for which Philo also offers an allegorical interpretation, no obvious didactic reading of the laws of the cult suggests itself, while the very specificity of the laws and their peculiarities provide an inviting target for allegory, which must have been difficult for Philo to resist. Sometimes, as with the burnt offering, it appears that he restrained himself and stopped short of full allegorization, but at other times, as with the ritual of the red cow, he did not.

It is also true that despite the difficulties cultic material presents, Philo was not incapable of a nonallegorical interpretation of such material. His interpretations of the peace offering (*Spec. Laws* 1.212-25) and the sin offering (1.226-46), for example, largely avoid allegory. While he treats the elements of these sacrifices as morally meaningful, the difference between his approach to them and to the burnt offering is striking. He explains the absence of brain and heart on the altar for the peace offering in terms that recall his interpretation of the burnt offering: "The altar of God should not be approached by the container in which mind had its lair when it came forth to tread the pathless wilds of injustice" (*Spec. Laws* 1.215). But he goes on to explain the offering of the fat, the lobe of the liver, and the kidneys in quite different terms:

The fat is the richest part and acts as a protection to the inwards, serving as a covering and a source of richness to them and benefiting them by the softness of its contact. The kidneys are chosen because of their relation to the testicles and generative organs. . . . The lobe is a sample tribute from the most important of the inwards, the liver. (*Spec. Laws* 1.216)

It is interesting that Philo introduces the discussion of the parts of the peace offering that are to be placed on the altar with an unusual admission that the reasons for the laws are not transparent:

What could be the reason why the law, when setting apart the lobe of the liver and the kidneys and the fat as a tribute reserved from the animals sacrificed, did not include either the heart or the brains, since the dominant principle resides in one or another of them. And I expect the same question will present itself to not a few of those who read the holy scriptures with their understanding rather than their eyes. If such persons after examination find a more convincing reason, they will benefit both themselves and me; if not I beg them to consider whether that which has commended itself to my mind will stand the test. (*Spec. Laws* 1.213-14)

Surely Philo must have been much tempted to engage in allegorical interpretation here as he had just done for the burnt offering, and I am hard-pressed to explain why he resisted the temptation here as he did not for the high priest's robe, the ritual of the red cow, or the laws of kashrut, to return to the examples cited above.

Philo's treatment of the laws concerning priests in *On the Special Laws* leaves no doubt of the high regard in which he holds them. Here, for example, is Philo's explanation of the prohibition on a priest marrying a harlot:

A harlot is profane in body and soul, even if she has discarded her trade and assumed a decent and chaste demeanour, and he is forbidden even to approach her, since her old way of living was unholy. Let such a one indeed retain in other respects her civic rights as she has been at pains to purge herself from her defilements, for repentance from wrongdoing is praiseworthy. Nor let anyone else be prevented from taking her in marriage, but let her not come near to the priest. For the rights and duties of the priesthood are of a special kind, and the office demands an even tenor of blamelessness from birth to death. (*Spec. Laws* 1.102)

In another context Philo might have understood the harlot to represent lust and other desires from which the soul, represented by the priest, must free itself. Here the former harlot remains a former harlot, and the priest remains a priest. Thus Philo reads the law as setting priests apart from the rest of the people of Israel with a higher level of holiness.

A similar attitude toward priests is evident in the discussion of Lev 22:10: "No lay person shall eat of the sacred donations." Philo explains that non-priests may not eat consecrated foods because "like pay for unlike worth is inequality, and inequality is the fountain of evil." Priests are to the people of Israel as pilots are to sailors on a merchant vessel or as captains and admirals are to oarsmen and marines on warships (*Spec. Laws* 1.121). Thus the perquisites of priesthood, restricted to priests and priests alone, show that priests are deserving of their exalted status.

To sum up, while Philo sometimes treats the cult and the priests involved in it allegorically, he does not resort to allegory to eliminate the difficulties posed by a hereditary priesthood. Rather, he follows the Torah in claiming elevated status for the descendants of Aaron, and he insists that that status is entirely appropriate.

Philo was not the only Alexandrian Jewish author to confront the problem of the Torah's hereditary priesthood. So too did the author of the *Letter of Aristeas*, who wrote sometime in the second century B.C.E. as Aristeas, a fictional Greco-Egyptian civil servant in the Ptolemaic court.[25] The *Letter* includes a description of an embassy to Jerusalem and a meeting with the high priest Eleazar, resplendent in his priestly robes (*Ep. Arist.* 96–99), who offers his visitors a philosophical interpretation of the dietary laws of the Torah (121–71). It also offers a flattering portrait of the priests of Jerusalem as they perform the temple service:

In its exhibition of strength and in its orderly and silent performance the ministration of the priests could in no way be surpassed. All of them, self-bidden, carry out labors involving great toil, and each has his appointed charge. Their service is unceasing. . . . Complete silence prevails, so that one might suppose that not a person was present in the place, though those performing the service amount to some seven hundred—besides the great multitude of persons bringing sacrifices to be offered—but everything is done with reverence and in a manner worthy of the great divinity. (92–95)[26]

But the glory of the Jerusalem priests according to the *Letter of Aristeas* pales beside that of the seventy-two elders chosen by Eleazar, six from each tribe, to go to Alexandria to translate the Torah. They are men "most excellent and of outstanding scholarship," of "distinguished parentage," proficient not only in Jewish but also in Greek literature, experienced ambassadors, expert in the law, who "zealously cultivated the quality of the mean . . . eschewing a crude and uncouth disposition," neither proud nor haughty, and they are deeply devoted to Eleazar, their altogether admirable leader (*Ep. Arist.* 121–23).[27] For the *Letter of Aristeas*, then, the learned elders stand out because of their merit. The priests, defined by mere ancestry, fade into the background.

It is illuminating to contrast the treatments of the biblical priesthood by Philo and the author of the *Letter of Aristeas* with the claims for the priests of Egypt of Chaeremon, a Stoic philosopher who was a contemporary of Philo and spent some of his career in Alexandria. According to one of the ancient notices, Chaeremon was also a *hierogrammateus*, a type of Egyptian priest expert in hieroglyphs. His works included a treatise on hieroglyphs and a history of Egypt; they survive only in fragments.[28] Among the fragments is this description of the priests of Egypt:

They chose the temples as the place to philosophize. . . . They renounced every employment and human revenues, and devoted their whole life to contemplation and vision of the divine. Through this vision they procured for themselves honour, security, and piety; through contemplation they procured knowledge; and through both a certain esoteric and venerable way of life. For to be always in contact with divine knowledge and inspiration keeps them far from all kinds of greediness, represses the passions, and incites them to live a life of understanding. . . . They were always seen near the gods, or rather their statues, either carrying or preceding them in a procession or setting them up with order and dignity. And each of these acts was no empty gesture, but an indication of some allegorical truth.[29]

It seems to me safe to assume that this description bears a rather tenuous connection to reality. It is highly unlikely that the priests of Egypt as a group shared a philosophical longing to contemplate the divine, especially since many of them attained their positions not because they led exemplary lives but because they belonged to priestly families. Philo and the author of the *Letter of Aristeas* would surely have been no more false to reality had they described the priests of Jerusalem in similar terms. But the Torah does not make it easy to understand philosophy and piety as requirements for priestly service. Rather, the office belongs to all male descendants of Aaron, who are entitled to serve as priests as long as they are sound in body. Thus the *Letter of Aristeas* reserves its highest praise for the elders, who have achieved their place through merit. Chaeremon, on the other hand, had no Torah to inhibit him. The rules for membership in the priesthoods of Egypt were not available in a single authoritative text known to every native expert and even to the rank and file. Furthermore, in contrast to the situation of the Jews, there was a wide variety of priesthoods in Egypt, a land long noted for the dazzling multiplicity of its gods. This in itself made knowledge of individual rules less likely.

More than the author of the *Letter of Aristeas*, Philo makes the most of the few indications the Torah provides that priestly status reflects some kind of merit. Thus he devotes considerable attention to the Levites, whom the Torah depicts as having earned their quasi-priestly status. According to a passage in Exodus (32:25-29), the Levites were chosen to serve the Lord as a reward for their slaughter of the offending Israelites after the incident of the golden calf. This passage, which shows no sign of P's subordination of Levites to priests, is particularly helpful to Philo in his purposeful conflation of priests and Levites because it has Moses praise the Levites for "fill[ing] their hands" (Exod 32:29), that is, ordaining themselves, through the slaughter;[30] P applies this terminology to priests alone, not to the Levites, whose dedication to temple service is described in different language.[31]

Philo makes use of this incident in several nonallegorical contexts. In *On the Special Laws*, he points to it as the reason for the choice of the tribe of Levi for the priesthood:

The nation has twelve tribes, but one out of these was selected on its special merits for the priestly office, a reward granted to them for their gallantry and godly zeal on an occasion when the multitude was seen to have fallen into sin. (1.79)

Philo tells the story of the Levites' slaughter of the worshipers of the golden calf in more detail in *On the Life of Moses* (2.170-73), emphasizing that priesthood was a reward for their zeal. He alludes to the story again in *On the Special Laws* to explain why the Levites were rewarded with the cities of refuge (3.124-27). The Torah does not offer a clear resolution to the tension between the picture of the priesthood of the Levites, on the one hand, and the limitation of priesthood to Aaron and his descendants alone, on the other. Nor does Philo as he exploits the stories about the Levites to lend the priesthood a certain amount of merit at least at the moment of its institution.

Philo likes the story of the Levites' zeal during the incident of the golden calf so much that he makes use of it in the allegorical treatises as well despite the allegorization of priests that eliminates the tension between ancestry and piety in these treatises. The Levites' slaughter of the relatives and neighbors who worshiped the calf represents the soul's or the virtuous man's excision of the desires of the body and all irrational elements (*On Drunkenness* 65–71 [men]; *On Flight and Finding* 88–92 [souls]). He offers a similar alleogorical interpretation of the zealous act of slaughter with which Phinehas, the grandson of Aaron, won the covenant of priesthood for himself and his descendants (Num 25:1-13) (*Allegorical Interpretation* 3.242; *On the Posterity of Cain* 182–83;

On Drunkenness 73–74).[32] Indeed, the passage in *On Drunkenness* concludes by invoking Phinehas. Perhaps because Phinehas was already a priest at the time of his zealous deed, Philo does not embrace this story as enthusiastically as the story of the Levites and the golden calf, treating it only once, and there briefly, in a nonallegorical context (*On the Life of Moses* 1.304).

But even if Philo can suggest that the priesthood was established on the basis of merit, the Torah makes it difficult to claim that it was passed down on that basis. Understandably Philo does not confront this problem directly. Yet he does at times imply the superior merit of priests in every generation. In *On the Special Laws*, for example, in his explication of Deuteronomy's provision for an appellate level of the judicial system consisting of "the levitical priests, or the magistrate in charge at the time" (Deut 17:8-9), Philo claims that priests make particularly suitable judges (*Spec. Laws* 4.191). This is because their service of the greatest of kings inspires them to keep their minds clear and to avoid error—thus the prohibition on strong drink for priests when they officiate (Lev 10:8-9). Philo goes on to identify the "magistrate in charge" as the high priest on whom he confers prophetic powers: "The true priest is necessarily a prophet, advanced to the service of the truly Existent by virtue rather than by birth, and to a prophet nothing is unknown" (*Spec. Laws* 4.192). The claim that the high priest's status reflects virtue rather than birth is a remarkable revision of the plain sense of the Torah and of the practice of centuries.

Yet for all his admiration for priests, when Philo attempted an extended treatment of Jewish practitioners of true philosophy comparable to Chaeremon's account of the priests of Egypt, he found his subjects not in the descendants of Aaron, but in the Therapeutae (*On the Contemplative Life*). Members of this voluntary community were more promising subjects because, as Philo writes at the beginning of the *Hypothetica*, his account of another voluntary community, the Essenes, "Their persuasion is not based on birth [*genos*] . . . , but on their zeal for virtue and desire to promote brotherly love" (*Hypothetica* 11.2).

In his account of the Therapeutae, Philo seeks to demonstrate the philosophical excellence of the way of life of these devotees of the philosophy of Moses much as Chaeremon depicts the philosophical excellence of the priests of Egypt. Both accounts belong to a body of Greco-Roman texts that offer idealized accounts of the lives of philosophical holy men; the descriptions of the Brahmans and gymnosophists in Philostratus's *Life of Apollonius of Tyana* are also examples. The ascetic regimen Chaeremon attributes to the Egyptian priests plays on long-held Greek ideas about the antiquity and sanctity of Egypt, as well as its strangeness.[33] For example, Chaeremon offers considerable detail about the diets of his priests. He notes their restraint in regard to wine and oil and their avoidance of any foods from outside Egypt. Some are vegetarians. They also avoid cows, that is, female cattle, and twin male animals, as well as males that are blemished, piebald, of unusual shape, or tame or that resemble sacred animals or human beings.[34]

Philo's account of the Therapeutae is noticeably less colorful.[35] The emphasis is on the asceticism of the Therapeutae, who become so absorbed in their study of wisdom that they sometimes forget to eat (*Contempl. Life* 34–35). Indeed, since the Therapeutae subsist on bread and water at all times, even on the Sabbath (*Contempl. Life* 36–37), Philo is able to avoid discussing the oddities of Jewish dietary laws, which are irrelevant to this highly ascetic regimen.[36] Perhaps the avoidance of the exotic was intended to emphasize the truly philosophical character of the Therapeutae. It is worth noting that Philo also avoids exoticism in the *Hypothetica*'s account of the Essenes, who surely provide promising raw material for such an effort, as Josephus's account in the *Jewish War* (2.119-61) demonstrates. Elsewhere, as we have seen, Philo vigorously defends the philosophical significance of the ritual laws against Greeks who, like Strabo, admired the Jews' belief in the one God, but not their ritual laws.[37] The account of the Therapeutae, on the other hand, makes such a defense unnecessary by largely avoiding ritual laws.

One aspect of Philo's discussion of the meals of the Therapeutae is particularly noteworthy for our purposes. First, he explains the lifelong avoidance of wine by the Therapeutae by noting the abstinence of priests before they officiate at sacrifices (*Contempl. Life* 74), a law of the Torah that, as we have seen, serves him well elsewhere too (*Spec. Laws* 4.191). He also explains the meals of the Therapeutae, consisting of leavened bread and salt mixed with hyssop, as intended to avoid comparison with the unleavened bread of the showbread and unmixed salt displayed with it[38] that constitute the "simplest and purest food . . . assigned to the highest caste, namely the priests, as a reward for their ministry" (*Contempl. Life* 81–82; see Lev 24:5-9). It is a remarkable tribute to priests to claim that even the Therapeutae, the devotees of the true wisdom, self-selected by their piety, are not worthy of the pure meal reserved for the sons of Aaron.[39]

It seems to me that Philo has some success in suggesting that the original occupants of the priestly office deserved the status they acquired for themselves because of their exceptional loyalty to the Lord. His hints that their descendants too are suited to the office not only by birth but also by merit are less persuasive, though his effort in the face of a rather recalcitrant biblical narrative is a good indication of how much he would have liked to be able to claim merit for them. If in the end Philo is unable to resolve the tension between a hereditary priesthood and his ideals of holiness, it is surely because the Torah itself makes such a resolution impossible for someone committed to the preservation of its practices.

Perhaps his concern for real priests made it inevitable that Philo would worry also about the problem expressed in the phrase "a kingdom of priests," the problem of the relationship between this group distinguished by ancestry and occupation and the people of Israel as a whole. Indeed he is among the handful of Jewish authors in the Second Temple period to quote or allude clearly to the phrase "a kingdom of priests," which he knew in its Septuagint translation, *basileion hierateuma*, a royal priesthood. Apparently he understood *basileion* as a noun since both of the times he uses the phrase (*On Sobriety* 66; *On Abraham* 56) he inserts *kai* between the two words.

Philo sometimes represents Israel as a kingdom of priests mediating between God and the rest of the nations as 3 Isaiah does (Isa 61:5-6).[40] Thus Abraham's descendants are "the nation dearest of all to God, which . . . has received the gift of priesthood and prophecy on behalf of all mankind" (*On Abraham* 98). But unlike 3 Isaiah, Philo understands Israel's priesthood not as a promise of material reward but rather as an indication of spiritual greatness. Israel is "a nation destined to be consecrated above all others to offer prayers for ever on behalf of the human race that it may be delivered from evil and participate in what is good" (*On Moses* 1.149). This passage does not sound so different from Eleazar's claim in the *Letter of Aristeas*, trumping Chaeremon's claims for the Egyptian priests before Chaeremon made it: "The priests who are the guides of the Egyptians, have looked closely into many things and are conversant with affairs, have named us 'men of God' [*anthrōpoi theou*], a title applicable to none others but only to him who reveres the true God. The rest are men of food and drink and raiment" (*Ep. Arist.* 140). For the *Letter of Aristeas*, then, despite the fact that membership in the Jewish people is normally hereditary, the requirements of Judaism make such membership an indication of merit as well. Yet Eleazar does not connect this claim to priesthood in any way, and, as we have seen, the *Letter* is considerably more enthusiastic about elders, who achieve their role by merit, than priests.

Elsewhere Philo makes clear the priestly aspect of his sense of Israel as a nation "consecrated above all others":

The Jewish nation is to the whole inhabited world what the priest is to the State [*polis*]. For the holy office in very truth belongs to the nation because it carries out all the rites of purification and both in body and soul obeys the injunctions of the divine laws. (*Spec. Laws* 2.163)

The Torah of course makes priests responsible for many aspects of its rituals of purification.

Philo works out the egalitarian implications of "a kingdom of priests" (or "a kingdom and priests") in a number of passages. Perhaps the most concrete instance of the effort to give all Jews a share in the priesthood appears in the discussion of marriage regulations for priests. Like some other ancient readers, Philo interprets Leviticus as restricting the high priest to a bride from a priestly family. He then emphasizes that in contrast to the high priest, ordinary priests may marry any woman of Israelite descent,

partly because the restrictions required to maintain [ordinary priests'] purity are slight, partly because the law did not wish that the nation should be denied altogether a share in the priestly clanship or be entirely excluded from it. . . . Sons-in-law are sons to their fathers-in-law, and the latter are fathers to the former. (*Spec. Laws* 1.111)

In the centuries before the turn of the era, as we saw in Chapter 1, some Jews read Leviticus as requiring that even ordinary priests marry women of priestly descent. It is possible that Philo knows this position and here intends to offer a rationale for rejecting it, but the works that require such marriages, the *Book of the Watchers, Aramaic Levi*, and 4QMMT, are all Palestinian and predate Philo by almost two centuries at the least. Further, Josephus, whose pronounced pride in priestly descent is untouched by any anxiety about merit, seems quite unaware of such a requirement, so it is more likely that support for it had simply disappeared by Philo's time. It is noteworthy that Philo's explanation for the permission given ordinary priests to marry nonpriestly women reflects an elevated view of priestly status even as it expresses a certain discomfort with boundaries within the Jewish people. This discomfort prepares us for Philo's other efforts at inclusion.

Philo's discussion of why the sin offering is consumed by the priests to the exclusion of the one who brings the offering (Lev 6:22; *Spec. Laws* 1.242-43) also makes an effort to expand the ranks of priesthood to include all Israel. This law of the Torah does not appear to be a very promising starting point for an effort to demonstrate the priestly status of all Israel, but Philo argues as follows: First, restricting consumption to priests honors the one bringing the offering, because the guests at the meal he has provided are of such high status. Next, it assures him that he has been forgiven because otherwise the meal would not be permitted to priests. Finally, Philo notes without further explanation that it is significant that no priest with bodily blemish may perform the sacrifice. Presumably his point is that this restriction makes the honor of providing the priests with their meal even greater.[41] But it is the remarkable conclusion Philo draws from these arguments that is most important for our purposes: "In fact he encourages those who no longer tread the path of wrongdoing with the thought that their resolution to purify themselves has given them a place in the sacerdotal caste and advanced

them to equal honor with the priest" (*Spec. Laws* 1.243). Presumably the
equal honor lies in providing the priests' feast, though someone looking
at the practice through a different lens might draw a rather different
conclusion about its implications for the status of priests. Yet if the reading seems somewhat forced, perhaps that makes it stronger evidence for
the depth of Philo's conviction on this point.

Philo also uses the Passover sacrifice to demonstrate the priesthood of
all Israel. This is an easier task than the one he attempts with the sin offering since the Passover sacrifice is the only sacrifice offered by laymen
on their own behalf.

In this festival many myriads of victims from noon till eventide are offered by the
whole people, old and young alike, raised for that particular day to the dignity
of the priesthood. For at other times the priests according to the ordinance of
the law carry out both the public sacrifices and those offered by private individuals. But on this occasion, the whole nation performs the sacred rites and acts as
priest with pure hands and complete immunity. (*Spec. Laws* 2.145)[42]

Philo's insistence that the Israelites' priestly activity is undertaken
with "pure hands and complete immunity" recognizes the anomalous
nature of this sacrifice, the only one the Torah leaves in the hands of the
head of the household. Philo goes on to suggest a historical explanation
for this deviation from standard practice: At the time of the Exodus, the
Israelites were so overcome with joy at leaving behind the idolatry of the
land of Egypt that in their enthusiasm they offered sacrifice without
waiting for the priests (*Spec. Laws* 2.146). This explanation is strikingly
different from the Torah's rationale for the sacrifice as the means for
providing the blood to mark the homes of the Israelites and to protect
them from the slaying of the firstborn sons that God was about to visit
on the Egyptians. Although priests are mentioned as a group as the children of Israel stand before Mt. Sinai shortly after they have left Egypt
(Exod 19:22), the Torah's account of the first Passover sacrifice gives no
hint of the existence of priests.

In *Questions and Answers on Exodus* (1.10), the Passover sacrifice provides Philo with another occasion for expounding the priestly character
of the whole people of Israel. I shall consider only the portions of the interpretation of greatest interest for our purposes. Again Philo offers a
historical explanation for the slaughter of the Passover sacrifice by the
laity, that at the time of the Exodus from Egypt no priesthood had yet
been established, an explanation not entirely consistent with the comments in *On the Special Laws* noted above. But then Philo goes on to suggest that God "deemed [the people of Israel] (all) equally worthy of
sharing in the priesthood and in freedom as well, since all who were of
the same nation had given evidence of equal piety." Further,

He thought it just and fitting that before choosing the particular priests He should grant priesthood to the whole nation in order that the part might be adorned through the whole, and not the whole through a part . . . And also that the nation might be an archetypal example to the temple-wardens and priests and those who exercise the high priesthood in carrying out the sacred rites.

Thus Philo claims here that the priesthood of all Israel is not only chronologically prior to the selection of a distinct group of priests but also ontologically prior: the nation is the archetype of the priesthood, even of the high priesthood.

To say that Philo was preoccupied with the problem of the priesthood for a kingdom of priests would be an exaggeration. The idea of a kingdom of priests hardly plays the central role in his thought that it does in the *Book of Jubilees*, for example. Still, the passages discussed here point to something significant. The biblical injunction that all Israelites are to slaughter the paschal lamb was not of Philo's making, but had he wished to play down the implications, he certainly could have done so. Or he could have resolved the tension between priests and the priesthood of all Israel allegorically, by turning priests into souls. He does not do so, I suspect, out of the same considerations that sometimes led him to restrain himself in his allegorizing of the cult: he did not wish to undermine the actual conduct of sacrifices. Rather, he seeks other opportunities to actualize the notion of a kingdom of priests. Indeed, there is a concrete aspect to at least one of Philo's attempts at a solution: intermarriage between priests and women from nonpriestly families. But perhaps the most powerful is the claim of *Questions and Answers on Exodus*: it is the "nation" that is the "archetypal example" for priests and even for the high priest.

Chapter 6

"The Children of Abraham Your Friend"
The End of Priesthood, the Rise of Christianity,
and the Neutralization of Jewish Sectarianism

In the summer of the year 70, four years after the beginning of the Jewish revolt against Rome, four Roman legions were massed outside Jerusalem, where the rebels had gathered for their last stand. The commander of the legions was the future emperor Titus; he had recently replaced his father, Vespasian, who had been acclaimed emperor by the legions in the east and was now on his way to Rome to assert his claim to the office. The most important building in Jerusalem, symbolically and strategically, was the temple, yet Josephus reports that Titus had determined to spare it against the advice of some of his generals (*Jewish War* 6.237-43).[1] Indeed, Josephus claims that when one of his soldiers impulsively set fire to it, Titus attempted to have the fire extinguished (*Jewish War* 6.252-59). No matter what Titus intended, the temple burned to the ground (*Jewish War* 6.260-66). The conquest of the city was completed in the weeks that followed, and Jerusalem was left in ruins (*Jewish War* 6.392-413).

Josephus reports that the conditions of the siege had brought an end to the sacrificial cult shortly before the destruction of the temple (*Jewish War* 6.94-95). The destruction made the cessation of the cult permanent, though it took many decades for most Jews to appreciate this, and not only because it takes some time for the consequences of momentous events to become clear. Rather, the example of the First Temple suggested that the loss of the Second Temple would not be permanent. Roughly seventy years after the destruction of the First Temple by the Babylonians, some of the descendants of the Judean elite returned to Jerusalem from their exile in Babylonia and rebuilt the temple with the permission of the Persians, who had in the meantime toppled the Babylonian empire. It is no accident that Baruch, the scribe of the prophet Jeremiah, serves as the visionary of two of the apocalypses written in the wake of the destruction of the Second Temple.[2] Jeremiah, after all, prophesied not only the destruction of the First Temple, which he and Baruch witnessed, but also the restoration of the people to their land after seventy years. In attributing their visions to Baruch, the authors drew on these associations, even if one of the apocalypses suggests that the earthly temple is unnecessary and will never be restored.[3] Another apocalypse from the years after 70 takes as its hero Ezra, the scribe who brought the Torah to the Jews at the behest of the Persians three-quarters of a century or so after the return; the figure of Ezra thus recalls the fact of restoration after the Babylonian exile and points to the coming restoration of Jerusalem that is a central theme of his visions. With the model of the First Temple in mind, then, many Jews in the first century expected that their grandchildren would again offer sacrifices in a new temple, though they differed among themselves as to whether that new temple would be built by human hands like its predecessors or would descend from heaven like the Jerusalem of Ezra's visions (*4 Ezra* 7:26, 10:40-55, 13:36).

And many Jews were probably not as distressed by the loss of the Second Temple as their ancestors had been by the lost of the First Temple.[4] We have seen that even while the Second Temple was still standing, some critics believed that it lacked the luster of the First Temple. Indeed, the author of the *Book of Dreams* (*1 Enoch* 83-90), which has usually been dated to the time of the Maccabean Revolt, goes so far as to claim that its cult was polluted from the very start (*1 Enoch* 89:73),[5] and the radical sectarians at Qumran appear to have given up on it completely.[6] After the destruction, *2 Baruch* compares the Second Temple unfavorably to the First Temple (*2 Bar.* 68:6).[7]

With the destruction of the temple, the descendants of Aaron were deprived of their defining task. This loss was surely a blow to their prestige, which was perhaps already in decline. While the texts from either side of the Maccabean Revolt critical of the priestly establishment reflect the views of a pious minority, the unseemly reality of the last decades before the destruction of the Second Temple could have had an impact on the standing of priests in the eyes of a larger group of Jews. In 35 B.C.E., when Herod became jealous of the popularity of the young high priest Aristobulus III, his own brother-in-law and the last Hasmonean to serve in that role (Josephus, *Jewish War* 1.437), he arranged his murder. From then on, he chose high priests from priestly families without any previous association with the position. To limit still further their potential as rivals to his power, almost all came from Alexandria or Babylonia, and he did not permit them to serve for life. When the Romans assumed direct rule of Judea in 6 C.E., they continued Herod's practice. From the time of Herod, then, the most obvious qualifications of occupants of the office of high priest, who often served only briefly, were likely to be wealth and an aptitude for flattering their rulers. Inevitably, the traditional prestige of the office was greatly diminished.[8]

And there was another important difference between the loss of the Second Temple and the loss of the First Temple. When the Second Temple was built, it stood alone as an institution capable of unifying and providing definition for a people lacking a king or political independence. By the time of its destruction, although the Jews again lacked both king and independence, another institution, the Torah, had come to stand with the temple at the center of Judaism. From one point of view the Torah served to support and strengthen the temple, but it was also an independent source of power; not only could its interpreters offer guidance to the people at large, they could also tell priests what to do. Thus the loss of the temple, especially if it was understood to be temporary, was likely less traumatic than it had been in 586 B.C.E.

But the evidence for the Bar Kokhba revolt (132–35 C.E.), limited though it is, demonstrates that as the seventieth anniversary of the destruction neared many Jews had not given up the goal of restoring of the temple. The revolt may have been set off by Hadrian's plans to turn Jerusalem into a Roman colony, Aelia Capitolina, which would have made the rebuilding of the Jewish temple impossible.[9] Among the coins the rebels minted are silver tetradrachms bearing images of the temple with the ark of the covenant.[10] Silver and bronze coins of various sizes bear the legends "Jerusalem" and "For the freedom of Jerusalem"; these legends are probably slogans announcing one of the goals of the revolt rather than statements that the goal had been achieved.[11]

The title Bar Kokhba used for himself was not king, but *něśî' yiśra'ēl,* "prince of Israel."[12] It is attested on both documents and coins,[13] and ultimately it points to the central place of temple and priesthood in the goals of the revolt. This title goes back to Ezekiel, who uses it instead of "king" for the descendants of David in his vision of the restored temple and community of Israel. There, as we have seen, it appears to be part of an effort to subordinate royal power to priestly power. In several texts from among the Dead Sea Scrolls, the hero of the eschatological battle is called "prince of the congregation," without any hint that the title "prince" is intended to limit the power of the leader it designates. The dominant form of messianic expectation in the Dead Sea Scrolls, however, is of two messiahs, priestly and royal, and in the *War Scroll,* in which the prince of the congregation figures prominently, the high priest is even more important.[14]

Bar Kokhba's use of the title *nāśî'* indicates military leadership as in the Dead Sea Scrolls, and Bar Kokhba also imitates the pattern of dual leadership found there. His partner is Eleazar the Priest, an otherwise unknown figure whose name and title appear on some of the coins from the revolt.[15] There is no reason to believe that Bar Kokhba and his supporters knew the Dead Sea Scrolls, but they draw inspiration from texts such as Ezekiel, Haggai, and Zechariah, and perhaps from more recent traditions that shared the Dead Sea Scrolls' interest in dual messianism.[16] It surely did not escape their notice that the building of the Second Temple was the work of such a pair of leaders, Zerubbabel the descendant of David and Joshua the high priest. While the *Book of Jubilees* and the Dead Sea Scrolls treat the priestly leader as the more important of the two messiahs, Haggai and Zechariah clearly view Zerubbabel as the dominant figure. It is the prophets' version of the pattern of dual leadership that is reflected in the Bar Kokhba revolt, where there can be no doubt that Bar Kokhba was the dominant figure. Some scholars have taken the presence of a priestly leader alongside Bar Kokhba and the interest in the restoration of the temple and its cult as evidence that priests played an important part in the revolt.[17] This inference may well be correct, but it is important to insist that the desire to see the temple rebuilt and the cult restored would hardly have been restricted to priests. Indeed, with the passage of time, the memory of the diminished state of the office of high priest in the century before the destruction of the temple had surely faded, and the prestige of the office along with the priesthood more generally may have risen even in the absence of the institution that gave priests their central task. Unfortunately, the evidence available for reconstructing these developments is extremely limited.

With the bloody failure of Bar Kokhba's revolt and the establishment of Aelia Capitolina, it became painfully evident that no Third Temple would be built seventy years after the destruction of the Second Temple. Bar Kokhba's revolt was the last Jewish attempt in antiquity to set in motion the rebuilding of the temple. But there was one further attempt, undertaken not by Jews but by the emperor Julian in the middle of the fourth century, out of motives entirely different from those of Bar Kokhba and his supporters.[18]

At the time of Bar Kokhba's defeat, Christians were a small and persecuted minority. The centuries between Bar Kokhba and Julian saw the continued expansion of Christianity, its rising influence, and eventually its legalization and adoption as the official religion of the Roman state. When Julian became emperor in 361, Christianity had been the dominant religion of the empire for almost half a century. Julian was a committed pagan Platonist, and during his brief reign he made a serious effort to undo the Christianizing work of his imperial predecessors. The effort came to an end with his death in battle against the Persians in 363. The plan to rebuild the temple in Jerusalem reflected Julian's support for the traditional religious practices of the empire before it became Christian, but it was also intended as a blow against the upstart religion for which the demise of the Jerusalem temple was an important element of propaganda. The details of the effort to rebuild the temple are obscure, but the cessation of the work, which the Christian accounts understand as miraculous intervention to prevent the achievement of Julian's sacrilegious goals, appears to have been the result of a fire, perhaps caused by an earthquake.[19]

We know very little about how Jews responded to Julian's plan. Rabbinic literature is silent about it.[20] The fourth-century inscription on the Western Wall that quotes with slight variation a passage from Isaiah, "You shall see, and your heart shall rejoice; / your bones shall flourish like grass" (Isa 66:14), has been read as a reaction to Julian's plan, but this is by no means certain.[21] Christian sources depict the Jews as extremely enthusiastic about the project. Although the picture is drawn for polemical purposes and serves to heighten satisfaction at the disappointment of their hopes, it does not seem unlikely that many Jews were excited about the opportunity even as the rabbinic elite remained cautiously aloof. Whatever the Jewish reaction, the project itself was short-lived. With Julian's death, the empire returned to Christian control, and Jews had to reconcile themselves to the postponement of the rebuilding of the temple to the dawn of the messianic age.

Ancestry and Merit after the Destruction

In the Second Temple period, as we have seen, some Jews struggled to constitute themselves as a kingdom of priests despite the fact that the Torah singles out a particular group to serve the priestly people as its priests. Some Jews were also troubled that this priesthood was hereditary and thus that priests distinguished by ancestry but not necessarily by piety were responsible for the temple crucial to the well-being of the Jewish people. Anxiety about a hereditary priesthood led some Jews to further anxiety about the character of the Jewish people, also defined, at least to a large extent, by ancestry rather than merit.

With the destruction of the temple, the problems priesthood created for the pious inevitably became less troubling. As I shall try to show, the memory of the temple retained its power even as Jews realized that its loss was more than a temporary inconvenience. The rabbis devoted a remarkable amount of attention to rules related to an institution that had been rendered inoperative, while the synagogues of Roman Palestine recalled the lost temple physically, in their ornamentation, and verbally, in their liturgy. It is perhaps not surprising that inscriptions and the synagogue practice ratified by the rabbis indicate that priestly ancestry remained a source of prestige even in the absence of the temple. Yet the same evidence also makes clear the limits of its claims. With the deferral of the restoration of the temple to messianic times, priesthood might still be valued, but the advantages accruing to actual priests were more token than real.

Yet, I shall argue, the decline of the significance of priestly ancestry among Jews was followed by the widespread and thorough embrace of a definition of the Jewish people based on ancestry. This definition served as an implicit rejection of sectarian definitions restricting membership to the worthy alone. Perhaps the loss of the temple contributed in some small way to this redefinition: the diminution in status of priests meant that their piety or lack of it was no longer a subject of much concern, and thus priests no longer constituted a glaring example of the tension between ancestry and merit. The most important cause of the whole-hearted embrace of ancestry, however, was the rise of Christianity. As Christians claimed to have taken the place of the old Israel, some re-jected the language of ethnicity altogether ("In Christ there is neither Jew nor Greek" [Gal 3:28]), while others claimed that they constituted a new people defined not by genealogy but by merit. Against these claims, Jews insisted—as much to themselves as to Christians—on the contin-ued viability of the old Israel and the guarantee of redemption inherent in descent from Abraham. Thus, despite the emergence of the concept of conversion to Judaism in the later Second Temple period, Jews after the destruction chose to embrace an understanding of membership in the people of Israel in which merit was de-emphasized and the implica-tions of the possibility of conversion ignored. This understanding was accepted by the rabbis, the religious elite of the postdestruction period, as well as the larger community. It is noteworthy that the rabbis largely ignored the implications of conversion, a process they regulated and ac-cepted, as they resisted the temptation of a sectarian definition of Israel, like that of the Qumran community, in which only the worthy counted as Jews. One of the most important consequences of the embrace of an-cestry by rabbis and other Jews was the reassurance it offered: the merit of the ancestors guaranteed the redemption of their descendants.

Rabbis and Priests

Though their successors came to enjoy wide recognition among other Jews, the rabbis of the centuries immediately following the destruction ap-pear to have been an elite without much of a following.[22] Yet the primary literary evidence for Judaism in the period after 70 is rabbinic literature. For Jewish society beyond the circles of the rabbis, the main evidence is the remains of synagogues, with all the difficulties of interpretation posed by material evidence. Both bodies of evidence offer some insight into the place of priesthood in postdestruction Jewish society.

The rabbis understood themselves as heirs of the Pharisees, though recent scholarship has suggested that this is less than the full story,[23] and they count as their predecessors a number of figures from the period before the destruction. Still, the emergence of the rabbinic movement was intimately linked in the rabbis' telling to the destruction of the temple, as can be seen in the story of Yohanan b. Zakkai's escape from the Roman siege of Jerusalem.[24] The rabbis' claim to authority, like that of the Pharisees according to Josephus (*Jewish War* 2.162), was based on expertise in interpretation of the Torah. The elaborate system of regulations they developed governing virtually all aspects of life is to a considerable extent a result of such interpretation, even if sometimes the interpretation was employed to demonstrate that an already existing practice could be derived from the Torah. As we saw in the halakhic works from among the Dead Sea Scroll, the enterprise of extending the laws of the Torah was already underway in the period of the Second Temple, and a considerable body of recent scholarship has been devoted to the question of similarities and differences between the halakhah of the Dead Sea Scrolls and of the rabbis in both content and approach.[25]

As religious experts who owed their prestige to learned expertise in the Torah rather than ancestral connection to the temple, the rabbis might have been expected to view the loss of the temple with a certain satisfaction even if they preferred not to confess to it. Yet precisely as experts in Torah, the rabbis also had to acknowledge the central place in the ideal order of the temple, its sacrificial cult, and its priests, as well as the laws of purity and tithing.[26] Though no longer of practical concern, priests and sacrifices of necessity figure prominently in the tannaitic midrashim to Leviticus and Numbers since these works are structured as commentaries. The Mishnah too gives considerable space to these subjects, though with its topical organization it might have ignored them had it wished to. Instead it devotes one of its six orders, *Qodašin* (Holy Things), to sacrifices and another, *Ṭoharot* (Purities), to laws of purity that were no longer in force in the absence of the temple and the sacrificial system. The Yerushalmi lacks gemara for both of these orders, presumably because they were no longer of practical interest, but while the Bavli contains gemara for only one tractate of *Ṭoharot*, it provides gemara for almost all of *Qodašin* despite the fact that the cult was by then far in the past.

Not only did the rabbis continue to devote attention to the cult because of its importance in the Torah, but they also understood its restoration as one of the key elements of the messianic era, as the liturgy makes abundantly clear.[27] One might imagine that in their heart of hearts most rabbis would not have rejoiced to see rabbinic learning replaced by service before the altar as the highest form of prestige. Yet at the end of the nineteenth and beginning of the twentieth century, in the waning days of the Lithuanian yeshivot, R. Israel Meir Ha-Kohen, the head of the yeshiva of Radin, known as the *Ḥafeṣ Ḥayyim* after his most important book, encouraged several students to study the order of *Qodašin*. This order did not form part of the standard curriculum in the Lithuanian yeshivot, but the messiah might arrive at any moment, and the *Ḥafeṣ Ḥayyim* wanted to be sure that there would be experts versed in the laws of sacrifice to participate in the reestablishment of the temple cult.[28] Thus the *Ḥafeṣ Ḥayyim* lived in expectation of an age in which priests would once again perform their ancient function. But the restoration of the temple did not mean the displacement of rabbis by priests; rather, in that new age, priests would be guided by those with rabbinic learning. Indeed, it is significant that the rabbis allowed the idea of a priestly messiah to fall by the wayside, embracing instead the other member of the pair envisioned by Haggai and Zechariah, the royal messiah descended from David. This messiah is sometimes paired with a messiah descended from Ephraim, a sure sign that the old priestly-royal pairing had fallen out of favor.

The *Ḥafeṣ Ḥayyim* lived almost two millenia after the destruction of the Second Temple, but there is considerable continuity between his attitude toward priests and those expressed in of the rabbis of antiquity. Most of the Mishnah consists of legal rulings, but *m. 'Abot* is a collection of sayings of rabbis and great figures of the period before the destruction about how to live life; it thus provides an unusual window into the rabbis' view of the world. It opens with an account of the transmission of the Torah from Moses at Mt. Sinai to Joshua, the elders, the prophets, the men of the great assembly, and finally, to the rabbis themselves (*m. 'Abot* 1:1). Priests are pointedly omitted from the chain. One passage in *m. 'Abot* treats priests with considerable respect: "There are three crowns: the crown of Torah, the crown of priesthood, and the crown of kingship. But the crown of a good reputation is better than all of them" (*m. 'Abot* 4:13).[29] Yet a passage from the sixth chapter of *m. 'Abot*, a later addition to the tractate,[30] provides a revealing counterpoint to this saying: "The Torah is greater than priesthood and kingship, for kingship requires thirty qualifications, and priesthood twenty-four, but the Torah requires forty-eight things" (*m. 'Abot* 6:5).[31] Mastery of the Torah, of course, differs from kingship and priesthood in that it is not linked to ancestry.

Some scholars have suggested that priests were competing with rabbis for leadership of the Jewish community in the centuries following the destruction of the temple.[32] The evidence for this picture is quite limited, but regardless of whether there was actual competition, there is undoubtedly an inherent tension between the ideal of Torah study and the claims of priestly ancestry sanctified by long tradition and by the Torah itself. The tension can be seen clearly in a passage from the Mishnah that ranks Jews by their ancestry: priest, Levite, Israelite, *mamzēr*, *nātîn*, proselyte, freed slave (*m. Horayot* 3.8). Such a hierarchy appears to have been widely embraced: epigraphic evidence shows that even after the failure of the second revolt and the end of any realistic expectation of rebuilding the temple in the near term, priestly ancestry continued to be a source of pride among Jews.[33] The passage from the Mishnah shows that, all other things being equal, the rabbis too embraced a hierarchy determined by ancestry.[34] The passage concludes, however, by insisting that a *mamzēr* learned in Torah outranks a high priest ignorant of Torah, a claim that surely would not have been accepted by most other Jews.

It is also worth noting that while Torah study was in principle accessible to any male Jew with the proper intellectual endowment and motivation, in practice only those with considerable resources were likely to have had time for the learning that the office of rabbi required. Thus it is not surprising that the office of rabbi seems to have run in particular families: many rabbis were the sons of rabbis, and at least in Babylonia, rabbis often married daughters and sisters of rabbis.[35] Indeed, a few rabbis came from priestly families,[36] which must have constituted a significant portion of the Jewish upper classes.[37] In other words, ancestry continued to play a crucial role in securing the status of the devotees of Torah study.[38]

The rabbis' ambivalence about priests can also be seen in their discussion of Aaron's status relative to Moses. In a passage that appears in slightly different form in two tannaitic midrashim, *Sifra* (*Vayyiqrā'* 2) and *Sifre Numbers* (58), the rabbis claim that God spoke only to Moses, not, as the Torah sometimes suggests, to his brother Aaron, the progenitor of the priesthood, as well. For the rabbis, of course, Moses was the prototype of the rabbinic sage, and the claim that God spoke to him but not to Aaron serves to exalt rabbis at the expense of priests. Yet the discussion of the same question that opens another tannaitic midrash, the *Mekilta* (*Pisḥa'* 1), shows that the rabbis did not entirely reject the claims of priesthood:[39]

And the Lord Spoke unto Moses and Aaron in the Land of Egypt Saying. From this I might understand that the divine word was addressed to both Moses and Aaron. When, however, it says: "And it came to pass on the day when the Lord spoke unto Moses in the land of Egypt" (Ex. 6.28), it shows that the divine word was addressed to Moses alone and not to Aaron. If so, what does Scripture mean to teach by saying here, "unto Moses and Aaron?" It merely teaches that just as

Moses was perfectly fit to receive the divine words, so was Aaron perfectly fit to receive the divine words. And why then did He not speak to Aaron? In order to grant distinction to Moses.[40]

For the *Mekilta*, then, Moses is more equal than Aaron.

Yet the passage goes on to claim that in their dealings with Pharaoh, Aaron was Moses' equal. It continues:

Rabbi says: *unto Moses and Aaron*. I might understand that the one preceding in the scriptural text actually had precedence over the other. But in the passage: "These are that Aaron and Moses to whom the Lord said," etc. (Ex. 6.26), Aaron is mentioned first. Scripture thus declares that both were equal, the one as important as the other.[41]

For the rabbis, as for the Torah, there can be no doubt that Moses was far and away superior to his older brother. Nor is it surprising to find the rabbis insisting that worthy though Aaron may have been, Moses alone received revelation. What is perhaps surprising is how far the rabbis are willing to go in praising Aaron.

Of course, it is easier to praise the progenitor of the priesthood, who has special claims to status that other priests do not and who was safely in the past, than to embrace contemporary priests. The rabbis do, however, acknowledge the special status of contemporary priests in some limited ways. Priests are to be called first to the Torah (*m. Giṭṭin* 5:8), though the motive, "for the sake of peace," perhaps suggests that the Mishnah is simply ratifying the reigning custom. The rabbis also regulate the recitation of the priestly blessing, a ritual legislated by the Torah, for the synagogue;[42] the performance of this ritual gave priests an ongoing role in the synagogue that could be performed by them alone. Even in the post-temple era, the rabbis expect priests to continue to observe the laws binding on them alone (Leviticus 21) that were not impossible to observe in the absence of the temple: limitations on marriage partners and avoidance of cemeteries and funerals of all but close relatives.[43]

This complex relationship between rabbis and priests is reminiscent in some respects of the relationship between scribes and priests in the Second Temple period. I argued above that the tension between scribes and priests has been overstated, and it seems to me possible to make a similar case for priests and rabbis. In the Second Temple period, as we have seen, the failings of priests caused anxiety and distress to many of the pious. One significant difference between the situation of the pious of the Second Temple period and the rabbis, of course, is that for the rabbis the absence of the temple made the piety of priests a less urgent concern. Despite the fact that priests continued to stand at the center of the ideal order defined by the Torah, the stakes were now much lower. Thus rabbis may occasionally accuse contemporary priests of arrogance and ignorance,[44] but the pious of the Second Temple period had accused them of far worse, for the loss of the temple deprived priests of the opportunity to defile holy things and commit sacrilege. As we have seen, efforts to resolve the problems posed by a hereditary priesthood in the Second Temple period resulted in the conflation of the offices of scribe and priest as in the *Book of the Watchers*' picture of Enoch. The rabbis do not go so far as to make a single biblical hero both rabbi and priest, but their willingness, at least in some moods, to place Aaron but little below Moses is surely an indication of a positive attitude if not toward contemporary priests, then at least toward the ideal priest.

Synagogues and Temple

As long as the Second Temple stood, synagogues functioned in its shadow, supplementing rather than replacing the sacrificial cult of the house of the Lord. With its destruction, they took on new importance.[45] The decoration of the synagogues reflects a sensibility quite different from that of the rabbis, and rabbinic literature too suggests some distance between the rabbis and the culture of the synagogues.[46] Thus the remains of the synagogues are of great interest in part because they allow us some access to the vast majority of Jews outside the circles of the rabbis. It is important to keep in mind, however, that the bulk of the evidence for synagogues comes from the fourth century and later.[47] Thus most of it is somewhat later than the rabbinic texts on which I have chosen to focus; both the Mishnah and the halakhic midrashim cite tannaim, rabbis of the first two centuries, though the Mishnah was published only at the beginning of the third century, while the halakhic midrashim were redacted somewhat later. But I do not believe that the picture of rabbinic attitudes I have sketched would change greatly if I had chosen texts from the Palestinian rabbis more closely contemporary with the synagogue remains, such as the Talmud Yerushalmi, *Genesis Rabbah*, or *Leviticus Rabbah*.

It is clear that the absent temple left its mark on the synagogues. Some synagogues faced east on the model of the tabernacle, as the Tosefta (*t. Megilla* 3.22) demanded. Others faced the location of the temple.[48] Synagogue inscriptions refer to the synagogue with expressions associated with the temple, such as "holy" and "holy place."[49] But perhaps the richest evidence, if the most difficult to interpret,[50] comes from the mosaics decorating the synagogue floors.[51] Despite the diversity, certain elements are quite widespread. These common elements show clearly that even when the temple and the cult were lost, they were not forgotten. The object most frequently depicted in mosaics is the menorah, an object intimately associated with the temple cult. The menorah often appears with a shofar, a lulav, and an etrog. Torah shrines flanked by pairs of incense shovels and of the four objects just mentioned are also common.[52] Like the menorah, the shofar and the incense shovel must evoke the temple and its cult.[53]

On the floor of the nave of many synagogues, the Torah shrine and its accompanying symbols appear as part of a complex of symbols and scenes. On a number of floors, the image of the Torah shrine is placed at the front with a zodiac circle in the center and a scene of lions or other animals flanking a large wreath elsewhere. Some floors also include a biblical scene or scenes.[54] In Seth Schwartz's reading, "The floors . . . tend to suggest a movement from the world, in idealized form—nature scenes, scenes from biblical narrative—through the heavens (the zodiac circle), to the temple cult, and back to the reality of the synagogue."[55] Thus the floors reflect a piety in which the absent temple continues to hold a central place.

The temple also plays an important role in the *piyyutim*, the elaborate liturgical poetry of the synagogue that began to flourish in the sixth century. In the acrostics signing their work, several of the early *payyetanim* identify themselves as priests,[56] and some scholars have argued that their interest in the temple and the priestly courses reflects a peculiarly priestly sensibility,[57] a point to which I shall return below. Many *piyyutim* were composed for occasions that inevitably recalled the temple, as, for example, the Avodah service of the Day of Atonement, in memory of the ceremony of the scapegoat, or the Ninth of Av, the anniversary of the destruction of the temple.[58] One popular subject of the early *piyyutim* of particular interest for our purposes was the priestly courses.[59] Some *piyyutim* enumerate all twenty-four courses that had officiated in the temple in successive weeks; many of these were composed for the Ninth of Av or for other dates associated with the destruction.[60] Other *piyyutim* treat a single course; these have been associated with a custom of announcing in synagogue the name of the priestly course that would have officiated in the temple on that Sabbath.[61]

The *piyyutim* are not the only indication of interest in the priestly courses in the synagogues of late antique Palestine. Inscriptions listing the twenty-four courses and juxtaposing each one with a Galilean city or village have been found in several locations in Israel as well as in the village of Bayt al-ḥādir in Yemen; most of the inscriptions are on stone plaques that were presumably placed on synagogue walls.[62] The place-names in the inscriptions reflect traditions that are also known from the *piyyutim*, which often play on place-names in their praise of the courses.

In light of the interest in the temple evident in the synagogue mosaics, the inscriptions listing the priestly courses and the attention the
piyyutim lavish on the courses are hardly surprising. The association of
the priestly courses with particular cities and villages in the Galilee in
the inscriptions and the *piyyutim* is more difficult to explain.[63] While
priests must have participated in the shift of the center of gravity of the
Jewish population from Judea to Galilee in the period after the destruction of the temple and the Bar Kokhba revolt, it is clear that the courses
did not move as a group, each to take up residence in a single location.[64]
In other words, the lists of the inscriptions and their echoes in the *piyyutim* reflect something other than actual priestly residential patterns.
Perhaps because the scholarly discussion has been preoccupied with
questions of historicity, the worldview that lies behind the lists has received little attention.[65] Without attempting a thorough discussion of
this question, which would have to consider the contemporary significance of the specific sites in Galilee, I would suggest that the idealized
picture of the twenty-four courses residing intact in Galilee constitutes
an implicit claim that Jewish life in Galilee effectively continues the institutions of temple times. The presence of inscriptions listing the
courses and their Galilean locations outside the Galilee, not only in
other parts of the land of Israel but even in Yemen, also demands explanation; at the very least, it suggests that the claim the lists imply was not
merely a matter of local pride.

Several scholars have recently argued for a resurgence of priestly
power in the fifth, sixth, and seventh centuries after a period of eclipse,
a resurgence to be explained at least in part by the power vacuum
caused by the end of the patriarchate in the early fifth century. They invoke a variety of types of evidence in support of this claim, including testimonies from Christian sources. The interest of the *piyyutim* in the
temple service and the priestly courses is taken to reflect renewed
priestly ascendancy, as is the appearance of the hekhalot literature, understood following Rachel Elior's forceful reading as a repository of
priestly traditions.[66]

The Christian evidence marshaled in support of the claim of the
prominence and power of priests in the period after the end of the patriarchate certainly deserves further attention, but the view that Jewish
texts that demonstrate interest in the temple or its priests necessarily reflect priestly authorship or a situation of priestly power is deeply problematic. It did not require priests in power to build buildings or set a
liturgy that expressed yearning for the restoration of the temple or nostalgia for the sons of Aaron performing the tasks the Torah assigns
them.[67] It is also worth remembering that priests in the postdestruction

period are no more likely to have been of one mind about issues than were priests before the destruction. Indeed, since some rabbis were themselves priests, the tension between, for example, rabbis and wealthy priests in Sepphoris does not reveal the world view of priests as a group.[68] Nor is it surprising that priestly families were prominent among the wealthy of Sepphoris, just as it is not surprising that some rabbis—a different elite, but an elite nonetheless—came from priestly families.

Priestly Interests and Priestly Power

Finally, it is worth noting that despite the way synagogues so actively re-called the temple, their remains offer little evidence that priests held a particularly exalted place in them. As we have seen, rabbinic law grants priests certain privileges in the synagogue service and a specified liturgical role; in so doing, it appears to be ratifying common synagogue practice. In this light it is interesting that donor inscriptions from the synagogues show that priestly ancestry was a source of pride but give no indication that priests as a group had a special status in the synagogue.[69] The lack of emphasis on priestly ancestry in the inscriptions is a striking contrast to the commemoration of the priestly courses. It might suggest that reverence for priesthood was oriented toward the past: while the priests of temple times were a worthy subject for liturgical poetry, actual priests in an era without a temple were not very different from everyone else.

Altogether, despite the fact that the rabbis had reason to be less nostalgic for the temple than did their contemporaries, their attitude toward priests was not very different. For rabbis and other Jews alike, priestly ancestry deserved acknowledgment, but it was not of overwhelming importance for society or even for the conduct of the synagogue liturgy. Indeed, the loss of the temple had a certain democratizing effect. The remembered temple was the place of all Jews equally, laypeople and priests alike; priestly ancestry no longer meant a special intimacy with the holy place and its rituals. With priests as a group deprived of the political power that was once theirs, it was easier for the rabbis to hold the positive attitude toward priesthood as an institution and the illustrious ancestor of all priests seen in the texts considered above. Real priests were no longer a source of anxiety because they no longer wielded significant influence, nor did they exercise the functions that once made their piety a source of pressing concern. Their behavior now had no more impact on the fate of Israel than did the behavior of any other Jew. Under these circumstances, the rabbis could afford to be generous.

Ancestry and Merit for a Holy People

If the destruction of the temple ultimately permitted a more relaxed attitude toward the failings of priests, it intensified the problem of the failings of the people of Israel as a whole. The requirements of monotheistic
theodicy placed the blame for the destruction squarely on the Jewish
people, thus emphasizing their unworthiness and heightening the tension between the ideal of a holy people and the reality of a genealogical
requirement for membership in that people. It is true that there were efforts to offer other kinds of explanations. Several passages in rabbinic
literature claim that Israel was held to a higher standard than other nations, as do *4 Ezra* and *2 Baruch*, thus hinting that the destruction was, if
not unfair, then at least not as black a mark as it might at first appear.
Another rabbinic tactic was to point to God's own grief at the punishment he imposed on his people, suggesting as subtly as possible that the
punishment was excessive.[70] But the dominant response was to insist
that the Jewish people was at fault; in the words of the festival liturgy,
"Because of our sins we were exiled from our land."[71]

The first-person plural of the liturgy is significant. It is not the language of a pious remnant amid a sinful majority, but the language of a
community that includes sinners in its midst. While *4 Ezra* reserves salvation for the few (7:45-61; 8:17-22), the rabbinic responses, even those
that try to shift the blame away from the people of Israel, do not differ-
entiate between a righteous remnant and a larger group of sinners. This
point should not be taken for granted. Like the Qumran community,
the rabbis could have attempted to separate a pious few from a majority
that through its sins had brought on disaster, and they could have
pointed to the words of Isaiah and other prophets as a warrant for this
step. Instead, they chose to embrace the dominant view of the Bible,
that Israel is a people defined by ancestry, judged and punished, forgiven and restored, as a community. They may have considered ordinary
Jews ignorant and careless in their religious practices, but they insisted
that they were not excluded from salvation.[72] This is true of the rabbis of
antiquity and of their heirs in the Middle Ages.

My understanding of the rabbis' rejection of a sectarian understanding of Israel differs somewhat from that of Shaye J. D. Cohen, although I
have been influenced by his argument.[73] While previous scholarship
tended to see Yavneh through the lens of the Council of Nicea, as the
moment at which the Pharisees triumphed over the other sects that had
been their opponents, for Cohen Yavneh represents "the creation of a
society which tolerates disputes without producing sects."[74] The Mishnah with its preservation of dissenting opinions is the most striking
piece of evidence for this development. The identification of the rabbis
with the Pharisees, assumed by most scholars, is too simple; even if many

or most of the rabbis at Yavneh had been Pharisees before 70, there is no sign of sectarian consciousness there.[75] The new outlook at Yavneh was made possible by the destruction of the temple, the primary locus of sectarian dispute in the period before 70.[76]

One difficulty with Cohen's picture is that the evidence for the disappearance of the sects after the destruction of the temple is elusive.[77] But more important for my purposes, even if the pre-70 sects did not survive long in the post-temple era, it would not necessarily mean the end of sectarianism.[78] As I have just noted, the prophetic idea of a righteous remnant has the potential to elicit a sectarian response to any disaster. The reaction to the destruction of the temple in *4 Ezra* is a good example; it has sectarian implications that could easily have been actualized in the right communal circumstances—and perhaps were, though we do not know. So too the devastation caused by the Bar Kokhba revolt and its suppression might have led the rabbis to separate themselves from the mass of Jews as much as possible, at least rhetorically. In fact, the rabbis' refusal of a sectarian self-understanding and embrace of the people as a whole was to a certain extent rhetorical. That is, the rabbis' embrace of an Israel consisting of all Jews is not so much an acceptance of other Jews in their sinfulness and variety as an effort to impose the rabbis' notion of Israel on other Jews, to insist that, whether they like it or not, all Jews are part of the holy people. In other words, one cannot take the "we" of the liturgy's "Because of our sins, we were exiled from our land" as a reflection of communal solidarity without further evidence from the specific historical context, which is unfortunately, rarely available.

Nonetheless, there can be no mistaking the antisectarian character of the rabbis' picture of the people of Israel and the central place it gives to ancestry.[79] Clearly there is ample precedent for this emphasis in biblical literature. But the importance of ancestry in rabbinic rhetoric is not simply a return to the biblical picture of Israel. Rather, I believe, it is a response to the emerging self-definition of Christians.[80]

Christians and Ethnic Identity

From the beginning Christianity claimed to transcend the old ethnic identifications. In Paul's famous formulation, in Christ, "There is neither Jew nor Greek, there is neither slave nor free, there is neither male nor female" (Gal 3:28), while the Book of Revelation speaks of creating a new people out of the saved of all the nations: thus the Lamb has "ransomed men for God from every tribe and tongue and people and nation, and ha[s] made them a kingdom and priests to our God" (Rev 5:9-10).[81]

Dispensing with the old distinctions does not mean that Christians dispensed with the language of ethnicity and race, as Denise Kimber

Buell has recently argued.[82] Thus Christians soon claim to be a third race in opposition to pagans and Jews.[83] But the Christian race differs from other nations or races because it is constituted not by birth but by merit. This is clear in a passage from the *Shepherd of Hermas* that Buell discusses at some length.[84] The *Shepherd of Hermas* is an apocalypse from the second century, probably written in Rome, though its language is Greek. In a vision, Hermas sees a tower that represents the church (*Sim.* 9.13.1), built of stones from twelve different mountains. The interpreting angel explains that the mountains represent the tribes (*phylai, Sim.* 9.17.1) or nations (*ethnē, Sim.* 9.17.2) of the earth. Although the stones are of many colors when they are mined from the mountains, when they are placed in the tower they become white; they represent those who "heard and believed" (*Sim.* 9.17.3-4). Indeed, according to the angel, the tower represents "the race (*genos*) of the righteous" (*Sim.* 9.17.5).[85] Thus the Christian race is not a race into which one is born. Rather, it is made up of people born into other races and nations who become part of the new race on the basis of righteousness. Of course, by some point in Christian history, perhaps late in the fourth century, being a Christian was in fact largely a matter of birth. But if the self-understanding of the *Shepherd of Hermas* was no longer accurate, it had not ceased to be relevant since the idea of Christianity as an identity that transcended birth was enshrined in the New Testament and other works from the early period.

It is also worth noting that Christian priesthood never becomes a hereditary office. The earliest Christians were self-consciously egalitarian; for John of Patmos, as we have seen, all of the saved were priests. Nonetheless, a religious hierarchy quickly emerged, but leadership was determined not by ancestry but by merit or at least some other form of status.[86] Of course, as the Christianization of the empire advanced, family ties and social connections became an increasingly important source of status within the church; one has only to think of the connections among the Cappadocian Fathers, the brothers Basil of Ceaserea and Gregory of Nyssa and their friend Gregory Naziansen.[87] But while certain families may have contributed more than their fair share to the ranks of bishops, there never developed a hereditary class of religious functionaries in Christianity, in part, perhaps, because of the value placed on celibacy. The avoidance of a hereditary priesthood did not, however, protect the priesthood from periodic complaints of corruption, and eventually the institution itself and the notion of mediation it entailed came under attack. Unlike the Jewish thinkers considered here, the Protestants who transformed the idea of a kingdom of priests into the idea of the priesthood of all believers were not constrained by the Torah's insistence on an actual class of hereditary priests.

Let me return now to Paul's famous formula of the transcendence of difference in Christ. Its conclusion is also important for our purposes.

There is neither Jew nor Greek, there is neither slave nor free, there is neither male nor female; for you are all one in Christ Jesus. And if you are Christ's, then you are Abraham's offspring, heirs according to the promise. (Gal 3:28-29)

Paul does not simply claim that the difference between Jews and gentiles is no longer relevant; he insists that gentiles too have become children of Abraham, and he supports this radical claim by means of exegesis of the Jews' own authoritative scriptures. The central point is that God's promise to Abraham for his offspring (Gen 12:7; 22:17-18) uses a singular form; thus "offspring" can only mean Christ (Gal 3:16), and one who is Christ's is thus also Abraham's offspring (Gal 3:29). The method by which Paul arrives at this conclusion demonstrates the other aspect of the challenge Christians posed for Jews: not only did they deny the Jews a special status conferred by birth, they also claimed the Jewish scriptures for themselves and asserted that they had a better way of reading them than did the Jews.

Children of Abraham

The sketch of the rabbis' distinctive understanding of the people of Israel that follows draws primarily on liturgical texts. They are a rich source for this understanding, and because they formulate the rabbis' views for the larger community that recites them, the views they express were particularly influential. Of course, no liturgical text explicitly acknowledges the Christian challenge to the uniqueness of the Jewish claim to Abraham. Yet the challenge illumines the recurrent interest of the liturgy in the patriarchs. The 'Amidah, the central prayer of each service, which dates to rabbinic times, begins:

Blessed are you, Lord our God and God of our ancestors, God of Abraham, God of Isaac, and God of Jacob, the great, the mighty, and the awesome God, God most high, who bestows kindness and creates everything, who remembers the good deeds of the ancestors and brings a redeemer to their children's children, with love, for the sake of his name.

In other words, Jews are assured of salvation not because of their own deeds but because of the piety of their ancestors.[88] A few blessings later the 'Amidah asks God's forgiveness because "we have sinned." Not only does the first-person plural maintain the unity of the people of Israel, rejecting any separation of the sinner from the rest of the Jewish people, but the perspective of the first blessing renders the sins less than catastrophic.

The *'Amidah* is not the only place the liturgy invokes Israel's ancestors to guarantee its salvation. The inclusion of the story of the binding of Isaac (Genesis 22) in the morning liturgy reflects the same idea, as is explicit in the prayer that follows the biblical passage:

May it be your will, Lord our God and God of our ancestors, that you remember on our behalf the covenant with our ancestors. Just as Abraham our father overcame his compassion for his only son and wished to slaughter him in order to do your will, so may your compassion overcome your anger at us.

The presence of the binding of Isaac in the liturgy is hardly innocent. The story was clearly a subject of contention between Jews and Christians.[89] As early Christians came to read it as a type of the crucifixion, Jews responded by developing their own theory of the redemptive power of Isaac's ordeal, and it is clear that at least some Jews had the crucifixion in view as they read Genesis. Thus *Genesis Rabbah*, composed in Palestine in the fourth and fifth centuries, comments on Gen 22:6, "And Abraham took the wood of the burnt offering and laid it on Isaac his son": "like the one who bears his cross on his shoulder" (*Gen. Rab.* 56.3). Later some Jewish texts insisted that Abraham had not held back his hand as ordered by the angel, that Isaac had died on the altar and had been resurrected.[90] The Christian use of the story appears to have left its mark on synagogue art as well.[91] The prayer following the recitation of Genesis 22, then, serves to appropriate this crucial event for the Jews as physical descendants of the patriarchs.

The clearest expression of the view that Jews can rely on ancestry when merit fails is found in the prayer that follows the binding of Isaac in the introductory morning service. The Babylonian Talmud (*b. Yoma* 87b) quotes the opening lines as a prayer for the Day of Atonement, and there is no reason to doubt that the opening lines point to the prayer more or less as we know it. The prayer begins by confessing collective unworthiness:

Master of the Universe, not because of our righteousness do we dare to beseech you, but because of your great mercy. For what are we? What are our lives? What is our goodness? What is our righteousness? What is our ability to save? What is our strength? What is our might? What can we plead before you, Lord our God and God of our ancestors? Are not all the mighty ones like nothing before you, and men of renown, as though they had never existed, and the wise, as if they lacked understanding? For most of their deeds are worthless, and the days of their lives are vanity before you, for "man has no advantage over the beasts; for all is vanity." (Eccl 3:19)

But even if Jews lack merit and life is potentially meaningless, they should not despair. Their ancestry assures God's concern for them and gives life meaning:

But we are your people, the children of your covenant, the children of Abraham your friend, to whom you made an oath on Mt. Moriah, the offspring of Isaac his only son, who was bound on the altar, the congregation of Jacob your first born son. . . . Happy are we, how good is our portion, how pleasant is our lot, how beautiful our inheritance! Happy are we that twice everyday, evening and morning, we recite, "Hear O Israel: The Lord our God is one Lord." (Deut 6:4)

This prayer abounds in the language of ancestry. Jews are the children of Abraham and the offspring of Isaac. Isaac is called Abraham's only son in an echo of the language in which God demands his sacrifice (Gen 22:2), though the designation is patently false since Abraham has an older son, Ishmael. Finally, Jacob, whose distinction among the patriarchs is that all his sons are heirs to the covenant and whose other name is the name of the people itself, Israel, is called God's firstborn son. If Christians claimed to have a path to salvation available to all who chose it, regardless of birth, this prayer answers that Jews were promised salvation simply on the basis of birth, without any particular effort on their part, though their texts also told them that they must strive to fulfill the terms of God's covenant with those ancestors whose merit guaranteed their salvation.

The idea that God's relationship with the people of Israel is a result of his love for Israel's ancestors goes back to the Book of Deuteronomy:

Behold, to the Lord your God belong heaven and the heaven of heavens, the earth with all that is in it; yet the Lord set his heart in love upon your ancestors and chose their descendants after them, you above all peoples, as at this day. Circumcise therefore the foreskin of your heart, and be no longer stubborn. For the Lord your God is God of gods and Lord of lords, the great, the mighty, and the awesome God, who is not partial and takes no bribe. (Deut 10:14-17)[92]

This is not the only place that Deuteronomy uses the Lord's love of Israel's ancestors to explain his relationship with their descendants (see Deut 4:37), and Deuteronomy also invokes the Lord's love of the descendants and his oaths to their ancestors to explain why he chose such an insignificant people (Deut 7:6-8). In none of these instances does Deuteronomy claim that the descendants, the people Moses addresses and, implicitly, the actual audience of the work at the time of its publication in the late seventh century B.C.E., were worthy of being chosen. Deuteronomy uses the fact of chosenness to exhort Israel to holiness; in all of these instances the Lord's love is linked to the demand that Israel keep the covenant and obey the Lord's commands (Deut 4:40; 7:9-11; 10:17-11:1). Further, if Israel fails to be a holy people and earns the Lord's wrath by violating his commands, Deuteronomy insists that it will be appropriately punished (e.g., Deuteronomy 29-30). The promise of restoration rests on the people's repentance.

The formulation of the first blessing of the 'Amidah, "the great, the mighty, and the awesome God," was clearly influenced by the passage from Deuteronomy quoted above. Yet by insisting that despite their sins Jews can count on their ancestors' bond with God to assure their salvation, this passage and the other passages from the liturgy go beyond anything in Deuteronomy or elsewhere in the Bible. Deuteronomy never claims that the Lord's love of Israel's ancestors or his oaths to them will protect the descendants, except perhaps indirectly: God's faithfulness to those who love him extends for a thousand generations (Deut 7:11). In the liturgy, the appeal to the merit of the ancestors passes over punishment and repentance, two crucial elements of the Deuteronomic schema. The authors of the liturgy apparently believed that punishments sufficient to the sins of any future generations had already taken place—the destruction of the temple, the failure of the Bar Kokhba revolt, the triumph of Christianity. All but the last act of the collective drama of the people of Israel is over. Individual Jews continue to live their lives, to sin and repent, to perform good deeds, and eventually to face their judgment. The drama of their fates is being played out at every moment. But Israel as a people has already been punished once and for all. All that remains is to await the messiah. The prominence in the liturgy of the merit of the ancestors as a guarantee of redemption suggests that in the face of a painful reality, some saw reassurance that redemption was on the way as more necessary than exhortation to repentance.

I conclude my discussion of the liturgy with a passage from the Mishnah that offers a clear statement of the rabbis' inclusive view of Israel, a passage that eventually became part of the liturgy: "All Israel has a portion in the world to come." In its original context, the opening of *m. Sanhedrin* 10:1, the passage is preceded by several chapters concerned with the rules for imposing the death penalty. Thus it offers a remarkable statement of the power of Jewish ancestry: because of their membership in the Jewish people even criminals deserving of death in this world have not forfeited their share in the world to come. After this opening, the remainder of *m. Sanhedrin* 10:1 and much of the chapter that follows go on to note beliefs and behaviors that disqualify Jews from the life of the world to come as well as individuals and groups who have been deprived of their share in that world. But despite the willingness to exclude some Jews, the point is clear: Jews who have not distinguished themselves by specific and primarily ideological sins can count on eternal life. It is worth noting, however, that two of the three complete manuscripts of the Mishnah that survive lack the positive statement about the fate of all Israelites in *m. Sanhedrin* 10:1, which begins instead with the list of those who have no share in the world to come. Yet even without the positive introduction, the negative list points to the positive conclusion, implying that those not mentioned in it have a share in the world to come. The manuscript evidence may then suggest that the positive formulation was added later to make certain that no one missed the point.[93]

The positive formulation and the proof text that accompanies it (Isa 60:21) in *m. Sanhedrin* 10:1 were eventually detached from the list of reasons for exclusion from the world to come that follows and placed at the beginning of the version of *m. 'Abot* used in the synagogue. Liturgical use guaranteed a wider audience for this passage than for *m. Sanhedrin* or the Mishnah generally. It is not clear when the passage from *m. Sanhedrin* was added to *m. 'Abot*, but an anonymous commentary to *m. 'Abot* found in Maḥzor Vitry discusses its significance.[94] The addition, the commentary explains, is intended to prevent the ignorant who hear *m. 'Abot* in synagogue from despairing that their sins prevent them from repenting and enjoying redemption.

There is, to be sure, considerable tension between this insistence on the redemption of all Israel and the exhortations to moral accountability so prominent in *m. 'Abot* and throughout rabbinic literature: "Consider three things, and you will not fall into sin: Know from whence you came, where you are going, and before whom you are fated to give an account" (*m. 'Abot* 3:1); "This world is like a vestibule before the world to come. Prepare yourself in the vestibule so that you may enter the banquet hall" (*m. 'Abot* 4:16). Surely no one who took the message of *m. 'Abot* to heart could doubt that many Jews would be found wanting when they stood before the divine judge. Yet, as in the *Book of Jubilees*, the emphasis on individual self-scrutiny stands side by side with the belief in collective salvation.

Synagogue Inscriptions and the People of Israel

We have seen that the synagogue mosaics provide important evidence for the way the temple was remembered. While it is more difficult to bring material evidence to bear on the question of how the people who built the synagogues and prayed in them understood the people of Israel to be constituted, donor inscriptions from the synagogues are of some interest for the question. Seth Schwartz has recently argued that the inscriptions reflect communities that saw themselves as self-contained units, each one a miniature people of Israel.[95] This understanding is reflected in their terminology for the community: "Israel," "holy congregation," "members of the holy community," "people."[96] Further, the inscriptions offer rather little evidence of hierarchy within the community beyond references to priestly ancestry, as noted above,

Levitical ancestry, or the use of the honorific "rabbi." It seems unlikely that the communities were as egalitarian as the inscriptions imply, but it is significant that the donors, who were presumably somewhat wealthier than most members of the community, chose to represent themselves and the community as they did.[97]

Further, each community is separated from other such communities not by claims to greater piety or by ideological differences of any kind but by geography, and at least some inscriptions understood the miniature Israels as part of a larger Israel.[98] One inscription, from the Jericho synagogue of the sixth or early seventh century, is particularly striking:

May they be remembered for good, may their memory be for good, all the holy congregation, great and small, whom the King of the Universe helped so that they pledged and made the mosaic. May He who knows their names and those of their sons and the members of their household, inscribe them in the book of life with all the righteous. (They are) friends to all Israel. Peace [Amen].[99]

The inscription's inclusion of all members of the community is emphatic: "all the holy congregation, great and small." Further, the inscription connects the members of the community of Jericho to the larger community of the Jewish people: they are "friends to all Israel." Schwartz notes that the explicit reference to the larger Israel is unusual but not unique: "May there be peace on this place and on all the places of Israel" appears on the lintels of two somewhat earlier synagogues. Indeed the very use of the term "Israel" invokes the larger entity.[100]

The inscriptions, then, offer no explicit definition of the people of Israel. Yet they imply an inclusive understanding in which all Jews, both great and small, form part of the holy people, the understanding also reflected in the liturgy that was presumably in use in the synagogues in which the inscriptions were recorded.

Christianity and Conversion to Judaism

I have argued that the rabbis attempted to trump the Christian claim to constitute a people saved on the basis of merit by insisting that the people of Israel was saved by virtue of its ancestry, a less transient possession, after all, than merit. But they could have responded quite differently and redefined the Jewish people precisely on the basis of merit. As we have seen, Jews had recognized for some time that birth was not the only way to become a member of the Jewish people. Gentiles who so desired could convert to Judaism. The rabbis' acceptance of conversion was not merely passive; they devoted considerable energy to regulating a process marked by a diversity of approaches in the later Second Temple period and to achieving a careful definition of the status of converts.

Nor was the embrace of conversion confined to literature known only to the rabbinic elite: the daily *'Amidah* prays for God's mercy on "the righteous and the pious, the elders of your people, the house of Israel, and the remnant of their scribes, the proselytes, and us."

In principle, the possibility of conversion should have transformed ideas of Jewish identity, moving them away from ancestry toward choice or merit, and recent books by Shaye J. D. Cohen[101] and Christine E. Hayes[102] have emphasized its significance for rabbinic definitions of the Jewish people. For Hayes,

> The rabbis broke with the rigid and highly impermeable group boundary prevalent in Second Temple Jewish sources and established a more clearly permeable one. They did this by championing the older Torah vision of Israel as a nation, yes, but a nation bound by a divine Covenant. In other words, biological filiation remained a value, but it was not deemed the only factor in determining group membership. . . . Through the formal recognition of conversion, the rabbis created a legal and ritual process whereby biological fact was to be understood as altered by legal fiction.[103]

Hayes's claim that the boundaries the rabbis set up were more permeable than those of Second Temple sources would be somewhat less startling if she had spelled out here what she makes explicit elsewhere in the book: the Second Temple sources she has in mind are *Jubilees*, 4QMMT, and perhaps other texts from Qumran that, in her view, share the "holy seed" ideology of the Book of Ezra.[104] I disagree with Hayes's reading of 4QMMT,[105] but she is certainly correct that *Jubilees* does not allow for the possibility of a gentile becoming a Jew. Yet, as Hayes herself recognizes, outside of sectarian circles, which viewed most Jews as children of darkness, and *Jubilees*, notions of Jewish identity in the Second Temple period were quite fluid.[106] The opposition to the assimilation of gentiles into the Jewish people in *Jubilees* reflects a situation in which the majority accepted such a process, perhaps without any formal ritual of conversion, as I argued in Chapter 2.[107]

It is clear that Hayes, like most moderns (I include myself among them), prefers the rabbis' view of Jewish identity in which, as she puts it, "genealogy and biological filiation were not dispensed with, but . . . were overcome"[108] to the exclusively genealogical view of *Jubilees*. Indeed, Hayes's book as a whole can be read as a defense of the rabbis against charges of inward-looking exclusivism. Thus, for example, after arguing persuasively that the notion of gentile impurity is an innovation of the tannaim, she suggests that it be understood not as a way of deterring Jews from entering mixed marriages, for which it would surely have been ineffective, but rather as "a resistance to, a contestation of, competing characterizations of mixed marriages that is striking in its very *leniency.*"[109] I suspect that Hayes's desire to defend the rabbis leads to overestimating the importance of conversion not only in social reality but even in the rabbis' own rhetoric.

Cohen summarizes his view of the development of rabbinic ideas about Jewish identity thus:

> The boundary between Us and Them is a combination of religion or "culture" . . . and ethnicity or "birth." . . . In a number of passages Philo, Josephus, and the rabbis explicitly acknowledge the duality of the boundary, but do not seem to realize that its two aspects are fundamentally irreconcilable. The identity system that would attain canonical form in rabbinic Judaism was a union of disparate elements, Jewishness as a function of religion and Jewishness as a function of descent.[110]

Cohen locates the origins of the idea of conversion in the conquests of the Hasmoneans that led Idumeans and Itureans to become Judeans, a process against which I understand the *Book of Jubilees* to be reacting (Chapter 2 above). The process had both a political and a religious aspect.[111] The rabbis undertook to regulate the process and develop a ritual to enact the transformation.[112] They also devoted considerable energy to defining the status of converts and of the offspring of unions of born Jews and converts as well as Jews and gentiles, as Hayes too notes.[113] Yet, Cohen points out, "Rabbinic hegemony and the political setting of Jewish communities from late antiquity to early modern times jointly ensured that Jewishness would be neither elusive nor problematic."[114] Thus for Cohen, in contrast to Hayes, the normalization of the process of conversion by the rabbis is part of a larger concern to clarify boundaries, not to lower them.[115] On this Cohen seems to me more persuasive than Hayes.

Cohen and Hayes are undoubtedly correct in their claim that the idea of conversion makes rabbinic Judaism something other than a religion of ancestry or, in Cohen's terms, an ethnic religion. Yet I believe they overestimate the actual impact of the idea. This is perhaps inevitable; a study of rabbinic views of conversion necessarily focuses on texts concerned with conversion. But the passages from the liturgy just discussed suggest that while the idea of conversion had the potential to transform ideas about Jewish identity, its actual impact was very limited. Converts were seen as exceptions to the rule rather than as exemplars of a new set of rules. The limited impact of conversion is perhaps in part because of its association with Christianity. After a certain point, of course, most Christians were the children of Christians, and baptism became less a ritual of conversion than a rite of passage. Further, the opposite side of Christianity's self-understanding as a religion of converts, open to all, is that there is no salvation outside the church. Precisely because they defined Israel by ancestry, some rabbis thought it unfair to exclude all others from salvation; thus they claim that righteous gentiles have a share in the world to come (*t. Sanh.* 13.2).[116]

Kingdom of Priests or Children of Abraham?

I would like to conclude by returning to the phrase that was the starting point of this book, "a kingdom of priests." It is significant that the rabbis showed little interest in the phrase.[117] The *Mekilta*'s comment on Exod 19:6 is worth noting:

> The sages said: The Israelites before they made the Golden Calf were eligible to eat of the holy things. But after they made the Golden Calf these holy things were taken from them and given to priests exclusively. (*Baḥodeš* 2)[118]

This interpretation takes the phrase "a kingdom of priests" quite literally, but restricts its relevance to a time far in the past, robbing it of any contemporary significance. As we have seen, Philo offered a similarly historical explanation for the fact that the Passover sacrifice is offered not by priests but by heads of household: priests did not yet exist as a separate group at the time of the first Passover sacrifice. But Philo goes on to draw a moral with profound implications for the time after the Exodus: the nation is the archetype of the priesthood (*Questions and Answers on Exodus* 1.10). Not so the passage from the *Mekilta*.

Indeed the rabbis' lack of interest in the phrase "a kingdom of priests" is itself suggestive. The problem the phrase embodied for Jews in the Second Temple period had in a sense been resolved by the destruction of the temple. In the days when the priests performed a crucial service, sinful priests were a constant reminder that birth did not guarantee piety. With the temple gone, sinful priests were a less powerful reminder of this still relevant truth. Perhaps this made the embrace of the dominant biblical understanding of the people of Israel as the children of Abraham, a community defined by birth and judged as a whole, less difficult. Converts were not to be excluded, but they were exceptions who did nothing to change the essential logic of Jewish community. In the face of a Christian empire that claimed they were no longer the heirs to God's promises to their ancestors, Jews came to insist that their very birth promised them redemption despite their own failings.

Notes

Introduction

1. Nor does it receive much attention in rabbinic literature. See Daniel R. Schwartz, "'Kingdom of Priests'—a Pharisaic Slogan?" in *Studies in the Jewish Background of Christianity*, Wissenschaftliche Untersuchungen zum Neuen Testament 60 (Tübingen: Mohr [Siebeck], 1992) 57–66.

2. Unless otherwise noted, translations of books of the Bible and Apocrypha are taken from the Revised Standard Version (RSV). The story appears to bring together three different stories of rebellion: of the Levites, of the "leaders of the assembly" (Num 16:2), and of Dathan and Abiram. The insistence on the holiness of the entire people comes from the revolt of the leaders of the assembly. See Israel Knohl, *The Sanctuary of Silence: The Priestly Torah and the Holiness School* (Minneapolis: Fortress, 1995) 73–85, for a recent discussion.

3. Paul D. Hanson *The Dawn of Apocalyptic: The Historical and Sociological Roots of Jewish Apocalyptic Eschatology*, rev. ed. (Philadelphia: Fortress, 1979) 68, calls this passage "an astonishing democratization of the formerly exclusive sacerdotal office." This view is quoted (from the first edition [1975]) and rejected by Joseph Blenkinsopp, *Isaiah 56-66*, Anchor Bible 19B (New York: Doubleday, 2003) 226. Blenkinsopp sees the passage as an instance of the theme of the despoiling of the Egyptians that he finds elsewhere in 3 Isaiah, including Isa 60:5-7, 16. I have criticized Hanson's larger argument (Martha Himmelfarb, *Ascent to Heaven in Jewish and Christian Apocalypses* [New York: Oxford University Press, 1993] 26–28), and I think he is mistaken to suggest that the prophet is advocating a change in cultic personnel. But the rhetoric of the passage is indeed remarkable, and to subsume it under the heading of "despoiling the Egyptians" fails to do it justice.

4. Thus I disagree with Schwartz, who seems to believe that this outer-directed sense of Israel as a priestly people among the nations of the world "does not supply any support for the inner-Jewish application of the verse" ("'Kingdom,'" 58).

5. I single out this passage because it can more confidently be attributed to Isaiah of Jerusalem than many of the other passages referring to a remnant in Isaiah 1-39. The language of Isa 1:27, 4:2-6, 6:13, and 10:20-22 shows significant points of contact with post-exilic prophecy, thus making it likely that these passages are later additions to the words of Isaiah of Jerusalem. See Joseph Blenkinsopp, *Isaiah 1-39*, Anchor Bible 19 (New York: Doubleday, 2000) 110–11 and comments to the passages noted.

6. Thus the corpus of laws in the Torah for the stranger, *gēr*, dwelling among the people in the land, reflecting the exceptional status of non-Israelite residents of the land.

7. The designation "foreign" perhaps belongs in quotation marks because there is reason to believe that some of those whom Ezra and Nehemiah treated as foreigners viewed themselves as Israelites or at least as worshipers of the God of Israel. Thus Nehemiah's enemy Tobiah the Ammonite bears a Yahwist name, and Neh 2:20 hints that Tobiah and Sanballat do not consider themselves foreigners.

8. The genealogy of Ruth 4:18–22 is widely regarded as a later addition, but opinions about Ruth 4:17, which makes the connection to David, are divided. See Edward F. Campbell, Jr., *Ruth*, Anchor Bible 7 (Garden City, N.Y.: Doubleday, 1975) 169, 172–73.

9. See, e.g., Shaye J. D. Cohen, *The Beginnings of Jewishness: Boundaries, Varieties, Uncertainties* (Berkeley: University of California Press, 1999) 156–74.

10. See Shaye J. D. Cohen, "Religion, Ethnicity, and 'Hellenism' in the Emergence of Jewish Identity in Maccabean Palestine," in *Religion and Religious Practice in the Seleucid Kingdom*, ed. Per Bilde et al. (Aarhus: Aarhus University Press, 1990) 204–23; and idem, *Beginnings*, 109–39.

11. The fragment of Clearchus is preserved in Josephus, *Against Apion* 1.176-83; see also Menahem Stern, *Greek and Latin Authors on Jews and Judaism* (Jerusalem: Israel Academy of Sciences and Humanities, 1974–84) 1.47-52.

12. The term "Judaism" is first attested in 2 Maccabees (2:21, 8:1, 13:48).

13. Knohl, *Sanctuary*, argues that this passage comes from H, not P (96–97).

14. Menahem Haran, *Temples and Temple Service in Ancient Israel* (rept. with corrections, Winona Lake, Ind: Eisenbrauns, 1985) 58–71, argues that while the early sources—J, E, and the non-Deuteronomic portions of the former prophets—accept the idea that any Israelite can sacrifice at an altar, it is their more or less unanimous view that priests serving in *temples* were of Levitical descent. The story about Micah's temple supports the point: in this out-of-the-way spot, the proprietor of the temple was prepared to use one of his sons as a priest, but much preferred to employ a Levite when that became possible (Haran, *Temples*, 78).

15. Some scholars argue that a tribal basis for priesthood is a later construct. Because there is little clear evidence for the existence of a tribe of Levi in early biblical sources, they see the tribe as a later invention intended to find a genealogical place for an important group that had originally constituted a guild, though membership in the guild may well have been passed on from father to son given the highly specialized nature of the profession. See, e.g., Baruch A. Levine, *Numbers 1–20*, Anchor Bible 4A (New York: Doubleday, 1993) 280–86. Against this view, see Haran, *Temples*, 71–83.

16. The precise figures are 4,289 priests and 341 Levites. So too almost a century later Ezra discovers that the group of Israelites assembled to return to Judea lacks Levites altogether, and he must make strenuous efforts to find some (Ezra 8:15-20).

17. John R. Bartlett, "Zadok and His Successors at Jerusalem," *Journal of Theological Studies* n.s. 19 (1968): 1–18.

18. For discussion of the view of Zadok as a Canaanite priest employed by David and arguments in favor of his Aaronide lineage, see Frank Moore Cross, *Canaanite Myth and Hebrew Epic: Essays in the History of the Religion of Israel* (Cambridge, Mass.: Harvard University Press, 1973) 207–15. Haran argues for Zadok's Levitical lineage in somewhat different terms (*Temples*, 70–82).

19. On the one temple, see Gideon Bohak, "Theopolis: A Single-Temple Policy and Its Singular Ramifications," *Journal of Jewish Studies* 50 (1999): 3–16. On the one text, see Martha Himmelfarb, "The Torah between Athens and Jerusalem: Jewish Difference in Antiquity," in *Ancient Judaism in Its Hellenistic Context*, ed. Carol Bakhos, Supplements to the Journal for the Study of Judaism 95 (Leiden: Brill, 2005).

Chapter 1

1. This is a schematic account of a far more complex situation. For a consideration of the history of the priesthood between the destruction and the rebuilding of the Jerusalem temple, see Joseph Blenkinsopp, "The Judaean Priesthood during the Neo-Babylonian and Achaemenid Periods: A Hypothetical Reconstruction," *Catholic Biblical Quarterly* 60 (1998): 25–43.

2. Two descendants of David, Sheshbazzar (Ezra 1) and Zerubbabel (Ezra 2-6; Zechariah 3-4), play significant roles in the community of the return. On other Davidide governors, see Carol L. Meyers and Eric M. Meyers, "Jerusalem and Zion after the Exile: The Evidence of First Zechariah," in *"Sha 'arei Talmon": Studies in the Bible, Qumran, and the Ancient Near East Presented to Shemaryahu Talmon*, ed. Michael Fishbane and Emmanuel Tov (Winona Lake, Ind.: Eisenbrauns, 1992); and Eric M. Meyers, "The Persian Period and the Judean Restoration: From Zerubbabel to Nehemiah," in *Ancient Israelite Religion: Essays in Honor of Frank Moore Cross*, ed. Patrick D. Miller, Paul D. Hanson, and S. Dean McBride (Philadelphia: Fortress, 1987).

3. E.g., *Jewish War* 2.261-63; *Antiquities* 18.85-87; 20.97-98, 169–71.

4. My translation.

5. The term "wisdom" appears only in chap. 1 of the Book of Daniel, and it is restricted to Daniel and his friends.

6. Translations differ considerably: "from that which is in charge of the Levitical priests" (RSV and New Revised Standard Version); "at the dictation of the levitical priests" (Revised English Bible, Jerusalem Bible). The New Jewish Publication Society version resorts to implicit emendation: "When he is seated on his royal throne, he shall have a copy of this Teaching written for him on a scroll by the levitical priests"; a note to "by" reads, "Nuance of Heb. *milliphne* uncertain."

7. I have modified the translation of RSV, which reads "direct" for "teach."

8. I am much influenced by an unpublished paper by Steven D. Fraade, "'They Shall Teach Your Statutes to Jacob': Priest, Scribe, and Sage in Second Temple Times," which argues that most of the scribes of the Second Temple period known to us by name were also priests.

9. For a discussion of the process of composition, see George W. E. Nickelsburg, *1 Enoch 1: A Commentary on the Book of 1 Enoch, Chapters 1–36; 81–108*, Hermeneia (Minneapolis: Fortress, 2001) 25, 132, 229, 278, 290–92. Nickelsburg is agnostic about whether chaps. 6–11, the narrative of the fall of the angels and its aftermath, formed part of the original work, although he believes that chaps. 12–16 represent an interpretation of the traditions of chaps. 6–11 (229).

10. My translation.

11. Nickelsburg, *Commentary*, 230. My reading of this portion of the *Book of the Watchers* is influenced by the work of Annette Yoshiko Reed, "'What the Fallen

Angels Taught': The Reception-History of the *Book of the Watchers* in Judaism and Christianity" (Ph.D. diss., Princeton University, 2002), revised as *Fallen Angels and the History of Judaism and Christianity: The Reception of Enochic Literature* (Cambridge: Cambridge University Press, 2005); and idem, "Heavenly Ascent, Angelic Descent, and the Transmission of Knowledge in 1 Enoch 6-16," in *Heavenly Realms and Earthly Realities in Late Antique Religions*, ed. Ra'anan S. Boustan and Annette Yoshiko Reed (Cambridge: Cambridge University Press, 2004).

12. James C.VanderKam, *Enoch and the Growth of an Apocalyptic Tradition*, Catholic Biblical Quarterly Monograph Series 16 (Washington, D.C.: Catholic Biblical Association, 1984) 104–5. At the conclusion of the *Astronomical Book*, chaps. 81–82 elaborate the picture of Enoch as scribe, but they are unlikely to have formed part of the original *Astronomical Book*. Nickelsburg, *Commentary*, connects them to the *Book of the Watchers*. For a critique of Nickelsburg's position, Annette Yoshiko Reed, "The Textual Identity, Literary History, and Social Setting of 1 Enoch: Reflections on George Nickelsburg's Commentary on 1 Enoch 1-36; 81-108," *Archiv für Religionsgeschichte* 5 (2003): 279–96.

13. All translations of the *Book of the Watchers* are taken from Nickelsburg, *Commentary*. In *1 Enoch* 15:1, Nickelsburg translates, "Enoch, righteous man and scribe of truth." The Aramaic is no longer extant for either *1 Enoch* 12:4 or 15:1. The Greek for *1 Enoch* 12:4 is *grammateus tēs dikaiosynēs*; for *1 Enoch* 15:1, *grammateus tēs alētheias*. Aramaic *qušta'* could be translated by either *dikaiosynē*, righteousness, or *alētheia*, truth. See Nickelsburg's discussion of his translation and the meaning of the two phrases (*Commentary*, 270).

14. Reed, "Heavenly Ascent," 61–66.

15. Himmelfarb, *Ascent*, 75–77.

16. VanderKam, *Enoch*, 179–80.

17. See the seminal article of George W. E. Nickelsburg, "Enoch, Levi, and Peter: Recipients of Revelation in Upper Galilee," *Journal of Biblical Literature* 100 (1981): 576–87.

18. See Himmelfarb, *Ascent*, 11–12 for a more detailed discussion and references.

19. Haran, *Temples*, 276–88.

20. See the *Book of Dreams* (*1 Enoch* 89:73) for an explicit claim to this effect; the Apocalypse of Weeks in the *Epistle of Enoch* (*1 Enoch* 93:9-10, 91:11) omits the Second Temple from its historical schema altogether, a silence that Nickelsburg, *Commentary*, reads as a rejection (447). See also Himmelfarb, "Temple and Priests in the *Book of the Watchers*, the Animal Apocalypse, and the Apocalypse of Weeks" (forthcoming).

21. For a more detailed discussion of heaven as temple with references to other literature, see Himmelfarb, *Ascent*, 14–20.

22. Exodus offers instructions for the building of the sanctuary and an account of the building (chaps. 25–27, 36–39); 1 Kings describes the building of Solomon's temple (chaps. 6–7), for which there is a parallel account in 2 Chronicles 3-4; and Ezekiel offers a plan for the restored temple (chaps. 40–42).

23. For biblical parallels, see Exod 26:1 (curtains of the sanctuary); 1 Kings 6:29; Ezek 41:17-19.

24. For biblical parallels, see Exod 25:18-22; 1 Kings 6:23-28. Ezekiel's holy of holies (Ezek 41:3-5, 17-24) does not contain a throne of cherubim until the glory of the Lord returns on the chariot throne (Ezek 43:1-5).

25. Nickelsburg, *Commentary*, 265–66.

26. Nickelsburg, *Commentary*, 271, treats Enoch's intercession as part of his

role as scribe and emphasizes the prophetic aspects of that role; he also notes possible priestly connections.

27. On this point, see Nickelsburg's admirably cautious formulation in, "Enoch, Levi," 586.

28. Nickelsburg, "Enoch, Levi," 585–86.

29. Ibid. See also David Suter, "Fallen Angel, Fallen Priest: The Problem of Family Purity in 1 Enoch 6-16," *Hebrew Union College Annual* 50 (1979): 115–35.

30. Nickelsburg, *Commentary*, 271–72.

31. See the discussion in Chapter 3 below.

32. Nickelsburg takes issue with my claim that *Psalms of Solomon* is not directed against priests in particular, but does not mention my claim for CD (both in Himmelfarb, *Ascent*, 21) (*Commentary*, 272). I am now inclined to accept Nickelsburg's reading of the *Psalms of Solomon*.

33. In his edition of *1 Enoch*, Michael A. Knibb emends this clause to "you lusted after the daughters of men" (in consultation with Edward Ullendorff, *The Ethiopic Book of Enoch: A New Edition in Light of the Aramaic Dead Sea Scrolls* [Oxford: Clarendon Press, 1978] 2.100). The emendation is accepted by Matthew Black in his translation (in consultation with James C. VanderKam, *The Book of Enoch or 1 Enoch: A New English Edition*, Studia in Veteris Testamenti Pseudepigrapha [Leiden: Brill, 1985] 152). The emendation eliminates one instance of a figurative use of "blood" from the passage, but my argument stands without it.

34. See the discussion of Jacob Milgrom, *Leviticus 1-16*, Anchor Bible 3 (New York: Doubleday, 1991) 310–13, in his discussion of the sacrifices of Lev 5:1-13.

35. Nickeslburg, "Enoch, Levi," 585.

36. Eibert J. C. Tigchelaar, *Prophets of Old and the Day of the End: Zechariah, the Book of Watchers and Apocalyptic* (Leiden: Brill, 1996) 198–203.

37. See Martha Himmelfarb, "Levi, Phinehas, and the Problem of Intermarriage at the Time of the Maccabean Revolt," *Jewish Studies Quarterly* 6 (1999): 1–23. The *Book of Jubilees*, as we shall see in the next chapter, does perceive a problem in the Hasmonean period, but its perception reflects its distinctive understanding of the people of Israel. (This claim represents a development of my position in the article cited in this note.)

38. Nickelsburg, *Commentary*, 230.

39. For the text and translation of *Aramaic Levi*, I use Robert A. Kugler, *From Patriarch to Priest: The Levi-Priestly Tradition from Aramaic Levi to Testament of Levi*, Society of Biblical Literature Early Judaism and Its Literature 9 (Atlanta: Scholars Press, 1996). I was unable to make use of Jonas C. Greenfield, Michael E. Stone, and Esther Eshel, *The Aramaic Levi Document: Edition, Translation, Commentary*, Studia in Veteris Testamenti Pseudepigrapha 19 (Leiden: Brill, 2004); or of Henryk Drawnel, *An Aramaic Wisdom Text from Qumran: A New Interpretation of the Levi Document*, Supplements to the Journal for the Study of Judaism 86 (Leiden: Brill, 2004); both works appeared after I had completed this chapter.

40. It uses a solar calendar, and it refers to Enoch's condemnation of Levi's descendents (*Ar. Levi* 102). See Jonas Greenfield and Michael E. Stone, "Remarks on the Aramaic Testament of Levi from the Geniza," *Revue biblique* 86 (1979): 224–25.

41. The discussion of *Aramaic Levi* here is based on my discussion in "Levi, Phinehas," 3–6.

42. The text is extremely fragmentary here, but the fragments can be supplemented by comparison to *Jubilees* 30, which either drew on *Aramaic Levi* directly or shared a source with it (Kugler, *From Patriarch*, 36–37, 83–86).

43. Robert A. Kugler, "Halakic Interpretive Strategies at Qumran: A Case Study," in *Legal Texts and Legal Issues: Proceedings of the Second Meeting of the International Organization for Qumran Studies, Cambridge 1995, Published in Honour of Joseph M. Baumgarten,* ed. Moshe Bernstein, Florentino García Martínez, and John Kampen, Studies on the Texts of the Desert of Judah 23 (Leiden: Brill, 1997) 133–35, particularly n. 15; this represents a change from his interpretation in *From Patriarch,* 103.

44. The plural form is difficult, but does not figure in the interpretation of *Aramaic Levi.*

45. This reading of Josephus requires textual emendation, but the emendation has been widely accepted. See the note there, *Josephus IV: Jewish Antiquities, Book I–IV,* trans. Henry St. J. Thackeray, Loeb Classical Library (London: William Heinemann; New York: G. P. Putnam's Sons, 1930) 452.

46. On the use of *zōnâ* in this sense, John Kampen, "4QMMT and New Testament Studies," in *Reading 4QMMT: New Perspectives on Qumran Law and History,* ed. John Kampen and Moshe J. Bernstein, Society of Biblical Literature Symposium Series 2 (Atlanta: Scholars Press, 1996) 135–38. See also Kampen, "The Matthean Divorce Texts Reexamined," in *New Qumran Texts and Studies: Proceedings of the First Meeting of the International Organization for Qumran Studies, Paris 1992,* ed. George J. Brooke with Florentino García Martínez, Studies on the Texts of the Desert of Judah 15 (Leiden: Brill, 1994) 149–67, and Kugler, "Halakic Interpretive Strategies," 131–40.

47. Here I disagree with Kugler, *From Patriarch,* 108–10. For my view, see, briefly, below, the section on *Aramaic Levi,* and in more detail, my "Earthly Sacrifice and Heavenly Incense: The Law of the Priesthood in *Aramaic Levi* and *Jubilees,*" in *Heavenly Realms,* ed. Boustan and Reed, 104–16.

48. RSV: stock.

49. Elisha Qimron and John Strugnell, *Qumran Cave 4.V: Miqsat Ma'aśe ha-Torah,* Discoveries in the Judaean Desert 10 (Oxford: Clarendon Press, 1994).

50. "Holy" in this passage is a reconstruction.

51. Qimron, "The Halakha," in *Qumran Cave 4.V,* 171–75; Himmelfarb, "Levi, Phinehas," 6–11, arrives at the same conclusion but criticizes Qimron's argument. See also Lester L. Grabbe, "4QMMT and Second Temple Jewish Society," in *Legal Texts,* ed. Bernstein, García Martínez, and Kampen, 103n. 54, who criticizes Qimron's arguments in "The Halakha" and expresses sympathy for the other position, but remains agnostic.

52. Joseph M. Baumgarten, quoted by Qimron and Strugnell, *Qumran Cave 4.V,* 55, note to line 75, and Qimron, "The Halakha," in *Qumran Cave 4.V,* 171n. 178a; Carolyn J. Sharp, "Phinean Zeal and the Rhetorical Strategy in 4QMMT," *Revue de Qumran* 18 (1997): 216–17. Kugler, "Halakic Interpretive Strategies," 135–36, thinks the text too obscure to permit a conclusion, but criticizes Qimron and Strugnell for suggesting one with too much certainty.

53. Himmelfarb, "Levi, Phinehas."

54. Christine E. Hayes, *Gentile Impurities and Jewish Identities: Intermarriage and Conversion from the Bible to the Talmud* (New York: Oxford University Press, 2002) 82–89.

55. See Chapter 2.

56. Remarkably, Qimron considers the passage from *Aramaic Levi* (which he calls *Testament of Levi*) "a clear example of a ruling in favour of endogamy" ("The Halakha," in *Qumran Cave 4.V,* 174).

57. Hayes, *Gentile Impurities,* 83–84.

58. Michael E. Stone, "Lists of Revealed Things in Apocalyptic Literature," in *Magnalia Dei: The Mighty Acts of God. Essays on the Bible and Archeology in Memory of G. Ernest Wright,* ed. Frank M. Cross, Werner Lemke, and Patrick D. Miller (Garden City, N.Y.: Doubleday, 1976) 444n. 1.

59. Nickelsburg, *Commentary,* 262.

60. Himmelfarb, *Ascent,* 72–73.

61. On the divine council, see Cross, *Canaanite Myth,* 186–90; E. Theodore Mullen, *The Assembly of the Gods,* Harvard Semitic Monographs 24 (Chico, Calif.: Scholars Press, 1980) 175–209.

62. On this last point, see Nickelsburg, "Enoch, Levi," 580.

63. The evidence about the name is actually somewhat complicated. The Greek manuscripts usually give the name as Joshua ben Sira ben Eleazar (Sir 50:27). The surviving Hebrew (MS B) gives it as Simon ben Joshua ben Eleazar ben Sira. The grandson's reference to "my grandfather Joshua" (RSV: Jesus) in the prologue to his translation confirms the first name according to the Greek. For the Hebrew text of ben Sira, see Pancratius C. Beentjes, *The Book of Ben Sira in Hebrew,* Ssupplements to Vetus Testamentum 68 (Leiden: Brill, 1997).

64. For discussion and references, see Patrick W. Skehan, trans. and notes, and Alexander A. Di Lella, intro. and commentary, *The Wisdom of Ben Sira,* Anchor Bible 39 (New York: Doubleday, 1987) 576–80.

65. E.g., Di Lella, *Ben Sira,* 576–80; also Randal A. Argall, *1 Enoch and Sirach: A Comparative and Conceptual Analysis of the Themes of Revelation, Creation, and Judgment,* Early Judaism and Its Literature 8 (Atlanta: Scholars Press, 1995) 66–73.

66. See, e.g., James A. Sanders, *The Psalms Scroll of Qumran Cave 11 (11QPs^a),* Discoveries in the Judaean Desert 4 (Oxford: Clarendon Press, 1965) 83–85; idem, *The Dead Sea Psalms Scroll* (Ithaca, N.Y.: Cornell University Press, 1967) 112–17; Celia Deutsch, "The Sirach 51 Acrostic: Confession and Exhortation," *Zeitschrift für die alttestamentliche Wissenschaft* 94 (1982): 400–409.

67. Lester L. Grabbe, *Priests, Prophets, Diviners, Sages: A Socio-historical Study of Religious Specialists in Ancient Israel* (Valley Forge, Pa.: Trinity Press International, 1995) 171–74.

68. E.g., Helge Stadelmann, *Ben Sira als Schriftgelehrter,* Wissenschaftliche Untersuchungen zum Neuen Testament 2/6 (Tübingen: Mohr [Siebeck], 1980) 13–26; Saul Olyan, "Ben Sira's Relationship to the Priesthood," *Harvard Theological Review* 80 (1987): 262–63, 275–76.

69. All translations of ben Sira are taken from the RSV unless otherwise indicated; the RSV offers a translation of the Greek text of ben Sira.

70. Ben Sira's term for this profession or calling is *sōpēr* or *grammateus* (Sir 38:24); the term appears only once in this passage but in a prominent spot, the very beginning of the account. The literal translation "scribe" seems hardly adequate for the activities ben Sira describes. Thus the Revised English Bible translates "scholar," while Michael E. Stone ("Ideal Figures and Social Context: Priest and Sage in the Early Second Temple Age," in *Ancient Israelite Religion,* ed. Miller, Hanson, and McBride, 575–86) uses "sage" and Johannes Marböck ("Sir. 38, 24–39,11: Der schriftgelehrte Weise. Eine Beitrag zu Gestalt und Werk ben Siras," in *La sagesse de l'ancien testament,* ed. Maurice Gilbert, 2nd ed.; Bibliotheca ephemeridum theologicarum lovaniensium 51 [Louvain: Louvain University Press, 1990] 293–316) calls this figure "der schriftgelehrte Weise." Although ben Sira fails to mention Ezra in his Praise of the Fathers, his lofty understanding of the functions of the scribe surely reflects the career of the most famous biblical

figure to bear the title "scribe" (so too Marböck, "Sir. 38,24–39,11," 297–99; see P. Höffken, "Warum schwieg Jesus Sirach über Esra?," *Zeitschrift für die alttestamentliche Wissenschaft* 87 [1975]: 184–201, for a very different position).

71. One of these visions (Zechariah 3) is of a scene in the heavenly court, and the speeches of the participants clarify the action. In another (Zech 2:5-9), Zechariah encounters an angel with a measuring rod in hand who explains that he is going off to measure Jerusalem.

72. See Michael Fishbane, "The Qumran Pesher and Traits of Ancient Hermeneutics," *Proceeding of the Sixth World Congress of Jewish Studies* (Jerusalem: World Union of Jewish Studies, 1977) 97–114; idem, *Biblical Interpretation in Ancient Israel* (Oxford: Clarendon Press, 1985) 447–57, for discussion of the form and its ancient Near Eastern background.

73. Martha Himmelfarb, *Tours of Hell: An Apocalyptic Form in Jewish and Christian Literature* (Philadelphia: University of Pennsylvania Press, 1983) 50–60.

74. The Book of Malachi also dates to the Persian period, but it contains no references to Persian kings or contemporary figures.

75. On deeds as defining prophets for ben Sira, see Burton L. Mack, *Wisdom and the Hebrew Epic: Ben Sira's Hymn in Praise of the Fathers* (Chicago: University of Chicago Press, 1985) 28.

76. This is a literal translation of the Greek. There is no Hebrew extant. RSV translates "according to the word"; the verse is numbered Sir 49:6 in RSV.

77. See Mack, *Wisdom*, 30–32, for the offices ben Sira implies for Moses and other reasons for believing that ben Sira understood Moses as a prophet.

78. Mack, *Wisdom*, 32, 104–7; Mack notes that Moses occupies an office that later divides into several different offices (105).

79. Thus Mack, *Wisdom*, 106–7.

80. Thus Mack, *Wisdom*, 30–31.

81. RSV: "two anointed"; the Hebrew, šěnê běnê-hayyiṣhār, is an unusual term, and I prefer the literal translation.

82. For discussion of this type of dual leadership, see David Goodblatt, *The Monarchic Principle: Studies in Jewish Self-Government in Antiquity* (Tübingen: Mohr-Siebeck, 1994) 57–59. Goodblatt also finds support for what he calls the "doctrine of the diarchy" in the Torah's picture of Moses and Aaron working side by side (59–60); I find this claim less persuasive. For an extended treatment that emphasizes the lack of evidence for the high priest's political power, see Deborah W. Rooke, *Zadok's Heirs: The Role and Development of the High Priesthood in Ancient Israel*, Oxford Theological Monographs (Oxford: Oxford University Press, 2000) 125–51.

83. On the governors of Yehud, Lester L. Grabbe, *Judaism from Cyrus to Hadrian. Volume One: The Persian and Greek Periods* (Minneapolis: Fortress, 1992) 73–84, esp. 74–75; Carol L. Meyers and Eric M. Meyers, *Haggai, Zechariah 1–8*, Anchor Bible 25B (Garden City, N.Y.: Doubleday, 1987) 9–17.

84. Thus Goodblatt, *Monarchic Principle*, 7–23. Rooke, *Zadok's Heirs*, argues that throughout this period the high priest had authority over the cult alone (see esp. the summaries of her arguments on pp. 120–22 [Persian period] and 325–27 [hellenistic period]). For a cautious endorsement of the view that high priests exercised political power in the hellenistic period, see James C. VanderKam, *From Joshua to Caiaphas: High Priests after the Exile* (Minneapolis: Fortress; Assen: Van Gorcum, 2004) esp. x, 122–24.

85. Mack, *Wisdom*, 84–87, 167–71. I argue below for a more radical reading of ben Sira's approach to Israelite kingship that resolves the "anomaly" Mack finds

(86) in what he perceives as ben Sira's failure to resolve the tension between the royal high priesthood and absent kingship.

86. There is surprisingly little clear evidence for the expectation of a Davidic messiah in texts of the Second Temple period; it consists of the *Psalms of Solomon, 4 Ezra,* and some texts from Dead Sea Scrolls. For discussion, see John J. Collins, *The Scepter and the Star: The Messiahs of the Dead Sea Scrolls and Other Ancient Literature,* The Anchor Bible Reference Library (New York: Doubleday, 1995) 49–73.

87. The Greek differs slightly: "in the days of heaven" (RSV: "all the days of heaven").

88. I have modified the translation of RSV, which reads, "as the days of the heavens."

89. Himmelfarb, "Levi, Phinehas," 22–23.

90. The Hebrew of the first two-thirds of the verse reads, *wĕgam bĕrîtô 'im dāwid ben yišay lĕmaṭēh yĕhûdâ / nahǎlat 'eš lipnê kĕbôdô nahǎlat 'ahǎrôn lĕkol zar'ô*. Stadelmann reads *'eš* in the second stich as *'îš* and translates thus: "Und auch Sein Bund mit David . . . ist das Erbe eines Mannes vor dem Angesicht Seiner Herrlichkeit, das Erbe Aarons für alle seine Nachkommen"; the "man before the face of his glory" is Aaron, whose descendants have inherited the covenant with David (*Ben Sira,* 156–58; quotation, 157). I find the Hebrew extremely difficult to construe, and I am afraid that it will not bear the meaning Stadelmann assigns it. P. W. Skehan emends the Hebrew "in light of G and the parallelism," to "*nahǎlat 'îš libnô lĕbaddô,*" which he translates, "Was an individual heritage through one son alone" (Skehan and Di Lella, *Wisdom of Ben Sira,* 508, 510). The meaning of the comparison remains less than clear even after this emendation.

91. So in Hebrew; in Greek, only Sir 45:26.

92. The translation of the Hebrew is taken from the notes of the *Oxford Annotated Apocrypha, Expanded Edition,* ed. Bruce M. Metzger (New York: Oxford University Press, 1977) 196. The Greek reads, "May he entrust to us his mercy! / And let him deliver us in our days!"

93. Nehemiah too is credited with repairing walls and buildings (Sir 49:13), but the activities of Hezekiah are more clearly parallel to Simon's. Simon repaired and fortified the temple and laid foundations for retaining walls, dug a cistern, and fortified the city against siege. Hezekiah fortified the city, provided water, and withstood a siege. Simon does everything Hezekiah did and also repairs the temple. See Mack, *Wisdom,* 35, for Simon as king-like.

94. Compare the Hebrew of Sir 45:24, the covenant with Phinehas, "the law of the covenant of peace"; see Stadelmann, *Ben Sira,* 161.

95. Stadelmann, *Ben Sira,* 160.

96. Pancratius C. Beentjes, "'The Countries Marvelled at You': King Solomon in Ben Sira 47:12–22," *Bijdragen, Tijdschrift voor filosofie en theologie* 45 (1984): 9–11.

97. The Greek of Sir 47:19 does not contain anything that could be construed as "but." The Hebrew offers the connective *w,* which could mean "but" in the proper context, but can also mean "and."

98. Beentjes, "'The Countries,'" 9–11. I cannot agree with Beentjes' view that ben Sira's understanding of Solomon's wrongdoing differs from that of the Deuteronomic history, which reports that Solomon's foreign wives led him into idolatry in his old age (1 Kings 11:1-13). Beentjes notes the absence of reference to idolatry or to the foreignness of Solomon's wives in ben Sira's account ("'The Countries,'" 8–9). But the law of the king itself associates the multiplication of wives with idolatry: "And he shall not multiply wives for himself lest his heart turn

away." Surely this suggests that the wives are foreign, a likely circumstance for a king, since there is no reason why the multiplication of Israelite wives would lead to idolatry. Compare 1 Kings 11:3: "And his wives turned his heart away."

99. "He will never blot out the posterity of him who loved him; / so he gave a remnant to Jacob, / and to David a root of his stock" (Sir 47:22). The Hebrew of the verse is incomplete, and the last two cola especially are severely damaged. They read, "he gave to [ ], and to [ ]," but they do not preserve any traces of the name David. Thus it is possible that the Hebrew concluded somewhat differently from the Greek, although it should be noted that in this verse the extant Hebrew is quite close to the Greek.

100. Stadelmann, *Ben Sira*, 161–63.

101. Stone, "Ideal Figures," 580.

102. E.g., Theophil Middendorp, *Die Stellung Jesu ben Siras zwischen Judentum und Hellenismus* (Leiden: Brill, 1973) 113, 125.

103. In addition to Nickelsburg, whose position is discussed below, see also, e.g., Gabriele Boccaccini, *Beyond the Essene Hypothesis: The Parting of the Ways between Qumran and Enochic Judaism* (Grand Rapids, Mich.: Eerdmans, 1998) 68–79; and idem, *Roots of Rabbinic Judaism: An Intellectual History, From Ezekiel to Daniel* (Grand Rapids, Mich.: Eerdmans, 2002) 89–103; James C. VanderKam, "The Interpretation of Genesis in 1 Enoch," in *The Bible at Qumran: Text, Shape, and Interpretation*, ed. Peter W. Flint with the assistance of Tae Hun Kim (Grand Rapids, Mich.: Eerdmans, 2001) 142–43; Benjamin G. Wright III, "'Fear the Lord and Honor the Priest': Ben Sira as Defender of the Jerusalem Priesthood," in *The Book of Ben Sira in Modern Research: Proceedings of the First International Ben Sira Conference 28–31 July 1996, Sosterberg, Netherlands*, ed. Pancratius C. Beentjes (Berlin: de Gruyter, 1997) 218–21.

104. Nickelsburg, *Commentary*, 50.

105. Ibid., 60–61.

106. Reed, "Heavenly Ascent," 55–61.

107. Reed, "Textual Identity," 291–92; Nickelsburg, *Commentary*, 62–64.

108. Thus James C. VanderKam, "2 Maccabees 6, 7a and Calendrical Change in Jerusalem," *Journal for the Study of Judaism in the Persian, Hellenistic, and Roman Period* 12 (1981): 57n. 20, sees the contrast between the tone of the *Astronomical Book* and that of *Jubilees* as evidence for his view that the solar calendar was the cultic calendar of the period before the Maccabean Revolt.

109. Wright, "'Fear the Lord,'" 189–222. See also Argall, *1 Enoch and Sirach*, and Gabriele Boccaccini, *Middle Judaism: Jewish Thought 300 B.C.E. to 200 C.E.* (Minneapolis: Fortress, 1991) 77–92.

110. So too Boccaccini, *Middle Judaism*, 77–92.

111. Wright, "'Fear the Lord.'"

112. Ibid., 192–95.

113. Ibid., 191.

114. Ibid., 218–22.

115. Ibid, 204–8.

116. The most difficult part of these passages to reconcile with a solar calendar is Sir 43:7. VanderKam, who believes that before the hellenistic reform the Jerusalem temple used a solar calendar, admits that the Hebrew text of Sir 43:7 is probably incompatible with a solar calendar, but argues that the Greek, Syriac, and Latin of the passage are not ("The Origin, Character, and Early History of the 364-Day Calendar: A Reassessment of Jaubert's Hypotheses," *Catholic Biblical Quarterly* 41 [1979]: 407–10).

117. Wright, "'Fear the Lord,'" 214–17 ("domesticating," 217).

118. Wright, "'Fear the Lord,'" 213–14.

119. See Himmelfarb, *Ascent*, 75–77, 102–14.

120. Wright, "'Fear the Lord,'" 208–12.

121. Reed, "Heavenly Ascent," 61–66; idem, *Fallen Angels*, 44–49.

122. Reed, *Fallen Angels*, 70–71, quotation, 71; see also 43–44.

123. Argall, *1 Enoch and Sirach*, 230, argues that they betray knowledge of the version of the story that appears in the *Book of the Watchers*.

124. Reed, *Fallen Angels*, 69–71.

125. There is no consensus about the existence or nature of intermediate stages between the third- or second-century B.C.E. Aramaic work and the second-century C.E. Greek Christian document. Thus, for example, some of the references to a royal priesthood in the *Testament of Levi* are obviously Christian in their current form, but some scholars have suggested that the figure of the sword-wielding priest originated in a document designed to serve as propaganda for the Hasmoneans. For arguments for such a document, see Kugler, *From Patriarch*, 216–19, and references there. This document, which would have drawn on *Aramaic Levi* and in turn served as the immediate source for the *Testament of Levi*, is of course entirely hypothetical. Marinus de Jonge criticizes Kugler's arguments for an intermediate document in "Levi in Aramaic Levi and the Testament of Levi," in *Pseudepigraphic Perspectives: The Apocrypha and Pseudepigrapha in Light of the Dead Sea Scrolls (Proceedings of the International Symposium of the Orion Center for the Study of the Dead Sea Scrolls and Associated Literature, 12–14 January, 1997)*, ed. Esther G. Chazon and Michael Stone, with the collaboration of Avital Pinnick (Leiden: Brill, 1999), 84–89.

126. For this figure, see Kugler, *From Patriarch*, 93.

127. The last part of the instructions, 51–60, repeats and summarizes some of the material that comes before it. This has led some scholars to suggest that this portion is not original to the text. See Kugler, *From Patriarch*, 108, for references. *Jubilees'* version of the instructions includes keeping the garments free of blood and covering blood (*Jub.* 21:17), subjects that *Aramaic Levi* treats only in this concluding portion (*Ar. Levi* 53, 56). Thus if the conclusion of the instructions is a later addition to *Aramaic Levi*, it had already been added by the time *Jubilees* was written.

128. Kugler, *From Patriarch*, 108–10.

129. Himmelfarb, "Earthly Sacrifice," 104–16.

130. See Kugler, *From Patriarch*, 128n.230, for those who hold this position.

131. Kugler, *From Patriarch*, 128–29.

132. On Joseph, see ibid., 127–28, 223.

133. Cf. Kugler, *From Patriarch*, 129, and Stone, "Ideal Figures," 578–79.

134. It appears that a considerable portion of the text has been lost (Kugler, *From Patriarch*, 85).

135. Kugler's reading of this passage as promising first fruits to *Levites* rather than priests in opposition to the command of the Torah (*From Patriarch*, 86) is part of his overall reading of *Aramaic Levi* as critical of the priestly establishment and sometimes in contradiction to the Torah. But surely the context, Levi's imminent elevation to priesthood, suggests that it is Levi's priestly descendants the text has in view.

136. This form is conjectural; the noun appears only twice in the Bible (Gen 49:10, the passage above, and Prov 30:17), both times in the construct.

137. Greenfield and Stone, "Remarks," 223–24.

138. Kugler, *From Patriarch*, 117 n. 196.
139. The *Testament of Levi* must be used with even greater caution than usual on this topic. It represents Jesus as a royal priest (chap. 18), to be sure, but this picture clearly served Christian ends. See de Jonge, "Levi," 88–89.
140. All quotations from Josephus's *Life* and *Against Apion* are taken from *Josephus I: The Life, Against Apion*, trans. Henry St. J. Thackeray, Loeb Classical Library (Cambridge, Mass.: Harvard University Press; London: William Heinemann, 1976; first printed, 1926).

Chapter 2

1. For a consideration of the evidence from Qumran, see James C. VanderKam, *The Book of Jubilees*, Guides to Apocrypha and Pseudepigrapha (Sheffield: Sheffield Academic Press, 2001) 143–46.
2. The term "specified" (thus Joseph M. Baumgarten and Daniel R. Schwartz, "Damascus Document," in *Damascus Document, War Scroll, and Related Documents*, vol. 2 of *The Dead Sea Scrolls: Hebrew, Aramaic, and Greek Texts with English Translations*, ed. James H. Charlesworth [Tübingen: Mohr (Siebeck); Louisville: John Knox, 1995]), is *mědûqdaq*.
3. The figures for manuscripts of biblical books come from James C. VanderKam, *The Dead Sea Scrolls Today* (Grand Rapids, Mich.: Eerdmans, 1994) 30. The figure for *Jubilees* comes from James C. VanderKam, "The Jubilees Fragments from Qumran Cave 4," in *The Madrid Qumran Congress: Proceedings of the International Congress on the Dead Sea Scrolls, Madrid, 18–21 March, 1991*, ed. Julio Trebolle Barrera and Luis Vegas Montaner, Studies on the Texts of the Desert of Judah 11 (Leiden: Brill, 1992) esp. 2.642–43. The doubtful manuscript is 4Q217.
4. James C. VanderKam, "Das chronologische Konzept des Jubiläenbuches," *Zeitschrift für die alttestamentliche Wissenschaft* 107 (1995): 81–85; idem, *Jubilees*, 95–96.
5. VanderKam, "Chronologische Konzept," 86–96; idem, *Jubilees*, 94–95.
6. Thus James C. VanderKam, "The Origins and Purposes of the *Book of Jubilees*," in *Studies in the Book of Jubilees*, ed. Matthias Albani, Jörg Frey, and Armin Lange, Texte und Studien zum antiken Judentum 65 (Tübingen: Mohr Siebeck, 1997) 20–22.
7. For more detailed discussion, Martha Himmelfarb, "Torah, Testimony, and Heavenly Tablets: The Claim to Authority of the *Book of Jubilees*," in *A Multiform Heritage: Studies on Early Judaism and Christianity in Honor of Robert A. Kraft*, ed. Benjamin G. Wright, Homage Series (Atlanta: Scholars Press, 1999) 19–29. For a collection of the material *Jubilees* indicates as contained in the heavenly tablets and the suggestion that the heavenly tablets constitute a sort of oral torah, see Florentino García Martínez, "The Heavenly Tablets in the Book of Jubilees," in *Studies in the Book of Jubilees*, ed. Albani, Frey, and Lange, 243–60.
8. For a very different understanding of the relationship between *Jubilees* and the heavenly tablets, Cana Werman, "The '[*tôrâ*] and the [*tě'ûdâ*]' Engraved on the Tablets," *Dead Sea Discoveries* 9 (2002): 75–103 (Hebrew original, "The 'Torah' and the 'Te'udah' on the Tablets," *Tarbiz* 68 [1998–99]: 473–92). Werman argues that *Jubilees* claims to be a copy of the heavenly tablets. Werman's article first appeared at the same time as my "Torah, Testimony," so I was unable to respond to her arguments. See also Ben Zion Wacholder, "*Jubilees* as Super

Canon: Torah-Admonition versus Torah-Commandment," in *Legal Texts*, ed. Bernstein, García Martínez , and Kampen, 195–211. Wacholder argues that *Jubilees* understands itself as more authoritative than the Torah and that the community at Qumran accepts this view.

9. For a brief history of the scholarship, see VanderKam, "Origins and Purposes," 4–16. VanderKam himself prefers a date between 160 and 150 (20).

10. Thus VanderKam, "2 Maccabees 6, 7a."

11. VanderKam, "Jubilees Fragments," 639–40.

12. Jacob also offers a sacrifice at the conclusion of his treaty with Laban at Gal-ed (Gen 31:54). *Jubilees* passes over the altar and sacrifice in silence, perhaps because it viewed the occasion as unsuitable (*Jub.* 29:5-8).

13. See Himmelfarb, "Earthly Sacrifice," 118–22, for *Jubilees'* attitude toward incense.

14. For arguments in favor of direct dependence, see Cana Werman, "Levi and Levites in the Second Temple Period," *Dead Sea Discoveries* 4 (1997): 220–21. The law of the priesthood figures prominently in Werman's discussion, but she considers other points as well. Michael E. Stone also claims direct dependence of *Jubilees* on *Aramaic Levi* ("Enoch, Aramaic Levi and Sectarian Origins," *Journal for the Study of Judaism in the Persian, Hellenistic, and Roman Period* 19 [1988]: 159n. 2, 170). It is true that there are significant differences between *Aramaic Levi* and *Jubilees*, but it is characteristic of *Jubilees* to reshape its sources. For a brief discussion of the views of scholars who argue against direct dependence in favor of a common source, see Kugler, *From Patriarch*, 146–47; for his defense of this position based on the relationship of *Jub.* 30:1-32:9 to *Aramaic Levi*, see pp. 147–55. James C. VanderKam, "Isaac's Blessing of Levi and His Descendants in *Jubilees* 31," in *The Provo International Conference on the Dead Sea Scrolls: Technological Innovations, New Texts, and Reformulated Issues*, ed. Donald W. Parry and Eugene Ulrich, Studies on the Texts of the Desert of Judah 30 (Leiden: Brill, 1999) 513–18, also argues that an indirect relationship is more likely.

15. All quotations of *Jubilees* are from the translation of James C. VanderKam, *The Book of Jubilees*, Corups Scriptorum Christianorum Orientalium 511; Scriptores Aethiopici 88 (Louvain: Peeters, 1989).

16. For the view that such a book existed, see Florentino García Martínez, "4QMess Ar and the *Book of Noah*," in *Qumran and Apocalyptic: Studies on the Aramaic Texts from Qumran*, Studies on the Texts from the Desert of Judah (Leiden: Brill, 1992). For the view that it did not, see Cana Werman, "Qumran and the Book of Noah," in *Pseudepigraphic Perspectives*, ed. Chazon and Stone.

17. On the choice of Levi as priest in *Jubilees* and related texts, see James Kugel, "Levi's Elevation to the Priesthood in Second Temple Writings," *Harvard Theological Review* 86 (1993): 1–64; Kugler, *From Patriarch*, 155–69; James C. VanderKam, "*Jubilees'* Exegetical Creation of Levi the Priest," *Revue de Qumran* 17 (1996): 359–73; Werman, "Levi and Levites," 216–22.

18. While the lack of antecedent for the pronouns of these verses at first leaves it unclear whether it is Jacob or Levi offering sacrifice, the identity of the officiant becomes clear by *Jub.* 32:5: "This was his gift because of the vow which he had made that he would give a tithe along with their sacrifices and their libations." This can only be Jacob. So too *Jub.* 32:7, "He was eating happily there— he, all his sons, and his men—for the seven days," can only refer to Jacob.

19. The Ethiopic is *mak^wannen*. I would like to thank Annette Reed for her assistance with the Ethiopic here and below. Despite the English translation, *Jubilees'* "prince" is not connected etymologically to the title *nāśî'* that Ezekiel gives

to the royal figure in his program of restoration (Ezek 44:3; 45:16, 17, 22, etc.), nor does it typically serve as a translation for this title in the Ethiopic Bible.

20. The first Hasmonean to call himself king was one of John Hyrcanus's sons, either Aristobolus or Alexander Jannai (Emil Schürer, *The History of the Jewish People in the Age of Jesus Christ (175 B.C.–A.D. 135)*, vol. 1, rev. and ed. Geza Vermes, Fergus Millar, and Matthew Black, lit. ed., Pamela Vermes [Edinburgh: T. & T. Clark, 1973] 216–17); even after adoption of the new title, they continued to call themselves priests. See the convenient listing of coin legends, 1.603–5. See also the discussion of Goodblatt, *Monarchic Principle*, 66–71.

21. For a convenient summary of the complex evidence, see J. Collins, *Scepter*, 74–83. Goodblatt (*Monarchic Principle*, 70) seems to me correct to question the view expressed by Collins (77) and others that the sect's own organization echoed the eschatological royal-priestly duo.

22. Thus Goodblatt, *Monarchic Principle*, 71. Contrast J. Collins, *Scepter*, who rightly points out that during the Hasmonean era the idea is attested only in texts from the Dead Sea Scrolls or associated with them, which he takes as evidence that the expectation was "a distinctive trait" of the movement (95).

23. For the delineation of H material outside the Holiness Code, I follow Knohl, *Sanctuary*. I am much indebted to his work for my understanding of H and P. He does not treat the subject of purity in either corpus, however.

24. I owe my understanding of P's attitude toward impurity largely to the work of Jacob Milgrom and especially his *Leviticus 1–16*. I am also influenced by the critiques of aspects of Milgrom's position in Knohl, *Sanctuary*, 225–30, and Hyam Maccoby, *Ritual and Morality: The Ritual Purity System and Its Place in Judaism* (Cambridge: Cambridge University Press, 1999) 165–81.

25. For the identification of this passage as Holiness material, see Knohl, *Sanctuary*, 99–100.

26. Following Knohl, *Sanctuary*, I take H to be later than P.

27. This verb is used in this sense also in Jeremiah (31:1-2, 9), Psalms (106:38), and perhaps Micah (4:11).

28. See Cana Werman, "The Rules of Consuming and Covering Blood in Priestly and Rabbinic Law," *Revue de Qumran* 16 (1995): 621–36 (Hebrew original: "Consumption of the Blood and Its Covering in the Priestly and Rabbinic Traditions," *Tarbiz* 63 [1993–94]: 173–83) for aspects of this subject noted in her title. I cannot accept Werman's view that *Jubilees* is engaged in a polemic against the halakhah of the sages.

29. For an analysis of Leviticus 17, see Baruch J. Schwartz, "The Prohibition Concerning the 'Eating' of Blood in Leviticus 17," in *Priesthood and Cult in Ancient Israel*, ed. Gary A. Anderson and Saul M. Olyan, Journal for the Study of the Old Testament Supplement Series 125 (Sheffield: Sheffield Academic Press, 1991) 34–36.

30. Betsy Halpern-Amaru, *Rewriting the Bible: Land and Covenant in Post-Biblical Jewish Literature* (Valley Forge, Pa.: Trinity Press International, 1994) 25–54; on this point, see p. 28.

31. Ibid., 44–45, 48–54.

32. In addition to the two discussed below, *Jubilees* treats the stories of Joseph and Potiphar's wife (*Jub.* 39:5-11), in which the forbidden relations are avoided because of Joseph's piety, and the story of Judah and Tamar (*Jub.* 41:8-28), in which *Jubilees* is eager to play down Judah's guilt. On the problems the stories of Reuben and Bilhah and Judah and Tamar pose for *Jubilees*, see Gary A. Anderson, "The Status of the Torah before Sinai: The Retelling of the Bible in the

Damascus Covenant and the Book of Jubilees," *Dead Sea Discoveries* 1 (1994): 19–29. For a discussion of all four stories and their implications for *Jubilees*' views on acceptable marriage partners, see Betsy Halpern-Amaru, *The Empowerment of Women in the* Book of Jubilees (Leiden: Brill, 1999) 108–32.

33. My translation.

34. RSV: "you," following the Greek, Syriac, and the targum.

35. Judah Goldin, "The Youngest Son, or Where Does Genesis 38 Belong?" *Journal of Biblical Literature* 96 (1977): 37–38.

36. Presumably Reuben and Bilhah could have been condemned to death as adulterers (Lev 20:10) as well, but *Jubilees* clearly sees the sin as incest. The prohibition of sexual relations with one's father's wife appears also in Leviticus 18 without a punishment (Lev 18:8).

37. See Jacob Milgrom, "The Concept of Impurity in *Jubilees* and the *Temple Scroll*," *Revue de Qumran* 16 (1993–94): 281–82, on *Jubilees*' extension of impurity to forbidden sexual relations.

38. The heavenly tablets ordain that a man is not to lie with his father's wife because it is "impure"; the man and woman are to die together because "they have done something impure" (*Jub.* 33:10). "There is to be nothing impure" in God's chosen people (*Jub.* 33:11). Moses is to order the Israelites to observe this law because "it is an impure thing" (*Jub.* 33:13). No man who commits this sin will be allowed to live because he is "despicable and impure" (*Jub.* 33:14). All who commit this sin are "impure, something detestable, a blemish, and something contaminated" (*Jub.* 33:19).

39. See the discussion of Jacob Milgrom, *Leviticus 17-22*, Anchor Bible 3A, (New York: Doubleday, 2000) 1538–39. Milgrom believes that the prohibition applies even after the death of the father or divorce of his wife. If the father is still alive, he notes, the forbidden sexual relations also constitute adultery.

40. It is perhaps worth noting, however, that Paul criticizes the Corinthian community for tolerating a man engaging in the same sin (1 Cor 5:1). But Paul's rhetoric suggests that it is precisely the exceptional nature of the sin that draws his attention: even the pagans do not engage in such behavior.

41. For a perceptive discussion of *Jubilees*' reworking of the story of the rape of Dinah, see Cana Werman, "*Jubilees* 30: Building a Paradigm for the Ban on Intermarriage," *Harvard Theological Review* 90 (1997): 1–22.

42. Geza Vermes, "Leviticus 18:21 in Ancient Jewish Bible Exegesis," in *Studies in Aggadah, Targum and Jewish Liturgy in Memory of Joseph Heinemann* (Hebrew), ed. Jacob J. Petuchowski and Ezra Fleischer (Jerusalem: Magnes Press and Hebrew Union College Press, 1981) 108–24.

43. Vermes, "Leviticus 18:21," 119–20. Hayes, *Gentile Impurities*, 74–77, suggests that *Jubilees* takes sexual relations with foreigners to cause moral impurity (as Hayes calls H's type of impurity), so that the profanation of seed that occurs in the marriage (as for Ezra) becomes defiling as well. Although this is not the place for a discussion, I am not convinced that the concern for profanation of seed Hayes points to in Ezra, *Jubilees*, and elsewhere should be understood as a type of purity. Further, while there can be no doubt that *Jubilees* draws on the Torah and other biblical material to develop its own laws, Hayes does not consider the significance of *Jubilees*' conception of the heavenly tablets, which permits it to invent new laws without the sort of exegetical justification the rabbis would have required.

I must also note that Hayes misunderstands my comments on *Jubilees* (78). The purity law to which I refer ("Sexual Relations and Purity in the Temple

202 Notes to Pages 70–73

Scroll and the Book of Jubilees," *Dead Sea Discoveries* 6 [1999]: 35) is not "forbidden sexual relations with Gentiles," as Hayes suggests in brackets in the quotation, but rather the law of a woman after childbirth ("Sexual Relations," 25–27); I never refer to the prohibition of marriage with gentiles as a purity law.

44. Deut 7:1-5 warns against marriage with both sons and daughters of the inhabitants of the land. Exod 34:15-16 warns against daughters only, and the account of the apostasy of the Israelites at Baal Peor in Num 25:1-11 dramatizes the dangers of foreign women.

45. Halpern-Amaru, *Empowerment of Women*, 103–25, 147–49.

46. Knohl, *Sanctuary*, 180–89.

47. Eberhard Schwarz, *Identität durch Abgrenzung: Abgrenzungsprozesse in Israel im 2. vorchristlichen Jahrhundert und ihre traditionsgeschichtlichen Voraussetzungen: Zugleich ein Beitrag zur Erforschung des Jubiläenbuches,* Europäische Hochschulschriften 162 (Frankfurt: Peter Lang, 1982) 108–11, carefully gathers the evidence and offers a cautious assessment. John C. Endres, *Biblical Interpretation in the Book of Jubilees,* Catholic Biblical Quarterly Monograph Series 18 (Washington, D.C.: Catholic Biblical Association, 1987) 137, assumes rather than demonstrates that "widespread miscegenation constituted the major problem" in *Jubilees'* time, which he also places in the context of the hellenistic reform.

48. In addition to the passage from 1 Maccabees discussed below, Schwarz, *Identität,* 108–10, cites passages from Josephus, the *Testament of Levi,* and *t. Sukkah* about priests who marry foreign women or allow their daughters to marry foreign men. None of these sources is even roughly contemporary with the Maccabean Revolt, and all are problematic as evidence for Schwarz's claim on other grounds as well (Himmelfarb, "Levi, Phinehas," 17–19).

49. Himmelfarb, "Levi, Phinehas," 19–21. Schwarz, *Identität,* 108, cites this passage with appropriate caution.

50. Himmelfarb, "Levi, Phinehas," 21–23.

51. In "Levi, Phinehas," I argue that *Jubilees* is not preoccupied with intermarriage, as others have claimed, but rather was reworking its source, *Aramaic Levi,* to reflect its view of the people of Israel as a kingdom of priests. While I still think we need to take account of *Jubilees'* use of *Aramaic Levi,* I argue below that there is a plausible historical explanation for *Jubilees'* concern, but the historical explanation requires a somewhat later date for *Jubilees* than the early Hasmonean period.

52. Victor Tcherikover, *Hellenistic Civilization and the Jews* (Philadelphia: Jewish Publication Society of America, 1959; New York: Atheneum, 1974) 90–116; Schürer, *History of the Jewish People* vol. 2, rev. and ed. Vermes, Millar, and Black, lit. ed., Pamela Vermes (Edinburgh: T. & T. Clark, 1979) 1–20, 85–183.

53. In the course of the revolt, Judah is reported to have attacked two pagan cult sites (1 Macc 5:44, 68; 2 Macc 12:26 [the same incident reported in 1 Macc 5:44]); later, in the 150s, his brothers occasionally did the same (1 Macc 10:84, 11:4, 13:43-48).

54. Uriel Rappaport, "Jewish Religious Propaganda and Proselytism in the Period of the Second Commonwealth" (Ph.D. diss., Hebrew University of Jerusalem, 1965) 79–80, 82 (Hebrew); idem, "The Hellenistic Cities and the Judaization of the Land of Israel in the Hasmonean Period" (Hebrew), in *Doron; Eighteen Articles in Honor of the Sixtieth Birthday of Prof. Bentsiyon Kats,* ed. Shmuel Perlman and Binyamin Shimron (Tel Aviv: Mif'al ha-Shikhpul, Bet ha-Hotsa'ah le-Or shel Histadrut ha-Studentim be-Universitat Tel-Aviv, 1967) 228–29. For criticism and development of Rappaport's position in see Morton Smith, "The

Gentiles in Judaism, 125 B.C.E.–C.E. 66," in *The Cambridge History of Judaism:* Vol. 3, *The Roman Period,* ed. William Horbury, W. D. Davies, and John Sturdy (Cambridge: Cambridge University Press, 1999) 198–213, and S. J. D. Cohen, "Religion," esp. 211–18. See also S. J. D. Cohen, *Beginnings,* 110–19. Seth Schwartz, "Israel and the Nations Roundabout: 1 Maccabees and the Hasmonean Expansion," *Journal of Jewish Studies* 42 (1991): 16–38, argues that 1 Maccabees' hostile attitude toward the Jews' gentile neighbors must predate Hyrcanus's conquests and the assimilation of the Idumeans into the Jewish population. But perhaps 1 Maccabees' hostility is a reaction to doubts about the process of assimilation, intended to demonstrate that the Hasmoneans were true defenders of their people and their Judaism despite the incorporation of the Idumeans.

55. S. J. D. Cohen, "Religion," 214, points to Jeremiah's inclusion in a list of circumcised, yet uncircumcised, nations (Jer 9:24-25) and to Herodotus's report that the "Syrians" in Palestine practice circumcision (*Histories* 2.104.3). Cohen rejects Josephus's claim (*Antiquities* 8.262; *Against Apion* 1.168-71) that Herodotus meant only the Jews.

56. For the passage from Ptolemy, *Historia Herodis,* preserved in Ammonius, *De Adfinium Vocabulorum Differentia,* see Stern, *Greek and Latin Authors,* 1.356.

57. S. J. D. Cohen, "Religion," 218–21; idem, *Beginnings,* 125–39.

58. S. J. D. Cohen, *Beginnings,* 156–74, esp. 169.

59. Rappaport, "Propaganda," 79–80, 82; idem, "Hellenistic Cities," 228–29. S. J. D. Cohen attempts to make sense of the differing views of the three ancient historians who discuss the incident, Josephus, Ptolemy, and Strabo, in "Religion," 211–16; idem, *Beginnings,* 116–18. Smith, "Gentiles," 203–4, follows Rappaport in understanding the process by which Idumeans became Jews as one of gradual assimilation; he sees it as based on an alliance between the Hasmoneans and the leaders of the Idumean countryside, perhaps hastened along by a show of force on Hyracanus's part. He discounts Josephus's account of Hyrcanus's conquest as propaganda, though he cannot decide whether it is pro-Jewish propaganda from Josephus himself or anti-Hasmonean propaganda going back to Nicholas of Damascus. He also suggests that the passage from Josephus could be read to mean that the Idumeans already practiced circumcision and that Hyrcanus required them to align their mode of circumcision with that of the Jews. This is perhaps a bit strained. On the Idumeans in Egypt in the first century, see Uriel Rappaport, "Les Iduméens en Égypte," *Revue de philologie* 43 (1969): 74–75, following Friederich Zucker, "Doppelinschrift spätptolemäischer Zeit aus der Garnison von Hermopolis Magna," *Abhandlungen der Preussischen Akademie der Wissenschaften,* Philosophisch-historische Klasse 6 (1937): 1–63; Rappaport suggests a special connection between one of the first century inscriptions and the onomasticon of Marissa (76–77).

60. Halpern-Amaru, *Empowerment of Women,* 155.

61. See Cana Werman, "The Attitude Towards Gentiles in the Book of Jubilees and Qumran Literature Compared with Early Tanaaic Halakha and Contemporary Pseudepigrapha" (Ph.D. diss., Hebrew University of Jerusalem, 1995) 256–57 (Hebrew); and idem, "*Jubilees* 30," 6–10, for detailed analysis of the story in *Jubilees.*

62. Some scholars have seen in *Jubilees* 30 a polemic against the Samaritans, another neighboring group subjugated by the Hasmoneans. I agree with Werman, "Attitude," 256n. 73, that this is unlikely; see also Reinhard Plummer, "The *Book of Jubilees* and the Samaritans," *Eglise et théologie* 10 (1979): 164–78.

63. Werman, "Attitude," 177–99.

204 Notes to Pages 76–78

64. Rebecca later refers to these wives as Hittites (*Jub.* 27:8, which parallels Gen 27:46).

65. Werman rejects the idea that Esau represents contemporary Idumeans and sees him rather as representing gentiles in general for *Jubilees* ("Attitude," 197–99).

66. R. H. Charles, *The Book of Jubilees or the Little Genesis* (London: Adam & Charles Black, 1902) lxii.

67. Rappaport, "Hellenistic Cities," 228–29.

68. For the connection of wars to recent history, see James C. VanderKam, *Textual and Historical Studies in the Book of Jubilees*, Harvard Semitic Monographs 14 (Missoula, Mont.: Scholars Press, 1977) 217–38: correspondences between Judah Maccabee's campaigns and this war and Jacob's battle against seven Amorite kings (34:1-9) point to an early Hasmonean date for *Jubilees*. Robert Doran, "The Non-Dating of Jubilees: Jub 34–38; 23:14-32 in Narrative Context," *Journal for the Study of Judaism in the Persian, Hellenistic, and Roman Period* 20 (1989): 1–11, argues that the needs of *Jubilees'* narrative provide a sufficient explanation for the introduction of Jacob's military exploits. Werman, "Attitude," expresses skepticism about previous attempts to find references to contemporary events in the book in her introductory comments (11–26) and throughout the work as noted above in relation to Esau.

69. Thus Doron Mendels, *The Land of Israel as a Political Concept in Hasmonean Literature* (Tübingen: Mohr-Siebeck, 1987) 57–88, esp. 73–81, argues on the basis of the extent of the land in *Jubilees* for a date shortly after the conquest of Idumea, which he dates to 125 B.C.E.

70. Dan Barag, "New Evidence on the Foreign Policy of John Hyrcanus I," *Israel Numismatic Journal* 12 (1992–93): 1–12. Barag notes that Martin Hengel, *Judaism and Hellenism: Their Encounter in Palestine during the Early Hellenistic Period*, trans. John Bowden (Philadelphia: Fortress, 1974) 1.62, argued decades ago that Hyrcanus's conquest dated to around 110 B.C.E. on the basis of the tomb inscriptions, the latest of which dates to 112/11.

71. Werman, "Attitude," 273–74, takes the texts she considers as reflecting "priestly halakhah"; Halpern-Amaru, *Empowerment of Women*, 156–57, refers to "a protesting priestly voice" (156). In addition to the passages I discuss here both Werman and Halpern-Amaru mention Pesher Nahum (4Q169 3–4 ii 9), "kings, princes, priests, and people, with the proselyte accompanying them." For the claim that these texts reflect priestly attitudes toward converts, see Daniel R. Schwartz, "On Two Aspects of a Priestly View of Descent at Qumran," in *Archeology and History in the Dead Sea Scrolls: The New York University Conference in Memory of Yigael Yadin*, ed. Lawrence H. Schiffman, Journal for the Study of the Pseudepigrapha Supplement Series 8; JSOT/ASOR Monographs 2 (Sheffield: Sheffield Academic Press, 1990) 165–66.

72. Joseph M. Baumgarten, "The Exclusion of 'Netinim' and Proselytes in 4Q Florilegium," in *Studies in Qumran Law* (Leiden: Brill, 1977), argues that the exclusion is not from the eschatological temple but from an inner circle of the eschatological community (82–84); this allows him to harmonize the views of the *Damascus Document* and 4QFlorilegium (82). His argument rests on analogies between Qumran law and rabbinic law and does not consider the possibility that conversion might have been controversial in some circles.

73. For the placement of this fragment in the eschatological schema, see Devorah Dimant, partially based on earlier transcriptions by John Strugnell, *Qumran Cave 4.XXI: Parabiblical Texts, Part 4: Pseudo-Prophetic Texts*, Discoveries in the Judaean Desert 30 (Oxford: Clarendon Press, 2001) 100, 249.

74. Hayes, *Gentile Impurities*, 82–91.

75. Werman, "Attitude," 256.

76. Ibid., 139.

77. Different strands of the Torah take different approaches. See the discussion in Moshe Weinfeld, *Deuteronomy and the Deuteronomic School* (1972; Winona Lake, Ind.: Eisenbrauns, 1992) 229–32. Weinfeld notes that while H warns that both the *gēr* and the native Israelite will become impure if they eat anything that dies by itself (Lev 17:15), Deuteronomy forbids Israelites to eat such an animal and suggests that they give it to the *gēr* instead (Deut 14:21) (*Deuteronomy*, 230). See also Knohl, *Sanctuary*, 182.

78. Halpern-Amaru, *Empowerment of Women*, 154–59; Hayes, *Gentile Impurities*, 73–81, 89–91. Hayes does not seem to know Halpern-Amaru's book.

79. Unlike Hayes, Halpern-Amaru does see *Jubilees'* rejection of foreign wives as reflecting anxiety about their bad influence; male foreigners, however, are unacceptable marriage partners simply because of their maternal ancestry (*Empowerment of Women*, 158).

80. Hayes, *Gentile Impurities*, 74.

81. Halpern-Amaru, *Empowerment of Women*, 154–55.

82. Hayes suggests, correctly in my view, that *Jubilees* denies the possibility of conversion (*Gentile Impurities*, 77); thus it is confusing when she writes that according to *Jubilees* there can be no marriage with foreigners, "*not even with converts*" (78; emphasis in the original).

83. James Kugel emphasizes this point in "The Holiness of Israel and the Land in Second Temple Times," in *Texts, Temples, and Traditions: A Tribute to Menahem Haran*, ed. Michael V. Fox et al. (Winona Lake, Ind.: Eisenbrauns, 1996) 25–29.

84. The most influential exponent of this point of view is James VanderKam. The paragraph above is a very condensed summary of his "Origins and Purposes," 19–22. He lists Klaus Berger, *Das Buch der Jubiläen*, Jüdische Schriften aus hellenistisch-römischer Zeit II.3 (Gütersloh: Gerd Mohn, 1981), Schwarz, *Identität*, and Endres, *Biblical Interpretation* ("Origins and Purposes," 13–16) as sharing his view of the context for the writing of *Jubilees*.

85. Cana Werman, "The Book of Jubilees in Its Hellenistic Context," *Zion* 66 (2001): 275–96 (Hebrew), reads *Jubilees* as responding to some of the same issues but dates the book to around 100 B.C.E. (296).

86. Albert I Baumgarten, *The Flourishing of Sects in the Maccabean Era: An Interpretation* (Leiden: Brill, 1997).

87. My understanding of the sociology of sectarianism is particularly influenced by the work of Bryan Wilson. See, e.g., Wilson, "The Sociology of Sects," in *Religion in Sociological Perspective* (Oxford: Oxford University Press, 1982).

88. The relationship between these two texts and the communities they reflect is complex. I shall have more to say about these texts in chapter 4.

89. Baumgarten and Schwartz, "Damascus Document."

90. I discuss the sectarianism of the *Damascus Document* and the *Rule of the Community* in chapter 4.

91. *Jubilees* has also been treated as a proponent of the priestly halakhah many scholars find in the Dead Sea Scrolls. For references, see Himmelfarb, "Sexual Relations," 11nn. 3–4. In my view, aside from the calendar, the connections are not particularly striking (33–36). For a reading of *Jubilees* as containing a variety of halakhic traditions, not only sectarian, see Menahem Kister, "Some Aspects of Qumran Halakhic," in *Madrid Qumran Congress*, ed. Trebolle Barrera and Vegas Montaner, 2.581–88.

92. Philip R. Davies, *Behind the Essenes: History and Ideology in the Dead Sea Scrolls*, Brown Judaic Studies 94 (Atlanta: Scholars Press, 1987) 121–23, also notes the absence of the language of the pious remnant from *Jubilees* 1 in the course of his comparison of that chapter to the accounts of the emergence of the remnant in the Apocalypse of Weeks and the first several columns of the *Damascus Document.*

93. On the use of the plant in the Dead Sea Scrolls and related texts, see Patrick A. Tiller, "The 'Eternal Planting' in the Dead Sea Scrolls," *Dead Sea Discoveries* 4 (1997): 312–35 (on *Jubilees*, 323–24).

94. Menahem Kister, "Concerning the History of the Essenes—A Study of the *Animal Apocalypse*, the *Book of Jubilees* and the *Damascus Covenant*," *Tarbiz* 56 (1986–87): 1–15 (Hebrew), reads this passage in *Jubilees* as describing the emergence of the sect. In my view he fails to account for the use of generational language here.

95. This scenario seems particularly difficult to reconcile with a date for *Jubilees* shortly after the Maccabean Revolt. The mention of the defilement of the holy of holies certainly recalls the events of the revolt, but during the revolt, the defilement of the holy of holies was the work of foreigners, and the outcome of the revolt was liberation from those foreigners. In *Jubilees*' scenario, the defilement is the work of Jews, and God's response is to turn Israel over to the nations. Thus it is not the revolt itself that is alluded to here. The events *Jubilees* predicts are to take place in the future, and not an imminent future. Still, surely it would be odd to introduce elements at once reminiscent of the recent past yet so totally transformed immediately after the revolt. If *Jubilees* belongs to the reign of John Hyrcanus, the problem is less acute.

Chapter 3

1. Elisha Qimron, with a bibliography by Florentino García Martínez, *Temple Scroll: A Critical Edition with Extensive Reconstructions* (Beer-Sheva: Ben-Gurion University of the Negev Press; Jerusalem: Israel Exploration Society, 1996).

2. Joseph M. Baumgarten, *Qumran Cave 4.XIII: The Damascus Document (4Q266-273)*, Discoveries in the Judaean Desert 18 (Oxford: Clarendon Press, 1996).

3. Yigael Yadin, *The Temple Scroll* (Jerusalem: Israel Exploration Society, 1983) 1.277–80, under the influence of the work of Gedalia Alon. For a similar view, see Florentino García Martínez, "El Rollo del Templo y la halaká sectaria," in *Simposio Biblico Español, Salamanca, 1982*, ed. Natalio Fernández Marcos, Julio C. Trebolle Barrera, and Javier Fernández Vallina (Madrid: Universidad Complutense, 1984) 611–22, esp. 612, 622.

4. Joseph M. Baumgarten et al., *Qumran Cave 4.XXV: Halakhic Texts*, Discoveries in the Judaean Desert 35 (Oxford: Clarendon Press, 1999).

5. Maurice Baillet, *Qumran Grotte 4.III (4Q482-4Q520)*, Discoveries in the Judaean Desert 7 (Oxford: Clarendon Press, 1982).

6. Qimron and Strugnell, *Qumran Cave 4.V.*

7. Eyal Regev, "The Temple Impurity and Qumran's 'Foreign Affairs' in the Early Hasmonean Period," *Zion* 64 (1999): 135–56 (Hebrew), argues that the laws included in 4QMMT all have to do with the problem of the purity of the temple, which the authors of the work saw as compromised by the priestly establishment. The laws of genital discharge could potentially find a place in a composition with these concerns since a priest and in some circumstances even a layperson who failed to observe these rules properly could defile the temple.

8. The precise contours of the Pharisees' purity practices are controversial, which is not surprising given the nature of the evidence. For an argument for a minimalist view, though one that would accept my formulation, see E. P. Sanders, "Did the Pharisees Eat Ordinary Food in Purity?" in *Jewish Law from Jesus to the Mishnah: Five Studies* (London: SCM Press; Philadelphia: Trinity Press International, 1990) 131–254. Sanders offers a critique of the work of Gedalia Alon (154–66) and, in great detail, of Jacob Neusner (esp. 166–84, but the entire essay is largely a response to Neusner).

9. My debt to Milgrom, particularly *Leviticus 1-16*, will be evident in what follows, although I disagree with him on a number of points.

10. Milgrom has argued that the impurities that require sacrifice as part of the process of purification were understood to pollute the sanctuary from afar ("Israel's Sanctuary: The Priestly 'Picture of Dorian Gray,' " *Revue biblique* 83 [1976]: 392–93; idem, *Leviticus 1-16*, 254–78). He deduces this from the fact that these sacrifices always include a *ḥaṭṭā't* (Lev 12:6; 14:12, 19; 15:14, 30), the purification offering intended to cleanse the sanctuary of the pollution caused by the person bringing the sacrifice. A woman in a state of menstrual impurity or a man who has had seminal emission can avoid polluting the sanctuary by taking care not to enter it. It is impossible, however, for a person bearing one of the more severe types of impurity to avoid polluting the sanctuary since his impurity affects it even from afar. Still, despite the inevitability of pollution in these cases, the *ḥaṭṭā't* sacrifice provides a remedy. I am inclined to agree with Maccoby, *Ritual*, 165–92, that Milgrom is not persuasive on this point. For Milgrom's response to Maccoby, see *Leviticus 23-27*, Anchor Bible 3B (New York: Doubleday, 2000) 2458–63.

11. According to Haran, the priestly school responsible for P goes back to the time of Ahaz in the late eighth century and flourished under Hezekiah at the turn of the eighth to the seventh century (*Temples*, 146–47). Fortunately for us, the date of P is not of great importance for us since it had surely reached its final form well before the later Second Temple period, the era of concern for us.

12. Haran, *Temples*, 221.

13. Knohl, *Sanctuary*, 134–35.

14. This is a point that Milgrom has argued forcefully; see *Leviticus 1-16*, 42–47, and elsewhere. For the opposing view, see, e.g., Baruch A. Levine, *In the Presence of the Lord: A Study of Cult and Some Cultic Terms in Ancient Israel* (Leiden: Brill, 1974). In Milgrom's view the priestly elimination of the demonic realm left human beings in the role of God's opponents: it is human sin and impurity that defiles the sanctuary, with the danger that, left unpurified, the sanctuary will no longer be a suitable dwelling for God. I am inclined to accept Knohl's view that P's laws for the sanctuary are concerned only with ritual laws; see his critique of Milgrom in *Sanctuary*, 225–30. For Milgrom's response to Knohl's critique, see *Leviticus 23-27*, 2440–46.

15. See Milgrom, *Leviticus 1-16*, 43–44, 887–89.

16. Milgrom, *Leviticus 1-16*, points to the origins of both rituals in an understanding of impurity as demonic (43–44), but argues that the rite of the scapegoat has been substantially transformed (43, 1071–79) while the rite of purification from skin affliction has not (832–35; comparison to rite of scapegoat, 834).

17. This remarkable circumstance has elicited less comment than one might have expected, perhaps because it fits so poorly with notions of purity laws as primitive. Milgrom, *Leviticus 1-16*, comments on it briefly (869). See Maccoby, *Ritual*, 126–28.

18. The RSV translation, which I cite here, translates *niddâ* as "filthy." In my view a more literal translation is to be preferred in light of Lamentations' use of the technical terminology of impurity including a form of *ṭm'*, impure or unclean (Lam 1:9), and the reference to the law of skin eruptions noted below.

19. Even Milgrom, who believes that P understands violations of the moral laws of the Torah to pollute the sanctuary (*Leviticus 1-16*, 21–26), does not suggest that P attributes immorality to the bearers of impurity, only that immorality pollutes the sanctuary as does impurity.

20. For a treatment of the laws of purity that seeks to explicate the system, see Milgrom, *Leviticus 1-16*, 976–1000.

21. Shaye J. D. Cohen, "Menstruants and the Sacred in Judaism and Christianity," in *Women's History and Ancient History*, ed. Sarah B. Pomeroy (Chapel Hill: University of North Carolina Press, 1991) 275, 277, reads the omission in Leviticus 15 of bathing for the purification of the menstruant as purposeful and raises the possibility that the Mishnah's silence on the same subject means that the requirement of immersion is a development of the amoraic period. It seems to me, however, that Milgrom is correct when he argues that for P impurity is always brought to an end with ablutions; thus Leviticus 15 fails to mention bathing for the menstruant and the *zābâ* because it assumes it (*Leviticus 1-16*, 934–35).

22. I follow Knohl's division of the priestly corpus into P and H in *Sanctuary*, and I accept his view that H follows P.

23. Thus I think Jonathan Klawans's designation of the impurity with which H is concerned as "moral" (*Impurity and Sin in Ancient Judaism* [New York: Oxford University Press, 2000] esp. 26–31) is problematic.

24. I owe the insight about H's transformation of P's use of the term *niddâ* to the junior paper (spring 1993) of Lauren Eichler, now Rabbi Lauren Eichler Berkun.

25. In addition to the three certain manuscripts, there are two other possible manuscripts (Sidnie White Crawford, *The Temple Scroll and Related Texts*, Companion to the Qumran Scrolls 2 [Sheffield: Sheffield Academic Press, 2000] 12–15).

26. For a detailed, column-by-column, listing of the content of the *Temple Scroll*, see Johann Maier, *The Temple Scroll: An Introduction, Translation and Commentary*, Journal for the Study of the Old Testament: Supplement Series 34 (Sheffield: JSOT Press, 1985) 8–19. For a useful introduction to the *Temple Scroll*, see Crawford, *Temple Scroll*.

27. For somewhat different analyses, see Andrew M. Wilson and Lawrence Wills, "Literary Sources of the *Temple Scroll*," *Harvard Theological Review* 75 (1982): 275–88; Michael Owen Wise, *A Critical Study of the Temple Scroll from Qumran Cave 11*, Studies in the Ancient Oriental Civilizations 49 (Chicago: Oriental Institute of the University of Chicago, 1990); and Florentino García Martínez, "Sources et redaction du *Rouleau du temple*," *Henoch* 13 (1991): 219–32 (a lengthy review of Wise, *Critical Study*).

28. Lawrence H. Schiffman, "The Temple Scroll and the Systems of Jewish Law of the Second Temple Period," in *Temple Scroll Studies: Papers Presented at the International Symposium on the Temple Scroll, Manchester, December 1987*, ed. George J. Brooke, Journal for the Study of the Pseudepigrapha: Supplement Series 7 (Sheffield: JSOT Press, 1989) 239–40.

29. The style of the *Temple Scroll* and its modes of exegesis have been the subject of considerable discussion. See, e.g., Gershon Brin, *Issues in the Bible and the Dead Sea Scrolls* (Tel Aviv: Tel Aviv University and HaKibbutz Hameuchad, 1994) 162–230 (Hebrew); Phillip R. Callaway, "Extending Divine Revelation:

Micro-Compositional Strategies in the *Temple Scroll*," in *Temple Scroll Studies*, ed. Brooke, 149–62; and Dwight D. Swanson, *The Temple Scroll and the Bible: The Methodology of 11QT*, Studies on the Texts of the Desert of Judah 14 (Leiden: Brill, 1995). For some interesting comments on the scroll's style in relation to its goals, see Aharon Shemesh and Cana Werman, "Halakhah at Qumran: Genre and Authority," *Dead Sea Discoveries* 10 (2003): 110–11.

30. Émile Puech, *Qumrân Grotte 4. XVIII: Textes hébreux (4Q521-4Q528, 4Q576-4Q579)*, Discoveries in the Judaean Desert 25 (Oxford: Clarendon Press, 1998) 87. Before the publication of 4Q524, Yadin (*Temple Scroll* 1.386–90) had dated the *Temple Scroll* to the time of John Hyrcanus, or even earlier, on the basis of a number of considerations, including the laws of kingship (cols. 57–59). After Yadin but before the publication of 4Q524, several scholars made more detailed arguments for the laws of kingship as reflecting the conditions of Hasmonean rule in the late second or early first century. See Martin Hengel, James H. Charlesworth, and Doron Mendels, "The Polemical Character of 'On Kingship' in the Temple Scroll: An Attempt at Dating 11QTemple," *Journal of Jewish Studies* 37 (1986): 28–38; and Lawrence H. Schiffman, "The King, His Guard and the Royal Council in the *Temple Scroll*," *Proceedings of the American Academy of Jewish Research* 54 (1987): 237–59.

31. Yadin took the *Temple Scroll* to be a sectarian document. See, e.g., *Temple Scroll*, esp. 1.398; and, idem, "Is the Temple Scroll a Sectarian Document?" in *Humanizing America's Iconic Book: Society of Biblical Literature Centennial Addresses 1980*, ed. Gene M. Tucker and Douglas A. Knight (Chico, Calif.: Scholars Press, 1980) 153–69. Both Milgrom and Baumgarten follow Yadin on this point. For Milgrom, see, e.g., "The Qumran Cult: Its Exegetical Principles," in *Temple Scroll Studies*, ed. Brooke, 165–80; the very title is revealing. For a recent example in J. Baumgarten's work, see his introduction to 4QTohorot in Baumgarten et al., *Qumran Cave 4. XXV*, 79–92. Baumgarten's view that the Qumran texts reflect Sadducean law, which goes beyond the sect's own compositions, might provide some justification for proceeding this way, but he does not seem to feel the need to defend this approach. For an argument for treating the *Temple Scroll* as sectarian despite its differences from clearly sectarian works such as the *Damascus Document*, see Shemesh and Werman, "Halakhah at Qumran," 124–28. On the other hand, Schiffman has consistently maintained the view that the *Temple Scroll* stands at some distance from sectarian compositions, although the details of his view have changed somewhat over time. For a summary statement, now more than a decade old, however, see Lawrence H. Schiffman, "The *Temple Scroll* and the Nature of Its Law: The Status of the Question," in *The Community of the Renewed Covenant: The Notre Dame Symposium on the Dead Sea Scrolls*, ed. Eugene Ulrich and James VanderKam, Christianity and Judaism in Antiquity Series 10 (Notre Dame: University of Notre Dame Press, 1994) 37–55.

32. For the view that the sect inherited the work, see Florentino García Martínez, "The Temple Scroll and the New Jerusalem," in *The Dead Sea Scrolls after Fifty Years: A Comprehensive Assessment*, ed. Peter W. Flint and James C. VanderKam, with the assistance of Andrea E. Alvarez (Leiden: Brill, 1999) 2.441–42; Crawford, *Temple Scroll*, 26–29.

33. For the dates of the other manuscripts of the *Temple Scroll*, see Crawford, *Temple Scroll*, 12–15.

34. While Wilson and Wills, "Literary Sources," consider the purity laws of cols. 48–51 as part of a source used by the *Temple Scroll*, Phillip R. Callaway, "Source Criticism of the Temple Scroll: The Purity Laws," *Revue de Qumran* 12

(1985–87): 213–22, refutes their argument, to my mind persuasively. Wise (*Critical Study*, 133–39) takes Callaway's arguments into account, but understands the purity laws as a distinctive body of material that summarizes the purity rules of the author's own community, as does García Martínez ("Sources et redaction," 228–31; "The Temple Scroll," 437), following him.

35. Scholars have long noted the contradiction between the rule for the wilderness camp of Numbers and the assumption of Leviticus 15 and Numbers 19 that those with abnormal genital flow and corpse impurity live at home. (The stringency of the law of the war camp relative to Leviticus 15 represents not a contradiction but an acknowledgment of the special holiness of the war camp, in which, according to Deuteronomy, the Lord himself is present [Deut 23:15].) Knohl, *Sanctuary*, 86, 184–85, explains the contradiction between the laws of the wilderness camp and the purity laws by arguing that Num 5:1-4 derives from the Holiness school. The expansion of the categories of impurity that require exclusion from the camp reflects H's extension of holiness to the land as a whole: H applies to the land purity rules that P applies only to the sanctuary. (Knohl sees the editorial hand of H in Numbers 19, but understands the passage as primarily the work of P [92–94].)

Milgrom, however, claims that there is no contradiction between Num 5:1-4 and the P passages because the camp of the passage in Numbers is not the land as a whole but the war camp of the wilderness period only (*Leviticus 17–22*, 1354–55). But the laws of the camp in Deuteronomy are presented as laws intended for use after entrance into the land, the camp is explicitly designated a war camp (Deut 23:10), and the only type of impurity mentioned is that of nocturnal emission (Deut 23:11), appropriately for a camp with an all-male population. The camp in Numbers, on the other hand, is clearly outside the land; it appears in the context of the narrative of the wandering in the wilderness. It is not called a war camp, and it explicitly mentions women (Num 5:3). In both cases, however, we are given a rationale for the stringent purity measures: the presence of the Lord in the camp.

I believe there are other problems with Knohl's argument. First, there is no unambiguous statement in H that the land can be defiled by the types of impurity that concern P. Second, it is worth remembering that unlike the laws of Leviticus 12–15 and Numbers 19, the rules of exclusion from the camp are explicitly placed outside the land, in the wilderness. Finally, even if the entire land is susceptible to defilement by physical impurity and the laws of the wilderness camp are properly understood as intended for life in the land, it is not clear how exclusion from the camp would protect the land. The exiles, after all, would live within the land even if they were outside the camp. It is worth remembering that Num 5:3 explains the stringency of its rules by appealing to the presence of the Lord in Israel's camps, as Deuteronomy does. No such explanation appears in H's other legislation intended to protect the land from defilement.

36. I do not understand there to be a significant difference between "the whole sanctuary" (*TS* 45.8) and "the whole city of the sanctuary" (*TS* 45.11–12). See Sara Japhet, "The Prohibition of the Habitation of Women: The Temple Scroll's Attitude toward Sexual Impurity and Its Biblical Precedents," *Comparative Studies in Honor of Yochanan Muffs, Journal of the Ancient Near Eastern Society* 22 (1993): 75n. 25, 86; and Baruch A. Levine, "The Temple Scroll: Aspects of Its Historical Provenance and Literary Character," *Bulletin of the American Schools of Oriental Research* 232 (1978): 14–17.

37. Enough survives in 4Q271 to show that the context, Sabbath laws, laws of

prayer, and the prohibition on communicating with ghosts, is the same in 4QD as in CD. Thus there is no reason to see CD as an abridgment of this portion of 4QD.

38. Yadin, *Temple Scroll* 1.287-88; Milgrom, "Studies in the Temple Scroll," *Journal of Biblical Literature* 97 (1978): 513; idem, "Qumran Cult,"174; idem, "The Scriptural Foundations and Deviations in the Laws of Purity of the *Temple Scroll*," in *Archeology and History*, ed. Schiffman, 89–91; Lawrence H. Schiffman, "Exclusion from the Sanctuary and the City of the Sanctuary in the Temple Scroll," *Hebrew Annual Review* 9 (1985): 308.

39. Japhet, "Prohibition," 76–79, 83–87. "Source" is a euphemism for genitals that appears in Leviticus (12:1, 20:18) and the *Temple Scroll.*

40. Yadin, *Temple Scroll* 1.331.

41. See especially Milgrom, "Studies in the Temple Scroll," 512–18, and idem, "First Day Ablutions at Qumran," in *Madrid Qumran Congress*, ed. Trebolle Barrera and Vegas Montaner, 2.561-70.

42. To be more precise, the *Temple Scroll* requires such bathing of a man who has had a nocturnal emission (*TS* 45.7-10). It goes on to require a three-day period of exclusion from the sanctuary for the man who has had a seminal emission in the course of sexual relations (*TS* 45.11-12). It does not mention a procedure for purification. The inference that it intends the bathing decreed for the impurity caused by nocturnal emission to apply to the impurity caused by sexual intercourse is reasonable.

43. Milgrom, "Studies in the Temple Scroll," 515n. 44.

44. Yadin, *Temple Scroll* 1.277-80. Yadin is influenced particularly by Gedalia Alon, "The Bounds of the Laws of Levitical Cleanness," in *Jews, Judaism, and the Classical World: Studies in Jewish History in the Times of the Second Temple and Talmud* (Jerusalem: Magnes Press, 1977).

45. For a discussion of the lack of evidence for the seclusion of menstruants in turn-of-the-era Judaism, see Sanders, "Did the Pharisees?" 149–51, 155–62.

46. See also the *Temple Scroll*'s instructions for building booths on the roofs of the structures in the third courtyard for the leaders of the people (*TS* 42.10-17). On both these points, see the discussion of Israel Knohl, "Post-Biblical Sectarianism and the Priestly Schools of the Pentateuch: The Issue of Popular Participation in the Temple Cult on Festivals," in *Madrid Qumran Congress*, ed. Trebolle Barrera and Vegas Montaner, 2.606-7, esp. n. 14.

47. Charlotte Hempel, *The Damascus Texts* (Companion to the Qumran Scrolls, 2; Sheffield: Sheffield Academic Press, 2000) 21.

48. Cana Werman, however, has expressed skepticism about whether the title "Book of the Divisions of the Times in their Jubilees and in their Weeks" is actually a reference to *Jubilees*, which refers to itself as Torah-Teudah (conversation with the author, Nov. 7, 2002); the translation is from Baumgarten and Schwartz, "Damascus Document."

49. All translations of material from 4QD unless otherwise noted are taken from Baumgarten, *Qumran Cave 4.XIII*. For my "rule of skin eruptions" above, Baumgarten translates, "rule of *ṣaraʻat.*" For material that appears only in CD, the translation is that of Florentino García Martínez and Eibert J. C. Tigchelaar, *The Dead Sea Scrolls Study Edition* (Leiden: Brill; Grand Rapids, Mich.: Eerdmans, 1997–98).

50. Baumgarten's reconstruction yields the somewhat redundant *zeh mišpaṭ* [*tôra*]*t haṣṣāraʻat*, for the parallel in 4Q266 6 i 13 (Baumgarten, *Qumran Cave 4.XIII*).

51. See also, "And the rule [*mišpaṭ*] for a scall of the head or the bea[rd]" (4Q266 6 i 5; parallel in 4Q273 4 ii 10, which breaks off after the first letter of "head"); and, "[And] the law [*mišpaṭ*] [of a woman who has a discharge]" (4Q272 1 ii 7). All come at the beginning of the relevant laws with the exception indicated above.

52. Introductions: the laws of purification for one with skin eruptions (Lev 14:2). Conclusions: the laws of permitted and prohibited animals (Lev 11:46); the laws of the impurity of the parturient (Lev 12:7); the laws of eruptions of fabrics and leather (Lev 13:59), a topic not treated in 4QD; the offering of the poor man with skin eruptions (Lev 14:32); the laws of eruptions generally (Lev 14:54, 57); the laws of genital discharge (Lev 15:32). The same usage also appears in Lev 6:2, 7, 18 and Lev 7:1, 11, introducing different types of sacrifice; Num 5:29, concluding the laws of the woman suspected of adultery; and Num 6:13, 21, introducing sections of the laws of the Nazirite.

53. The first item following the heading prohibits vowing any unjust gain to the altar. It is worth noting that the Torah juxtaposes vowing and the term *tôrâ* in Num 6:21: "This is the law [*tôrâ*] for the Nazirite who takes a vow." Unlike the purity laws, however, the passage on donations to the sanctuary is not closely linked to a single passage in the Torah. There are other places in the *Damascus Document* (e.g., CD 10.14, 15.7, 16.12) where *mišpaṭ* means something like "rule," but it is not in the construct nor is it used as the heading or conclusion for a specific set of laws.

54. This rubric involves some reconstruction by Baumgarten; most important, the word *'al* appears only in 4Q266, where it is crossed out.

55. As Shemesh and Werman note ("Halakhah at Qumran," 115).

56. For a list of occurrences in Leviticus 11–15, see note 52 above. I count Lev 14:54, 57 as a single instance. Elsewhere in the Torah, the term appears seven times as an introduction and twice as a conclusion.

57. I discuss these laws in more detail in "Impurity and Sin in 4QD, 1QS, and 4Q512," *Dead Sea Discoveries* 8 (2001): 16–17.

58. See Baumgarten, *Qumran Cave 4.XIII*, 54.

59. See Himmelfarb, "Impurity and Sin," 16, for more detailed discussion of the treatment of the terms *sapaḥat* and *mam'eret*.

60. The preserved text begins with the definition of *sapaḥat*, a term that appears at the very beginning of Leviticus's discussion (Lev 13:2). Leviticus then switches to the variant form *mispaḥat* (13:6-8). The term *sapaḥat* appears again only in the summary of the laws of eruptions in Lev 14:56. The laws of skin eruptions in 4QD conclude with a discussion of scall of the head or beard, which comes toward the end of Leviticus's procedures for judging the purity status of skin eruptions (Lev 13:29-37); the concluding formula has been preserved (4Q266 6 i 13/4Q272 1 ii 2).

61. In the single manuscript containing the laws of the parturient, the discussion of the woman with abnormal flow concludes in the middle of a line and the discussion of the parturient begins on the next line (4Q266 6 ii 4–5). But despite this possible indication of a new unit, the absence of an introductory phrase with *mišpaṭ* and the active rearrangement of the material of Leviticus 12–15 to place the impurity of the parturient together with the other types of impurity of genital discharge strongly suggest that the parturient is here treated as a third type of *zābâ*.

62. Milgrom, *Leviticus 1–16*, 934.

63. My translation.

64. My translation.

65. Both fragments in which the passage is preserved contain the opening heading. While 4Q266 6 i breaks off before the end of the passage, 4Q272 1 ii 7 contains the opening heading for the topic that follows, female genital discharge.

66. I have added "one" to Baumgarten's translation (*Qumran Cave 4.XIII*, 53, 190). If the first 'ô *ǎšer*, is translated, "or one who," then this 'ô *ǎšer* too should be translated "or one who." The translation of García Martínez and Tigchelaar rightly treats the two instances of 'ô *ǎšer* equally, thus suggesting that the passage discusses three categories of men: "Regula[tion concerning the man with a disch]arge. Eve[ry man] [with a di]scha[rge from his flesh, or who brings upon himself a] lustful thought or who[. . .]" (*Dead Sea Scrolls* 1.625).

67. The words "bathe in water" are Baumgarten's reconstruction, as his transcription of the Hebrew indicates, but in the translation the words are not placed in brackets (*Qumran Cave 4.XIII*, 190). I have corrected this error in the quotation above.

68. I have combined Baumgarten's translations of the two relevant fragments (*Qumran Cave 4.XIII*, 53, 190). I indicate lacunae only where neither fragment preserves the text, and I have not made any effort to show the actual size of the lacunae.

69. Baumgarten points out that *m. Zabim* 2.2 exempts discharge from being considered a sign of *zāb* impurity if it can be connected to sexual stimulation (*Qumran Cave 4.XIII*, 54; idem, "Zab Impurity in Qumran and Rabbinic Law," *Journal of Jewish Studies* 45 [1994]: 275). But his comment on the passage in 4QD, "It would appear from the context that a discharge resulting from lustful thoughts was considered as coming under the category of *zab* and would therefore be defiling" (*Qumran Cave 4.XIII*, 54), is somewhat misleading. Any discharge is defiling, but according to Leviticus 15 normal seminal emission defiles for a much shorter period than abnormal discharge and far less effort is required to remove the impurity.

70. My proposal leaves room for several other words on the line.

71. It is frustrating that the phrase "his contact is like that of " (4Q266 6 i 16; 4Q272 1 ii 5) breaks off where it does. Perhaps contact with the *zāb* is compared to contact with the *niddâ*, apparently the subject a few lines later (4Q272 1 ii 9–10).

72. Charlotte Hempel, *The Laws of the Damascus Document: Sources, Tradition and Redaction*, Studies on the Texts of the Desert of Judah 29 (Leiden: Brill, 1998) 37–38, considers the assumption of participation to be characteristic of the legal material in the *Damascus Document.*

73. Trans. Joseph M. Baumgarten, in Baumgarten et al., *Qumran Cave 4.XXV.* This translation reflects the restoration *wĕ'im tēṣē['mē'îš ši]kbat hazzera'*. Milgrom restores the text differently, *wĕ'im tēṣē['mimmenû ši]kbat hazzera'*, in "4QTOHO-RA[a]: An Unpublished Qumran Text on Purities," in *Time to Prepare the Way in the Wilderness: Papers on the Qumran Scrolls by Fellows of the Institute for Advanced Studies of the Hebrew University, Jerusalem, 1989–1990*, ed. Devorah Dimant and Lawrence H. Schiffman, Studies on the Texts of the Desert of Judah 16 (Leiden: Brill, 1995) 59–68. (Baumgarten's first discussion of the text, "The Laws about Fluxes in 4QTohora[a] [4Q274]," in *Time to Prepare the Way*, ed. Dimant and Schiffman, 1–8, also uses this restoration.) In Milgrom's reading, the man with the seminal

emission is the man referred to in the previous line as counting the days of purification. Milgrom argues that the touch of this man defiles after the seminal emission because as a former *zāb* (in Leviticus's sense) who has not yet completed the waiting period before the ritual of purification, he was still somewhat impure even before the seminal emission; the seminal emission serves to increase his impurity so that his touch is now defiling. This argument rests on Milgrom's view that 4QTohorot A implies first-day ablutions for the impurities it discusses ("4QTOHORA^a," 66–67). The attribution by 4QD of a defiling touch to a man who has had a nocturnal emission is virtually certain even if the attribution of such a touch to the man who has had a seminal emission during sexual intercourse is less so. It seems to me that the passage in 4QD strengthens the case for Baumgarten's reading of 4QTohorot A, in which the defiling touch is independent of the previous state of purity of the man who has had the seminal emission.

74. See Milgrom, *Leviticus 1–16*, 934–35.

75. Indeed, Hempel, *Laws*, considers the purity laws of the *Damascus Document* part of the stratum of 4QD that does not show a connection to a specific community (26).

76. The words "pregnant woman" are preserved, but not enough else survives to be certain of the nature of the transgression. See Joseph M. Baumgarten, "A Fragment on Fetal Life and Pregnancy in 4Q270," in *Pomegranates and Golden Bells: Studies in Biblical, Jewish and Near Eastern Ritual, Law, and Literature in Honor of Jacob Milgrom*, ed. David P. Wright, David N. Freedman, and Avi Hurvitz (Winona Lake, Ind.: Eisenbrauns, 1995) 445–48.

77. Menahem Kister, "Notes on Some New Texts from Qumran," *Journal of Jewish Studies* 44 (1993): 280–81.

78. On the *Damascus Document*'s attitude toward women, see Eileen Schuller, "Women in the Dead Sea Scrolls," in *Dead Sea Scrolls after Fifty Years*, ed. Flint and VanderKam, 2.123–31.

79. Thomas O. Lambdin, trans., "The Gospel of Thomas (II, 2)," in *The Nag Hammadi Library in English*, ed. James M. Robinson (San Francisco: Harper and Row, 1977) 130.

80. See the discussion of David Winston, "Philo and the Rabbis on Sex and the Body," in *Hellenism and Hebraism Reconsidered: The Poetics of Cultural Influence and Exchange I (Poetics Today* 19 [1998]), ed. David Stern, 43–53.

81. While Baumgarten has to supply the *zābâ* after "rule of," the term does appear in the next line, and the context leaves no doubt that it should appear at the beginning of the passage.

82. The beginning of the passage is preserved in 4QD 272 1 ii 7–18; 4QD 266 6 ii 1–2 preserves the conclusion of the discussion of the *niddâ*.

83. Baumgarten et al., *Qumran Cave 4.XXV*, 83–87. The most important piece of evidence for this claim appears in 4QTohorot B^b 1 ii 7–10:

And those [who receive] th[e lust]ration water shall (first) immerse themselves in water and be cle[an]sed of [human?] corpse defilement [and of every] other [defilement when the pri]est [spr]inkles the lustration water upon them to purify [them, for they cannot] [be sanctified] unless they are cleansed and their flesh is c[lean.]

See also Shaye J. D. Cohen's discussion of the Karaite practice of sprinkling for purification from menstrual impurity, in "Purity, Piety, and Polemic: Medieval Rabbinic Denunciations of 'Incorrect' Purification Practices," in *Women and Water: Menstruation in Jewish Life and Law*, ed. Rahel R. Wasserfall, Brandeis Series on Jewish Women (Hanover, N.H.: Brandeis University Press, 1999) 93–94.

84. The beginning of the rule of the *zābâ* and the material about the menstruant discussed so far appear in 4Q272 1 ii. The passage about to be discussed, concerning the man who has sexual relations with the menstruant, stands at the beginning of 4Q266 6 ii, which continues with discussion of the woman with abnormal genital discharge and the woman who has given birth. Thus 4QD's discussion of the man who has sexual relations with the menstruant appears to be the end of its treatment of the menstruant, just as this topic also concludes Leviticus 15's discussion of the menstruant.

85. See Milgrom, *Leviticus 1–16*, 940, for a discussion of the absence of a prohibition in P. I am not sure that P is as obsessed with purity as Milgrom thinks; the purity laws discussed here obviously thought it insufficiently obsessed.

86. Himmelfarb, "Impurity and Sin," 21–22. Baumgarten's comment on this passage, "The association of impurity with sin [*ʿāwôn*] is characteristic of the Qumran outlook" (*Qumran Cave 4.XIII*, 56), thus ignores Leviticus 18 and 20.

87. Baumgarten, *Qumran Cave 4.XIII*, uses "anything hallowed"; I have changed the translation slightly to make it clear that 4QD and Leviticus here use the same term, *qōdeš*.

88. Milgrom, *Leviticus 1–16*, 751–52.

89. One of these is the rule just cited, for the woman after childbirth. Another law relevant to laypeople is the prohibition of eating one's share of the well-being offering while bearing any type of impurity (Lev 7:20-21) (Milgrom, *Leviticus 1–16*, 751–52). A passage in Numbers implies a prohibition of eating the paschal sacrifice, a sacrifice to be consumed by laypeople, while suffering from corpse impurity (Num 18:11, 13). The most concentrated set of prohibitions for priests appears in Lev 22:3-9, where priests in various states of impurity are forbidden to eat holy food.

90. The Torah also applies the rule of waiting for sunset to types of impurity that have nothing to do with genital flow, such as the impurity caused by contact with the carcass of a forbidden insect or animal (Lev 11:24, 25, 27, 28, 31), eating a permitted animal that dies of itself, or contact with its carcass (Lev 11:39-40). So too one who enters a house that has been shut because it is afflicted with eruptions becomes impure until evening (Lev 14:46). The Holiness Code decrees that one who eats an animal unfit for consumption because it died on its own or was killed by other animals is impure until evening (Lev 17:15). The Torah also decrees that impurity disappears only at evening for those who engage in the various aspects of the manufacture of the ashes of the red cow. The priest in charge of the sacrifice of the cow (Num 19:7), the person who burns the cow (Num 19:8), and the person who gathers the ashes (Num 19:10) all become impure and must launder, bathe, and wait until evening to return to a state of purity. The person who sprinkles the waters on those impure from contact with a corpse also becomes impure, as does anyone who touches the waters, and the impurity lasts until evening (Num 19:21), although here the text is not as clear as it might be. The only type of impurity that lasts more than a single day for which the Torah legislates an evening terminus is the impurity caused by contact with a corpse, the type of impurity removed by sprinkling with waters containing the ashes of the red cow (Num 19:19).

91. Baumgarten, *Qumran Cave 4.XIII*, 56; and, Joseph M. Baumgarten, "The Pharisaic-Sadducean Controversies about Purity and the Qumran Texts," *Journal of Jewish Studies* 31 (1980): 157–61; Lawrence H. Schiffman, "Pharisaic and Sadducean Halakhah in Light of the Dead Sea Scrolls: The Case of Tevul Yom," *Dead Sea Discoveries* 1 (1994): 285–99.

92. Martha Himmelfarb, "The Polemic against the *Tebul Yom*: A Reexamination," in *New Perspectives on Old Texts: Proceedings of the Tenth International Symposium of the Orion Center for the Study of the Dead Sea Scrolls and Associated Literature, January 9–11 2005*, ed. Esther G. Chazon, Ruth A. Clements, and Besty Halpern-Amaru (Leiden: Brill, forthcoming).

93. Baumgarten (*Qumran Cave 4.XIII*, 56) compares the passage in 4QD to Num 19:20, which threatens a bearer of corpse impurity who does not undergo purification with being cut off from among the congregation because he has defiled the sanctuary, but neither the crime nor the terminology is very close to 4QD.

94. The text is fragmentary, but it is difficult to imagine an interpretation of the surviving letters,]*led lĕmēneqet bĕṭôh*[, that does not involve a nurse.

95. Milgrom, *Leviticus 1–16*, 746, raises the possibility that the infant was to undergo immersion with the mother at the end of the seven- or fourteen-day period of more intense impurity.

96. See, e.g., Joseph M. Baumgarten, "The Purification Rituals in *DJD* 7," in *The Dead Sea Scrolls: Forty Years of Research*, ed. Devorah Dimant and Uriel Rappaport, Studies on the Texts of the Desert of Judah 10 (Jerusalem: Magnes Press and Yad Izhak Ben-Zvi; Leiden: Brill, 1992) 199–209; Florentino García Martínez, "The Problem of Purity: The Qumran Solution," in *The People of the Dead Sea Scrolls: Their Writings, Beliefs and Practices*, by Florentino García Martínez and Julio Trebolle Barrera, trans. Wilfred G. E. Watson (Leiden: Brill, 1995) 139–57; Klawans, *Impurity and Sin*, 67–91. Baumgarten comments on the conflation of sin and impurity in 4QD in his commentary to it (*Qumran Cave 4.XIII*, 56, 146) and elsewhere ("Zab Impurity," 275).

97. In "Impurity and Sin," I treat the *Damascus Document*, the *Rule of the Community*, and 4QRitual of Purification B (4Q512).

98. For 4QD's list of transgressors, which I omit from my discussion here, see Himmelfarb, "Impurity and Sin," 26–27.

99. Himmelfarb, "Impurity and Sin," 13–14, for further discussion.

100. The expression *timṣā' yādāh* and variations appear a number of other places in the Bible (Jud 9:38; 1 Sam 10:7; Isa 10:10, 14; Hos 2:9; Job 31:25; Eccl 9:10), but it means "afford" only in one other instance (Lev 25:28).

101. Lev 5:11; 14:22, 30, 31, 32. It is also used for sacrifices that do not involve substitution (Num 6:21; Ezek 46:7), and it appears in other contexts as well with the meaning "afford" (Lev 25:26 [perfect], 47; 27:8).

102. The conclusion of the rule for skin eruptions is preserved, and as noted above, the laws of skin eruptions in 4QD follow the order of the Torah, where the sacrifice is treated at the end of the discussion.

103. Although it is very fragmentary, 4Q266 6 ii 2–4 seems to contain the complete treatment of the woman with abnormal discharge, and there is no indication of a discussion of sacrifice.

104. Baumgarten argues that the description of the place of service in the temple indicates that the priest in question is the high priest (*Qumran Cave 4.XIII*, 51, to l. 7).

105. See, e.g., the influential programmatic essay of Ya'aqov Sussman, "The History of Halakha and the Dead Sea Scrolls-Preliminary Observations on Miqṣat Ma'aśe Ha-Torah (4QMMT)," *Tarbiz* 59 (1989–90): 11–76 (Hebrew) (English translation without extensive annotation: "Appendix I: The History of Halakha and the Dead Sea Scrolls: Preliminary Observations on MIQṢAT MA'AŚE HA-TORAH [4QMMT]," in *Qumran Cave 4.V*, ed. Qimron and Strugnell,

179–200). The literature on this topic is now considerable. Eyal Regev, "Were the Priests All the Same? Qumranic Halakhah in Comparison with Sadducean Halakhah," *Dead Sea Discoveries* 12 (2005): 158–88, has recently argued against the view that the Dead Sea Scrolls and the Sadducees are regularly in agreement on halakhic matters. He sees them as two separate schools growing out of the common halakhah of the period before the hellenistic reform (184). While Regev is persuasive on many individual points, I hope I have shown that his view that a single legal tradition emerges from the Dead Sea Scrolls is untenable.

106. See Himmelfarb, "Sexual Relations," 25–27.

Chapter 4

1. On Chronicles' attitude toward the survivors of the northern kingdom, see H. G. M. Williamson, *Israel in the Book of Chronicles* (London: Cambridge University Press, 1977) 139–40 (summary), and Sara Japhet, *The Ideology of the Book of Chronicles and Its Place in Biblical Thought* (Frankfurt am Main: Peter Lang, 1989) 325–34.

2. On the terms themselves, see Hengel, *Judaism and Hellenism* 1.1–2. On the idea of Judaism as growing out of the encounter with Hellenism, see S. J. D. Cohen, *Beginnings*, 109–39, esp. 132–39.

3. Thus, e.g., Bryan Wilson: "An individual chooses to be a sectarian, and he is normally required to show some mark of merit (by knowledge of doctrine; by quality of life; the recommendation of members in good standing; initiations or ritual performances, and so on) in order to be accepted as a member" (*Religion*, 92).

4. The sect as a sociological category emerged in discussions of Christianity in western Europe, and there is no equivalent to the church against which the sect is defined in Second Temple Judaism. The temple establishment had jurisdiction over only one aspect, however important, of religious life. Nor was there ever an official definition of orthodoxy as there was for Christians. The picture is further confused by Josephus's use of the Greek term *hairesis* in his account of the Pharisees, Sadducees, and Essenes. The term is usually translated "sect," though Josephus does not seem to have intended to identify these groups as sects in the modern, sociological sense. On the history of the term and the problems of using it outside the context for which it was originally developed, see, e.g., Wilson, *Religion*, 100–105.

5. There is an enormous literature on the *Damascus Document*, the *Rule of the Community*, and the structure of the sect. In my notes I refer only to the works most relevant to the points I am trying to make.

6. To the best of my knowledge, no single recent article reviews the various theories proposed. Perhaps the complexity of the subject makes the task impossible. For a pre-4QMMT review, see John J. Collins, "The Origin of the Qumran Community: A Review of the Evidence," in *To Touch the Text: Biblical and Related Studies in Honor of Joseph A. Fitzmyer, S.J.*, ed. Maurya P. Horgan and Paul J. Kobelski (New York: Crossroad, 1989); Collins assumes continuity between the community of CD and the *yaḥad* and thus does not address the question of the relationship between them. For a recent effort to consider that question including a brief review of the literature, see Charlotte Hempel, "Community Origins in the *Damascus Document* in the Light of Recent Scholarship," in *Provo International Conference*, ed. Parry and Ulrich.

7. See, e.g., Philip S. Alexander, "The Redaction-History of Serekh ha-Yaḥad: A Proposal" *Revue de Qumran* (1996): 437–53; Philip R. Davies, "Redaction and Sectarianism in the Qumran Scrolls," in *Sects and Scrolls: Essays on Qumran and Related Topics*, South Florida Studies in the History of Judaism 134 (Atlanta: Scholars Press, 1996); Hempel, *Laws*; Sarianna Metso, *The Textual Development of the Qumran Community Rule* (Leiden: Brill, 1997).

8. This is the picture suggested by Philip R. Davies; see *The Damascus Covenant: An Interpretation of the "Damascus Document"* (Journal for the Study of the Old Testament: Supplement Series 25 (Sheffield: JSOT Press, 1982) esp. 198–201, and idem, *Behind the Essenes*, esp. 107–34.

9. Eyal Regev, "The *Yaḥad* and the *Damascus Covenant*: Structure, Organization, and Relationship," *Revue de Qumran* 21 (2003): 233–62, considers many of the same features of the two works that I consider. He concludes, as I do, that the *Damascus Document*'s community is more hierarchical than the *yaḥad*. I am not persuaded, however, by his claim that comparison of institutions shows that the *yaḥad* preceded the community of the *Damascus Document*.

10. See Albert I. Baumgarten, "The Zadokite Priests at Qumran: A Reconsideration," *Dead Sea Discoveries* 4 (1997): 140–41, and Robert A. Kugler, "Priesthood at Qumran," in *Dead Sea Scrolls after Fifty Years*, ed. Flint and VanderKam, 2.93–94n. 1, for the history of the discussion.

11. E.g., 4QMMT for explicit criticism and the *Temple Scroll* for implicit.

12. The clearest indication of this view is 4QFlorilegium (4Q174) I 6–7. For discussion relevant to the point here and references to others who have treated this issue, see Devorah Dimant, "*4QFlorilegium* and the Idea of the Community as Temple," in *Hellenica et Judaica: Hommages à Valentin Nikiprowetzky* [*z"l*], ed. André Caquot, Mireille Hadas-Lebel, and Jean Riaud (Leuven: Peeters, 1986) esp. 174–80, 184–89.

13. E.g., 4QFlorilegium, the *Temple Scroll*, 4QNewJerusalem.

14. 4QShirShabb.

15. E.g., 4QMMT, the *Temple Scroll*, 4QD.

16. For a convenient collection of references, see Kugler, "Priesthood," 108.

17. For references, see Kugler, "Priesthood," 109–12.

18. Aharon Shemesh, "The Origins of the Laws of Separatism: Qumran Literature and Rabbinic Halacha," *Revue de Qumran* 18 (1997): 223–41, argues that the sect understood biblical laws governing relations with other Israelites to apply only to the sectarians' dealings with other members of the sect; Jews who were not members of the sect are not considered to be "kinsmen" or "brothers."

19. All translations of the *Rule of the Community* are taken from Michael A. Knibb, *The Qumran Community* (Cambridge: Cambridge University Press, 1987).

20. All translations of the portion of the *Damascus Document* known from the Geniza (CD) are taken from Baumgarten and Schwartz, "Damascus Document."

21. "Light" is clear, but "children of" is Baumgarten's restoration; see his commentary to this line in *Qumran Cave 4.XIII*, 32.

22. Baumgarten and Schwartz argue that the manuscript reading at CD 13.14, *libnê haššaḥar*, "to the Sons of Dawn," is correct. Thus the passage prohibits buying and selling not with outsiders, but with members of the sect, because it would be wrong to derive material benefit from dealings with fellow members ("Damascus Document," 55n. 203).

23. See most recently Robert A. Kugler, "Priesthood at Qumran: The Evidence of References to Levi and Levites," in *Provo International Conference*, ed. Parry and Ulrich, 477–79.

24. For discussion of the passages in question, see Kugler, "Levi and Levites," 467–70.

25. Milgrom, "Qumran Cult," 176–77. The position he now rejects appeared in "Studies in the Temple Scroll," 503–4.

26. For discussion of these laws, Lawrence H. Schiffman, "Legislation Concerning Relations with Non-Jews in the *Zadokite Fragments* and in Tannaitic Literature," *Revue de Qumran* 11 (1983): 379–89.

27. But the placement of the *gēr* with the poor and the needy rather than the widows and orphans reflects the Holiness Code's law of the Israelite who has become poor (Lev 25:35-38). This difficult passage commands that the impoverished Israelite be treated as a resident alien, *gēr wĕtôšāb* (Lev 25:35). While the meaning of the passage is somewhat obscure, it suggests a relationship between the categories of the poor and the *gēr*. Further, the difficult language actually calls the impoverished Israelite *gēr wĕtôšāb*, thus blurring the boundaries between Israelite and *gēr*.

28. For discussion (though not of this point), see Joseph M. Baumgarten, "The Disqualifications of Priests in 4Q Fragments of the 'Damascus Document': A Specimen of the Recovery of pre-Rabbinic Halakha," in *Madrid Qumran Congress*, ed. Trebolle Barrera and Vegas Montaner, 2.503–13.

29. Metso, *Textual Development*, esp. 105–6. Alexander, "Redaction-History," argues that in the absence of compelling evidence to the contrary, the version of the *Rule of the Community* in the manuscripts that are earlier on paleographic grounds should be understood as the earlier form of the text. Alexander wrote in knowledge of Metso's thesis but before the publication of her book. For my purposes the direction of the development of the *Rule of the Community* is not crucial because, in my view, even the version that mentions Zadokites grants power to the community as a whole.

30. For a dissent before the publication of the 4QS fragments, see Davies, *Behind the Essenes*, 51–72.

31. See the summary of the discussion in A. Baumgarten, "Zadokite Priests," 140–41, and Kugler, "Priesthood," 2.93n. 1. Alison Schofield and James C. VanderKam, "Were the Hasmoneans Zadokites?" *Journal of Biblical Literature* 124 (2005): 73–87, have recently argued that the Hasmoneans were probably themselves Zadokites.

32. Daniel R. Schwartz, "Introduction: On the Jewish Background of Christianity," in *Studies in the Jewish Background of Christianity*, 20; idem, "Qumran Between Priestliness and Christianity," in *The Scrolls of the Judaean Desert: Forty Years of Research*, ed. Magen Broshi et al. (Jerusalem: Bialik Institute and Israel Exploration Society, 1992) 179 (Hebrew).

33. A. Baumgarten, "Zadokite Priests," 142–53. See also Charlotte Hempel, "Interpretative Authority in the Community Rule Tradition," *Dead Sea Discoveries* 10 (2003): 74–80. Hempel discusses the second and third of the passages quoted above (1QS 5.8-10, 1QS 5.20–22) in both their 1Q and 4Q versions. She sees them as preserving material from different periods, with earlier, more democratic material juxtaposed with material that accords priests (sons of Aaron) a greater role even in 4QS, perhaps under the influence of 1QS (77–79).

Zadokites play a prominent role in two other scrolls in addition to the *Rule of the Community*, the *Rule of the Congregation* (1QSa) and the *Rule of Benedictions* (1QSb). Baumgarten suggests that because both of these short rules were copied in the same manuscript as the Cave 1 version of the *Rule of the Community*, they may reflect the views of only a small group and can hardly be taken as a groundswell of support for the new position ("Zadokite Priests," 152–53). See also Hempel, "The Earthly Essene Nucleus of 1QSa," *Dead Sea Discoveries* 3 (1996): 253–69. Hempel argues that the central portion of 1QSa (1.6–2.11a), which she sees not as a messianic rule but as a rule very close to the *Damascus Document*, has also undergone a "Zadokite recension" (257–61). All of the instances of Zadokite or priestly authority in 1QSa that Baumgarten notes (1QSa 1.2, 1.24, 2.3) juxtapose Zadokites with others as in 1QS. The clearest instance of Zadokite authority in any of the texts in this manuscript is 1QSb 3.22–25, a blessing of the Zadokite priests.

34. Regev, "*Yaḥad* and *Damascus Covenant*," 235–40, argues that the term "council" actually refers to local communities that formed the *yaḥad*; if so, even the 4QS version of this passage grants authority to the (local) group as a whole.

35. Hempel, "Interpretative Authority," 79, points out that 1QS is more expansive on this point than is 4QS.

36. See discussion and references to the occurrences of the different titles in Charlotte Hempel, "Community Structures," in *Dead Sea Scrolls after Fifty Years*, ed. Flint and VanderKam, 2.79–82.

37. Baumgarten and Schwartz, "Damascus Document," translate "Examiner" with an uppercase "e."

38. As noted by Dimant, "*4QFlorilegium*," 188. See also 1QSa 2.5–9 and 1QM 7.4–5. For a broader discussion of these passages, see Aharon Shemesh, "'The Holy Angels Are in Their Council': The Exclusion of Deformed Persons from Holy Places in Qumranic and Rabbinic Literature," *Dead Sea Discoveries* 4 (1997): 193–201.

39. Klawans, *Impurity and Sin*, 76–79, makes a similar observation.

40. It is used, however, elsewhere in the Bible, when Bathsheba purifies herself after menstruation (2 Sam 11:4).

41. Lev 26:43: "But the land shall be left by them, and enjoy its sabbaths while it lies desolate without them; and they shall make amends for their iniquity"; Num 35:33: "No expiation can be made for the land, for the blood that is shed in it, except by the blood of him who shed it."

42. In addition to 4Q512, there are two other manuscripts containing purification liturgies, 4Q284 and 4Q414, recently published in Baumgarten et al., *Qumran Cave 4.XXV*.

43. In his publication of the fragments Baillet, *Qumrân Grotte 4.III*, 263, suggests that cols. 3–7 and 9–11 of the work treat sexual impurity; col. 4, priests; col. 8, skin eruptions; frag. 67, eruptions of houses; and col. 12, corpse impurity. As J. Baumgarten, "Purification Rituals," 200, comments, "Not all of these identifications are equally convincing."

44. See the discussion of J. Baumgarten, *Qumran Cave 4.XXV*, 83–87.

45. The conflation of categories of impurity in a halakhic context is also suggested in 4QTohorot A (4Q274). This very fragmentary text contains rules for the separation of bearers of one type of impurity from bearers of a different type. It is thus remarkable that its first three preserved lines describe an impure man drawing on terminology associated with different types of impurity in Leviticus. Because the impure man occupies a "bed of sorrow" and a "seat of sighing" (trans. Baumgarten, *Qumran Cave 4.XXV*), J. Baumgarten argues that he has abnormal genital flow; abnormal genital flow is the only type of male impurity that makes bedding and seat impure (Lev 15:4–6) ("Laws about Fluxes," 3–4; Baumgarten et al., *Qumran Cave 4.XXV*,101–2). Milgrom identifies the man in question as afflicted with skin eruptions because the passage goes on to insist

on his isolation, quoting Lev 13:45, "He shall call out, 'Unclean! Unclean!'" directing a man with skin eruptions to warn others of his presence ("4QTOHO-RAa," 61.)

46. J. Baumgarten, "Purification Liturgies," 203.

47. J. Baumgarten, "Purification Rituals," 200–201, 208, notes that the term *niddâ* is used in 4Q512 in a variety of contexts that do not appear to concern menstrual impurity.

48. Klawans, *Impurity and Sin*, 76–78; he uses the phrase in quotation marks on p. 77. He also refers to "grave sinfulness in general" (76) and "grave sin in general" (77). Eyal Regev has recently argued in somewhat different terms that the Qumran community understood the temple to have been defiled by the *moral* impurity of its contemporaries ("Abominated Temple and a Holy Community: The Formation of the Notions of Purity and Impurity in Qumran," *Dead Sea Discoveries* 10 [2003]: 243–78).

49. The "purity" of the community, *ṭāhorat hārabbîm*, has been the subject of discussion ever since the discovery of the Dead Sea Scrolls; for a recent treatment, including a review of earlier discussions, see Friedrich Avemarie, "'Tohorat ha-Rabbim' and 'Mashqeh ha-Rabbim'—Jacob Licht Reconsidered," in *Legal Texts*, ed. Bernstein, García Martínez, and Kampen, 215–29.

50. Jonathan Klawans, "Impurity of Immorality in Ancient Judaism," *Journal of Jewish Studies* 48 (1997): 9; idem, *Impurity and Sin*, 82–85. This understanding of the meaning of the pure food and drink of the community is by no means certain, although there is support for such usage in some of the appearances of the term *ṭāhorâ* in the *Temple Scroll* and perhaps 4QMMT (Avemarie, "'Tohorat ha-Rabbim,'" 222–24). The Torah's use of the root *ṭhr*, on the other hand, suggests a different understanding of 1QS's *ṭāhorat hārabbîm*. The Torah never uses the noun *ṭāhorâ* of food, but it does term some forbidden animals "impure" (Lev 11:4-8; Deut 14:7-9, 19), and it refers to permitted birds as "pure" (Deut 14:11). It also decrees that contact with the corpse of an impure swarming thing renders impure earthen vessels and their contents, dampened food and drink, and ovens and stoves (Lev 11:33–35). Thus it is possible that in referring to its food as *ṭāhorâ* the Qumran community was simply emphasizing that it met the standards of the Torah. Surely there were many whose food did not; in an agricultural society without refrigeration avoiding prohibited contact with the corpses of impure creatures was probably not an easy task. Indeed, Sanders, "Did the Pharisees?" 246–47, suggests that the Pharisees may have been the only laypeople who actually observed these laws. (Sanders reads Lev 11:33-35 as concerned with insects as well as the eight creatures that swarm on the earth listed in Lev 11:29–30 [138], but this does not seem to me to be the plain sense of Leviticus.) For a recent argument for the view that concern for purity was widespread in ancient Israel, drawing in part on archeological evidence, Eyal Regev, "Pure Individualism: The Idea of Non-Priestly Purity in Ancient Judaism," *Journal for the Study of Judaism in the Persian, Hellenistic, and Roman Period* 31 (2000): 176–202. There is no indication in the Torah that pure food, as opposed to consecrated food, must be eaten in a state of purity.

51. Knibb, *Qumran Community*, argues against the view that the second passage is a continuation of the first on the grounds that the first constitutes a separate paragraph in the manuscript passage and that the second passage is preceded by an introductory formula: "These are the rules by which the men of perfect holiness shall walk with one another" (1QS 8.20). He prefers to read the two passages as alternate forms of the rule, reflecting the development of the rule

over time (136). In addition to the passage about baptism cited above, the section about membership in the community that follows the penal code twice refers to exclusion from the pure food for those who violate the rules, although the relationship between the rulings of the two passages is less than clear.

52. Moshe Weinfeld, *The Organizational Pattern and the Penal Code of the Qumran Sect*, Novum Testamentum et Orbis Antiquus 2 (Fribourg: Éditions Universitaires; Göttingen: Vandenhoeck & Ruprecht, 1986).

53. Mariano San Nicolò, "Zur Vereinsgerichtbarkeit im hellenistischen Ägypten," in ΕΠΙΤΥΜΒΙΟΝ: *Heinrich Swoboda Dargebracht* (Reichenberg: Stiepel, 1927) 280–81, with references to the rules.

54. My translation is inspired by the RSV translation of *'erwat dābār* in Deut 24:1 as "some indecency."

55. On this phrase, J. Baumgarten, "Purification Rituals," 201.

56. He notes, however, that one early discussion understood 1QS 3.4–5, "He shall not be made clean by atonement or purified by waters for purification, or made holy by seas and rivers, or purified by any water for washing," as evidence for a polemic against baptism (J. Baumgarten, "Purification Rituals," 199; the reference is to M. H. Gottstein, "Anti-Essene Traits in the Qumran Scrolls," *Vetus Testamentum* 4 [1954]: 145–46).

57. Knibb, *Qumran Community*, 110–11.

58. For an interesting discussion of the parallels between Qumran literature, particularly 1QS, and the thought of John the Baptist as far as it can be recovered, see David Flusser, "The Baptism of John and the Dead Sea Sect," in *Essays on the Dead Sea Scrolls in Memory of E. L. Sukenik*, ed. Yigael Yadin and Chaim Rabin, assisted by Jacob Licht (Jerusalem: Hekhal Ha-Sefer, 1961) 209–39, esp. 209–17 (Hebrew).

59. D. Schwartz, "Jewish Background," 19–24; idem, "Qumran Between"; and, from a somewhat different angle, idem, "Law and Truth: On Qumran-Sadducean and Rabbinic Views of Law," in *Dead Sea Scrolls: Forty Years of Research*, ed. Dimant and Rappaport, 239.

60. D. Schwartz, "Jewish Background," 21–22; idem, "Qumran Between," 179–80; idem, "Law and Truth," 238.

61. D. Schwartz, "Jewish Background," 21; idem, "Qumran Between," 179.

62. D. Schwartz, "Jewish Background," 22–24; idem, "Qumran Between," 180; idem, "Law and Truth," 239. He illustrates this point with passages drawn from the *Hodayot* (all three articles) and the *Community Rule* ("Qumran Between" and "Law and Truth").

63. The comparison to Christianity is central to D. Schwartz's "Jewish Background" and "Qumran Between"; it is noted briefly in his "Law and Truth," where the idea of rabbinic Judaism as a solution to the problem appears. It is worth noting that Schwartz suggests that the rise of Christianity may have played a role in shaping the rabbinic attitude that the law is not the means to an end, but the end in itself (230) but he does not develop this suggestion.

64. D. Schwartz, "Law and Truth," 239.

65. Krister Stendahl, "Paul and the Introspective Conscience of the West," *Harvard Theological Review* 56 (1963): 199–215; reprinted in *Paul among Jews and Gentiles and Other Essays* (Philadelphia: Fortress, 1976).

66. This point of view was pioneered by Lloyd Gaston, whose essays on this theme are collected in *Paul and the Torah* (Vancouver: University of British Columbia Press, 1987). It has been further developed by John G. Gager, *The Origins of Anti-Semitism* (New York: Oxford University Press, 1983) 197–264. See also

Gager, *Reinventing Paul* (New York: Oxford University Press, 2000), and the account of traditional views and recent developments there (21–75).

67. Thus Jeffrey L. Rubenstein, "Nominalism and Realism in Qumranic and Rabbinic Law: A Reassessment," *Dead Sea Discoveries* 6 (1999): 157–83, who discusses Schwartz's examples of rabbinic nominalism and argues that rabbinic attitudes toward law include both nominalist and realist strands; Rubenstein claims that the most pronounced form of nominalism does not appear until the fifth century (183).

68. The literature on Revelation, like that for other books of the New Testament, is huge. As in the section of the chapter on the Dead Sea Scrolls, I limit my references to the most relevant scholarship.

69. For a study of the theme with different concerns and assumptions about John's relationship to Judaism, see Elisabeth Schüssler Fiorenza, *Priester für Gott: Studien zum Herrschafts- und Priestermotiv in der Apokalypse*, Neutestamentliche Abhandlungen n.f. 7 (Munster: Aschendorff, 1972).

70. John W. Marshall, *Parables of War: Reading John's Jewish Apocalypse* (Waterloo, Ontario: Wilfrid Laurier University Press, 2001). Marshall dates the book quite precisely, between the summer of 68 and the late spring of 70 C.E. (*Parables*, 88–97), but Marshall's argument holds even if we accept a date under Domitian in the late first century, the time favored by much of late twentieth-century scholarship.

71. David Frankfurter, "Jews or Not? Reconstructing the 'Other' in Rev 2:9 and 3:9," *Harvard Theological Review* 94 (2001): 403–25.

72. The RSV translation, "practice immorality," is too weak. The Greek *porneusai* is the equivalent of the Hebrew root *znh*, to be a harlot, and like it, it has clear sexual connotations.

73. For criticism of several recent proponents of the view that the synagogues of Satan are Jews with whom John's community is in conflict, see Marshall, *Parables*, 12–16. Marshall is more cautious than Frankfurter in characterizing the opponents John addresses; they are "a group of people who do not stand in opposition to Rome and the wider Greco-Roman culture in the way John does" (124–34; quotation, 133).

74. Frankfurter, "Jews or Not?" 418–20.

75. Frankfurter worries that this contentious question does not show up in John's criticism of his opponents ("Jews or Not?" 422n. 81).

76. Frankfurter, "Jews or Not?" 410–12. Frankfurter also treats the description of the 144,000 from the tribes of Israel as those who "have not defiled themselves with women, for they are virgins" (Rev 14:4) as an instance of commitment to purity in the service of holy war. See Adela Yarbro Collins, *Crisis and Catharsis: The Power of the Apocalypse* (Philadelphia: Westminster Press, 1984) 127–31, and Richard Bauckham, *The Climax of Prophecy: Studies on the Book of Revelation* (Edinburgh: T&T Clark, 1993) 230–31. The relationship of this passage to the elaboration of purity laws in the Second Temple period seems to me less clear-cut. The Qumran sectarians lived in an all-male community presumably because it is easier for a man to maintain the state required for holy war and fellowship with the angels if he avoids sexual relations and other physical contact with women. Still, *emolunthēsan*, the term that RSV translates "defiled themselves," does not appear to be part of the technical vocabulary of purity for the Greek Bible; it does not appear in the Septuagint's translation of the purity laws of Leviticus. It is used of nonritual defilement in 3 Isaiah (Isa 59:3, 65:4) and of rape in Zech 14:2. Thus I disageree with Bauckham, who claims that the term

refers to "ritual defilement" (*Climax of Prophecy*, 231). Further, there is no indication that members of the community at Qumran were expected to be virgins; it is worth noting that some of the Therapeutae according to Philo had left behind wives when they came to join the group (*On the Contemplative Life* 18). Here, then, John's picture goes significantly beyond what we know from elsewhere in Second Temple Judaism.

77. Marshall, *Parables*, 16–18, 141–48.

78. Ibid., 192.

79. The RSV translation, "saints," has a Christian ring that I prefer to avoid. John likes this term; he uses it fourteen times. See Marshall, *Parables*, 21n. 21, for a list of occurrences.

80. On the 144,000 as Jews rather than Christians, see Marshall, *Parables*, 18–21.

81. Marshall argues that all Israel remains in the default position in heaven (*Parables*, 185–89). In response to my argument here Marshall has pointed out (e-mail correspondence, March 21, 2003) that at the time John wrote, there were far fewer than 144,000 Jews who were followers of Jesus. Thus the number should not be taken to represent a minority of the Jews but rather the ideal Jewish people. I accept Marshall's point about the small size of the Jesus movement, but I remain convinced that John's sectarian logic means that for him, as for Ezekiel, the ideal Israel represented by the 144,000 is necessarily a minority.

82. See Frankfurter, "Jews or Not?" 413–15.

83. See Bauckham, *Climax of Prophecy*, 230–31, on somewhat different grounds.

84. Himmelfarb, *Ascent*, esp. 49–51, 66–69.

85. Some manuscripts read "Levitical priests," the translation of NJPS. This reading would not change my argument. Blenkinsopp, *Isaiah 1–39*, 190–91, sees the passage in Isaiah 2 not as the words of Isaiah of Jerusalem but as a post-exilic composition. Thus it is perhaps contemporary with the last chapter of the book, which belongs to 3 Isaiah (Isaiah 56–66), the portion of the book that is entirely post-exilic.

86. The visionary portion of Revelation begins with John's entrance into the heavenly throne room (Rev 4:1–2). The throne, surrounded by living creatures (Rev 4:6–7), develops the picture of Ezekiel's chariot throne (Ezekiel 1), which Ezekiel identifies as the heavenly counterpart to the cherubim throne of the holy of holies on earth (Ezek 10:15, 20). Before the throne is a sea of glass (Rev 4:6), presumably the heavenly version of the "molten sea," an enormous bronze basin in Solomon's temple (1 Kings 7:23). The four living creatures and the twenty-four elders who sit on thrones around the throne of God worship the Lamb with harps and golden bowls of incense (Rev 5:6), identified as the prayers of the saints. When the fifth seal is opened, John sees the souls of the martyrs under the heavenly altar (Rev 6:9). After the seventh seal is opened, an angel with a golden censer offers incense to mix with the prayers of the saints on the golden altar (Rev 8:3–5). At the sound of the seventh trumpet, the heavenly temple is opened and the ark of the covenant within is revealed (Rev 11:19). Angels emerge from the temple with their sickles to reap the earth (Rev 14:14–20). Seven angels take seven golden bowls of wrath and fill the heavenly "temple of the tent of witness" with smoke as they bring seven plagues on the earth (Rev 15:5–8). A voice from the temple marks the beginning and end of the pouring out of the plagues (Rev 16:1, 17).

87. Himmelfarb, *Ascent*, esp. 22–23.

Chapter 5

1. Josephus, *Jewish War* 5.205; idem, *Jewish Antiquities* 18.159-60, 19.276, 20.100.
2. Josephus, *Jewish Antiquities* 20.100. Josephus refers to Tiberius Julius Alexander's role as a Roman official at several points in the *Jewish War* (2.220, 309; 5.45; 6.237).
3. The Wisdom of ben Sira was translated into Greek by ben Sira's grandson in 132 B.C.E. in Egypt. It is also possible that the *Book of the Watchers* and *Jubilees* were available in Greek in Egypt in Philo's day. But Philo gives no sign of familiarity with any of these works, which is perhaps not surprising given his focus on the Torah and his very different view of the world.
4. Daniel R. Schwartz, "Philo's Priestly Descent," in *Nourished with Peace: Studies in Hellenistic Judaism in Memory of Samuel Sandmel*, ed. Frederick E. Greenspahn, Earle Hilgert, and Burton L. Mack, Homage Series 9 (Chico, Calif.: Scholars Press, 1984), argues that Jerome's report of Philo's priestly lineage in *De illustribus viris* 11 is correct. Schwartz also argues that priests played an important role in the Alexandrian Jewish community ("The Priests in *Ep. Arist.* 310," *Journal of Biblical Literature* 97 [1978]: 567-71).
5. For examples, see Hengel, *Judaism and Hellenism* 1.255-67.
6. Strabo, *Geographica* 16.2.35-40; Stern, *Greek and Latin Authors* 1.294-311.
7. All translations of Philo are taken from the Loeb Classical Library edition, *Philo*, vols. 1–5, trans. F. H. Colson and G. H. Whitaker; vols. 6–10, trans. Colson; supplement vols. 1 and 2, trans. Ralph Marcus (Cambridge, Mass.: Harvard University Press; London: William Heinemann, 1966–71).
8. D. Schwartz, "Jewish Background," 16–18, comments that Philo's defense of observance of the law in this passage is "hardly cogent" (quotation, 17).
9. Other Alexandrians resented the Jews for their support of the Romans and the privileges the Romans granted them. Further, the Roman policy of exempting citizens of Greek cities from the poll tax encouraged residents of Alexandria who were not citizens, including many Jews, to attempt to be declared citizens. The Jews based their claim on the special privileges they enjoyed. The claim was vehemently rejected by many of the Greco-Egyptian citizens (John M. G. Barclay, *The Jews in the Mediterranean Diaspora from Alexander to Trajan [323 B.C.E.-117 C.E.]* [Edinburgh: T&T Clark, 1996] 48–51).
10. Barclay, *Jews in the Mediterranean Diaspora*, 51–71.
11. Isaak Heinemann, *Philons griechische und jüdische Bildung: Kulturvergleichende Untersuchungen zu Philons Darstellung der jüdischen Gesetze* (Breslau: M&H Marcus, 1932) 52–57, 78–81; Valentin Nikiprowetzky, "La spiritualisation des sacrifices et le culte sacrificiel au temple de Jérusalem chez Philon d'Alexandrie," *Études philoniennes* (Paris: Éditions du Cerf, 1996) 79–84 (article first published in *Semitica* 17 [1967]: 97–116). It is remarkable that Nikiprowetzky never cites Heinemann.
12. Philo notes the difference between priests and Levites at some points in his work (e.g., *Spec. Laws* 1.156).
13. Nadab and Abihu, two of the very few priests known by name from the Torah's narrative, play a role in Philo's allegorical treatises, interpretations of Genesis, as does Phinehas, who is a priest at the time of his zealous act but stands in line to be high priest. See J. W. Earp, "Index of Names," in *Philo*, vol. 10, for references.
14. For discussion of Philo's allegorization of the cult, see Heinemann, *Philons Bildung*, 46–51, 57–62; Nikiprowetzky, "Spiritualisation," 84–90.

15. For a full development of this theme, see *On Dreams* 1.206-18; *On the Migration of Abraham* 102–3. For Aaron as logos in a noncultic context, see *On Dreams* 2.185-90. On Philo's allegory of the high priest, see Jean Laporte, "The High Priest in Philo of Alexandria," in *The Studia Philonica Annual: Studies in Hellenistic Judaism* 3; *Heirs of the Septuagint: Philo, Hellenistic Judaism and Early Christianity: Festschrift for Earle Hilgert*, ed. David T. Runia, David M. Hay, and David Winston (Atlanta: Scholars Press, 1991) 71–82.

16. *On Dreams* 1.215 (the portion of the passage omitted above); *On the Migration of Abraham* 102–3.

17. *On Dreams* 1.207.

18. The logos of the soul is identified with the Levites in another passage (*On the Sacrifices of Abel and Cain* 119). See also discussion in Laporte, "High Priest," 74–79.

19. Nikiprowetzky, "Spiritualisation," 87, quotes this passage, but the paragraph number in his note is mistaken.

20. For discussion, see Nikiprowetzky, "Spiritualisation," 86–88. He includes the following passages on the offering of virtues or aspects of the soul: *On the Sacrifices of Abel and Cain* 84, *On the Preliminary Studies* 106, *On Flight and Finding* 18–19, and *On Dreams* 2.232; and on the offering of the soul itself: *On Drunkenness* 152, *On the Migration of Abraham* 67, and *On Dreams* 2.67 (not 217), 183.

21. See Nikiprowetzky, "Spiritualisation," 90–96.

22. Ibid., 92–93.

23. Ibid., 94.

24. See, e.g., *Spec. Laws* 1.80, 85, 86, 97; there are many more examples in *On the Special Laws* and the rest of Philos's work. For a complete listing, see Peder Borgen, Kåre Fuglseth, and Roald Skarsten, *The Philo Index: A Complete Greek Word Index to the Writings of Philo of Alexandria* (Grand Rapids, Mich.: Eerdmans; Leiden: Brill, 2000). Philo uses the terms "allegory" or "to allegorize" only rarely in his writings, and at least in *On the Special Laws*, they mean allegory in general or in the abstract (*Spec. Laws* 1.269, 287, 327; 2.29, 147; I believe this is a complete list).

25. For the difficulties in offering a more precise date, see Emil Schürer, *The History of the Jewish People in the Age of Jesus Christ (175 B.C.–A.D. 135)* vol. 3, p. 1, rev. and ed. Geza Vermes, Fergus Millar, and Martin Goodman, organizing ed. Matthew Black, lit. ed. Pamela Vermes (Edinburgh: T&T Clark, 1986) 679–84.

26. All translations of the *Letter of Aristeas* are taken from Moses Hadas, *Aristeas to Philocrates (Letter of Aristeas)* (New York: Harper and Brothers, 1951). I also make use of its Greek text.

27. Aristeas's elaborate description of the virtues of these elders is perhaps intended to recall the more austere qualifications of the elders Moses chose to help him with his administrative responsibilities: "capable men who fear God, trustworthy men who spurn ill-gotten gain" (Exod 18:21), "men who are wise, discerning, and experienced" (Deut 1:13). Note that LXX of Deut 1:15, reporting Moses' implementation of the plan, preserves all three adjectives, while MT is down to two.

28. For the testimonia and fragments of Chaeremon's work, see Pieter Willem van der Horst, *Chaeremon: Egyptian Priest and Stoic Philosopher* (Leiden: Brill, 1984).

29. Van der Horst, *Chaeremon*, frag. 10.

30. Although he explicitly acknowledges the difference between priests and Levites at some points in his work (e.g., *Spec. Laws* 1.156), often Philo ignores

the subordination of Levites to priests demanded by the priestly source of the Torah, treating the Levites as full priests. *On Flight and Finding* 93 shows awareness of the distinction: Levites, priests, and those who commit homicide unintentionally are all ministers of God.

31. On the differences between the processes for priests and Levites, see B. Levine, *Numbers 1–20*, 273–74.

32. Similar allegories about Phinehas appear also in *On the Confusion of Tongues* (57) and *On the Change of Names* (108), but without emphasis on the reward of the covenant of priesthood.

33. David Frankfurter, "The Consequences of Hellenism in Late Antique Egypt: Religious Worlds and Actors," *Archiv für Religionsgeschichte* 2 (2000): 172–73.

34. Van der Horst, *Chaeremon*, frag. 10.6-7 (pp. 18–21).

35. Despite the differences, scholars have long pointed to similarities of vocabulary and other details in Chaeremon's description of the Egyptian priests and Philo's description of the Therapeutae. But the similarities, are more likely to reflect a common milieu than than Philo's dependence on Chaeremon. See van der Horst, *Chaeremon*, 56n. 1 to frag. 10, and references there.

36. See the comments of Valentin Nikiprowetzky, "Le *De Vita Contemplativa* revisité," *Études philoniennes*, 204 (first published in *Sagesse et religion: Colloque de Strasbourg, 20–22 Octobre 1976* [Paris: Presses Universitaires de France, 1979] 105–25).

37. See discussion at the beginning of this chapter and n. 6 for reference.

38. According to Lev 24:7 in the LXX; the MT does not mention salt.

39. See also Valentin Nikiprowetzky, "Les suppliants chez Philon d'Alexandrie," *Études philoniennes*, 41–43 (first published in *Revue des études juives* 122 [1963]: 241–78).

40. D. Schwartz, "'Kingdom,'" 65–66, emphasizes this point. I shall try to show below that he is wrong to claim that Philo understands the priesthood of all Israel in internal terms only in relation to the paschal sacrifice.

41. Thus also Colson in his note there (240–41).

42. Elsewhere Philo writes of the Passover sacrifice, "As commanded by law, the whole nation acts as priest" (*On the Life of Moses* 2.224).

Chapter 6

1. Though there are certainly grounds for suspicion, Tessa Rajak, *Josephus: The Historian and His Society* (Philadelphia: Fortress, 1984) 206–11, and Martin Goodman, "Trajan and the Origins of the Bar Kokhba War," in *The Bar Kokhba War Reconsidered*, ed. Peter Schäfer, Texte und Studien zum antiken Judentum 100 (Tübingen: Mohr Siebeck, 2003) 24, are inclined to accept Josephus's claim.

2. These are *2 (Syriac) Baruch* and *3 (Greek) Baruch*. Two other apocalypses were written in response to the destruction, *4 Ezra* and *the Apocalypse of Abraham*. On the responses of *2 Baruch* and *4 Ezra*, see Michael E. Stone, "Reactions to Destructions of the Second Temple: Theology, Perception and Conversion," *Journal for the Study of Judaism in the Persian, Hellenistic, and Roman Period* 12 (1981): 195–204.

3. It is *3 Baruch* that considers the earthly temple unnecessary. The visionary's ascent through the heavens to the heavenly temple is described there, and the heavenly temple alone is required to keep the cosmos functioning properly.

4. For a similar view, see Shaye J. D. Cohen, "The Temple and the Synagogue," in *Cambridge History of Judaism*, ed. Horbury, Davies, and Sturdy, 307–9.

5. Nickelsburg (*Commentary*, 360–61) now suggests that the allusion to Judah and the events of the Maccabean Revolt in the work are not original and prefers an earlier date, at the end of the third century B.C.E.

6. The Essenes, however, did not break off contact with the temple altogether (Josephus, *Jewish Antiquities* 18.19). See Albert I. Baumgarten, "Josephus on Essene Sacrifice," *Journal of Jewish Studies* 45 (1994): 169–83.

7. R. H. Charles, trans., L. H. Brockington, rev., "The Syriac Apocalypse of Baruch," in *The Apocryphal Old Testament*, ed. H. F. D. Sparks (Oxford: Clarendon Press, 1984).

8. Martin Goodman, *The Ruling Class of Judaea: The Origins of the Jewish Revolt against Rome A.D. 66–70* (Cambridge: Cambridge University Press, 1987) 40–45; for discussion of the implications of a weakened priestly aristocracy for the fate of Judea under Roman rule, see pp. 29–50.

9. For a recent argument in favor of this view that places the establishment of Aelia Capitolina in the larger context of Roman imperial policy toward the Jews, see Goodman, "Trajan," 23–29. For a recent defense of the view that the establishment of Aelia Capitolina was a response to the revolt rather than a cause, see Yoram Tsafrir, "Numismatics and the Foundation of Aelia Capitolina—A Critical Review," in *Bar Kokhba War*, ed. Schäfer, 31–36.

10. For discussion of the images, see Leo Mildenberg, *The Coinage of the Bar Kokhba War*, trans. and ed. Patricia Erhart Mottahedeh (Aarau, Frankfurt-am-Main, Salzburg: Sauerländer, 1984) 33–45.

11. For a table of the occurrences of the legends, see Mildenberg, *Coinage*, 365–68. For understanding "For the freedom of Jerusalem" as a slogan rather than a method of dating, see pp. 30–31.

12. For the significance of the title, see Peter Schäfer, "Bar Kokhba and the Rabbis," in *Bar Kokhba War*, 15–20.

13. For the attestations, see Peter Schäfer, *Der Bar Kokhba-Aufstand: Studien zum zweiten jüdischen Krieg gegen Rom* (Tübingen: Mohr [Siebeck], 1981) 67.

14. For references and discussion, see J. Collins, *Scepter*, 58–64, 74–77.

15. For the dates and types of coins, see Mildenberg, *Coinage*, 29.

16. Schäfer, "Bar Kokhba," and David Goodblatt, "The Title *Nāśî'* and the Ideological Background of the Second Revolt," in *The Bar-Kokhva Revolt: A New Approach*, ed. Aharon Oppenheimer and Uriel Rapppaport (Jerusalem: Yad Izhak Ben Zvi, 1984) 113–32 (Hebrew); both argue that the ideology of the Bar Kokhba revolt owes more to such traditions than to the rabbis.

17. Goodblatt, "Title *Nāśî'*"; Dalia Ben-Haim Trifon, "Some Aspects of Internal Politics Connected with the Bar-Kokhva Revolt" (Hebrew), in *Bar-Kokhva Revolt*, ed. Oppenheimer and Rappaport, 13–26.

18. For a convenient account of Julian's dealings with the Jews and references to the literature, see Günter Stemberger, *Jews and Christians in the Holy Land: Palestine in the Fourth Century*, trans. Ruth Tuschling (Edinburgh: T&T Clark, 2000) 198–216. For an examination of the sources and the development of the story of the abortive attempt at rebuilding, see David B. Levenson, "A Source and Tradition Critical Study of the Stories of Julian's Attempt to Rebuild the Jerusalem Temple" (Ph.D. diss., Harvard University, 1979).

19. Fire caused by earthquake is the view of Michael Avi-Yonah, *The Jews of Palestine: A Political History from the Bar Kokhba War to the Arab Conquest* (New York: Schocken, 1976) 201–3, following Rufinus's account.

20. This has not prevented scholars from detecting a reaction. See, e.g., Avi-Yonah, *Jews of Palestine*, 197–98.

21. For the association, see Benjamin Mazar assisted by Gaalyah Cornfeld, *The Mountain of the Lord* (Garden City, N.Y.: Doubleday, 1975) 94. Stemberger, *Jews and Christians*, 209–10, embraces it, though cautiously.

22. Shaye J. D. Cohen, "The Rabbi in Second-Century C.E. Society," in *Cambridge History of Judaism*, ed. Horbury, Davies, and Sturdy, 3.961-77; Catherine Hezser, *The Social Structure of the Rabbinic Movement in Roman Palestine* (Tübingen: Mohr Siebeck, 1997) esp. 353–86; Seth Schwartz, *Imperialism and Jewish Society, 200 B.C.E. to 640 C.E.*, Jews, Christians, and Muslims from the Ancient to the Modern World (Princeton, N.J.: Princeton University Press, 2001) 103–28.

23. Shaye J. D. Cohen, "The Significance of Yavneh: Pharisees, Rabbis, and the End of Jewish Sectarianism," *Hebrew Union College Annual* 55 (1984) 36–42; Peter Schäfer, "Der vorrabbinische Pharisäismus," in *Paulus und das antike Judentum: Tübingen-Durham-Symposium in Gedenken an den 50. Todestag Adolf Schlatters (19. Mai 1938)*, ed. Martin Hengel and Ulrich Heckel, Wissenschaftliche Untersuchungen zum Neuen Testament 58 (Tübingen: Mohr, 1991).

24. For the sources and different views of their development, see Jacob Neusner, *Development of a Legend: Studies on the Traditions Concerning Yohanan ben Zakkai* (Leiden: Brill, 1970), and Peter Schäfer, "Die Flucht Johanan b. Zakkais aus Jerusalem und die Gründung des 'Lehrhauses' in Jabne," *Aufstieg und Niedergang der römischen Welt* II.19.2 (1979): 43–102.

25. For a useful history of the discussion, see Lawrence H. Schiffman, "Halakhah and Sectarianism in the Dead Sea Scrolls," in *The Dead Sea Scrolls in Their Historical Context*, ed. Timothy H. Lim (Edinburgh: T&T Clark, 2000).

26. See Stuart A. Cohen, *The Three Crowns: Structures of Communal Politics in Early Rabbinic Jewry* (Cambridge: Cambridge University Press, 1990) 158–63.

27. See, for example, the blessing in the *'Amidah* beginning, "Lord our God, accept your people Israel and their prayer." Other blessings in the daily *'Amidah* allude to the restoration of the temple service, while the restoration of sacrifice and the temple is a central subject of both the *'Amidah* for the additional service of the Sabbath and the *'Amidah* for the additional service for festivals.

28. Gedalyahu Alon, "The Lithuanian Yeshivas," in *The Jewish Expression*, ed. Judah Goldin (New York: Bantam Books, 1970) 452.

29. I follow the numeration of Hanokh Albeck, *The Six Orders of the Mishnah: Tractate Neziqin* (Jerusalem: Bialik Institute; Tel Aviv: Dvir, 1953) (Hebrew). In some other editions this passage is 4:17. Simeon is Simeon ben Yohai, who was active in the mid-second century.

30. The chapter is devoted to the praise of Torah study. It appears in slightly different form in *Kalla Rabbati*, chap. 8, and *Tanna' dēbê 'Eliyyāhû Zuta'*, chap. 17. It appears that the sixth chapter was added to *m. 'Abot* when it came to be recited in synagogue on Sabbath afternoons between Passover and Shavu'ot in order to provide a chapter for each of the six Sabbaths. Liturgical use of *m. 'Abot* is first attested in the academy of Sura; the practice spread to synagogues by the eleventh century. For references to the sources, see Leopold Zunz, *Jewish Sermons: Their Historical Development*, ed. Hanokh Albeck (trans. from the 2nd ed. of the German original, 1892; Jerusalem: Mosad Bialik, 1974) 197, 520n. 68 (Hebrew); idem, *Die Ritus des synagogalen Gottesdienstes, geschichtlich entwickelt* (Berlin: J. Springer, 1859) 85–86.

31. I follow the numeration of Albeck, *Mishnah*; in other editions, this mishnah is 6:6.

32. Thus Reuven Kimelman, "The Conflict between the Priestly Oligarchy and the Sages in the Talmudic Period (An Explication of PT *Shabbat* 12:3, 13c = *Horayot* 3:5, 48c)," *Zion* 48 (1983): 135–48 (Hebrew); see also Lee I. Levine, *The Rabbinic Class of Roman Palestine in Late Antiquity* (Jerusalem: Yad Izhak Ben-Zvi; New York: Jewish Theological Seminary, 1989; Hebrew original, 1985) 171–73; and idem, *The Ancient Synagogue: The First Thousand Years* (New Haven, Conn.: Yale University Press, 2000) 492–93. I have not been able to see Dalia Ben-Haim Trifon, "The Jewish Priests from the Destruction of the Temple to the Rise of Christianity" (Ph.D. diss., Tel Aviv, 1985) (Hebrew) 219–22, for reservations about this view (see S. A. Cohen, *Three Crowns*, 175n. 37 for the reference).

33. Margaret Williams, "The Contribution of Jewish Inscriptions to the Study of Judaism," in *Cambridge History of Judaism*, ed. Horbury, Davies, and Sturdy, 3.89.

34. Thus S. J. D. Cohen, "Rabbi," 941–42, 950; see also 978–79 for a list of other, similar rankings in tannaitic literature. In her consideration of this passage and passages from the two talmudim favoring sages over priests, Hayes, *Gentile Impurities*, 188–89, correctly insists that for the rabbis "Torah learning is supreme" (189), but overlooks the continued relevance of birth as long as it is subordinated to Torah learning.

35. S. J. D. Cohen, "Rabbi," 948–50, 975: "[The second-century rabbis'] status as elites depended as much, if not more, upon their wealth and birth as upon their intellectual and pietistic attainments."

36. S. J. D. Cohen, "Rabbi," 943n. 88; Hezser, *Social Structure*, 267–69.

37. On the picture of priests as wealthy in rabbinic texts, S. J. D. Cohen, "Rabbi," 943; L. Levine, *Rabbinic Class*, 171.

38. For the rabbis as "socially diverse," see Hezser, *Social Structure*, 257–66.

39. I would like to thank Peter Schäfer for his helpful comments on this passage.

40. Jacob Z. Lauterbach, trans., *Mekilta De-Rabbi Ishmael* (Philadelphia: Jewish Publication Society, 1933) 1.1.

41. Ibid., 1.2.

42. See L. Levine, *Ancient Synagogue*, 497–99, and references there. Some have read *m. Meg.* 4:5 as implying that priests played a dominant role in the synagogue liturgy; if so, as Levine notes, it stands alone.

43. For marriage laws, see Louis M. Epstein, *Marriage Laws in the Bible and the Talmud* (Cambridge, Mass.: Harvard University Press, 1942) 308–32.

44. Kimelman, "Conflict"; L. Levine, *Rabbinic Class*, 172.

45. Hanswulf Bloedhorn and Gil Hüttenmeister, "The Synagogue," in *Cambridge History of Judaism*, ed. Horbury, Davies, and Sturdy, 3.285, claim "solid archaeological evidence" for approximately seventy synagogues in the land of Israel; they also note literary evidence for approximately fifteen others whose location can be identified and approximately thirty-five places where the archaeological finds may include material from a synagogue. A note says that the article was updated for publication, which took place in 1999 (267n. 1).

46. L. Levine, *Ancient Synagogue* (esp. 440–70), and S. Schwartz, *Imperialism* (esp. 247–48), agree on this point despite their very different approaches to the material. See also Steven Fine, *This Holy Place: On the Sanctity of the Synagogue during the Greco-Roman Period*, Christianity and Judaism in Antiquity Series 11 (Notre Dame, Ind.: University of Notre Dame Press, 1997), and idem, "Between Liturgy and Social History: Priestly Power in Late Antique Palestinian Synagogues?" *Journal of Jewish Studies* 56 (2005): 1–9.

47. For a mid-third century date and a discussion of why the third century,

usually viewed as a time of economic decline and political crisis, should have been a time of synagogue building, L. Levine, *Ancient Synagogue*, 172–77. The explanation Levine favors is that building is "an act of reaffirmation in the face of economic and social stress" (177). S. Schwartz, *Imperialism*, 226–39, argues that synagogues did not become widespread until the fourth century.

48. S. J. D. Cohen "Temple," 320.

49. Ibid.

50. S. Schwartz, *Imperialism*, 246–47, emphasizes the difficulties for interpretation posed by the absence of texts that can be safely connected with the decoration of the synagogues. If the synagogues are not rabbinic institutions, rabbinic texts cannot automatically be presumed to illumine their decoration. Even the liturgy is problematic since the set liturgy of a later period had not yet emerged (250). Indeed the only text that can be used with any certainty to explain the decorative schema of the synagogues is the Bible.

51. The walls of some synagogues were covered with frescoes (Rachel Hachlili, *Ancient Jewish Art and Archaeology in the Land of Israel* [Leiden: Brill, 1988] 224), but very little of such walls survives.

52. L. Levine, *Ancient Synagogue*, 215.

53. Ibid., 215–19, discusses several theories about the significance of the depictions of torah shrines flanked by the symbols mentioned above. While the question of their meaning is certainly complicated, any interpretation that excludes allusion to the temple (216) seems to me highly implausible.

54. This is the characterization of S. Schwartz, *Imperialism*, 254–55.

55. S. Schwartz, *Imperialism*, 257.

56. Joseph Yahalom, *Poetry and Society in Jewish Galilee of Late Antiquity* (Tel Aviv: Hakibbutz Hameuchad, 1999) (Hebrew), 107.

57. Joseph Yahalom, *Priestly Palestinian Poetry: A Narrative Liturgy for the Day of Atonement* (Jerusalem: Magnes, 1996), esp. 56–58 (Hebrew), and idem, *Poetry and Society*, 111–16. See also L. Levine, *Ancient Synagogue*, 499–500, and references there. Rabbinic influence on the *piyyutim* is undeniable; see Michael D. Swartz, "Sage, Priest, and Poet: Typologies of Religious Leadership in the Ancient Synagogue," in *Jews, Christians, and Polytheists in the Ancient Synagogue: Cultural Interaction in the Greco-Roman Period*, ed. Steven Fine (New York: Routledge, 1999) 103, 114n. 20 and references there. So too, S. Schwartz, *Imperialism*, writes, "The *piyyut* offers unambiguous evidence for the rabbinization of liturgical practice in sixth century Palestine" (263).

58. A great deal has been written about *piyyutim* for the Day of Atonement and the Avodah service in particular. I have not seen the new collection of texts and translations by Michael D. Swartz and Joseph Yahalom, *Avodah: Ancient Poems for Yom Kippur* (University Park: Penn State University Press, 2005). Other recent contributions include Yahalom, *Priestly Palestinian Poetry*, and idem, *Poetry and Society*, 16–35; Michael D. Swartz, "Ritual about Myth about Ritual: Towards an Understanding of the *Avodah* in the Rabbinic Period," *Journal of Jewish Thought and Philosophy* 6 (1997): 135–55. For *piyyutim* on the Ninth of Av, see below.

59. Ezra Fleischer, "A *Piyyut* of Yannai the Cantor on the Priestly Courses," *Sinai* 64 (1969): 176–84 (Hebrew), writes, "It is clear beyond the shadow of a doubt that . . . almost all of the early *payyetanim* of the land of Israel composed *piyyutim* in their memory" (176).

60. See Fleischer, "A *Piyyut* of Yannai," 176n. 1, for a list of such *piyyutim*.

61. Ezra Fleischer, "New *Shiv'atot* on the Priestly Courses of the *Payyetan* Rabbi Pinḥas," *Sinai* 61 (1967): 30–36 (Hebrew); for a different type of evidence, see

Ephraim E. Urbach, "*Mishmarot* and *Ma'amadot*," *Tarbiz* 42 (1972–73): 309–13 (Hebrew).

62. For the texts of four of these inscriptions with notes, see Joseph Naveh, *On Stone and Mosaic: The Aramaic and Hebrew Inscriptions from Ancient Synagogues* (Jerusalem: Ha-Ḥevrah le-Ḥakirat Erets Yiśrael ve-Atikoteha, 1978) 87–89 (Hebrew) (inscriptions 51–52, Caesarea and Ashkelon), 91–92 (inscription 56, Kissufim), 142–43 (inscription 106, Bayt al-ḥādir); all but the last are very fragmentary. For an inscription housed in Nazareth, Hanan Eshel, "A Fragmentary Hebrew Inscription of the Priestly Courses?" *Tarbiz* 61 (1991–92): 159–61 (Hebrew). The most complete inscription, the one from Bayt al-hādir, was found on a column in a mosque.

63. For the influential claim that these traditions derive from a *baraita*, a tannaitic saying, of the twenty-four courses and their Galilean locations, see Samuel Klein, *Beiträge zur Geographie und Geschichte Galiläas* (Leipzig: Rudolf Haupt, 1909) esp. 94–95. This claim is rendered problematic by the discussion of Dalia [Ben-Haim] Trifon, "Did the Priestly Courses (*Mishmarot*) Transfer from Judaea to Galilee after the Bar Kokhba Revolt?" *Tarbiz* 59 (1989–90): 77–93 (Hebrew).

64. For a largely persuasive treatment of the problems, see Trifon, "Did the Priestly Courses Transfer?" Ze'ev Safrai, "Did the Priestly Courses (*Mishmarot*) Transfer from Judea to Galilee after the Bar Kokhba Revolt?: On D. Trifon's Article in *Tarbiz*, LIX [1989–90], pp. 77–93," *Tarbiz* 62 (1993): 287–92 (Hebrew), takes the sources as a more direct reflection of historical reality. It seems to me that Trifon has the better of the argument.

65. Trifon, "Did the Priestly Courses Transfer?" offers the promising suggestion that the lists reflect regional patriotism (84), but she does not develop the idea.

66. For the theory of resurgence that touches on the *piyyutim* and hekhalot texts but emphasizes Christian sources, see a series of articles by Oded Irshai: "Confronting a Christian Empire: Jewish Culture in the World of Byzantium," in *Cultures of the Jews: A New History*, ed. David Biale (New York: Schocken, 2002) 189–204; "The Role of the Priesthood in the Jewish Community in Late Antiquity: A Christian Model?" in *Jüdische Gemeinden und ihr christlicher Kontext in kulturräumlich vergleichender Betrachtung von der Spätantike bis zum 18. Jahrhundert*, ed. Christoph Cluse, Alfred Haverkamp, and Israel J. Yuval (Hannover: Hahnsche, 2003) 75–85; and "The Priesthood in Jewish Society of Late Antiquity," in *Continuity and Renewal: Jews and Judaism in Byzantine-Christian Palestine*, ed. Lee I. Levine (Jerusalem: Dinur Center, Yad Ben-Zvi, and Jewish Theological Seminary of America, 2004) 67–106 (an expanded Hebrew version of the previous article). For resurgence with particular attention to the *piyyutim*, Yahalom, *Poetry and Society*, 111–16. On the hekhalot texts as repositories of priestly traditions Rachel Elior, *Three Temples: On the Emergence of Jewish Mysticism*, trans. David Louvish (Oxford; Portland, Ore.: Littman Library of Jewish Civilization, 2004). As noted above, L. Levine, *Ancient Synagogue*, 492–93, suggests ongoing priestly power after the destruction; in an earlier publication, "Caeserea's Synagogues and Some Historical Implications," in *Biblical Archaeology Today, 1990: Proceedings of the Second International Congress on Biblical Archaeology, Jerusalem, June–July 1990* (Jerusalem: Israel Exploration Society, 1993) 670–74, he suggests two possibilities, ongoing priestly power or a resurgence of power in the fourth and fifth centuries, without a clear theory about the cause.

67. Fine, "Between Liturgy and Social History," arrives at a similar conclusion from a different angle of approach.

68. Here I differ with Kimelman, "Conflict," and L. Levine, *Rabbinic Class*, 171–73. See the comments of Trifon, "Some Aspects," 14–16.

69. Hayim Lapin, "Palestinian Inscriptions and Jewish Ethnicity in Late Antiquity," in *Galilee through the Centuries: Confluence of Cultures*, ed. Eric M. Meyers (Winona Lake, Ind.: Eisenbrauns, 1999) 265.

70. For Lamentation Rabbati, the midrash on the Book of Lamentations, which offers both types of response, see Shaye J. D. Cohen, "The Destruction: From Scripture to Midrash," *Prooftexts* 2 (1982): 18–39 (the sins of the nations: 30-33; God's grief: 33-35). For the theme of God's sadness at disasters that befall his people, including the destruction of the Second Temple, see Peter Kuhn, *Gottes Trauer und Klage in der rabbinischen Überlieferung (Talmud und Midrasch)* (Leiden: Brill, 1978).

71. This passage appears in the *'Amidah* for the additional service. Of course, the Jews of Palestine had not been exiled from their land; see Israel Jacob Yuval, "The Myth of the Jewish Exile from the Land of Israel: A Demonstration of Irenic Scholarship," *Common Knowledge* 12 (2006): 16–33. Yuval argues that the Jewish understanding of the destruction of the Second Temple as involving exile is determined in considerable part by Christian claims.

72. S. J. D. Cohen, "Rabbi," 959–61, characterizes the rabbis' attitude toward the *'ammê hā'āreṣ* as disdain rather than hatred.

73. S. J. D. Cohen, "Significance of Yavneh."

74. Ibid., 28–29; quotation, 29. The characterization of earlier scholarship and comparison to the Council of Nicea are Cohen's.

75. S. J. D. Cohen, "Significance of Yavneh," 36–42.

76. Ibid., 43–46.

77. Martin Goodman makes this important point in "Sadducees and Essenes after 70 C.E.," in *Crossing the Boundaries: Essays in Biblical Interpretation in Honour of Michael D. Goulder*, ed. Stanley E. Porter, Paul Joyce, and David E. Orton (Leiden and New York: Brill, 1994) 347–56. For S. J. D. Cohen's careful discussion of the evidence, see "Significance of Yavneh," 31–36.

78. Daniel Boyarin, *Border Lines: The Partition of Judaeo-Christianity* (Philadelphia: University of Pennsylvania Press, 2004), has recently offered an account of the emergence of rabbinic Judaism as a process parallel to the emergence of Christian orthodoxy. Just as the Christian process required a rejected other, the heretic, so did the Jewish process. This account calls into question Cohen's picture of the emergence of rabbinic Judaism, and Boyarin argues that the developments Cohen ascribes to Yavneh are late and Babylonian (151–201).

79. Although Boyarin touches only lightly on the role of ancestry in the rabbinic construction of Israel, he ends his book by noting the importance of the late rabbinic formulation "an Israelite, even if he sins, remains an Israelite" (*b. San.* 44a) (*Border Lines*, 224), a passage to which he also refers in the introduction (10).

80. Several recent studies have argued for the importance of Christianity in shaping Judaism in the centuries after the destruction. In addition to Boyarin, *Border Lines*, and S. Schwartz, *Imperialism*, I have been particularly influenced by Israel Jacob Yuval, *Two Nations in Your Womb: Mutual Perceptions of Jews and Christians* (Tel-Aviv: 'Alma / 'Am 'oved, 2000) (Hebrew).

81. All NT translations are taken from RSV.

82. Denise Kimber Buell, "Rethinking the Relevance of Race for Early Christian Self-Definition," *Harvard Theological Review* 94 (2001): 449–76; and idem, "Race and Universalism in Early Christianity," *Journal of Early Christian Studies* 10

(2002): 429–68. Buell criticizes as ideologically motivated the view that early Christians had transcended Jewish particularism in favor of a more universalistic view of humanity, noting that in antiquity ethnicity was not seen as immutable and that Christians continued to use ethnic categories in their polemics and self-presentation ("Rethinking," esp. 466–76). Buell's book, *Why This New Race?: Ethnic Reasoning in Early Christianity* (New York: Columbia University Press, 2005), appeared too late for me to take account of it here.

83. Marcel Simon, *Verus Israel: A Study of the Relation between Christians and Jews in the Roman Empire (135–425)*, trans. H. McKeating (New York: Oxford University Press for the Littman Library of Jewish Civilization, 1986; first French edition, 1948) 108–9; Buell, "Rethinking," 466–72.

84. Buell, "Race," 453–62. There are further complexities in the picture, for some stones are defective (*Sim.* 9.4.4-8, 9.6.3-7), but they are not relevant for us (see Buell, "Race," 455–58, for discussion). A convenient edition of the *Shepherd of Hermas* with both Greek and English is found in *Apostolic Fathers*, vol. 2, ed. and trans. Bart D. Ehrman, Loeb Classical Library (Cambridge, Mass.: Harvard University Press, 2003).

85. Buell, "Race," 454–55. Ehrman, *Apostolic Fathers*, translates, "race of the upright."

86. On the emergence of a religious hierarchy during the early centuries, see the classic work of Hans von Campenhausen, *Ecclesiastical Authority and Spiritual Power in the Church of the First Three Centuries*, trans. J. A. Baker (Stanford, Calif.: Stanford University Press, 1969).

87. For a discussion of the importance of social networks among the Christian elite after Constantine, see Elizabeth A. Clark, *The Origenist Controversy: The Cultural Construction of an Early Christian Debate* (Princeton, N.J.: Princeton University Press, 1992) esp. 11–42.

88. On the rabbinic idea of "merit of the fathers," see Arthur Marmorstein, *The Doctrine of Merits in Old Rabbinic Literature*, prolegomenon by R. J. Zwi Werblowsky (1920; New York: Ktav, 1968) 147–71; Ephraim E. Urbach, *The Sages: Their Concepts and Beliefs*, trans. Israel Abrahams (Jerusalem: Magnes Press, 1975) 496–511.

89. The relationship between Jewish and Christian treatments of the binding of Isaac has been the subject of considerable discussion. The pioneering study of Shalom Spiegel, *The Last Trial: On the Legends and Lore of the Command to Abraham to Offer Isaac as a Sacrifice: The Akedah*, trans. from the Hebrew, with an introduction, by Judah Goldin (Philadelphia: Jewish Publication Society, 1967), is cautious about the question of influence and its direction. Some scholars contend that early Christians drew on pre-Christian Jewish developments of the story; see, e.g., Geza Vermes, "Redemption and Genesis xxii—The Binding of Isaac and the Sacrifice of Jesus," in *Scripture and Tradition in Judaism: Haggadic Studies*, 2nd ed. (Leiden: Brill, 1973), and Alan F. Segal, "The Sacrifice of Isaac in Early Judaism and Christianity," in *The Other Judaisms of Late Antiquity* (Atlanta: Scholars Press, 1987). Others are skeptical; see, e.g., Philip R. Davies and Bruce D. Chilton, "The Aqedah: A Revised Tradition History," *Catholic Biblical Quarterly* 40 (1978): 514–46.

90. Spiegel, *Last Trial*, 26–37.

91. For an argument that the mosaic of the binding of Isaac in the Bet Alpha synagogue draws on elements of Christian depictions, see Marc Bregman, "The Riddle of the Ram in Genesis Chapter 22: Jewish-Christian Contacts in Late Antiquity," in *The Sacrifice of Isaac in the Three Monotheistic Religions: Proceedings of a*

Symposium on the Interpretation of the Scriptures Held in Jerusalem, March 16–17, 1995, ed. Frédéric Manns (Jerusalem: Franciscan Printing, 1995). See also Bianca Kühnel, "Jewish and Christian Art in the Middle Ages: The Dynamics of a Relationship," in *Juden und Christen zur Zeit der Kreuzzüge*, ed. Alfred Haverkamp, Vorträge und Forschungen 47 (Sigmaringen: Jan Thorbecke, 1999) 8–9. I would like to thank John Gager for this reference.

92. I have modified the translation of the RSV by substituting "ancestors" for "fathers" and "awesome" for "terrible." Both changes are intended to bring the translation of this passage in line with my translation of the first blessing of the '*Amidah* and thus to highlight the connections between them.

93. I am indebted to Israel Yuval and Peter Schäfer for discussion of this passage in their seminar, Christianity and the Rabbis in Late Antiquity, at Princeton University in Spring 2004. The manuscripts are the Cambridge (William Henry Lowe, ed., *The Mishnah on Which the Palestinian Talmud Rests from the Unique Manuscript Preserved in the University Library of Cambridge, Add. 470.1* [Cambridge: Cambridge University Press, 1883]) and the Kaufmann (Georg Beer, ed., *Faksimile-Ausgabe des Mischnacodex Kaufmann A 50* [Jerusalem: N.p., 1967–68]). The readings of these two manuscripts are not identical, however. The Cambridge manuscript begins, "Those who have no share," while the Kaufmann manuscript reads, "And those who have no share," which might suggest that there was originally a statement preceding it.

94. For the commentary, see A. Berliner, ed., *Commentar zu den Sprüchen der Väter, aus Machsor Vitry, mit Beiträgen* (Frankfurt: J. Kauffman, 1897). Berliner attributes the commentary to R. Jacob ben Samson, a student of Rashi. Israel Ta-Shma has shown that this attribution is incorrect; the commentary is a compilation, with extracts from the work not only of R. Jacob but of Rashi's grandson, Samuel ben Meir, and R. Ephraim of Regensburg ("On the Commentary to Avoth in Mahzor Vitry," *Kiryat Sefer* 42 [1966–67]: 507–8 [Hebrew]). Since it is a compilation, the commentary is not very useful for dating. Nor is Mahzor Vitry. Although its compiler died at the beginning of the twelfth century, many of the manuscripts of the work add material to the original form (Ernst Daniel Goldschmidt, "Mahzor Vitry," *Encyclopaedia Judaica* 11:737).

95. S. Schwartz, *Imperialism*, 275–89.

96. Ibid., 275.

97. Lapin, "Palestinian Inscriptions," 266; S. Schwartz, *Imperialism*, 284–87. Both make this claim in part on the basis of comparison to pagan and Christian inscriptions.

98. S. Schwartz, *Imperialism*, 287–88.

99. The translation is by Schwartz, *Imperialism*, 287–88, with discussion. For the Aramaic text of the inscription with notes, see Naveh, *On Stone and Mosaic*, 103–5 (inscription 69).

100. S. Schwartz, *Imperialism*, 288. "Israel" can be ambiguous, however, as Schwartz notes (288n. 39): At Gerasa, a Hebrew inscription reading "Peace on all Israel" is accompanied by a Greek inscription reading "Peace on the synagogue."

101. S. J. D. Cohen, *Beginnings*.

102. Hayes, *Gentile Impurities*.

103. Ibid., 160.

104. Ibid., 73–91; minority position: 81 (*Jubilees*) and, more clearly, 83 (4QMMT). Hayes understands the ideology of these texts as a concern for genealogical impurity, which she understands as a third type of impurity alongside

the ritual impurity discussed in Leviticus 12–15 and Numbers 15 and the moral impurity of the Holiness Code (Leviticus 17–26). I am not persuaded that the concern for holy seed is best understood in terms of purity.

105. For my reading of 4QMMT, see "Levi, Phinehas," 6–12. Hayes discusses my position and rejects it in *Gentile Impurities*, 82–86.

106. Hayes, *Gentile Impurities*, 197.

107. Hayes herself treats 4QMMT as representing a minority position (*Gentile Impurities*, 83); see also her comments about Second Temple texts that hold a position different from that of *Jubilees* (81).

108. Hayes, *Gentile Impurities*, 194.

109. Ibid., 162; italics hers.

110. S. J. D. Cohen, *Beginnings*, 343.

111. Ibid., 109–39, 342.

112. Ibid., 198–238, 342.

113. Ibid., 241–340; Hayes, *Gentile Impurities*, esp. 165–78.

114. S. J. D. Cohen, *Beginnings*, 343.

115. Ibid., 342.

116. David Novak, *The Image of the Non-Jew in Judaism: An Historical and Constructive Study of the Noahide Laws* (New York: Edward Mellen Press, 1983) 262–63.

117. See the discussion of D. Schwartz, "Kingdom," 62–63.

118. Lauterbach, *Mekilta*, 2.205.

Bibliography

Albani, Matthias, Jörg Frey, and Armin Lange, eds. *Studies in the Book of Jubilees.* Texte und Studien zum antiken Judentum 65. Tübingen: Mohr Siebeck, 1997.

Albeck, Hanokh. *The Six Orders of the Mishnah: Tractate Neziqin.* Jerusalem: Bialik Institute; Tel Aviv: Dvir, 1953. (Hebrew)

Alexander, Philip S. "The Redaction-History of Serekh ha-Yaḥad: A Proposal." *Revue de Qumran* 17 (1996): 437–56.

Alon, Gedalia. "The Bounds of the Laws of Levitical Cleanness." Pages 190–234 in *Jews, Judaism, and the Classical World: Studies in Jewish History in the Times of the Second Temple and Talmud.* Jerusalem: Magnes Press, 1977.

———. "The Lithuanian Yeshivas." Pages 448–64 in *The Jewish Expression,* ed. Judah Goldin. New York: Bantam Books, 1970.

Anderson, Gary A. "The Status of the Torah before Sinai: The Retelling of the Bible in the Damascus Covenant and the Book of Jubilees." *Dead Sea Discoveries* 1 (1994): 19–29.

Apostolic Fathers. Vol. 2. Ed. and trans. Bart D. Ehrman. Loeb Classical Library. Cambridge, Mass.: Harvard University Press, 2003.

Argall, Randal A. *1 Enoch and Sirach: A Comparative and Conceptual Analysis of the Themes of Revelation, Creation, and Judgment.* Early Judaism and Its Literature 8. Atlanta: Scholars Press, 1995.

Avemarie, Friedrich. " 'Tohorat ha-Rabbim' and 'Mashqeh ha-Rabbim'–Jacob Licht Reconsidered." Pages 215–29 in *Legal Texts,* ed. Bernstein, García Martínez, and Kampen.

Avi-Yonah, Michael. *The Jews of Palestine: A Political History from the Bar Kokhba War to the Arab Conquest.* New York: Schocken, 1976.

Baillet, Maurice. *Qumran Grotte 4.III (4Q482–4Q520).* Discoveries in the Judaean Desert 7. Oxford: Clarendon Press, 1982.

Barag, Dan. "New Evidence on the Foreign Policy of John Hyrcanus I." *Israel Numismatic Journal* 12 (1992–93): 1–12.

Barclay, John M. G. *The Jews in the Mediterranean Diaspora from Alexander to Trajan (323 B.C.E.–117 C.E.).* Edinburgh: T&T Clark, 1996.

Bartlett, John R. "Zadok and His Successors at Jerusalem." *Journal of Theological Studies,* n.s., 19 (1968): 1–18.

Bauckham, Richard. *The Climax of Prophecy: Studies on the Book of Revelation.* Edinburgh: T&T Clark, 1993.

Baumgarten, Albert I. *The Flourishing of Sects in the Maccabean Era: An Interpreta-tion.* Leiden: Brill, 1997.
———. "Josephus on Essene Sacrifice." *Journal of Jewish Studies* 45 (1994): 169–83.
———. "The Zadokite Priests at Qumran: A Reconsideration." *Dead Sea Discover-ies* 4 (1997): 137–56.
Baumgarten, Joseph M. "The Disqualifications of Priests in 4Q Fragments of the 'Damascus Document': A Specimen of the Recovery of Pre-Rabbinic Ha-lakha." Pages 503–13 in *Madrid Qumran Congress*, vol. 2, ed. Trebolle Barrera and Vegas Montaner.
———. "The Exclusion of 'Netinim' and Proselytes in 4Q Florilegium." Pages 87–96 in *Studies in Qumran Law*. Leiden: Brill, 1977.
———. "A Fragment on Fetal Life and Pregnancy in 4Q270." Pages 445–48 in *Pomegranates and Golden Bells: Studies in Biblical, Jewish and Near Eastern Ritual, Law, and Literature in Honor of Jacob Milgrom*, ed. David P. Wright, David N. Freedman, and Avi Hurvitz. Winona Lake, Ind.: Eisenbrauns, 1995.
———. "The Laws about Fluxes in 4QTohora[a] [4Q274]." Pages 1–8 in *Time to Prepare the Way*, ed. Dimant and Schiffman.
———. "The Pharisaic-Sadducean Controversies about Purity and the Qumran Texts." *Journal of Jewish Studies* 31 (1980): 157–70.
———. "The Purification Liturgies." Pages 200–212 in *Dead Sea Scrolls after Fifty Years*, vol. 2, ed. Flint and VanderKam.
———. "The Purification Rituals in *DJD* 7." Pages 199–209 in *Dead Sea Scrolls: Forty Years of Research*, ed. Dimant and Rappaport.
———. *Qumran Cave 4.XIII: The Damascus Document (4Q266–273)*. Discoveries in the Judaean Desert 18. Oxford: Clarendon Press, 1996.
———. "Zab Impurity in Qumran and Rabbinic Law." *Journal of Jewish Studies* 45 (1994) 273–77.
Baumgarten, Joseph M., and Daniel R. Schwartz. "Damascus Document." Pages 4–57 in *Damascus Document, War Scroll, and Related Documents*, vol. 2 of *The Dead Sea Scrolls: Hebrew, Aramaic, and Greek Texts with English Translations*, ed. James H. Charlesworth. Tübingen: Mohr (Siebeck); Louisville: John Knox, 1995.
Baumgarten, Joseph M., et al. *Qumran Cave 4.XXV: Halakhic Texts*. Discoveries in the Judaean Desert 35. Oxford: Clarendon Press, 1999.
Beentjes, Pancratius C. *The Book of Ben Sira in Hebrew*. Supplements to Vetus Tes-tamentum 68. Leiden: Brill, 1997.
———. "'The Countries Marvelled at You': King Solomon in Ben Sira 47:12–22." *Bijdragen, Tijdschrift voor filosofie en theologie* 45 (1984): 6–14.
Beer, Georg, ed. *Faksimile-Ausgabe des Mischnacodex Kaufmann A 50*. Jerusalem: N.p., 1967–68.
Berger, Klaus. *Das Buch der Jubiläen*. Jüdische Schriften aus hellenistisch-römischer Zeit II.3. Gütersloh: Gerd Mohn, 1981.
Berliner, A., ed. *Commentar zu den Sprüchen der Väter, aus Machsor Vitry, mit Beiträ-gen*. Frankfurt: J. Kauffman, 1897.
Bernstein, Moshe, Florentino García Martínez, and John Kampen, eds. *Legal Texts and Legal Issues: Proceedings of the Second Meeting of the International Organi-zation for Qumran Studies, Cambridge 1995, Published in Honour of Joseph M. Baum-garten*. Studies on the Texts of the Desert of Judah 23. Leiden: Brill, 1997.
Black, Matthew, in consultation with James C. VanderKam. *The Book of Enoch or 1 Enoch: A New English Edition*. Studia in Veteris Testamenti Pseudepigraphica. Leiden: Brill, 1985.

Blenkinsopp, Joseph. *Isaiah 1–39.* Anchor Bible 19. New York: Doubleday, 2000.
———. *Isaiah 56–66.* Anchor Bible 19B. New York: Doubleday, 2003.
———. "The Judaean Priesthood during the Neo-Babylonian and Achaemenid Periods: A Hypothetical Reconstruction." *Catholic Biblical Quarterly* 60 (1998): 25–43.
Bloedhorn, Hanswulf, and Gil Hüttenmeister. "The Synagogue." Pages 267–97 in *Cambridge History of Judaism,* vol. 3, ed. Horbury, Davies, and Sturdy.
Boccaccini, Gabriele. *Beyond the Essene Hypothesis: The Parting of the Ways between Qumran and Enochic Judaism.* Grand Rapids, Mich.: Eerdmans, 1998.
———. *Middle Judaism: Jewish Thought 300 B.C.E. to 200 C.E.* Minneapolis: Fortress, 1991.
____. *Roots of Rabbinic Judaism: An Intellectual History, From Ezekiel to Daniel.* Grand Rapids, Mich.: Eerdmans, 2002.
Bohak, Gideon. "Theopolis: A Single-Temple Policy and Its Singular Ramifications." *Journal of Jewish Studies* 50 (1999): 3–16.
Borgen, Peder, Kåre Fuglseth, and Roald Skarsten. *The Philo Index: A Complete Greek Word Index to the Writings of Philo of Alexandria.* Grand Rapids, Mich.: Eerdmans; Leiden: Brill, 2000.
Boustan, Ra'anan S., and Annette Yoshiko Reed, eds. *Heavenly Realms and Earthly Realities in Late Antique Religions.* Cambridge: Cambridge University Press, 2004.
Boyarin, Daniel. *Border Lines: The Partition of Judaeo-Christianity.* Philadelphia: University of Pennsylvania Press, 2004.
Bregman, Marc. "The Riddle of the Ram in Genesis Chapter 22: Jewish-Christian Contacts in Late Antiquity." Pages 127–45 in *The Sacrifice of Isaac in the Three Monotheistic Religions: Proceedings of a Symposium on the Interpretation of the Scriptures Held in Jerusalem, March 16–17, 1995,* ed. Frédéric Manns. Jerusalem: Franciscan Printing, 1995.
Brin, Gershon. *Issues in the Bible and the Dead Sea Scrolls.* Tel Aviv: Tel Aviv University, 1994. (Hebrew)
Brooke, George J., ed. *Temple Scroll Studies: Papers Presented at the International Symposium on the Temple Scroll, Manchester, December 1987.* Journal for the Study of the Pseudepigrapha Supplement 7. Sheffield: JSOT Press, 1989.
Buell, Denise Kimber. "Race and Universalism in Early Christianity." *Journal of Early Christian Studies* 10 (2002): 429–68.
———. "Rethinking the Relevance of Race for Early Christian Self-Definition." *Harvard Theological Review* 94 (2001): 449–76.
Callaway, Phillip R. "Extending Divine Revelation: Micro-Compositional Strategies in the *Temple Scroll.*" Pages 149–62 in *Temple Scroll Studies,* ed. Brooke.
———. "Source Criticism of the Temple Scroll: The Purity Laws." *Revue de Qumran* 12 (1985–87): 213–22.
Campbell, Edward F. Jr. *Ruth.* Anchor Bible 7. Garden City, N.Y.: Doubleday, 1975.
Charles, R. H. *The Book of Jubilees or the Little Genesis.* London: Adam & Charles Black, 1902.
Charles, R. H., trans., rev. L. H. Brockington. "The Syriac Apocalypse of Baruch." Pages 835–95 in *The Apocryphal Old Testament,* ed. H. F. D. Sparks. Oxford: Clarendon Press, 1984.
Chazon, Esther G., and Michael Stone, eds., with the collaboration of Avital Pinnick. *Pseudepigraphic Perspectives: The Apocrypha and Pseudepigrapha in Light of the Dead Sea Scrolls (Proceedings of the International Symposium of the Orion Center*

for the Study of the Dead Sea Scrolls and Associated Literature, 12–14 January, 1997). Leiden: Brill, 1999.

Clark, Elizabeth A. *The Origenist Controversy: The Cultural Construction of an Early Christian Debate.* Princeton, N.J.: Princeton University Press, 1992.

Cohen, Shaye J. D. *The Beginnings of Jewishness: Boundaries, Varieties, Uncertainties.* Berkeley: University of California Press, 1999.

———. "The Destruction: From Scripture to Midrash." *Prooftexts* 2 (1982): 18–39.

———. "Menstruants and the Sacred in Judaism and Christianity." Pages 273–303 in *Women's History and Ancient History,* ed. Sarah B. Pomeroy. Chapel Hill: University of North Carolina Press, 1991.

———. "Purity, Piety, and Polemic: Medieval Rabbinic Denunciations of 'Incorrect' Purification Practices." Pages 82–100 in *Women and Water: Menstruation in Jewish Life and Law,* ed. Rahel R. Wasserfall. Brandeis Series on Jewish Women. Hanover, N.H.: Brandeis University Press, 1999.

———. "The Rabbi in Second-Century C.E. Society." Pages 922–90 in *Cambridge History of Judaism,* vol. 3, ed. Horbury, Davies, and Sturdy.

———. "Religion, Ethnicity, and 'Hellenism' in the Emergence of Jewish Identity in Maccabean Palestine." Pages 204–23 in *Religion and Religious Practice in the Seleucid Kingdom,* ed. Per Bilde et al. Aarhus: Aarhus University Press, 1990.

———. "The Significance of Yavneh: Pharisees, Rabbis, and the End of Jewish Sectarianism." *Hebrew Union College Annual* 55 (1984): 27–53.

———. "The Temple and the Synagogue." Pages 298–325 in *Cambridge History of Judaism,* vol. 3, ed. Horbury, Davies, and Sturdy.

Cohen, Stuart A. *The Three Crowns: Structures of Communal Politics in Early Rabbinic Jewry.* Cambridge: Cambridge University Press, 1990.

Collins, Adela Yarbro. *Crisis and Catharsis: The Power of the Apocalypse.* Philadelphia: Westminster Press, 1984.

Collins, John J. "The Origin of the Qumran Community: A Review of the Evidence." Pages 159–78 in *To Touch the Text: Biblical and Related Studies in Honor of Joseph A. Fitzmyer, S.J.,* ed. Maurya P. Horgan and Paul J. Kobelski. New York: Crossroad, 1989.

———. *The Scepter and the Star: The Messiahs of the Dead Sea Scrolls and Other Ancient Literature.* The Anchor Bible Reference Library. New York: Doubleday, 1995.

Crawford, Sidnie White. *The Temple Scroll and Related Texts.* Companion to the Qumran Scrolls 2. Sheffield: Sheffield Academic Press, 2000.

Cross, Frank Moore. *Canaanite Myth and Hebrew Epic: Essays in the History of the Religion of Israel.* Cambridge, Mass.: Harvard University Press, 1973.

Davies, Philip R. *Behind the Essenes: History and Ideology in the Dead Sea Scrolls.* Brown Judaic Studies 94. Atlanta: Scholars Press, 1987.

———. *The Damascus Covenant: An Interpretation of the "Damascus Document."* Journal for the Study of the Old Testament Supplement Series 25. Sheffield: JSOT Press, 1982.

———. "Redaction and Sectarianism in the Qumran Scrolls." Pages 152–63 in *Sects and Scrolls: Essays on Qumran and Related Topics.* South Florida Studies in the History of Judaism 134. Atlanta: Scholars Press, 1996.

Davies, Philip R., and Bruce D. Chilton. "The Aqedah: A Revised Tradition History." *Catholic Biblical Quarterly* 40 (1978): 514–46.

De Jonge, Marinus. "Levi in Aramaic Levi and the Testament of Levi." Pages 71–89 in *Pseudepigraphic Perspectives,* ed. Chazon and Stone.

Deutsch, Celia. "The Sirach 51 Acrostic: Confession and Exhortation." *Zeitschrift für die alttestamentliche Wissenschaft* 94 (1982): 400–409.

Dimant, Devorah. *"4QFlorilegium* and the Idea of the Community as Temple."
Pages 165–89 in *Hellenica et Judaica: Hommages à Valentin Nikiprowetzky* [*z"l*],
ed. André Caquot, Mireille Hadas-Lebel, and Jean Riaud. Leuven: Peeters,
1986.

———. *Qumran Cave 4.XXI: Parabiblical Texts, Part 4: Pseudo-Prophetic Texts.* Partially based on earlier transcriptions by John Strugnell. Discoveries in the Judaean Desert 30. Oxford: Clarendon Press, 2001.

Dimant, Devorah, and Uriel Rappaport, eds. *The Dead Sea Scrolls: Forty Years of Research.* Studies on the Texts of the Desert of Judah 10. Jerusalem: Magnes
Press and Yad Izhak Ben-Zvi; Leiden: Brill, 1992.

Dimant, Devorah, and Lawrence H. Schiffman, eds. *Time to Prepare the Way in the
Wilderness: Papers on the Qumran Scrolls by Fellows of the Institute for Advanced
Studies of the Hebrew University, Jerusalem, 1989–1990.* Studies on the Texts of
the Desert of Judah 16. Leiden: Brill, 1995.

Doran, Robert. "The Non-Dating of Jubilees: Jub 34–38; 23:14–32 in Narrative
Context." *Journal for the Study of Judaism in the Persian, Hellenistic, and Roman Period* 20 (1989): 1–11.

Earp, J. W. "Index of Names." Pages 269–433 in *Philo,* vol. 10.

Elior, Rachel. *Three Temples: On the Emergence of Jewish Mysticism.* Trans. David Louvish. Oxford; Portland, Ore.: Littman Library of Jewish Civilization, 2004.

Endres, John C. *Biblical Interpretation in the Book of Jubilees.* Catholic Biblical Quarterly Monograph Series 18. Washington, D.C.: Catholic Biblical Association,
1987.

Epstein, Louis M. *Marriage Laws in the Bible and the Talmud.* Cambridge, Mass.:
Harvard University Press, 1942.

Eshel, Hanan. "A Fragmentary Hebrew Inscription of the Priestly Courses?" *Tarbiz* 61 (1991–92): 159–61 (Hebrew).

Fine, Steven. "Between Liturgy and Social History: Priestly Power in Late Antique Palestinian Synagogues?" *Journal of Jewish Studies* 56 (2005): 1–9.

———. *This Holy Place: On the Sanctity of the Synagogue during the Greco-Roman Period.* Christianity and Judaism in Antiquity Series 11. Notre Dame, Ind.: University of Notre Dame Press, 1997.

Fishbane, Michael. *Biblical Interpretation in Ancient Israel.* Oxford: Clarendon
Press, 1985.

———. "The Qumran Pesher and Traits of Ancient Hermeneutics." Pages
97–114 in *Proceedings of the Sixth World Congress of Jewish Studies.* Jerusalem:
World Union of Jewish Studies, 1977.

Fleischer, Ezra. "New *Shiv'atot* on the Priestly Courses of the *Payyetan* Rabbi
Pinḥas." *Sinai* 61 (1967): 30–56. (Hebrew)

———. "A *Piyyut* of Yannai the Cantor on the Priestly Courses." *Sinai* 64 (1969):
176–84. (Hebrew)

Flint, Peter W., and James C. VanderKam, eds., with the assistance of Andrea E.
Alvarez. *The Dead Sea Scrolls after Fifty Years: A Comprehensive Assessment.* 2 vols.
Leiden: Brill, 1999.

Flusser, David. "The Baptism of John and the Dead Sea Sect." Pages 209–39 in *Essays on the Dead Sea Scrolls in Memory of E. L. Sukenik,* ed. Yigael Yadin and Chaim
Rabin, assisted by Jacob Licht. Jerusalem: Hekhal Ha-Sefer, 1961. (Hebrew)

Fraade, Steven D. " 'They Shall Teach Your Statutes to Jacob': Priest, Scribe, and
Sage in Second Temple Times." Unpublished paper.

Frankfurter, David. "The Consequences of Hellenism in Late Antique Egypt: Religious Worlds and Actors." *Archiv für Religionsgeschichte* 2 (2000): 162–93.

————. "Jews or Not? Reconstructing the 'Other' in Rev 2:9 and 3:9," *Harvard Theological Review* 94 (2001): 403–25.

Gager, John G. *The Origins of Anti-Semitism.* New York: Oxford University Press, 1983.

————. *Reinventing Paul.* New York: Oxford University Press, 2000.

García Martínez, Florentino. "*4QMess Ar* and the *Book of Noah.*" Pages 1–44 in *Qumran and Apocalyptic: Studies on the Aramaic Texts from Qumran.* Studies on the Texts of the Desert of Judah 9. Leiden: Brill, 1992.

————. "The Heavenly Tablets in the Book of Jubilees." Pages 243–60 in *Studies in the Book of Jubilees,* ed. Albani, Frey, and Lange.

————. "The Problem of Purity: The Qumran Solution." Pages 139–57 in *The People of the Dead Sea Scrolls: Their Writings, Beliefs and Practices,* by Florentino García Martínez and Julio Trebolle Barrera. Trans. Wilfred G. E. Watson. Leiden: Brill, 1995.

————. "El Rollo del Templo y la halaká sectaria." Pages 611–22 in *Simposio Bíblico Español, Salamanca, 1982,* ed. Natalio Fernández Marcos, Julio C. Trebolle Barrera, and Javier Fernández Vallina. Madrid: Universidad Complutense, 1984.

————. "Sources et redaction du *Rouleau du temple.*" *Henoch* 13 (1991): 219–32.

————. "The Temple Scroll and the New Jerusalem." Pages 431–60 in *Dead Sea Scrolls after Fifty Years,* vol. 2, ed. Flint and VanderKam.

García Martínez, Florentino, and Eibert J. C. Tigchelaar. *The Dead Sea Scrolls Study Edition,* 2 vols. Leiden: Brill; Grand Rapids, Mich.: Eerdmans, 1997–98.

Gaston, Lloyd. *Paul and the Torah.* Vancouver: University of British Columbia Press, 1987.

Goldin, Judah. "The Youngest Son, or Where Does Genesis 38 Belong?" *Journal of Biblical Literature* 96 (1977): 27–44.

Goldschmidt, Ernst Daniel. "Mahzor Vitry." Pages 736–38 in vol. 11 of *Encyclopaedia Judaica.* Jerusalem: Keter Publishing House, 1972.

Goodblatt, David. *The Monarchic Principle: Studies in Jewish Self-Government in Antiquity.* Tübingen: Mohr-Siebeck, 1994.

————. "The Title *Nāśî'* and the Ideological Background of the Second Revolt." Pages 113–32 in *Bar-Kokhva Revolt,* ed. Oppenheimer and Rappaport. (Hebrew)

Goodman, Martin. *The Ruling Class of Judaea: The Origins of the Jewish Revolt against Rome A.D. 66–70.* Cambridge: Cambridge University Press, 1987.

————. "Sadducees and Essenes after 70 C.E." Pages 347–56 in *Crossing the Boundaries: Essays in Biblical Interpretation in Honour of Michael D. Goulder,* ed. Stanley E. Porter, Paul Joyce, and David E. Orton. Leiden: Brill, 1994.

————. "Trajan and the Origins of the Bar Kokhba War." Pages 23–30 in *Bar Kokhba War,* ed. Schäfer.

Gottstein, M. H. "Anti-Essene Traits in the Qumran Scrolls." *Vetus Testamentum* 4 (1954): 145–46.

Grabbe, Lester L. "4QMMT and Second Temple Jewish Society." Pages 89–108 in *Legal Texts,* ed. Bernstein, García Martínez, and Kampen.

————. *Judaism from Cyrus to Hadrian. Volume 1: The Persian and Greek Periods.* Minneapolis: Fortress, 1992.

————. *Priests, Prophets, Diviners, Sages: A Socio-historical Study of Religious Specialists in Ancient Israel.* Valley Forge, Pa.: Trinity Press International, 1995.

Greenfield, Jonas, and Michael E. Stone. "Remarks on the Aramaic Testament of Levi from the Geniza." *Revue biblique* 86 (1979): 214–30.

Hachlili, Rachel. *Ancient Jewish Art and Archaeology in the Land of Israel.* Leiden: Brill, 1988.

Hadas, Moses. *Aristeas to Philocrates (Letter of Aristeas)*. New York: Harper and Brothers, 1951.

Halpern-Amaru, Betsy. *The Empowerment of Women in the* Book of Jubilees. Leiden: Brill, 1999.

———. *Rewriting the Bible: Land and Covenant in Post-Biblical Jewish Literature*. Valley Forge, Pa.: Trinity Press International, 1994.

Hanson, Paul D. *The Dawn of Apocalyptic: The Historical and Sociological Roots of Jewish Apocalyptic Eschatology*. Rev. ed. Philadelphia: Fortress, 1979.

Haran, Menahem. *Temples and Temple Service in Ancient Israel*. Repr. with corrections. Winona Lake, Ind.: Eisenbrauns, 1985.

Hayes, Christine E. *Gentile Impurities and Jewish Identities: Intermarriage and Conversion from the Bible to the Talmud*. New York: Oxford University Press, 2002.

Heinemann, Isaak. *Philons griechische und jüdische Bildung: Kulturvergleichende Untersuchungen zu Philons Darstellung der jüdischen Gesetze*. Breslau: M&H Marcus, 1932.

Hempel, Charlotte. "Community Origins in the *Damascus Document* in the Light of Recent Scholarship." Pages 316–29 in *Provo International Conference*, ed. Parry and Ulrich.

———. "Community Structures." Pages 67–92 in *Dead Sea Scrolls after Fifty Years*, vol. 2, ed. Flint and VanderKam.

———. *The Damascus Texts*. Companion to the Qumran Scrolls 2. Sheffield: Sheffield Academic Press, 2000.

———. "The Earthly Essene Nucleus of 1QSa," *Dead Sea Discoveries* 3 (1996): 253–69.

———. "Interpretative Authority in the Community Rule Tradition." *Dead Sea Discoveries* 10 (2003): 59–80.

———. *The Laws of the Damascus Document: Sources, Tradition and Redaction*. Studies on the Texts of the Desert of Judah 29. Leiden: Brill, 1998.

Hengel, Martin. *Judaism and Hellenism: Their Encounter in Palestine during the Early Hellenistic Period*. Trans. John Bowden. 2 vols. Philadelphia: Fortress, 1974.

Hengel, Martin, James H. Charlesworth, and Doron Mendels. "The Polemical Character of 'On Kingship' in the Temple Scroll: An Attempt at Dating 11QTemple." *Journal of Jewish Studies* 37 (1986): 28–38.

Hezser, Catherine. *The Social Structure of the Rabbinic Movement in Roman Palestine*. Tübingen: Mohr Siebeck, 1997.

Himmelfarb, Martha. *Ascent to Heaven in Jewish and Christian Apocalypses*. New York: Oxford University Press, 1993.

———. "Earthly Sacrifice and Heavenly Incense: The Law of the Priesthood in *Aramaic Levi* and *Jubilees*." Pages 103–22 in *Heavenly Realms*, ed. Boustan and Reed.

———. "Impurity and Sin in 4QD, 1QS, and 4Q512." *Dead Sea Discoveries* 8 (2001): 9–37.

———. "Levi, Phinehas, and the Problem of Intermarriage at the Time of the Maccabean Revolt." *Jewish Studies Quarterly* 6 (1999): 1–23.

———. "The Polemic against the *Tebul Yom*: A Reexamination." In *New Perspectives on Old Texts: Proceedings of the Tenth International Symposium of the Orion Center for the Study of the Dead Sea Scrolls and Associated Literature, January 9–11 2005*. Ed. Esther G. Chazon, Ruth A. Clements, and Besty Halpern-Amaru. Leiden: Brill, forthcoming.

———. "Sexual Relations and Purity in the Temple Scroll and the Book of Jubilees." *Dead Sea Discoveries* 6 (1999): 11–36.

——. "Temple and Priests in the *Book of the Watchers*, the Animal Apocalypse, and the Apocalypse of Weeks." Forthcoming.

——. "The Torah between Athens and Jerusalem: Jewish Difference in Antiquity." Pages 113–29 in *Ancient Judaism in Its Hellenistic Context*, ed. Carol Bakhos. Supplements to the Journal for the Study of Judaism 95. Leiden: Brill, 2005.

——. "Torah, Testimony, and Heavenly Tablets: The Claim to Authority of the *Book of Jubilees*." Pages 19–29 in *A Multiform Heritage: Studies on Early Judaism and Christianity in Honor of Robert A. Kraft*. Homage Series. Ed. Benjamin G. Wright. Atlanta: Scholars Press, 1999.

——. *Tours of Hell: An Apocalyptic Form in Jewish and Christian Literature*. Philadelphia: University of Pennsylvania Press, 1983.

Höffken, P. "Warum schwieg Jesus Sirach über Esra?" *Zeitschrift für die alttestamentliche Wissenschaft* 87 (1975): 184–202.

Horbury, William, W. D. Davies, and John Sturdy, eds. *The Cambridge History of Judaism*: vol. 3, *The Roman Period*. Cambridge: Cambridge University Press, 1999.

Irshai, Oded. "Confronting a Christian Empire: Jewish Culture in the World of Byzantium." Pages 181–221 in *Cultures of the Jews: A New History*, ed. David Biale. New York: Schocken, 2002.

——. "The Priesthood in Jewish Society of Late Antiquity." Pages 67–106 in *Continuity and Renewal: Jews and Judaism in Byzantine-Christian Palestine*, ed. Lee I. Levine. Jerusalem: Dinur Center, Yad Ben-Zvi, and Jewish Theological Seminary of America, 2004. (Hebrew)

——. "The Role of the Priesthood in the Jewish Community in Late Antiquity: A Christian Model?" Pages 75–85 in *Jüdische Gemeinden und ihr christlicher Kontext in kulturräumlich vergleichender Betrachtung von der Spätantike bis zum 18. Jahrhundert*, Ed. Christoph Cluse, Alfred Haverkamp, and Israel J. Yuval. Hannover: Hahnsche, 2003.

Japhet, Sara. *The Ideology of the Book of Chronicles and Its Place in Biblical Thought*. Frankfurt am Main: Verlag Peter Lang, 1989.

——. "The Prohibition of the Habitation of Women: The Temple Scroll's Attitude toward Sexual Impurity and Its Biblical Precedents." *Comparative Studies in Honor of Yochanan Muffs*. *Journal of the Ancient Near Eastern Society* 22 (1993): 69–87.

Josephus. Trans. Henry St. J. Thackeray et al. 10 vols. Loeb Classical Library. Cambridge, Mass.: Harvard University Press; London: William Heinemann, 1926–65.

Kampen, John. "4QMMT and New Testament Studies." Pages 129–144 in *Reading 4QMMT: New Perspectives on Qumran Law and History*, ed. John Kampen and Moshe J. Bernstein. Society of Biblical Literature Symposium Series 2. Atlanta: Scholars Press, 1996.

——. "The Matthean Divorce Texts Reexamined." Pages 149–67 in *New Qumran Texts and Studies: Proceedings of the First Meeting of the International Organization for Qumran Studies, Paris 1992*. Ed. George J. Brooke with Florentino García Martínez. Studies on the Texts of the Desert of Judah 15. Leiden: Brill, 1994.

Kimelman, Reuven. "The Conflict between the Priestly Oligarchy and the Sages in the Talmudic Period (An Explication of PT *Shabbat* 12:3, 13c = *Horayot* 3:5, 48c)." *Zion* 48 (1983): 135–48. (Hebrew)

Kister, Menahem. "Concerning the History of the Essenes—A Study of the *Ani-*

mal Apocalypse, the *Book of Jubilees* and the *Damascus Covenant.*" *Tarbiz* 56 (1986–87): 1–18. (Hebrew)

———. "Notes on Some New Texts from Qumran." *Journal of Jewish Studies* 44 (1993): 280–90.

———. "Some Aspects of Qumran Halakhah." Pages 571–88 in *Madrid Qumran Congress*, ed. Trebolle Barrera and Vegas Montaner.

Klawans, Jonathan. *Impurity and Sin in Ancient Judaism.* New York: Oxford University Press, 2000.

———. "Impurity of Immorality in Ancient Judaism." *Journal of Jewish Studies* 48 (1997): 1–16.

Klein, Samuel. *Beiträge zur Geographie und Geschichte Galiläas.* Leipzig: Rudolf Haupt, 1909.

Knibb, Michael A. *The Ethiopic Book of Enoch: A New Edition in Light of the Aramaic Dead Sea Scrolls.* In consultation with Edward Ullendorff. Oxford: Clarendon Press, 1978.

———. *The Qumran Community,* Cambridge: Cambridge University Press, 1987.

Knohl, Israel. "Post-Biblical Sectarianism and the Priestly Schools of the Pentateuch: The Issue of Popular Participation in the Temple Cult on Festivals." Pages 601–9 in *Madrid Qumran Congress*, ed. Trebolle Barrera and Vegas Montaner.

———. *The Sanctuary of Silence: The Priestly Torah and the Holiness School.* Minneapolis: Fortress, 1995.

Kugel, James. "The Holiness of Israel and the Land in Second Temple Times." Pages 21–32 in *Texts, Temples, and Traditions: A Tribute to Menahem Haran*, ed. Michael V. Fox et al. Winona Lake, Ind.: Eisenbrauns, 1996.

———. "Levi's Elevation to the Priesthood in Second Temple Writings." *Harvard Theological Review* 86 (1993): 1–64.

Kugler, Robert A. *From Patriarch to Priest: The Levi-Priestly Tradition from Aramaic Levi to Testament of Levi.* Society of Biblical Literature Early Judaism and Its Literature 9. Atlanta: Scholars Press, 1996.

———. "Halakic Interpretive Strategies at Qumran: A Case Study." Pages 131–40 in *Legal Texts*, ed. Bernstein, García Martínez, and Kampen.

———. "Priesthood at Qumran." Pages 93–116 in *Dead Sea Scrolls after Fifty Years*, vol. 2, ed. Flint and VanderKam.

———. "Priesthood at Qumran: The Evidence of References to Levi and Levites." Pages 465–79 in *Provo International Conference*, ed. Parry and Ulrich.

Kuhn, Peter. *Gottes Trauer und Klage in der rabbinischen Überlieferung (Talmud und Midrasch).* Leiden: Brill, 1978.

Kühnel, Bianca. "Jewish and Christian Art in the Middle Ages: The Dynamics of a Relationship." Pages 1–15 in *Juden und Christen zur Zeit der Kreuzzüge*, ed. Alfred Haverkamp. Vorträge und Forschungen 47. Sigmaringen: Jan Thorbecke, 1999.

Lambdin, Thomas O., trans. "The Gospel of Thomas (II, 2)." Pages 124–38 in *The Nag Hammadi Library in English*, ed. James M. Robinson. San Francisco: Harper & Row, 1977.

Lapin, Hayim. "Palestinian Inscriptions and Jewish Ethnicity in Late Antiquity." Pages 239–68 in *Galilee through the Centuries: Confluence of Cultures*, ed. Eric M. Meyers. Winona Lake, Ind.: Eisenbrauns, 1999.

Laporte, Jean. "The High Priest in Philo of Alexandria." Pages 71–82 in *The Studia Philonica Annual: Studies in Hellenistic Judaism* 3; *Heirs of the Septuagint: Philo, Hellenistic Judaism and Early Christianity: Festschrift for Earle Hilgert*, ed. David T. Runia, David M. Hay, and David Winston. Atlanta: Scholars Press, 1991.

Lauterbach, Jacob Z., trans. *Mekilta De-Rabbi Ishmael.* Vol. 1. Philadelphia: Jewish Publication Society, 1933.

Levenson, David B. "A Source and Tradition Critical Study of the Stories of Julian's Attempt to Rebuild the Jerusalem Temple." Ph.D. diss., Harvard University, 1979.

Levine, Baruch A. *In the Presence of the Lord: A Study of Cult and Some Cultic Terms in Ancient Israel.* Leiden: Brill, 1974.

————. *Numbers 1–20.* Anchor Bible 4A. New York: Doubleday, 1993.

————. "The Temple Scroll: Aspects of Its Historical Provenance and Literary Character." *Bulletin of the American Schools of Oriental Research* 232 (1978): 5–23.

Levine, Lee I. *The Ancient Synagogue: The First Thousand Years.* New Haven, Conn.: Yale University Press, 2000.

————. "Caeserea's Synagogues and Some Historical Implications." Pages 666–78 in *Biblical Archaeology Today, 1990: Proceedings of the Second International Congress on Biblical Archaeology, Jerusalem, June-July 1990.* Jerusalem: Israel Exploration Society, 1993.

————. *The Rabbinic Class of Roman Palestine in Late Antiquity.* Jerusalem: Yad Izhak Ben-Zvi; New York: Jewish Theological Seminary, 1989. Hebrew original, 1985.

Lowe, William Henry, ed. *The Mishnah on Which the Palestinian Talmud Rests from the Unique Manuscript Preserved in the University Library of Cambridge, Add. 470.1.* Cambridge: Cambridge University Press, 1883.

Maccoby, Hyam. *Ritual and Morality: The Ritual Purity System and Its Place in Judaism.* Cambridge: Cambridge University Press, 1999.

Mack, Burton L. *Wisdom and the Hebrew Epic: Ben Sira's Hymn in Praise of the Fathers.* Chicago: University of Chicago Press, 1985.

Maier, Johann. *The Temple Scroll: An Introduction, Translation and Commentary.* Journal for the Study of the Old Testament: Supplement Series 34. Sheffield: JSOT Press, 1985.

Marböck, Johannes. "Sir. 38, 24–39,11: Der schriftgelehrte Weise. Eine Beitrag zu Gestalt und Werk ben Siras." Pages 293–316 in *La sagesse de l'ancien testament,* ed. Maurice Gilbert. 2nd ed. Bibliotheca ephemeridum theologicarum lovaniensium 51. Louvain: Louvain University Press, 1990.

Marmorstein, Arthur. *The Doctrine of Merits in Old Rabbinic Literature.* Prolegomenon by R. J. Zwi Werblowsky. 1920. Reprint, New York: Ktav, 1968.

Marshall, John W. *Parables of War: Reading John's Jewish Apocalypse.* Waterloo, Ontario: Wilfrid Laurier University Press, 2001.

Mazar, Benjamin, assisted by Gaalyah Cornfeld. *The Mountain of the Lord.* Garden City, N.Y.: Doubleday, 1975.

Mendels, Doron. *The Land of Israel as a Political Concept in Hasmonean Literature.* Tübingen: Mohr-Siebeck, 1987.

Metso, Sariana. *The Textual Development of the Qumran Community Rule.* Leiden: Brill, 1997.

Metzger, Bruce M. ed. *Oxford Annotated Apocrypha, Expanded Edition.* New York: Oxford University Press, 1977.

Meyers, Carol L., and Eric M. Meyers. *Haggai, Zechariah 1–8.* Anchor Bible 25B. Garden City, N.Y.: Doubleday, 1987.

————. "Jerusalem and Zion after the Exile: The Evidence of First Zechariah." Pages 121–35 in *"Sha'arei Talmon": Studies in the Bible, Qumran, and the Ancient Near East Presented to Shemaryahu Talmon,* ed. Michael Fishbane and Emmanuel Tov. Winona Lake, Ind.: Eisenbrauns, 1992.

Meyers, Eric M. "The Persian Period and the Judean Restoration: From Zerub-babel to Nehemiah." Pages 509–21 in *Ancient Israelite Religion*, ed. Miller, Hanson, and McBride.

Middendorp, Theophil. *Die Stellung Jesu ben Siras zwischen Judentum und Hellenismus.* Leiden: Brill, 1973.

Mildenberg, Leo. *The Coinage of the Bar Kokhba War.* Trans. and ed. Patricia Erhart Mottahedeh. Aarau, Frankfurt-am-Main, Salzburg: Sauerländer, 1984.

Milgrom, Jacob. "4QTOHORA^a: An Unpublished Qumran Text on Purities." Pages 59–68 in *Time to Prepare the Way*, ed. Dimant and Schiffman.

———. "The Concept of Impurity in *Jubilees* and the *Temple Scroll.*" *Revue de Qumran* 16 (1993–94): 277–84.

———. "First Day Ablutions at Qumran." Pages 561–70 in *Madrid Qumran Congress*, ed. Trebolle Barrera and Vegas Montaner.

———. "Israel's Sanctuary: The Priestly 'Picture of Dorian Gray.' " *Revue biblique* 83 (1976): 390–99.

———. *Leviticus 1–16.* Anchor Bible 3. New York: Doubleday, 1991.

———. *Leviticus 17–22.* Anchor Bible 3A. New York: Doubleday, 2000.

———. *Leviticus 23–27.* Anchor Bible 3B. New York: Doubleday, 2000.

———. "The Qumran Cult: Its Exegetical Principles." Pages 165–80 in *Temple Scroll Studies*, ed. Brooke.

———. "The Scriptural Foundations and Deviations in the Laws of Purity of the *Temple Scroll.*" Pages 83–99 in *Archeology and History*, ed. Schiffman.

———. "Studies in the Temple Scroll." *Journal of Biblical Literature* 97 (1978): 501–23.

Miller, Patrick D., Paul D. Hanson, and S. Dean McBride. *Ancient Israelite Religion: Essays in Honor of Frank Moore Cross.* Philadelphia: Fortress, 1987.

Mullen, E. Theodore. *The Assembly of the Gods.* Harvard Semitic Monographs 24. Chico, Calif.: Scholars Press, 1980.

Naveh, Joseph. *On Stone and Mosaic: The Aramaic and Hebrew Inscriptions from Ancient Synagogues.* Jerusalem: Ha-Ḥevrah le-Ḥaḳirat Erets Yiśrael ve-Atiḳoteha, 1978. (Hebrew)

Neusner, Jacob. *Development of a Legend: Studies on the Traditions Concerning Yohanan ben Zakkai.* Leiden: Brill, 1970.

Nickelsburg, George W. E. *1 Enoch 1: A Commentary on the Book of 1 Enoch, Chapters 1–36; 81–108.* Hermeneia. Minneapolis: Fortress, 2001.

———. "Enoch, Levi, and Peter: Recipients of Revelation in Upper Galilee." *Journal of Biblical Literature* 100 (1981): 575–600.

Nikiprowetzky, Valentin. "Le *De Vita Contemplativa* revisité." Pages 105–25 in *Sagesse et religion: Colloque de Strasbourg, 20–22 Octobre 1976.* Paris: Presses Universitaires de France, 1979. Reprint, pages 199–216 in *Études philoniennes.*

———. *Études philoniennes.* Paris: Éditions du Cerf, 1996.

———. "La spiritualisation des sacrifices et le culte sacrificiel au temple de Jérusalem chez Philon d'Alexandrie." *Semitica* 17 (1967): 97–116. Reprint, pages 79–96 in *Études philoniennes.*

———. "Les suppliants chez Philon d'Alexandrie." *Revue des études juives* 122 (1963): 241–78. Reprint, pages 11–43 in *Études philoniennes.*

Novak, David. *The Image of the Non-Jew in Judaism: An Historical and Constructive Study of the Noahide Laws.* New York: Edward Mellen Press, 1983.

Olyan, Saul. "Ben Sira's Relationship to the Priesthood." *Harvard Theological Review* 80 (1987): 261–86.

Oppenheimer, Aharon, and Uriel Rappaport. *The Bar-Kokhva Revolt: A New Approach.* Jerusalem: Yad Izhak Ben Zvi, 1984. (Hebrew)

Parry, Donald W., and Eugene Ulrich, eds. *The Provo International Conference on the Dead Sea Scrolls: Technological Innovations, New Texts, and Reformulated Issues.* Studies on the Texts of the Desert of Judah 30. Leiden: Brill, 1999.

Philo. Trans. F. H. Colson, G. H. Whitaker, and Ralph Marcus. 12 vols. Loeb Classical Library. Cambridge, Mass.: Harvard University Press; London: William Heinemann, 1966–71.

Plummer, Reinhard. "The *Book of Jubilees* and the Samaritans." *Eglise et théologie* 10 (1979): 147–78.

Puech, Émile. *Qumrân Grotte 4, XVIII: Textes hébreux (4Q521–4Q528, 4Q576–4Q579).* Discoveries in the Judaean Desert 25. Oxford: Clarendon Press, 1998.

Qimron, Elisha. *Temple Scroll: A Critical Edition with Extensive Reconstructions.* With a bibliography by Florentino García Martínez. Beer-Sheva: Ben-Gurion University of the Negev Press; Jerusalem: Israel Exploration Society, 1996.

Qimron, Elisha, and John Strugnell. *Qumran Cave 4.V: Miqṣat Maʿaśe ha-Torah.* Discoveries in the Judaean Desert 10. Oxford: Clarendon Press, 1994.

Rajak, Tessa. *Josephus: The Historian and His Society.* Philadelphia: Fortress, 1984.

Rappaport, Uriel. "The Hellenistic Cities and the Judaization of the Land of Israel in the Hasmonean Period." Pages 219–30 in *Doron; Eighteen Articles in Honor of the Sixtieth Birthday of Prof. Bentsiyon Kats,* ed. Shmuel Perlman and Binyamin Shimron. Tel Aviv: Mifʿal ha-Shikhpul, Bet ha-Hotsaʾah le-Or shel Histadrut ha-Studentim be-Universitat Tel-Aviv, 1967. (Hebrew)

———. "Les Iduméens en Égypte." *Revue de philologie* 43 (1969): 73–82.

———. "Jewish Religious Propaganda and Proselytism in the Period of the Second Commonwealth." Ph.D. diss., Hebrew University of Jerusalem, 1965. (Hebrew)

Reed, Annette Yoshiko. *Fallen Angels and the History of Judaism and Christianity: The Reception of Enochic Literature.* Cambridge: Cambridge University Press, 2005.

———. "Heavenly Ascent, Angelic Descent, and the Transmission of Knowledge in 1 Enoch 6–16." Pages 47–66 in *Heavenly Realms,* ed. Boustan and Reed.

———. "The Textual Identity, Literary History, and Social Setting of 1 Enoch: Reflections on George Nickelsburg's Commentary on 1 Enoch 1–36; 81–108." *Archiv für Religionsgeschichte* 5 (2003): 279–96.

———. " 'What the Fallen Angels Taught': The Reception-History of the *Book of the Watchers* in Judaism and Christianity." Ph.D. diss., Princeton University, 2002.

Regev, Eyal. "Abominated Temple and a Holy Community: The Formation of the Notions of Purity and Impurity in Qumran." *Dead Sea Discoveries* 10 (2003): 243–78.

———. "Pure Individualism: The Idea of Non-Priestly Purity in Ancient Judaism." *Journal for the Study of Judaism in the Persian, Hellenistic, and Roman Period* 31 (2000): 176–202.

———. "The Temple Impurity and Qumran's 'Foreign Affairs' in the Early Hasmonean Period." *Zion* 64 (1999) 135–56. (Hebrew)

———. "Were the Priests All the Same? Qumranic Halakhah in Comparison with Sadducean Halakhah." *Dead Sea Discoveries* 12 (2005): 158–88.

———. "The *Yaḥad* and the *Damascus Covenant*: Structure, Organization, and Relationship." *Revue de Qumran* 21 (2003): 233–62.

Rooke, Deborah W. *Zadok's Heirs: The Role and Development of the High Priesthood in Ancient Israel.* Oxford Theological Monographs. Oxford: Oxford University Press, 2000.

Rubenstein, Jeffrey L. "Nominalism and Realism in Qumranic and Rabbinic Law: A Reassessment." *Dead Sea Discoveries* 6 (1999): 157–83.

Safrai, Ze'ev. "Did the Priestly Courses (*Mishmarot*) Transfer from Judea to Galilee after the Bar Kokhba Revolt?: On D. Trifon's Article in *Tarbiz*, LIX [1989–90], pp. 77–93." *Tarbiz* 62 (1992–93): 287–92. (Hebrew)

San Nicolò, Mariano. "Zur Vereinsgerichtbarkeit im hellenistischen Ägypten." Pages 255–300 in *EIIITYMBION: Heinrich Swoboda Dargebracht.* Reichenberg: Stiepel, 1927.

Sanders, E. P. "Did the Pharisees Eat Ordinary Food in Purity?" Pages 131–254 in *Jewish Law from Jesus to the Mishnah: Five Studies.* London: SCM Press; Philadelphia: Trinity Press International, 1990.

Sanders, James. *The Dead Sea Psalms Scroll.* Ithaca, N.Y.: Cornell University Press, 1967.

———. *The Psalms Scroll of Qumran Cave 11 (11QPsᵃ).* Discoveries in the Judaean Desert 4. Oxford: Clarendon Press, 1965.

Schäfer, Peter. "Bar Kokhba and the Rabbis." Pages 1–22 in *Bar Kokhba War,* ed. Schäfer.

———. *Der Bar Kokhba-Aufstand: Studien zum zweiten jüdischen Krieg gegen Rom.* Tübingen: Mohr (Siebeck), 1981.

———. "Die Flucht Johanan b. Zakkais aus Jerusalem und die Gründung des 'Lehrhauses' in Jabne." *Aufstieg und Niedergang der römischen Welt* II.19.2 (1979): 43–102.

———. "Der vorrabbinische Pharisäismus." Pages 125–72 in *Paulus und das antike Judentum: Tübingen-Durham-Symposium in Gedenken an den 50. Todestag Adolf Schlatters (19. Mai 1938),* ed. Martin Hengel and Ulrich Heckel. Wissenschaftliche Untersuchungen zum Neuen Testament 58. Tübingen: Mohr, 1991.

———, ed. *The Bar Kokhba War Reconsidered.* Texte und Studien zum antiken Judentum 100. Tübingen: Mohr Siebeck, 2003.

Schiffman, Lawrence H. "Exclusion from the Sanctuary and the City of the Sanctuary in the Temple Scroll." *Hebrew Annual Review* 9 (1985): 301–20.

———. "Halakhah and Sectarianism in the Dead Sea Scrolls." Pages 123–42 in *The Dead Sea Scrolls in Their Historical Context,* ed. Timothy H. Lim. Edinburgh: T&T Clark, 2000.

———. "The King, His Guard and the Royal Council in the *Temple Scroll.*" *Proceedings of the American Academy of Jewish Research* 54 (1987): 237–59.

———. "Legislation Concerning Relations with Non-Jews in the *Zadokite Fragments* and in Tannaitic Literature." *Revue de Qumran* 11 (1983): 379–89.

———. "Pharisaic and Sadducean Halakhah in Light of the Dead Sea Scrolls: The Case of Tevul Yom." *Dead Sea Discoveries* 1 (1994): 285–99.

———. "The *Temple Scroll* and the Nature of Its Law: The Status of the Question." Pages 37–55 in *The Community of the Renewed Covenant: The Notre Dame Symposium on the Dead Sea Scrolls,* ed. Eugene Ulrich and James VanderKam. Christianity and Judaism in Antiquity Series 10. Notre Dame: University of Notre Dame Press, 1994.

———. "The Temple Scroll and the Systems of Jewish Law of the Second Temple Period." Pages 239–55 in *Temple Scroll Studies,* ed. Brooke.

———, ed. *Archeology and History in the Dead Sea Scrolls: The New York University Conference in Memory of Yigael Yadin.* Journal for the Study of the Pseudepigrapha Supplement Series 8. JSOT/ASOR Monographs 2. Sheffield: Sheffield Academic Press, 1990.

Schofield, Alison, and James C. VanderKam. "Were the Hasmoneans Zadokites?" *Journal of Biblical Literature* 124 (2005): 73–87.

Schuller, Eileen. "Women in the Dead Sea Scrolls." Pages 117–44 in *Dead Sea Scrolls after Fifty Years*, ed. Flint and VanderKam.

Schürer, Emil. *The History of the Jewish People in the Age of Jesus Christ (175 B.C.–A.D. 135)*. Vols. 1 and 2. Rev. and ed. Geza Vermes, Fergus Millar, and Matthew Black; lit. ed., Pamela Vermes. Edinburgh: T&T Clark, 1973–79.

———. *The History of the Jewish People in the Age of Jesus Christ (175 B.C.–A.D. 135)*. Vol. 3, p.1. Rev. and ed. Geza Vermes, Fergus Millar, and Martin Goodman; organizing ed., Matthew Black; lit. ed., Pamela Vermes. Edinburgh: T&T Clark, 1986.

Schüssler Fiorenza, Elisabeth. *Priester für Gott: Studien zum Herrschafts- und Priestermotiv in der Apokalypse*. Neutestamentliche Abhandlungen n.f. 7. Munster: Aschendorff, 1972.

Schwartz, Baruch J. "The Prohibition Concerning the 'Eating' of Blood in Leviticus 17." Pages 34–66 in *Priesthood and Cult in Ancient Israel*, ed. Gary A. Anderson and Saul M. Olyan. Journal for the Study of the Old Testament Supplement Series 125. Sheffield: Sheffield Academic Press, 1991.

Schwartz, Daniel R. "Introduction: On the Jewish Background of Christianity." Pages 1–26 in *Studies in the Jewish Background*.

———. " 'Kingdom of Priests'—a Pharisaic Slogan?" Pages 57–80 in *Studies in the Jewish Background*.

———. "Law and Truth: On Qumran-Sadducean and Rabbinic Views of Law." Pages 229–40 in *Dead Sea Scrolls: Forty Years of Research*, ed. Dimant and Rappaport.

———. "On Two Aspects of a Priestly View of Descent at Qumran." Pages 157–79 in *Archeology and History*, ed. Schiffman.

———. "Philo's Priestly Descent." Pages 155–71 in *Nourished with Peace: Studies in Hellenistic Judaism in Memory of Samuel Sandmel*, ed. Frederick E. Greenspahn, Earle Hilgert, and Burton L. Mack. Homage Series 9. Chico, Calif.: Scholars Press, 1984.

———. "The Priests in *Ep. Arist.* 310." *Journal of Biblical Literature* 97 (1978): 567–71.

———. "Qumran between Priestliness and Christianity." Pages 176–81 in *The Scrolls of the Judaean Desert: Forty Years of Research*, ed. Magen Broshi et al. Jerusalem: Bialik Institute and Israel Exploration Society, 1992. (Hebrew)

———. *Studies in the Jewish Background of Christianity*. Wissenschaftliche Untersuchungen zum Neuen Testament 60. Tübingen: Mohr (Siebeck), 1992.

Schwartz, Seth. *Imperialism and Jewish Society, 200 B.C.E. to 640 C.E.* Jews, Christians, and Muslims from the Ancient to the Modern World. Princeton, N.J.: Princeton University Press, 2001.

———. "Israel and the Nations Roundabout: 1 Maccabees and the Hasmonean Expansion." *Journal of Jewish Studies* 42 (1991): 16–38.

Schwarz, Eberhard. *Identität durch Abgrenzung: Abgrenzungsprozesse in Israel im 2. vorchristlichen Jahrhundert und ihre traditionsgeschichtlichen Voraussetzungen: Zugleich ein Beitrag zur Erforschung des Jubiläenbuches*. Europäische Hochschulschriften 162. Frankfurt: Peter Lang, 1982.

Segal, Alan F. "The Sacrifice of Isaac in Early Judaism and Christianity." Pages 109–30 in *The Other Judaisms of Late Antiquity*. Atlanta: Scholars Press, 1987.

Sharp, Carolyn J. "Phinean Zeal and the Rhetorical Strategy in 4QMMT." *Revue de Qumran* 18 (1997): 207–22.

Shemesh, Aharon. "'The Holy Angels Are in Their Council': The Exclusion of Deformed Persons from Holy Places in Qumranic and Rabbinic Literature." *Dead Sea Discoveries* 4 (1997): 178–206.

———. "The Origins of the Laws of Separatism: Qumran Literature and Rabbinic Halacha." *Revue de Qumran* 18 (1997): 223–41.

Shemesh, Aharon, and Cana Werman. "Halakhah at Qumran: Genre and Authority." *Dead Sea Discoveries* 10 (2003): 104–29.

Simon, Marcel. *Verus Israel: A Study of the Relations between Christians and Jews in the Roman Empire (135–425)*. Trans. H. McKeating. New York: Oxford University Press for the Littman Library of Jewish Civilization, 1986. First French edition, 1948.

Skehan, Patrick W., trans. and notes, and Alexander A. Di Lella, intro. and commentary. *The Wisdom of Ben Sira*. Anchor Bible 39. New York: Doubleday, 1987.

Smith, Morton. "The Gentiles in Judaism, 125 B.C.E.–C.E. 66." Pages 192–249 in *The Cambridge History of Judaism*, Vol. 3, ed. Horbury, Davies, and Sturdy.

Spiegel, Shalom. *The Last Trial: On the Legends and Lore of the Command to Abraham to Offer Isaac as a Sacrifice: The Akedah*. Trans. and with an introduction, by Judah Goldin. Philadelphia: Jewish Publication Society, 1967.

Stadelmann, Helge. *Ben Sira als Schriftgelehrter*. Wissenschaftliche Untersuchungen zum Neuen Testament 2/6. Tübingen: Mohr (Siebeck), 1980.

Stemberger, Günter. *Jews and Christians in the Holy Land: Palestine in the Fourth Century*. Trans. Ruth Tuschling. Edinburgh: T&T Clark, 2000.

Stendahl, Krister. "Paul and the Introspective Conscience of the West." *Harvard Theological Review* 56 (1963): 199–215. Reprint, pages 78–96 in *Paul among Jews and Gentiles and Other Essays*. Philadelphia: Fortress, 1976.

Stern, Menahem. *Greek and Latin Authors on Jews and Judaism*. 3 vols. Jerusalem: Israel Academy of Sciences and Humanities, 1974–84.

Stone, Michael E. "Enoch, Aramaic Levi and Sectarian Origins." *Journal for the Study of Judaism in the Persian, Hellenistic, and Roman Period* 19 (1988): 159–70.

———. "Ideal Figures and Social Context: Priest and Sage in the Early Second Temple Age." Pages 575–86 in *Ancient Israelite Religion*, ed. Miller, Hanson, and McBride.

———. "Lists of Revealed Things in Apocalyptic Literature." Pages 414–52 in *Magnalia Dei: The Mighty Acts of God. Essays on the Bible and Archeology in Memory of G. Ernest Wright*, ed. Frank M. Cross, Werner Lemke, and Patrick D. Miller. Garden City, N.Y.: Doubleday, 1976.

———. "Reactions to Destructions of the Second Temple: Theology, Perception and Conversion." *Journal for the Study of Judaism in the Persian, Hellenistic, and Roman Period* 12 (1981): 195–204.

Sussman, Ya'aqov. "Appendix I: The History of Halakha and the Dead Sea Scrolls: Preliminary Observations on MIQSAT MA'AŚE HA-TORAH [4QMMT]." Pages 179–200 in *Qumran Cave 4.V*, ed. Qimron and Strugnell.

———. "The History of *Halakha* and the Dead Sea Scrolls—Preliminary Observations on *Miqṣat Ma'aśe Ha-Torah* (4QMMT)." *Tarbiz* 59 (1989–90): 11–76. (Hebrew)

Suter, David. "Fallen Angel, Fallen Priest: The Problem of Family Purity in 1 Enoch 6–16." *Hebrew Union College Annual* 50 (1979): 115–35.

Swanson, Dwight D. *The Temple Scroll and the Bible: The Methodology of 11QT*. Studies on the Texts of the Desert of Judah 14. Leiden: Brill, 1995.

Swartz, Michael D. "Ritual about Myth about Ritual: Towards an Understanding of the *Avodah* in the Rabbinic Period." *Journal of Jewish Thought and Philosophy* 6 (1997): 135–55.

———. "Sage, Priest, and Poet: Typologies of Religious Leadership in the Ancient Synagogue." Pages 101–17 in *Jews, Christians, and Polytheists in the Ancient Synagogue: Cultural Interaction in the Greco-Roman Period*, ed. Steven Fine. New York: Routledge, 1999.

Swartz, Michael D., and Joseph Yahalom. *Avodah: Ancient Poems for Yom Kippur.* University Park: Penn State University Press, 2005.

Ta-Shma, Israel. "On the Commentary to Avoth in Maḥzor Vitry." *Kiryat Sefer* 42 (1966–67): 507–8. (Hebrew)

Tcherikover, Victor. *Hellenistic Civilization and the Jews.* Philadelphia: Jewish Publication Society of America, 1959. Reprint, New York: Atheneum, 1974.

Tigchelaar, Eibert J. C. *Prophets of Old and the Day of the End: Zechariah, the Book of Watchers and Apocalyptic.* Leiden: Brill, 1996.

Tiller, Patrick A. "The 'Eternal Planting' in the Dead Sea Scrolls." *Dead Sea Discoveries* 4 (1997): 312–35.

Trebolle Barrera, Julio, and Luis Vegas Montaner, eds. *The Madrid Qumran Congress: Proceedings of the International Congress on the Dead Sea Scrolls, Madrid, 18–21 March 1991.* 2 vols. Studies on the Texts of the Desert of Judah 11. Leiden: Brill, 1992.

Trifon, Dalia Ben-Haim. "Did the Priestly Courses (*Mishmarot*) Transfer from Judaea to Galilee after the Bar Kokhba Revolt?" *Tarbiz* 59 (1989–90): 77–93. (Hebrew)

———. "The Jewish Priests from the Destruction of the Temple to the Rise of Christianity." Ph.D. diss., Tel Aviv Unversity, 1985. (Hebrew)

———. "Some Aspects of Internal Politics Connected with the Bar-Kokhva Revolt." Pages 13–26 in *The Bar-Kokhva Revolt: A New Approach*, ed. Aharon Oppenheimer and Uriel Rappaport. Jerusalem: Yad Izhak Ben Zvi, 1984. (Hebrew)

Tsafrir, Yoram. "Numismatics and the Foundation of Aelia Capitolina—A Critical Review." Pages 31–36 in *Bar Kokhba War*, ed. Schäfer.

Urbach, Ephraim E. "*Mishmarot* and *Ma'amadot*." *Tarbiz* 42 (1972–73): 304–27. (Hebrew)

———. *The Sages: Their Concepts and Beliefs.* Trans. Israel Abrahams. Jerusalem: Magnes Press, 1975.

Van der Horst, Pieter Willem. *Chaeremon: Egyptian Priest and Stoic Philosopher.* Leiden: Brill, 1984.

VanderKam, James C. "2 Maccabees 6, 7a and Calendrical Change in Jerusalem." *Journal for the Study of Judaism in the Persian, Hellenistic and Roman Period* 12 (1981): 52–74.

———. *The Book of Jubilees.* Corpus Scriptorum Christianorum Orientalium 511. Scriptores Aethiopici 88. Louvain: Peeters, 1989.

———. *The Book of Jubilees.* Guides to Apocrypha and Pseudepigrapha. Sheffield: Sheffield Academic Press, 2001.

———. "Das chronologische Konzept des Jubiläenbuches." *Zeitschrift für die alttestamentliche Wissenschaft* 107 (1995): 80–100.

———. *The Dead Sea Scrolls Today.* Grand Rapids, Mich.: Eerdmans, 1994.

———. *Enoch and the Growth of an Apocalyptic Tradition.* Catholic Biblical Quarterly Monograph Series 16. Washington, D.C.: Catholic Biblical Association, 1984.

———. *From Joshua to Caiaphas: High Priests after the Exile.* Minneapolis: Fortress; Assen: Van Gorcum, 2004.

————. "The Interpretation of Genesis in 1 Enoch." Pages 129–48 in *The Bible at Qumran: Text, Shape, and Interpretation*, ed. Peter W. Flint, with the assistance of Tae Hun Kim. Grand Rapids, Mich.: Eerdmans, 2001.

————. "Isaac's Blessing of Levi and His Descendants in *Jubilees* 31." Pages 497–519 in *Provo International Conference*, ed. Parry and Ulrich.

————. "*Jubilees*' Exegetical Creation of Levi the Priest." *Revue de Qumran* 17 (1996): 359–73.

————. "The Jubilees Fragments from Qumran Cave 4." Pages 635–48 in *Madrid Qumran Congress*, ed. Trebolle Barrera and Vegas Montaner.

————. "The Origin, Character, and Early History of the 364-Day Calendar: A Reassessment of Jaubert's Hyothesis." *Catholic Biblical Quarterly* 41 (1979): 390–411.

————. "The Origins and Purposes of the *Book of Jubilees*." Pages 3–24 in *Studies in the Book of Jubilees*, ed. Albani, Frey, and Lange.

————. *Textual and Historical Studies in the Book of Jubilees*. Harvard Semitic Monographs 14. Missoula, Mont.: Scholars Press, 1977.

Vermes, Geza. "Leviticus 18:21 in Ancient Jewish Bible Exegesis." Pages 108–24 in *Studies in Aggadah, Targum and Jewish Liturgy in Memory of Joseph Heinemann*, ed. Jacob J. Petuchowski and Ezra Fleischer. Jerusalem: Magnes Press and Hebrew Union College Press, 1981. (Hebrew)

————. "Redemption and Genesis xxii—The Binding of Isaac and the Sacrifice of Jesus." Pages 193–227 in *Scripture and Tradition in Judaism: Haggadic Studies*. 2nd ed. Leiden: Brill, 1973.

Von Campenhausen, Hans. *Ecclesiastical Authority and Spiritual Power in the Church of the First Three Centuries*. Trans. J. A. Baker. Stanford, Calif.: Stanford University Press, 1969.

Wacholder, Ben Zion. "*Jubilees* as Super Canon: Torah-Admonition versus Torah-Commandment." Pages 195–211 in *Legal Texts*, ed. Bernstein, García Martínez, and Kampen.

Weinfeld, Moshe. *Deuteronomy and the Deuteronomic School.* Oxford: Clarendon Press, 1972. Reprint, Winona Lake, Ind.: Eisenbrauns, 1992.

————. *The Organizational Pattern and the Penal Code of the Qumran Sect.* Novum Testamentum et Orbis Antiquus 2. Fribourg: Éditions Universitaires: Göttingen: Vandenhoeck & Ruprecht, 1986.

Werman, Cana. "The Attitude towards Gentiles in the Book of Jubilees and Qumran Literature Compared with Early Tanaaic Halakha and Contemporary Pseudepigrapha." Ph.D. diss., Hebrew University of Jerusalem, 1995. (Hebrew)

————. "The Book of Jubilees in Its Hellenistic Context." *Zion* 66 (2001): 275–96. (Hebrew)

————. "Consumption of the Blood and Its Covering in the Priestly and Rabbinic Traditions." *Tarbiz* 63 (1993–4): 173–83. (Hebrew)

————. "*Jubilees* 30: Building a Paradigm for the Ban on Intermarriage." *Harvard Theological Review* 90 (1997): 1–22.

————. "Levi and Levites in the Second Temple Period." *Dead Sea Discoveries* 4 (1997): 211–25.

————. "Qumran and the Book of Noah." Pages 171–81 in *Pseudepigraphic Perspectives*, ed. Chazon and Stone.

————. "The Rules of Consuming and Covering Blood in Priestly and Rabbinic Law." *Revue de Qumran* 16 (1995): 621–36.

————. "The '[*tôrâ*] and the [*tě'ûdâ*]' Engraved on the Tablets." *Dead Sea Discoveries* 9 (2002): 75–103.

254   Bibliography

———. "The 'Torah' and the 'Te'udah' on the Tablets." *Tarbiẓ* 68 (1998–9): 473–92. (Hebrew)

Williams, Margaret. "The Contribution of Jewish Inscriptions to the Study of Judaism." Pages 75–93 in *Cambridge History of Judaism*, vol. 3, ed. Horbury, Davies, and Sturdy.

Williamson, H. G. M. *Israel in the Book of Chronicles.* London: Cambridge University Press, 1977.

Wilson, Andrew M., and Lawrence Wills. "Literary Sources of the *Temple Scroll.*" *Harvard Theological Review* 75 (1982): 275–88.

Wilson, Bryan. *Religion in Sociological Perspective.* Oxford: Oxford University Press, 1982.

Winston, David. "Philo and the Rabbis on Sex and the Body." *Hellenism and Hebraism Reconsidered: The Poetics of Cultural Influence and Exchange I*, ed. David Stern. *Poetics Today* 19 (1998): 41–62.

Wise, Michael Owen. *A Critical Study of the Temple Scroll from Qumran Cave 11.* Studies in Ancient Oriental Civilizations 49. Chicago: Oriental Institute of the University of Chicago, 1990.

Wright, Benjamin G, III. "'Fear the Lord and Honor the Priest': Ben Sira as Defender of the Jerusalem Priesthood." Pages 189–222 in *The Book of Ben Sira in Modern Research: Proceedings of the First International Ben Sira Conference 28–31 July 1996, Sosterberg, Netherlands*, ed. Pancratius C. Beentjes. Berlin: de Gruyter, 1997.

Yadin, Yigael. "Is the Temple Scroll a Sectarian Document?" Pages 153–69 in *Humanizing America's Iconic Book: Society of Biblical Literature Centennial Addresses 1980*, ed. Gene M. Tucker and Douglas A. Knight. Chico, Calif.: Scholars Press, 1980.

———. *The Temple Scroll.* 3 vols. Jerusalem: Israel Exploration Society, 1983.

Yahalom, Joseph. *Poetry and Society in Jewish Galilee of Late Antiquity.* Tel Aviv: Hakibbutz Hameuchad, 1999. (Hebrew)

———. *Priestly Palestinian Poetry: A Narrative Liturgy for the Day of Atonement.* Jerusalem: Magnes, 1996. (Hebrew)

Yuval, Israel Jacob. "The Myth of the Jewish Exile from the Land of Israel: A Demonstration of Irenic Scholarship," *Common Knowledge* 12 (2006): 16–33.

———. *Two Nations in Your Womb: Mutual Perceptions of Jews and Christians.* Tel-Aviv: 'Alma / 'Am 'oved, 2000. (Hebrew)

Zucker, Friederich. "Doppelinschrift spätptolemäischer Zeit aus der Garnison von Hermopolis Magna." *Abhandlungen der Preussischen Akademie der Wissenschaften: Philosophisch-historische Klasse* 6 (1937): 1–63.

Zunz, Leopold. *Jewish Sermons: Their Historical Development.* Ed. Hanokh Albek. Trans. from the 2nd ed. of the German original, 1892. Jerusalem: Mosad Bialik, 1974. (Hebrew)

———. *Die Ritus des synagogalen Gottesdienstes, geschichtlich entwickelt.* Berlin: J. Springer, 1859.

Index

Acknowledgments

It is a pleasant duty to thank the many people who have helped me in various ways in the writing of this book. It is a particular pleasure that the first three I mention are alumni of the Princeton Religion Department. I am grateful to Annette Reed, now of McMaster University, for many helpful conversations, particularly about the *Book of the Watchers*. David Frankfurter of the University of New Hampshire and John Marshall of the University of Toronto read and criticized the portion of Chapter 4 dealing with the Book of Revelation. David Runia of the University of Melbourne and Daniel Schwartz of Hebrew University offered helpful suggestions on a paper delivered at a conference at the Institute for Advanced Studies at Hebrew University in March 2001 that was the basis for Chapter 5. The final chapter of this book owes a great deal to Peter Schäfer of Princeton and Israel Yuval of the Hebrew University, who allowed me to sit in on their wonderful undergraduate course, "Christianity and the Rabbis in Late Antiquity," taught at Princeton in the spring of 2004. I am grateful to both of them for many thought-provoking conversations that semester. I would also like to thank Peter Schäfer for his helpful comments on a draft of that chapter. John Gager of Princeton offered helpful suggestions at a number of points. Gregg Gardner, a graduate student in the Department of Religion at Princeton, prepared the bibliography and performed service above and beyond the call of duty in proofreading and correcting the notes. Our department manager, Lorraine Fuhrmann, eased the burdens of my term as department chair; without her, this book would have taken even longer to complete. I would also like to thank the other members of the department staff, Pat Bogdziewicz and Kerry Smith, for all their help and good cheer. Tammy Williams provided timely advice about computer problems.

Part of Chapter 1 of this book originally appeared as "The Wisdom of the Scribe, the Wisdom of the Priest, and the Wisdom of the King

According to Ben Sira" in the festschrift for George Nickelsburg, *For a Later Generation: The Transformation of Tradition in Israel, Early Judaism, and Early Christianity*, ed. Randal A. Argal, Beverly A. Bow, and Rodney A. Werline (Harrisburg, Pa.: Trinity Press International, 2000) 89–99. I thank the Morehouse Publishing Company for permission to reprint it. Parts of Chapters 3 and 4 are drawn from "Sexual Relations and Purity in the Temple Scroll and the Book of Jubilees," *Dead Sea Discoveries* 6 (1999): 11–36; "Impurity and Sin in 4QD, 1QS, and 4Q512," *Dead Sea Discoveries* 8 (2001): 9–37; and "The Purity Laws of 4QD: Exegesis and Sectarianism," in *Things Revealed: Studies in Early Jewish and Christian Literature in Honor of Michael E. Stone*, ed. Esther G. Chazon, David Satran, and Ruth A. Clements (Leiden: Brill, 2004) 155–69. I thank Koninklijke Brill NV for permission to use this material.

Finally, I turn to my family. I owe my husband, Steven Weiss, far more than I can possibly thank him for. Here I will mention only that he read the manuscript of this book with great care and offered many helpful suggestions. Our children, Asher, Margaret, Ruth, and Abigail, now adults or almost adults, provided practical assistance of various kinds and offered loving encouragement, for which I am deeply grateful. I am also grateful to my mother, Judith Himmelfarb, whose love and kindness are unfailing, to my brothers and sisters and brothers-in-law and sisters-in-law, Edward and Sarah Himmelfarb, Miriam Himmelfarb, Anne Himmelfarb and Joel Schwartz, Sarah Himmelfarb and Ron Sass, Naomi Himmelfarb and Jack Mearns, Dan Himmelfarb and Carol Cardinale, and to my nephew, Benjamin Himmelfarb.

This book is dedicated to the memory of my father, Milton Himmelfarb. I deeply regret that my father's illness prevented him from reading and commenting on this manuscript as he did for my other books. I know the book would be a better one if it had had the benefit of his criticism. Jewish tradition teaches us to regard our parents as our teachers. Over the years my father taught me many things about Jewish texts and Jewish history, drawing on a broad and deep knowledge that was all the more impressive because it was not professional knowledge. I remember particularly how I first learned about the Documentary Hypothesis as I sat next to him in synagogue at the age of twelve or thirteen. During the reading of the Torah he would point out the characteristic language of the sources found in that Sabbath's portion, and he would explain how recognition of multiple sources illumined the reading. In his writings my father explored the tensions between the culture of modernity and the claims of Jewish tradition, insisting that modern Jews were the poorer if they failed to respond to those claims. That was what my father taught me in those conversations in synagogue, and it was a lesson he exemplified daily in his life.